Conversations On the Rise, Progress

William Moister

Nabu Public Domain Reprints:

You are holding a reproduction of an original work published before 1923 that is in the public domain in the United States of America, and possibly other countries. You may freely copy and distribute this work as no entity (individual or corporate) has a copyright on the body of the work. This book may contain prior copyright references, and library stamps (as most of these works were scanned from library copies). These have been scanned and retained as part of the historical artifact.

This book may have occasional imperfections such as missing or blurred pages, poor pictures, errant marks, etc. that were either part of the original artifact, or were introduced by the scanning process. We believe this work is culturally important, and despite the imperfections, have elected to bring it back into print as part of our continuing commitment to the preservation of printed works worldwide. We appreciate your understanding of the imperfections in the preservation process, and hope you enjoy this valuable book.

A HISTORY

OF

WESLEYAN MISSIONS.

A HISTORY

OF

WESLEYAN MISSIONS,

IN ALL PARTS OF THE WORLD,

FROM THEIR COMMENCEMENT TO THE PRESENT TIME.

Illustrated by Numerous Engravings.

BY THE
REV. WILLIAM MOISTER.

WITH AN INTRODUCTION BY THE REV. ELIJAH HOOLE, D.D.

THIRD AND REVISED EDITION.

LONDON:
ELLIOT STOCK, 62, PATERNOSTER, ROW, E.C.
1871.

PREFACE.

On returning home with impaired health, after many years of arduous Missionary labour in foreign lands, the author of this book was delighted to find such a general interest manifested by British Christians in the great and important work to which the best part of his life had been cheerfully devoted. As opportunities and health permitted, he felt a real pleasure in striving to maintain, foster, and increase this interest, by advocating the cause of Missions in the pulpit, on the platform, in the Sabbath-school, and on every fitting occasion. With the same object in view, he was induced to publish his "Memorials of Missionary Labours in Africa and the West Indies"—a work which was so favourably received that it soon passed into a third edition. This was followed by a volume of "Missionary Stories, Facts, and Incidents," drawn chiefly from the writer's personal recollections, observations, and journals, which has also had a wide circulation.

With improved health and a comparatively light pastoral charge, last year the author found leisure to prepare for the press, and to publish his "Conversations on the Rise, Progress, and Present State of Wesleyan Missions in various parts of the World." This work was intended more especially for the benefit of the rising generation, to show them what had been done during the century which had elapsed since the commencement of our Foreign Missions: but it met with such a favourable reception generally that a second edition was called for within a few months of its first publication. Instead, however, of re-publishing the book in its original form, the author was induced to re-write and re-arrange the whole, with a view to render it still more worthy of the high commendations it had received, and to make it such a "History of Wesleyan Missions in all Parts of the World," as might prove useful as a book of reference and general information for all classes. In carrying out this object, the conversational style has been dropped, to make room for a considerable quantity of new matter, and for some important information derived from valuable manuscripts and original letters of Mr. Wesley and Dr. Coke, recently come to hand, most of which have never before been published.

The author desires to express his grateful acknowledgments for valuable hints and suggestions which he has received from the Revs. Dr. Hoole, W. B. Boyce, James Calvert, and some other brethren, and for the aid which he has derived from their published works, as well as those of the Rev. Drs. Dixon, Jobson, Etheridge, Scott, Rule, and Horsford, and of the Rev. Messrs. Marsden, Churchill, Wilson, Playter, Caroll, Bleby, Duncan, Samuel, Morgan, McBrair, Fox, Smith, Broadbent, B. Shaw, W. Shaw, Holden, S. Young, R. Young, Williams, West, Barrett, Strachan, Hunt, Cargill, Arthur, Harvard, Hardy, Newstead, Robinson, and Piercy. These and many other authors, as well as the official records of the Society, have been laid under contribution, so far as matters of fact are concerned, in order to make the work as comprehensive and complete as was practicable within a compass of a single volume. The writer will receive with gratitude from his friends and brethren any further communications which may tend to make the work still more perfect in future editions; and whilst he commends his labours to the blessing of God, he will continue to contribute all the pecuniary profits which he may realise from the publication of this and his other works to the funds of the "Wesleyan Missionary Society."

W. M.

SEDBERGH, YORKSHIRE.

INTRODUCTION.

MISSIONS form the most pleasing part of the History of the Church. They carry us away from disputes concerning precedence among ecclesiastics, from quarrelling Synods, and from General Councils of doubtful authority; and exhibit the true life of Christianity, in the endeavours of holy men to spread the knowledge of the Gospel, and its salvation, among those who were ready to perish.

Missions also contribute their testimony to the truth of Christianity. In the Bible we read that God "hath made of one blood all nations of men to dwell on all the face of the earth, and hath determined the times before appointed, and the bounds of their habitations: that they should seek the Lord, if haply they might feel after Him, and find Him though he be not far from any one of us" (Acts xvii. 26, 27). If this declaration of inspired truth required any confirmation, that confirmation is found in the history of modern Missions. Men of all races have received the Gospel. The touch of grace, like "a touch of nature, makes the whole world kin." The 300 inhabitants of Easter Island, in the Pacific Ocean, 1,000 miles from any other land, dwelling among gigantic sculptures of unknown origin, and of remote antiquity, may not have been reached by Christian effort; but men of the same race in other Islands of the Pacific have been received into the fellowship of the Church. The same may be said of the inhabitants of the remote regions of Asia and Africa, which will in due time be reached by the leaven of the Gospel. "In Him shall all the families of the earth be blessed."

Science, the knowledge of language, and commerce have been much indebted to Missions. It must also be acknowledged that the success of modern Missions has been much indebted to the discoveries of science, and the extension of commerce, as well as to the unparalleled colonisation from the British shores. The use of steam by sea has brought remote places within easy distance of each other. Railroads and telegraphs have also increased the facility of communication. The abundance of gold in some lands, and the pressing over-population of the British Isles, have led to the peopling of whole regions, heretofore almost unknown, with civilised communities. While we exclaim with wonder, "What hath God wrought!" we acknowledge that the course of events under the Divine blessing has tended to produce the results over which we now rejoice.

The great extension of Wesleyan Missions so clearly and accurately stated in this volume, has taken place within living memory. There are members of the General Committee who were acquainted with William Warrener, the first Missionary sent to the West Indies. They knew Dr. Coke, the founder of the West India Missions, and who laid down the plan of Methodism in America, under Mr. Wesley's direction. They esteemed the men who accompanied the Doctor when he took his departure for the East; they also knew the Shaws of South Africa, the Morgans, the Davises, the Freemans, and other noble and devoted men who were the means of leavening Western Africa with Christian doctrine. They have seen Missionaries successively prepared and sent out to the utmost parts of the earth, little less than two thousand in number, and have witnessed a measure of liberality among poor and rich for the support of Missions unparalleled since the days of the Apostles. There has been no lack of men for the service; such as Threlfall, Whiteley, Hill, Baker, and others, who have obtained the crown of martyrdom. Eminent scholars, such as Gogerly, Clough, and Hardy; eloquent preachers, such as Arthur and Punshon; bold pioneers, such as Boardman, Pilmore, Black, Thomas, Lawry, Waterhouse, and Burt; diligent translators, such as Hunt, Hazelwood, Lyth, Calvert, Rule, Newstead, Fletcher, Boyce, Appleyard, and Tindall. Year after year bands of men whose hearts God had touched, have presented themselves to the Committee ready to go wherever the Church under the guidance of Divine Providence may send them, and they have had with them the true spirit and power of the Gospel. "God gave the Word, and great was the company of those that published it. Kings of armies did flee apace, and she that tarried at home divided the spoil."

English Methodism, "she that tarried at home," is represented by such advocates of Missions as Adam Clarke, Jabez Bunting, Richard Watson, James Buckley, Robert Smith, John James, and a host of laymen too numerous to mention, whose memories are embalmed in many hearts, and whose names are written in heaven. The effects of Missions on those who "tarried at home" cannot be overrated, enlargement of acquaintance with the condition of mankind in general; their idolatries, immoralities, and miseries; deep concern to find how greatly we have been "verily guilty concerning our brother," in having looked on with indifference while he was perishing, and even helping his tyrants and oppressors; a kindling of zeal on his behalf, and an accumulation of sorrow, and compassion, and indignation, which at length flooded the country and legislature, and secured the emancipation of the captives in-the West Indies, and the abolition of slavery throughout the world; and the suppression of the murder of women and children, and of the sick and aged in India, under the pretence of religion. All this was achieved in the face of the determined opposition of powerful parties in the State, and the cruellest scoffs and ridicule of men of wit and learning; and meantime evangelical piety was on the increase, the leaven of the Gospel permeating all classes of Society. The hand of God is to be seen in the work thus wrought.

But more extraordinary, if possible, were the effects produced among the heathen. In the West Indies the powerful superstition of Obeaism ceased, marriage and the sanctity of family life took the place of unbounded licentiousness; in Africa the Kaffir was found clothed and seated at the feet of Jesus; while from the uttermost parts of the earth—Australia, New Zealand, the Tonga Islands, and Fiji—were heard songs of praise, giving glory to the "Righteous One," with whom they had now become acquainted, by the Word of God and the power of the Holy Ghost, through the ministry of the messengers of the Churches.

A writer on Missions has said that "the Methodists make a great talk about any good they may do." He further proceeds to remark, "there is much in their system which cherishes a spirit of self-complacency and self-sufficiency. There is also about them too much of the spirit of display; they do nothing in a corner if the exhibition of it may bring them any credit with the world." —*Brown's History of Missions*, Vol. I. p. 547. We accept the caution against vainglory; but we are not to be restrained from declaring the wonderful works of the Lord, and from calling upon all who love and fear Him to unite with us in blessing and praising His holy name, because

INTRODUCTION.

"He is good, and His mercy endureth for ever." We can never sufficiently praise Him for the work He is now carrying on in the heathen world, and among His ancient people, the Jews, and for the promises of Holy Writ yet to be fulfilled: "It shall come, that I will gather all nations and tongues; and they shall come, and see My glory. And I will set a sign among them, and I will send those that escape of them unto the nations, to Tarshish (Spain), Pul (Asia), and Lud (Africa), that draw the bow, to Tubal (Russia), and Javan (Greece), to the isles afar off (Britain and American islands and continent), that have not heard My fame, neither have seen My glory; and they shall declare My glory among the Gentiles" (Isaiah lxvi. 18, 19).

It is now generally acknowledged that heathen people are to be converted to Christianity by the labours of their own countrymen chiefly. Missionaries may commence the work, and may for some time be necessary for its superintendence; but the main body of labourers must be natives. The Rev. Egerton Ryerson, now Dr. Ryerson, was the means of the conversion of Peter Jones, and of Shawundais, a native Indian chief, who still survives and is venerated as the Rev. John Sunday; and who, by the blessing of God, can count his converts and fellow-labourers among the Indians of Canada in great numbers. In the Hudson's Bay Territory, Henry Steinhaur and John Sinclair are native Missionaries. In Ceylon, Continental India, and Southern and Western Africa, in the highly favoured Tonga Islands, Fiji, and Rotumah Missions, the work is carried on to a large extent by native agents; and in other parts of the world ministers have been raised up, as the fruit of Missionary labour, who, for talents, zeal, and success, would compare favourably with the evangelists of any country in Christendom.

While this Introduction is passing through the press, authentic accounts are received of extensive awakenings and conversions in the South Sea Islands, in the West Indies, and in South Africa, reminding us of many similar scenes which have occurred on the Missions in past years under the faithful preaching of the Word of God. By Divine mercy there are multitudes before the throne of God in heaven the fruit of Missionary labour, and there are still greater multitudes preparing to join them in their happy employment. They come from the east and the west, and the north and the south, to sit down in the kingdom of God.

Protestant Missions for the conversion of the heathen to Christianity are not of a very ancient date, and the name of the Wesleys is connected with their earliest rise. It has been stated, on good authority, that "the Missionary spirit was a passion in the Wesley family when Christian Missions scarcely existed. John Wesley, the grandfather of the Wesleys, after being ejected from his church living in 1662, longed to go as a Missionary, first to Surinam, and afterwards to Maryland. Samuel Wesley, his son, when between thirty and forty years of age, formed a magnificent scheme to go as a Missionary to India, China, and Abyssinia: and in the last year of his life, most sincerely lamented that he was not young enough to go to Georgia. His sons, John and Charles, then at Oxford, caught his spirit, and actually went to Georgia, John Wesley having it particularly in view to preach the Gospel to the American Indians."—See *Life and Times of Samuel Wesley*, p. 432.

These stirrings of the Wesley family towards the heathen preceded the operations of the Societies which afterwards took up the work of Missions. The "Society for Promoting Christian Knowledge," founded in 1698, established a connection with the first Protestant Mission to the heathen, the Danish Mission to the Hindus at Tanquebar, in 1709. The "Society for the Propagation of the Gospel in Foreign Parts," incorporated in 1701, does not appear to have had any Missions to the heathen for many years after its formation. John Wesley did not acknowledge himself a Missionary of this Society when in America; nor would he receive a salary from them; but he furnished them with most valuable reports as to the state of the settlements and the proceedings of the clergymen employed by them. The journals of that eminent man show how his heart yearned over the heathen, and how willing he would have been to devote his life to their spiritual benefit. Divine Providence permitted his wish to be frustrated, and directed his course back to his native land for the accomplishment of a greater work than was possible, humanly speaking, among the scattered population of America at that time.

The circumstances connected with the introduction of Methodism into America are related at large in the pages of this work. Particulars are also given of the commencement of Methodist Missions to the heathen in the West Indies in 1786, as well as in other countries in after years. Many providential circumstances concurred to favour the benevolent work among the negroes at its commencement; and to the present day the blessing of God has rested upon it.

In reference to Missions, at this early date, Mr. S. D. Waddy is in possession of an original document of some value, and of more than usual interest. It is entitled, "A Plan of the Society for the establishment of Missions among the Heathen;" the annual subscription constituting a member being two guineas. The General Meeting of the Society to be held on the last Tuesday in January 1784. A List of Contributions is published, amounting to £66 8s. 0d., and a letter is addressed to the Rev. John Fletcher, of Madeley, requesting his co-operation. It is signed "Thomas Coke," who was no doubt the author of the following address:—

TO ALL THE REAL LOVERS OF MANKIND.

"THE present institution is so agreeable to the finest feelings of piety and benevolence, that little need be added for its recommendation. The candid of every denomination (even those who are entirely unconnected with the Methodists, and are determined so to be) will acknowledge the amazing change which our preaching has wrought upon the ignorant and uncivilised, at least throughout these nations; and they will admit that the spirit of a Missionary must be of the most zealous, most devoted, and self-denying kind: nor is anything more required to constitute a Missionary for the heathen nations than good sense, integrity, great piety, and amazing zeal. Men possessing all these qualifications in a high degree we have among us, and I doubt not but some of these will accept of the arduous undertaking, not counting their lives dear, if they may but promote the kingdom of Christ, and the present and eternal welfare of their fellow-creatures. And we trust nothing shall be wanting, as far as time, strength, and abilities will admit, to give the fullest and highest satisfaction to the promoters of the plan, on the part of

"Your devoted servants,

"THOMAS COKE,
"THOMAS PARKER.

"Those who are willing to promote the institution are desired to send their names, places of abode, and sums subscribed, to the Rev. Dr. Coke, in London, or Thomas Parker, Esq., Barrister-at-law, in York."

Animated by the spirit which dictated this "Address," Dr. Coke, encouraged by Mr. Wesley, never ceased his endeavours on behalf of Africa, the West Indies, and the

East. When nearly alone he had to bear the burden of providing means for the support of Missions, he was not discouraged. As a lover of humanity, and as a diligent student of prophecy, he looked forward with joy and confidence to the success of Missionary efforts; and the result showed that he had not been mistaken: he reaped a full and glorious reward.

In the year 1804, on the departure of the Doctor for America, a Committee was appointed to undertake the management of the Missions which had for more than twenty years chiefly devolved on himself, the Rev. Joseph Benson, president; William Marriot, Esq., treasurer; and Joseph Butterworth, Esq., secretary.

On Dr. Coke's appointment to India in 1813, the Society was reorganised, and in the course of a few years was placed upon its present permanent footing.

Many volumes of great interest relating to the Missions have been published, but in no case has an entire history of the whole been attempted, until Mr. Moister's publication of last year, addressed chiefly to youthful readers, which, meeting with much encouragement, has been improved and enlarged so as to form the volume now submitted to the reader. This undertaking has had the approval of the authorities of the Missionary Society, and its accomplishment is regarded as a fitting completion of the many works on Missions which the author's extensive personal knowledge and diligent researches have enabled him to publish, to the great advantage of the cause to which his life has been devoted.

ELIJAH HOOLE.

Wesleyan Mission House,
    Bishopsgate-street Within, London.

CONTENTS.

CHAP.		PAGE
I.	*EUROPE*	3
II.	*AMERICA*	51
III.	*THE WEST INDIES*	109
IV.	*WESTERN AFRICA*	155
V.	*SOUTHERN AFRICA*	206
VI.	*AUSTRALIA*	262
VII.	*NEW ZEALAND*	309
VIII.	*THE FRIENDLY ISLANDS*	352
IX.	*THE FIJI ISLANDS*	403
X.	*INDIA*	459
XI.	*CHINA*	511
XII.	*THE RETROSPECT*	533

HISTORY OF WESLEYAN MISSIONS.

CHAPTER I.

EUROPE.

ENGLAND, SCOTLAND, AND IRELAND—THE BRITISH ISLES—FRANCE, SWITZERLAND, AND GERMANY—GIBRALTAR, SPAIN, AND ITALY—MALTA AND THE MEDITERRANEAN.

IT has been admitted by writers of almost every shade of political opinion, that, at the commencement of the seventeenth century, religion and morality were at a very low ebb throughout the length and breadth of ENGLAND and the British Isles. The clergy of the Established Church, with few exceptions, were notoriously addicted to the pleasures of the world, and manifested little regard for the spiritual interests of their parishioners; whilst the ministers and members of Dissenting congregations exhibited a fearful lack of spiritual life in their religious worship and church organisations. The result was a general disregard for religion among all classes of people, and the prevalence of infidelity and crime in almost every part of the land. It was at this juncture, and in this special time of need, that God, in His providence, raised up the Rev. John Wesley, the founder of Methodism, his pious and devoted brother Charles, and other good men, who took a prominent part in that wonderful religious movement, which was so truly missionary in its character, being designed to "spread Scriptural holiness throughout the land."

Some difference of opinion has been expressed by persons who would be very exact in matters of history, as to the precise time and place of the origin of this great work. But it is not our province to decide whether Epworth or Oxford has the best claim to the honour of being regarded as the cradle of Methodism. In

JOHN WESLEY.

tracing the rise and progress of Wesleyan Missions, it may be sufficient to state very briefly the simple facts of the case. It was in the year 1729 that Messrs. John and Charles Wesley, who had been so piously trained at their Epworth home by their incomparable mother, began to hold religious meetings with some of their fellow students at Oxford, for their mutual edification. The peculiar strictness of their moral conduct, the systematic manner in which they economised their time, and the zeal and earnestness with which they laboured for the temporal and spiritual benefit of their fellow-men, exposed them to much persecution, and brought upon them by way of reproach, the name of *Methodists*. This innocent designation was ultimately accepted as one that could do nobody any harm, and which might serve to distinguish a body of people which were destined, in the order of Divine Providence, to become a numerous, powerful, and influential branch of the Christian Church, for the spread of the Gospel throughout the world.

The genuine missionary spirit which actuated the founder of Methodism from the very commencement of his career was beautifully exemplified in the readiness with which he took leave of his widowed mother, and embarked for America a few months after his dear father's death, in 1735. And although his pleasant dream of converting the Indians to the faith of the Gospel was not fully realized, there is sufficient evidence, in the touching records which he has given in his journals of the interviews and conversations which he had with red men of the West, that, if Providence had permitted, it was in his heart to live and die with them. The great Head of the Church designed John Wesley for a higher position than that of an individual missionary in the vast field of the world. He was to be the chief instrument in organizing a missionary system which should extend its influence not only to the simple children of the forest, who had such a warm place in his loving heart, but to "every nation and people and kindred and tongue." If Mr. Wesley's mission to Georgia was in some respects a failure, it was not useless or unfruitful. It was one of the links in that chain of circumstances which ultimately led to such wonderful results. In that far off land, and when tossing on the mighty ocean, Wesley was brought into contact with a class of men who were possessed of clearer views and stronger faith than he had ever known before. At the feet of these disciples of Christ the strong-minded theologian sat with the humility and meekness of a little child, to learn more fully the lessons of a Saviour's love. The work of evangelical enlightenment so hopefully commenced in the mind of Mr. Wesley through the instrumentality of the Moravian brethren in America, and on the voyage, was matured on his return to England by means of his hallowed intercourse with good Peter Böhler, one of their general superintendents or bishops. Then came the grand crisis, on that memorable Wednesday evening in the month of May, 1788, when Wesley was assembled with a few Christian brethren at a little meeting in Aldersgate-street. One of the members was reading Luther's preface to the Epistle to the Romans, when, about a quarter before nine o'clock, whilst the simple plan of justification by faith in the Lord Jesus Christ was being clearly set forth, the humble penitent seeker was enabled to believe to the full salvation of his soul. "I felt my heart strangely warmed," says Wesley, "and felt that I did trust in Christ—Christ alone—for salvation; and an assurance was given me that He had taken away *my* sins, even *mine*, and saved *me* from the law of sin and death."

From this eventful period in the history of the founder of Methodism may be dated the commencement of that wonderful career of evangelical labour which has been the admiration of the world. Having thus at length emerged from comparative darkness into the glorious light of the Gospel, and found for himself the pearl of great price, the heart of John Wesley burned within him to proclaim the way of salvation to the perishing sons of men. In connexion with his brother Charles, Mr. Whitfield, and others, who had been made partakers of the like precious faith, he went forth in the name and strength of the Lord to proclaim a present, free, and full salvation to penitent sinners. The churches in the metropolis, and other places in which these men of God had been wont occasionally to minister as duly authorized Clergymen, were soon closed against them, and they saw that their religious movement, which they intended for the quickening and revival of the established Church of England, would probably take another direction. Nothing daunted by the taunts, and sneers, and hostile attitude of wicked men, and willing to be led by Divine Providence, Wesley and his associates went out into the highways and hedges and, with all the power of loving entreaty, earnest exhortation, and sympathetic tears, they compelled men to come in to the Gospel feast.

Field preaching, to which Mr. Wesley and his coadjutors were at first driven by dire necessity, when they were excluded from the pulpits of the churches, soon became a popular institution, and congregations, sometimes numbering tens of thousands, might be seen assembled together in Moorfields, on Kennington Common,

GEORGE WHITFIELD.

and in other public places, listening with devout attention to the heralds of the Cross. Thus, without any contrivance of theirs, and owing to circumstances over which they had no control, multitudes were brought under the sound of the Gospel who would never have entered a church to hear it. The Divine influence which attended the preaching on the occasions of these miscellaneous gatherings was sometimes overwhelming; and it is believed that hundreds of sinners were saved, who might have been lost if the preachers had strictly confined themselves to canonical rules and regulations. Hence it appears, from the earliest stages of its history, Methodism was pre-eminently a child of Providence; every step that was taken being clearly indicated by an invisible but overruling Power.

Nor was the hand of Divine Providence less conspicuous in the circumstances which led to the erection of separate places of worship, and the employment of lay preachers to aid in carrying on the good work. Preaching in the open air answered very well during the summer months; but when the pelting rains, the bleak winds, and chilling frosts of autumn and winter came, the newly-gathered flocks required places of shelter in which they might worship God and enjoy those social means of grace which are so necessary for the maintenance of spiritual religion. Hence arose the necessity of the erection of those plain and humble sanctuaries, at first called "preaching houses," but afterwards more appropriately designated "chapels." As the work extended, and Methodist chapels and other preaching places were multiplied in various parts of the country, the necessity of an increase in the number of preachers was a natural consequence. Strange as it may appear, Mr. Wesley was still ardently attached to the church which had excluded him from her pulpits, and was anxious, as far as possible, to conform to her discipline; but with all his ingenuity he could not meet the demand for ministerial labour resulting from the success of the enterprise, so long as he confined the work to himself, his brother, and the few other Clergymen who joined with them in their pious but erratic course of proceeding. A selection was therefore made from among the converts of such as were most distinguished by their piety, zeal, and talents, and they were employed as prayer-leaders, exhorters, and occasional expounders of the Scriptures. The first person thus employed was a young man named Thomas Maxfield, who gave umbrage to his friend and patron, by ascending from the desk to the pulpit at the Foundry in his absence. The young aspirant would probably have received a severe rebuke, had it not been for the timely interposition of the mother of the Wesleys, who had heard him. "Take care," said the noble-minded woman to her indignant son, "what you do with respect to that young man, for he is as surely called to preach the Gospel as you are." Under the influence of such testimony, Mr. Wesley submitted to what he believed to be the order of God, and young Maxfield became the first of a long list of devoted men who faithfully and successfully preached the Gospel in the Methodist Connexion, without the imposition of episcopal hands.

The origin of class-meetings, band-meetings, love-feasts, watch-nights, and other means of grace peculiar to the Methodists, was no less remarkable in its providential aspect. The self-denying labours of the Wesleys, and their noble band of itinerant preachers would, in all probability, have been no more permanent in their results than those of other popular evangelists which might be named, had no provision been made for the systematic pastoral oversight of the new converts. But by a train of circumstances entirely unpremeditated, the founder of Methodism was led, step by step, to make arrangements for the spiritual edification and instruction of his people, and for their compact union in a well-organized Connexion. Respect was paid to the same principle of unity and cohesion in the formation of Societies, Circuits, and Districts, with their weekly, quarterly, and annual meetings, for the proper division of ministerial labour, and the exercise of general discipline. When the whole country was thus divided into separate spheres of evangelical labour, and every man at his post, it was a beautiful sight to see the venerable and apostolic Wesley mounted on his faithful steed, travelling with amazing rapidity from town to town, taking the general oversight of the work, in the true spirit of a primitive bishop.

The principal centres of Methodistic influence in England at the commencement of the enterprise were London, Bristol, and Newcastle-upon-Tyne, where large numbers of poor colliers, and the labouring classes generally, were brought under the influence of the Gospel, and many of them savingly converted to God. The work was afterwards extended to Leeds, Liverpool, Manchester, York, Norwich, Cornwall, and other counties, cities, towns, villages, and rural districts. In many places, in the course of time, beautiful chapels were erected, large congregations gathered, and interesting Societies organised, whilst considerable attention was paid to the training of the rising generation by the establishment of Sabbath and week-day schools in various parts of the kingdom. Nor was the mental improvement of junior Ministers, and the intellectual culture of our young men generally, neglected. Ordination to the full work of the ministry by the imposition of hands, having been adopted by the Conference, and all the attributes of a Christian Church having been given to the Wesleyan Societies, superior schools, colleges, and seminaries of learning were established in different places, some for the education of youth generally, and others for the training of our rising ministry exclusively. Thus did Methodism grow and expand in all its departments, till its influence had extended to almost every village and hamlet in England and Wales; and such were its power and respectability that it ultimately took its place among the most prominent and influential Noncomformist churches in the land. It might appear invidious to mention the names of individual Ministers who took a prominent part in the work of Methodism in this country at an early period; but the labours of such men as William Thompson, Samuel Bradburn, Joseph Benson, Adam Clarke, Richard Watson, Robert Newton, Jabez Bunting, and a host of others, will never be forgotten.

But whilst we rejoice over the success which has attended the mission of Methodism in England, we must not close our eyes to the solemn fact that much yet remains to be done. Rapid as has been the progress of our denomination in this highly favoured land, it has scarcely kept pace with the still more rapid increase of the population. If it be true that there are at the present time more unconverted sinners in England than there were in the days of Wesley and Whitfield, surely every body of professing Christians, and especially a missionary Church like ours, should be awake to the importance of the occasion. It is lamentable to contemplate the extent to which the Sabbath is desecrated and the worship of God neglected in many of our large cities and towns, as well as in many rural districts. Hence the necessity of falling back upon the great principles so clearly recognised and so highly prized by the early Methodists, and especially by our honoured founder, that every Methodist preacher should regard himself as in a certain sense a Home Missionary; that the people should be zealous, united, and liberal in the cause of God, remembering the well-known mottoes,

WESLEYAN SOLDIERS' CHURCH, ALDERSHOT.

"one and all," "all at work and always at work." To give every member of the community an opportunity of doing something towards the evangelisation of the long-neglected parts of our own country, our "Home Mission and Contingent Fund" has been established. This important fund, for the assistance of poor Circuits and for the support of the Gospel in destitute localities, was originated by Mr. Wesley himself; and, as recently amplified and extended in its operations, it is doing a great work. In addition to various grants made in aid of the ordinary circuit work of Methodism, it helps to sustain seventy-four Home Missionaries, and eleven Ministers who are appointed to labour for the benefit of Wesleyans in the Army and Royal Navy. The principal military station is at Aldershot, where two Wesleyan chaplains are usefully employed. It is an interesting sight to see the men marching to parade service on Sunday mornings; and it is still more pleasing to witness their devout attention to the Word of God. In connection with the Home Missionary work of Methodism, a useful sphere of labour is found, not only for Ministers, but also for the pious and devoted members of the church. Christian ladies have been usefully employed as visitors, and their labours have been made a blessing to many a poor family.

But it is time to travel northward, and to consider what Methodism has done for the people beyond the Border.

On Wednesday, the 24th of April, 1751, Mr. Wesley, accompanied by one of his preachers named Christopher Hopper, paid his first visit to SCOTLAND, not with the intention of preaching, however, but merely to make his observations on a country and people who had figured so prominently in general and ecclesiastical history, and in which he felt a lively interest. From their peculiar theological views, and from their high character for religion and morality, the founder of Methodism seems to have concluded that the Scots would have no desire for his ministrations. But in this he was mistaken. He had no sooner passed over the Tweed, than his presence in North Britain was hailed by many with evident tokens of gratitude and joy; and, at the earnest request of the people, he preached in various places, especially at Dunbar and Musselburgh, with a freedom and power which seemed to surprise both himself and his hearers.* The impression made upon Mr. Wesley's mind by this

---

* The character and aim of Methodism were not entirely unknown across the border at this early period. Both in Dunbar and Musselburgh small Societies of pious soldiers from John Haim's regiment of dragoons in Flanders had been formed, which were made a blessing to the townsmen; and it is believed that this

hasty visit appears to have been very favourable; for, adverting to it in his Journal, he says, "I know not why any should complain of the shyness of the Scots towards strangers. All I spoke with were as free and open with me as the people of Newcastle or Bristol; nor did any person move any dispute of any kind, or ask

HOME MISSION COTTAGE VISITOR.

visit of Mr. Wesley to North Britain was owing mainly to an invitation which he had received from a military officer then quartered at one of these places. This introduction of Methodism into Scotland, through the instrumentality of converted soldiers, is one of many instances which will come under our notice, as we trace the history of Missions, in which pious men connected with the Army and Navy have been the pioneers of the regular Missionary, and should tend to increase our interest in the spiritual welfare of these classes of our fellow-men.

me any question concerning my opinions." He was strongly urged by several influential persons to remain longer in Scotland; but his engagements in England obliged him reluctantly to decline the invitation. Under these circumstances, he says, "All I could do was to promise that Mr. Hopper would come back and spend a few days with them."

Mr. Wesley repeated his visit to North Britain the following year with evident pleasure; and, at intervals, his Preachers who were stationed in Northumberland responded to the calls which were made for their services beyond the Border, as they had opportunity. The results of these and subsequent visits of the founder of Methodism and his fellow-labourers in the Gospel was so satisfactory, that ultimately Wesleyan Ministers were regularly appointed to labour there, and the country was divided into Circuits, on the plan adopted in England and Wales. It may be freely admitted, however, without any reflection on the labourers or the system, that Methodism has not taken such deep root or had so extensive a range in Scotland as in some other parts of the British empire, for various reasons which might be easily assigned. It has, nevertheless, been made a great blessing to the country by reviving and stimulating to action other religious communities, as well as by directly promoting the personal salvation and religious edification of multitudes of people. Commodious places of worship have been erected and Societies formed in Edinburgh, Glasgow, Greenock, Leith, Dunbar, Dumbarton, Aberdeen, Dundee, Perth, and other places, and if comparatively little has been done by Methodism for the rural districts of Scotland, it is satisfactory to know that more ample provision is made for the religious instruction of the scattered population in the country by other churches than in many places. The cause of Methodism in North Britain has suffered severely for several years past from financial pressure, in the form of chapel debts and otherwise. But the noble movement recently inaugurated, for the purpose of raising the sum of £10,000 as a sustentation and extension fund, if well sustained, will no doubt afford considerable relief; and, with the blessing of God upon the labours of His faithful servants, there is ground to anticipate a bright and prosperous future for Methodism in Scotland, which already numbers *thirty-two Ministers and about four thousand church members.*

We must now turn our attention to IRELAND, a country which has so long been the great difficulty of statesmen and a source of anxiety to Christian philanthropists. The introduction of Methodism into the sister kingdom was attended by some interesting circumstances of a truly providential character, and which are deserving of notice. When Mr. Wesley landed in Dublin for the first time, on Sunday morning, the 9th of August, 1747, he found a small Society of zealous Methodists already organized, who, from their acquaintance with his character and writings, received him as their father and friend, although they had never seen him before. These earnest disciples of Christ had been gathered out of the world and brought to a saving knowledge of the truth through the instrumentality of Mr. Williams, one of Wesley's early Preachers, who had crossed over to Ireland some time before. The generous, bland, and courteous bearing of the Irish people seems to have made a favourable impression on the mind of the founder of Methodism from the very first; and on their part they showed that they duly appreciated the value and importance of that free, full, and present salvation which he and his associates came to offer for their acceptance. Hence, notwithstanding the hindrances arising from Popish darkness and superstition, the general poverty of the people, and the frequent losses from emigration, Ireland has proved a fruitful soil for Methodism.

Having a firm conviction that his labours would not be in vain in the Lord, Mr. Wesley frequently visited the Emerald Isle in after years, to regulate the affairs of the Societies, and to counsel and encourage the Preachers whom he appointed, from time to time, to labour there, as well as to proclaim from the fulness of his own heart the good news of salvation. In these hallowed labours he was nobly assisted by his devoted brother Charles and Dr. Coke, both of whom had a special regard for the Irish people. They often remained for weeks and months in succession, itinerating through different parts of the country; and when the leaders in London manifested some dissatisfaction at their long-continued absence from the metropolis, Mr. Wesley gave utterance to that memorable saying, "Have patience, and Ireland will repay you." Every person acquainted with the history of Methodism in the sister kingdom will be ready to admit that the most sanguine expectations of Wesley have been realized. Elegant chapels have been erected in Dublin, Cork, Belfast, and many other places, and at the town last named a college has been opened, which promises to be an honour to the Connexion. The very best kind of success has attended the faithful preaching of the Gospel by Wesleyan Mini-

WESLEYAN CHAPEL, THURLES, TIPPERARY, IRELAND.

sters in Ireland. Tens of thousands of precious souls have been won for Christ, under circumstances of difficulty and opposition, which strikingly illustrate the amazing power of Divine grace, as well as the special providence of God. On the occasion of one of his visits to Cork, Wesley was rudely assailed by the mob; but a party of British soldiers came to his rescue and, protected by them, he finished his sermon in peace, and great good was the result.

Among the numerous converts gathered out of the world, through the instrumentality of the early Methodist Preachers, were several

JOHN WESLEY AT CORK.

young men of more than ordinary ability and zeal in the cause of the Redeemer, who were called to go forth as Christian evangelists to preach the Gospel to their fellow-countrymen. The names of Thomas Walsh, Matthias Joyce, William Hamilton, Charles Graham, Gideon Ouseley, William Reilly, and some others, will ever be held in grateful remembrance, not only by Irish Methodists, but by Christian people of other lands. By the blessing of God upon the persevering efforts of these faithful servants of the Lord, and other zealous labourers with whom they were associated, or by whom they were succeeded, a great and glorious work was commenced in Ireland, which has continued to prosper to the present time, and which will never die. Had Irish Methodism kept her own since the time of her first organization, she would have presented to our view a Christian Church of large and fair proportions, and one which would have compared favourably with any other religious denomination in the land. But from the peculiar circumstances of the country, and the blighting influence of Popish superstition, there has been a constant stream of emigration flowing from the Emerald Isle, which has tended greatly to diminish her numbers and weaken her resources.

But whilst Ireland has thus been suffering loss from the removal of some of her best Christian citizens, America, Australia, Southern Africa, and other countries, have been enriched. Zealous Irish Methodists have frequently carried with them to the lands of their adoption the precious seed of the kingdom, which, when deposited in a fruitful soil, has brought forth an abundant harvest to the honour and glory of God. Some of the emigrants have been the pioneers of the regular Missionary in the distant lands in which they have settled; and we have met with them on various Mission Stations abroad, and have generally found them both able and willing to aid us in our noble enterprize. Although long since organized into a separate Conference, Irish Methodism has hitherto been largely indebted to the British Connexion, and especially to the Wesleyan Missionary Society, for the means to carry on the work at many of the poorer stations; and Ireland still presents to the view of the Christian philanthropist a field of home missionary labour deserving of more attention than it has yet received. The success of the past is well calculated to encourage increased exertion for the future. After many losses by emigration and otherwise, the Irish Connexion still numbers *one hundred and seventy-four ministers,* and *twenty thousand two hundred and eighty-six church members* in the respective Districts and Circuits into which the country is divided. It is hoped that the establishment of the Methodist College at Belfast, with the Rev. William Arthur, M.A. at its head, will give a fresh impetus to the cause in Ireland, and that still greater prosperity will be realized in time to come.

THE BRITISH ISLES.

After the brief sketches we have given of the origin and progress of Methodism in England, Scotland, and Ireland, it may be well to glance at some of the beautiful isles near our shores, before we cross the sea and proceed to distant lands. Far away to the north, in a cold and cheerless climate, are situated the ZETLAND ISLANDS, which possess a missionary history worthy of a brief record. The principal of these are, Mainland, Yell, Unst, Bressay, and Fula. Although so near to Scotland, these bleak and rocky isles long remained in a state of great spiritual destitution. It was not till a comparatively recent period that the Gospel, in the form of Wesleyan-Methodism, was introduced into them. This event was brought about by means strikingly illustrative of the special providence of God. John Nicholson, a native of one of these northern islands, wishing to better his position, left home in early life, and entered the British Army. During his absence he was brought to a saving knowledge of the truth, whilst attending the Methodist ministry in London, and joined the Society in Poplar. Having suffered much from ill-health, he obtained his discharge, and returned to his native land in 1819, in very poor circumstances as to this world, but possessed of the pearl of great price. His fellow-countrymen received him kindly, and supplied his temporal wants with their characteristic hospitality; and he, in return, from the fulness of his heart, proclaimed to them the glad tidings of

LERWICK, ZETLAND.

salvation according to his ability. At that time most of the people were, to a great extent, ignorant of spiritual things and very demoralized; but the earnest exhortations of Nicholson were blessed to the conversion of many, and others began to enquire what they must do to be saved. A general concern for religion having been thus awakened in the Zetland Islands, a number of inhabitants united in requesting that they might have Wesleyan Ministers sent to labour among them. This led to the appointment of the Rev. Dr. M'Allum, as a deputation from the British Conference, to visit the country, and to ascertain the real facts of the case.

The report of the deputation being favourable, and the necessity for the appointment of Missionaries immediately being apparent, at the Conference of 1822, it was arranged that the Revs. John Raby and Samuel Dunn should be sent to Zetland. They embarked soon afterwards, and arrived in safety at Lerwick, the capital of the islands, on the 3rd of October. The Missionaries were everywhere received with the liveliest demonstrations of gratitude and joy by a poor but simple-minded people, who were anxious to be instructed in the things of God. They prosecuted their labours from the first with evident tokens of Divine blessings, being assisted by John Nicholson, who still continued faithful, and many were brought to a saving knowledge of the truth. Dr. Clarke, who was President of the Conference that year, took a lively interest in the Mission, and at a subsequent period paid a personal visit to the islands, which was very encouraging and refreshing both to Ministers and people. Messrs. Raby and Dunn were succeeded in after years by the Rev. Messrs. Lewis, Thompson, Wears, Dickinson, Langridge, Hindson, Lowthian, Mackintosh, Mortimer, Stevenson, and others, and the good work was extended to most of the inhabited islands, with much toil, exposure, and discomfort to the Missionaries, but with unspeakable advantage and blessing to the people. At Lerwick, Walls, and other principal towns, tolerable chapels have been erected, Societies formed, and Sabbath-schools established; but from the comparative poverty of the inhabitants the cause is, to a great extent, still dependent upon the liberality of British Christians for its support. It has been sustained and carried on to the present time as an important branch of our Home Mission work, and as such it has a strong claim upon the benevolence of English Methodists.* *Six Ministers* are usefully employed in the Zetland Islands District, and the number of *church members is one thousand eight hundred and ninety-two.*

About midway between the north of England and Ireland, and directly opposite the seaport town of Whitehaven, with which it is in constant communication by means of steam-boats, lies the ISLE OF MAN. Methodism was introduced to this country in the year 1775, in a manner somewhat remarkable. A native of the island, having taken up his residence in Liverpool about that time, was induced to hear one of Mr. Wesley's preachers, when the word preached came with power to his heart, and led to his conversion. The new convert had no sooner found the pearl of great price than he felt deeply concerned for the spiritual welfare of his fellow-countrymen. He was anxious that a Missionary of the Cross should be sent to his native isle to make known to the poor deluded inhabitants the glad tidings of salvation, which had made him so happy. Seeing no prospect of securing the services of a regular Minister, he applied to a zealous Local Preacher named John Crook, and earnestly entreated him to undertake the Mission. Mr. Crook complied with the request, embarked for the Isle of Man, and landed in safety at Douglas on Sunday morning the 11th of March. He made known the object of his visit to the inhabitants of the town, and proceeded at once to preach the first Methodist sermon ever heard in that country. The service was held in the court-house, by the kind permission of the authorities, and the congregation was rather small; but in the evening the attendance was so large that Mr. Crook was obliged to preach in the open air, and a

---

* In 1859 a scheme was set on foot for the erection of a new chapel and minister's residence at Lerwick, the capital of Zetland, as a memorial of the Rev. Dr. Adam Clarke. The buildings were expected to cost about £2,000, towards which upwards of one-half was soon raised by an appeal to friends in Great Britain and other places. This new establishment will be an invaluable acquisition to the whole district, and a great improvement to the town of Lerwick, which has been for some time rising in importance.

gracious influence rested upon the people. At the close of his first day of labour in the Isle of Man, the lonely evangelist, being a perfect stranger in the place, was meditating what steps to take to obtain a lodging, when a warm-hearted Irishman, who had a brother a Methodist in his native land, came up and cordially invited him to his house for the night. A like-minded Scotchman supplied his wants on the following day. Thus encouraged by evident tokens of the providential care of his heavenly Father, as well as by the gracious influence which attended the word, Mr. Crook was induced to persevere in the good work in which he was engaged.

At a subsequent service held during the week, a servant of the Governor was convinced of sin, and led to seek the Lord; and on the following Sabbath his Excellency himself and the clergyman of the town were among the hearers of the humble Methodist preacher. The good work thus auspiciously commenced in Douglas was, on the occasion of a subsequent visit of Mr. Crook, extended to Peeltown, Castletown, and other places, where several persons were savingly converted to God, some of whom were ultimately called to preach the Gospel to their fellow-countrymen. Hence, when Mr. Wesley visited the island, in 1777, he was much pleased with what he saw, and on taking his leave he wrote in his Journal as follows, "Having now visited the island round, east, south, north, and west, I was thoroughly convinced that we have no such Circuit as this, either in England, Scotland, or Ireland." The result of this favourable impression which the founder of Methodism received on the occasion of his first visit to the Isle of Man, was the appointment of regular preachers to cultivate a field so fruitful and promising; and it is a pleasing fact that, from time to time, a glorious harvest has been reaped and laid up in the garner of the Lord. Commodious places of worship have, moreover, been erected in Douglas, Castletown, Ramsay, and Peel, which are the heads of so many Wesleyan Circuits, with their numerous country chapels and preaching places. The Isle of Man District numbers *ten Ministers and two thousand nine hundred and fourteen church members*, forming an interesting and important sphere of evangelical labour.

Passing round the extreme point of Cornwall, called the Land's End, we come to the SCILLY ISLES, the principal of which is called St. Mary's. Rugged and uninteresting as they may appear to the eye of the voyager, they justly claim a prominent place in the history of early Methodism. To these wild and rocky regions the glad tidings of salvation were conveyed by the Rev. Joseph Sutcliffe, in the year 1788, when he was stationed at St. Ives, in Cornwall. His colleagues were very loath to spare him for one week even, to go on this adventurous enterprise, every night being occupied with preaching appointments in the Circuit. But one day a Cornish Methodist called to say, that his men had agreed to forego a night's fishing, in order to take Mr. Sutcliffe to Scilly, that the people there might have an opportunity of hearing the Word of God. This was an opening of Providence which so influenced both preachers and people that they were afraid to obstruct the course of the zealous evangelist any longer. He therefore embarked with the fishermen, and on landing at St. Mary's, he stood up before the door of the inn and preached his first sermon in the open air, on the love of God to a lost and ruined world. He held another service in the evening, and discoursed on justification by faith in our Lord Jesus Christ. The people listened with devout attention to the humble Methodist preacher, and earnestly requested a continuance of his services; but he was obliged to hasten home for the present, promising to return again at the earliest possible opportunity.

On his second visit to the Scilly Isles, Mr. Sutcliffe spent a week in preaching to the people and in visiting from house to house. On this occasion he formed a small class of three members, who had formerly been connected with the Society in Cornwall. On visiting the islands for the third time, shortly afterwards, the zealous Missionary arranged to remain three weeks; but, in consequence of the prevalence of stormy weather, he was detained for three months. This was inconvenient to the St. Ives Circuit, but a great blessing to the inhabitants of the rocky isles; for at that time the only officiating clergyman was in poor health, and was only able to preach once a week, the prayers being read by a sailor. Mr. Sutcliffe was therefore allowed to preach once in the church, but more frequently in the court-house. During this protracted visit a number of persons were brought under religious influence, and thirty enquirers were united in Society, being determined to flee from the wrath to come. Having as yet no religious friends to entertain him, Mr. Sutcliffe was under the necessity of boarding at the inn. But such was the impression made upon the mind of his host by his holy walk and self-denying labours, that when he enquired for his bill, on his departure, he was politely told there was "nothing to pay," and that "the labourer was worthy of his meat." Land was also given for a chapel, which was soon afterwards built, and a Minister was appointed to live and labour among the people. Ever since the Scilly Isles were formed into a Wesleyan Circuit they have presented a useful and interesting sphere of labour, of great importance to the fishermen and others who have been resident there. *One Minister* is employed, and he has *one hundred and thirty church members* under his pastoral care.

On proceeding up the English Channel our attention is arrested by the chalky cliffs of the ISLE OF WIGHT. Or if we make our approach from the other side, a sail of from thirty to sixty minutes in the steamer will bring us from Portsmouth or Southampton to Ryde or Cowes, where we land amid scenes of surpassing beauty and loveliness. Considering the scenery and climate of this charming little isle, it is not surprising that it should be called the " Garden of England," or that it should have been selected as the occasional residence of royalty. But to the Wesleyan Methodist the Isle of Wight possesses an interest above all these considerations, by reason of its early religious history.

When Mr. Wesley paid his first visit to the island, on Tuesday, the 10th of July, 1753, he found a small Society already formed at Newport; but, after a lengthened residence in the town, we have never been able to ascertain by what means the work was first commenced. From Mr. Wesley's " Short History of the People called Methodists," we glean the interesting fact that one of his preachers had been on the ground before him; but who that preacher was, or whence he came, are questions which no one appears to be able to answer. The little flock at Newport received the founder of Methodism with gratitude and joy; and, on inquiring into their religious state, he records the pleasing circumstance that "several of them had found peace with God." He makes special mention of one, a pious female, who "had known her interest in Christ for eight years," having first heard of the way of salvation from a person who called at the island when on his passage to Pennsylvania. Mr. Wesley was not slow to follow up this good beginning. Hence we find him preaching in the market-place at half-past six o'clock in the evening and at five o'clock in the morning to large and attentive congregations. After another sermon on the following evening, he took his departure; but he appears to have been well pleased with his visit to the island, for he returned about three months afterwards, and renewed his efforts for the spiritual welfare of the people, by preaching morning and evening in the market-place at Newport as before, and by extending his visit to Shorwell, a village about six miles distant. "Surely," he wrote on leaving, "if there was any one here to preach the Word of God with power, a multitude would soon be obedient to the faith."

At subsequent periods Mr. Wesley visited the Isle of Wight repeatedly, and took a lively interest in the erection of the first Methodist chapel in Town-lane, Newport. For several years, however, the station was supplied with preachers from Portsmouth, and it was not till 1787 that a Wesleyan Minister was appointed to reside on the island, when a regular Circuit was formed embracing a number of preaching places in the rural districts. Ultimately, the good work was extended to Cowes, Ryde, Ventnor, Godshill, Yarmouth, Freshwater, and to almost every other town and village in the island. The blessing of God attended the word preached, and multitudes were brought to a saving knowledge of the truth, chapels were erected in various places, and Sabbath-schools established for the religious training of the rising generation. The island is now divided into *two Circuits*, with *six Ministers*, and *nine hundred and ninety church members*.

Among the early Wesleyan converts, in the Isle of Wight, was Elizabeth Wallbridge, the "Dairyman's Daughter," of worldwide fame, by means of the simple and touching narrative of the Rev. Legh Richmond. Elizabeth was brought to God through the instrumentality of the Rev. James Crabb, a Methodist Home Missionary; and she was for many years a truly pious and consistent member of our church. When she was taken ill, she went home to her parents, who lived in the cottage which stands directly opposite the Wesleyan chapel on Hale Common, near Arreton; and, there being no Minister of her own denomination in the country, she applied to the clergyman of the parish for spiritual counsel. This led to Mr. Richmond's acquaintance with her, and to the affecting account which he afterwards published of her earnest piety and happy death. The attempt to ignore the fact that the "Dairyman's Daughter" was a Wesleyan Methodist, by a marked silence on the subject, appears to have been a mistaken piece of policy, to gain for the narrative a wider circulation, as is clearly set forth in the interesting volume on "Methodism in the Isle of Wight," by the Rev. J. B. Dyson.

We must now call the attention of the reader to the CHANNEL ISLANDS, the principal of which are Jersey, Guernsey, Alderney, and Sark. From their proximity to the coast of France, they would hardly appear, at first sight, viewed in reference to their geographical position, to belong to England; but such is, nevertheless, the fact. They are the only remnants of the Norman dominions annexed to this country by William the Conqueror, and have ever since remained a part of the British empire, although the French language still prevails there to a considerable extent. The introduction of Methodism into those beautiful islands, and its extension thence to the Continent, may justly be classed among the most remarkable events of its missionary history.

Towards the latter part of the last century, Pierre Le Sueur, a native of Jersey, went to Newfoundland as a trader; and, whilst there, he was convinced of sin under the faithful ministry of the Rev. Lawrence Coughlan, who had been sent there as a Missionary, at the instance of Mr. Wesley. He returned to Jersey in 1775, with an awakened conscience; but his friends and neighbours, to whom he spoke of a change of heart, thought him mad; and he looked in vain for counsel or sympathy, till another convert, named John Fentin, more established in the faith than himself, came from Newfoundland, who afforded him the help which he required. With such counsel and fellowship Le Sueur soon found peace in believing; and he and his friend, Fentin, engaged at once in active Christian labours for the good of their fellow-countrymen. Their conversations, prayers, and exhortations, produced considerable excitement; and, in the course of a week or two, twelve persons were awakened to a sense of their danger, and joined them in their devotions. In 1779 a pious sea captain arrived in Jersey, who gladly united with the Methodists in their efforts to do good, boldly preaching in English, whilst Le Sueur continued his labours in French. In 1783 the little band of devoted Christians was further strengthened by the arrival of a few pious soldiers who had been recently converted, some in Winchester, and others in Southampton, through the instrumentality of Captain Webb, who had been successfully labouring in those places.

The Methodists of Jersey now wrote to England for a preacher; and when Mr. Wesley received the letter, which was forwarded to him by Jasper Winscombe, of Winchester, Robert Carr Brackenbury, Esq., a wealthy Methodist layman, was present. This gentleman had been brought to God some time before, and had just begun to preach; and, being able to preach in French as well as in English, he appeared to be just the man for the Channel Islands. Mr. Wesley told him so, when he nobly offered his services, and proceeded at once to Jersey. Having hired a house in St. Heliers, Mr. Brackenbury held meetings frequently for the religious instruction of all who were willing to attend; and preached the Gospel with great success in various parts of the island, being cordially assisted in his efforts to do good by Mr. Le Sueur and the pious soldiers, and their friends, whom he soon organized into a regular Methodist Society. As the work advanced, in 1786, Mr. Wesley sent Adam Clarke to Jersey, to assist Mr. Brackenbury; and so great was their success that they were soon able to report that "Societies were formed all over the island."

Methodism had been introduced into Guernsey the year before, when Dr. Coke, on visiting the islands, took thither a young French preacher named Jean de Quetteville, who had recently been brought to God and called to the work, and who was made instrumental in the conversion of many sinners. In 1787 Adam Clarke visited Alderney, where he succeeded in planting the standard of the Cross amid much opposition and peril. Whilst the good work was thus advancing in Jersey, Guernsey, and Alderney, the little isle of Sark was favoured with a few sparks of the heavenly fire, and the whole group became permeated with the leven of Methodism. The origin and progress of this remarkable work of God was watched by Mr. Wesley with feelings of deep interest, when, in the eighty-fifth year of his age, he paid a visit to the Channel Islands, accompanied by Dr. Coke. And when the venerable patriarch "saw the grace of God he was glad, and exhorted the people to cleave unto the Lord with purpose of heart." Thenceforward the cause continued to advance, commodious chapels were built in all the towns and villages, and, from year to year, vast multitudes were brought under the influence of the Gospel. There are now, in the respective Circuits of the Channel Islands District, *nineteen Wesleyan Ministers*, French and English, and *four thousand church members.*

Having thus briefly sketched the chief characteristics and results of the Home Missionary work of Methodism in England, Scotland, Ireland, and the British Isles, before we cross the sea to take a survey of the origin and progress of the enterprise in other lands, we may just note the principal statistics, in the aggregate, as far as ascertained. In connection with the various Wesleyan Districts and Circuits in Great Britain, there are *one thousand five hundred and ninety-eight Ministers* and *three hundred and sixty-six thousand, one hundred and twenty-two church members*, in view of which we may "thank God and take courage."

France, Switzerland, and Germany.

In the circumstances connected with the introduction of Methodism into France, and its establishment in various places on the European continent, we can scarcely fail to notice some

HOTEL DE VILLE, ARRAS.

beautiful illustrations of the providence and grace of God. The Lord sometimes works by strange means for the accomplishment of the purposes of His mercy. He frequently overrules evil for good, and causes the wrath of man to praise Him. This was clearly seen in many incidents connected with the war which so long prevailed between England and France in the early part of the present century. Among the prisoners who were taken by the French during that fierce struggle were a number of pious Methodists, who embraced every opportunity of edifying each other, and of seeking to promote the spiritual welfare of their fellow-sufferers in the land of their exile. As early as 1807 some of these wrote home to their friends, from the Arras prison, giving interesting accounts of earnest exhortations, the conversion of sinners, lively prayer-meetings, and happy class-meetings; and reporting as many as seventy persons united in Society at that place. Special mention is made of a dear Christian brother, named Jeremiah Taylor, whose zealous labours were made a great blessing to his fellow-prisoners.

Whilst the leaven of Divine truth was thus working on the Continent, a gracious movement commenced in this country among the French prisoners taken by the English. The unfortunate foreigners were regarded with feelings of sympathy and kindness by the British people generally. In some instances laudable efforts were made to alleviate the distress of the sufferers, by supplying them with clothing and such other temporal comforts as they could not otherwise have obtained, whilst, at the same time, every opportunity was embraced of communicating to them the light of the Gospel. Indeed, a regular Methodist Mission was at length organized for the benefit of the French prisoners of war, especially on the Medway, where seven thousand were confined in ten ships, which were anchored in the river, to receive them as they were brought in. This work of Christian charity originated in motives of pure benevolence, and was carried on in a manner worthy of the highest commendation.

Early in the year 1810, the Rev. William Toase, who was then stationed in the Sevenoaks Circuit, and who had a knowledge of the French language, received a polite invitation from the Commander of H. M. prison ship *Glory*, to visit and preach to the prisoners on board. This he did for the first time on the 7th of March, and the result of the experiment was so encouraging, that he repeated his visits as often as his other engagements would permit. The sanction of the Government authorities having been obtained, through the intervention of Dr. Coke, for the Wesleyan Ministers to visit all the other ships, at the following Conference Mr. Toase was appointed to Rochester, with the understanding that he should devote himself chiefly to this interesting department of Christian labour. This arrangement enabled the zealous Missionary,

CHATHAM.
(*Where many of the French Prisoners were Confined.*)

assisted by a pious French preacher named Kerpezdron, to establish preaching and teaching on board most of the prison ships connected with the depôt at Chatham. He also visited Portsmouth, where nine thousand French prisoners were confined in fifteen prisons, and where he met with the cordial co-operation of the

Rev. Messrs. Beal and Edmondson in making arrangements for their instruction. Similar missions were commenced at Plymouth, by Mr. Le Sueur from Jersey; and at Dartmouth by Mr. Etchells and others.

Thus was the Gospel of Christ faithfully preached to thousands of poor captives in their own tongue, who in the day of their adversity were disposed to attend to it in a manner which they perhaps would not have done under other circumstances. And there is reason to believe that by these means, and the schools which were established for the instruction of youths, the circulation of the Scriptures and other religious books, and the visits paid to the sick in the hospital, many were brought to a saving knowledge of the truth, and received impressions never to be effaced. At intervals, arrangements were made by the Government authorities for a *cartel*, when a considerable number of prisoners were liberated and permitted to return to France as invalids, or in exchange for English prisoners. On such occasions the most affecting scenes were witnessed when the liberated captives took leave of the Missionaries, whom they regarded as their friends and benefactors, and who, in some instances, had been made the means of their salvation. One would say, "When you preached to us the Word of Life, it sounded in our years as the voice of mercy and love, and was a source of consolation to our souls." "How can we forget," exclaimed another, "your labours among us? and be assured we shall feel it our indispensable duty to publish to our families and countrymen what the Methodists have done on our behalf." And, what is better still, they returned to their native land well supplied with copies of the sacred Scriptures and other good books, for their edification and for the instruction of their friends and countrymen. These evangelical labours among the French prisons were continued for three years, with manifest tokens of the presence and blessing of God, and with the most beneficial results to the poor sufferers. Many of those who had been brought to Christ during the time of their captivity, wrote the most pleasing and interesting letters to the Missionaries, after their return home, expressive of their sincere gratitude for the blessings which they had received at their hands.

There can be no doubt but the return of the French prisoners to their own country, under the circumstances we have described, would tend to prepare the way for the reception of the Gospel by their fellow-countrymen; and it was not long afterwards that direct and systematic efforts were made to introduce Methodism into France. When the war was over, which had so long kept the Continent of Europe in a state of constant ferment, the Missionaries in the Channel Islands turned their attention to the neighbouring coast, where some of their converts were already settled, and where the people generally manifested a willingness to hear the Gospel. In the year 1816, Mr. De Quitteville visited Normandy, and spent several weeks at Beuville, Periere, Condé, and Cherbourg, where he met with a kind reception, and preached to the people with evident tokens of the Divine blessing. Having formed a small Society of those who were awakened to a sense of their sinful state, and expressed a sincere desire to flee from the wrath to come, Mr. De Quitteville returned to Guernsey to resume the duties of his own station. In the early part of the following year Messrs. Toase, Ollivier, and Le Sueur, visited the coast at different times as they could be spared from their circuits, to build up the little flock, and to make known to all who were willing to hear, the way of salvation. Notwithstanding many difficulties, and considerable opposition from Popish priests and others, the good work continued to prosper, and neat little chapels were built, first at Periere, and then at Beuville, and other places.

In 1818 arrangements were made for the occupation of several stations on the coast by resident Missionaries with the hope of giving permanence to the work. Messrs. Le Sueur and Cook were appointed to Beuville, Periere and Condé, Mr. Kerpezdron to Mer, and Mr. Ollivier to Cherbourg, with Mr. Toase, resident in Jersey, as General Superintendent of the French Mission, under the direction of the Missionary Committee in London. The following year the Rev. John Hawtrey was appointed to labour in Paris where he was succeeded, after a considerable interval, during which the station was vacant, by Messrs. Cook, Toase, Newstead, and others who prosecuted the work with varied measures of success amid many difficulties and discouragements, till, by the blessing of God

NEW WESLEYAN CHAPEL, PARIS.

upon the labours of His servants, it reached its present position of importance and respectability. In 1862, a beautiful new chapel and mission premises were erected in the Rue Roquépine, where religious services are regularly held every Sabbath, and frequently during the week, in French and English, and occasionally in German, for the convenience and benefit of the inhabitants and the numerous visitors who frequently flock to the French capital. There also a book depôt has been established, and schools are conducted for the training of the rising generation, and the station is an important centre of light and influence in a dark benighted land. The work has also been extended to Chantilly, Rheims, Calais, and Boulogne, where there are a considerable number of English residents, who, by means of our Missionaries, are favoured with a Gospel ministry in their own tongue. At the same time an important work is carried on in French by native ministers, who have been raised up as the fruit of missionary labour. Since the organization of the French Conference in 1852, Methodism has been planted in various parts of the south of France and Switzerland, where it had not previously been introduced, and the noble band of faithful labourers who occupy the ground are pressing onward in their holy enterprise with heart and hope amid numerous difficulties, arising chiefly from Romish prejudice and the want of adequate means to carry on the work.

But Methodism in SWITZERLAND demands a distinct and separate notice, however brief. No true-hearted Wesleyan can regard with feelings of indifference the native land of the sainted John Fletcher, Vicar of Madeley. Although these mountainous regions were more highly favoured than many parts of the European continent in former times, by enjoying a larger measure of the light of Protestant Christianity, yet many districts were fearfully dark and demoralised, when, in 1839, the Missionaries in the south of France were induced to extend their labours to them. In the following year, a Missionary and an assistant were appointed to the Upper Alps, the very place where the celebrated Felix Neff had once laboured with such apostolic zeal and success, but which was now suffering from extreme spiritual destitution. Ultimately, a permanent station was established at Lausanne, in the Canton de Vaud; and, in 1867, a new chapel, college, and other ecclesiastical buildings were erected as a memorial of Mr. Fletcher, and for the benefit of his birth-place, towards the cost of which the Missionary Committee in London made a liberal grant from the Jubilee Fund. This institution, which is called the "Students' Home," is under the able superintendence of the Rev. James Hocart, and promises to be a valuable acquisition to the French

FLETCHER MEMORIAL CHAPEL AND COLLEGE, LAUSANNE.

Conference, as it affords the means of training labourers for every part of the work. From this centre of spiritual light and gospel influence, as well as from other mission stations in France and Switzerland, it may be reasonably hoped that, in time to come, the truth of God will go forth, which with His blessing, may prove effectual to the salvation of many souls, and tend to counteract the Popish superstition and infidelity which are so rife in those countries.

It is a pleasing fact that, notwithstanding the obstacles which have impeded the progress of the work at every stage from its very commencement, the servants of God have not been permitted to labour in vain or spend their strength for nought. Some precious sheaves have already been gathered into the garner of the Lord. In addition to results which can never be tabulated, there are now in connexion with the French Methodist Conference *thirty-five Missionaries, two thousand one hundred and fifty-eight church members*, and *two thousand six hundred scholars* in the Mission schools.

Methodism in GERMANY, both in its origin and subsequent course, appears to have been pre-eminently a child of Providence. About the year 1830 an industrious and respectable German named Christopher Gottlob Müller, had occasion to visit England on business; and whilst in this country, he was brought to a saving knowledge of the truth through the instrumentality of the Wesleyan ministry. On his return to Winnenden, in the kingdom of Wurtemberg, his native place, he made known to his friends and neighbours what a precious treasure he had found. Being a man of ardent temperament and unquenchable zeal, Mr. Müller exerted himself in every possible way to save the souls of his fellow countrymen. He held meetings for exhortation, prayer, and Christian fellowship, in different places, at stated intervals; and the effects produced by his humble efforts were of a very extraordinary character. From the commencement the special blessing of God rested upon the labours of His servant, and it is believed that in a short time scores and hundreds of sinners were savingly converted to God.

Those who were thus gathered out of the world Mr. Muller united in religious societies after the Methodist plan as he had seen it in England; and, if the discipline was not so perfect as could have been desired, it was better than none, as it kept the people together; and the good work continued to prosper. Every convert who was endowed with the gift of prayer or exhortation was immediately pressed into the service of the Lord by the zealous evangelist; and, in the course of a few years, their sphere of usefulness had so enlarged that he was enabled to report that his fellow-labourers in the Gospel were twenty-three in number, that his plan of village labour included twenty-six places, and that the number of persons admitted into his religious societies, after due examination and trial, was three hundred and twenty-six.

Long before the work had reached this point of prosperity, Mr. Müller had placed himself in communication with the Committee of the Wesleyan Missionary Society in London, with a view to obtain such aid and direction as they might be able to give. The Mission would no doubt have been taken up by the Society and prosecuted with vigour had the way been clear to do so. But there were certain peculiarities in the laws and ecclesiastical usages of the country, which seemed to render it inexpedient to send regular Wesleyan Missionaries from England to Germany at that early period. It was, therefore, considered best for the time being, to direct, encourage, and aid Mr. Müller and his coadjutors in every possible way in the prosecution of their noble enterprise, and to await the openings of Divine Providence with regard to future action. For the long period of twenty-eight years did this zealous servant of the Lord continue to labour under the direction of the Wesleyan Missionary Committee, by whom the necessary funds were supplied for carrying on the work. In the early part of the year 1858, worn out with incessant toil, but happy in the Saviour's love, good Mr. Müller was called to his reward in heaven; and his remains were conveyed to their last resting place amid the tears and lamentations of multitudes of people who had been benefitted by his labours.

The father and founder of the German Wesleyan Mission having been thus removed from the scene of his hallowed toil, it became necessary to take immediate steps to provide for carrying on the work. In the first place, the Rev. W. B. Pope, M.A., of Hull, was requested to visit Germany, and report to the Committee the state and requirements of the Mission. This led to the appointment, in 1859, of the Rev. John Lyth, D.D., to Winnenden, who for about five years rendered good service to the cause as General Superintendent of the German Mission. On the return of Dr. Lyth to England, he was succeeded in his office, in 1865, by the Rev. John C. Barratt; the Revs. John M. Morill, and George Terry, B.A., having taken part in the work in the interim. Nothwithstanding numerous difficulties which have presented themselves from time to time, a pleasing measure of success has been realised. The most encouraging feature of this mission has been the raising up of a large number of native evangelists to proclaim to their fellow-countrymen that Gospel which had made them so happy. By the blessing of God upon the agency employed, the work has expanded into *ten circuits*, supplied by *one English missionary* and *ten German ministers and assistants*, with *a membership of one thousand nine hundred and fifteen*, and *two hundred and sixty-one scholars* in the Mission schools.

Before we take our leave of this part of the European continent we must say a few words about SWEDEN, where a Wesleyan Mission was commenced in 1826; but, in consequence of peculiar circumstances, was ultimately relinquished. The first Missionary appointed to this country was the Rev. Joseph R. Stephens, who was sent there at the earnest request of a few English residents in Stockholm, with the double object of ministering to them, and of seeking to diffuse the light of the Gospel among the native inhabitants. He addressed himself to the study of the Swedish language with becoming diligence, and, in the mean time, he held religious services in English, which were highly appreciated by those who were able to profit by them. In 1830, Mr. Stephens was succeeded by the Rev. George Scott, D.D., who continued to labour in Sweden with much zeal and earnestness for about twelve years, amid many difficulties, but with considerable success. After a commodious chapel had been erected in Stockholm, and the work had made encouraging progress, a storm of persecution arose, and a spirit of intolerance was manifest by the civil and ecclesiastical authorities, which resulted in the withdrawal of the missionary, to the grief and disappointment of those who had been benefitted by his labours. It is believed, however, that the spiritual results of the mission during its continuance will be seen in the last great day. It is a pleasing fact, moreover, that the north of Europe is not left entirely without the benefit of our form of Christianity, the Methodist Episcopal Church of America having extensive and important Missions in Norway, as well as in France and Germany.

Gibraltar, Spain, and Italy.

The Wesleyan Mission to Gibraltar was attended with circumstances of a very gloomy character in its commencement; but afterwards the sun of prosperity shone upon it, and it has been made a blessing to thousands, especially of the military, who have been, from time to time, stationed there. It was about the beginning of the present century that a number of Methodist soldiers then quartered at Gibraltar, united in a petition to Dr. Coke that they and other residents at that celebrated military settlement, who felt their spiritual destitution, might be favoured with the services of a Wesleyan chaplain. This led to the appointment, in 1804, of the Rev. James M'Mullen, as the first Missionary to Gibraltar. He arrived there with his wife and child, after a stormy passage, in the month of September. On landing they found the yellow fever raging among the wasted population with more than its usual violence and malignity. The fatal disease had invaded almost every family, and there was scarcely a house in which there was not one dead. The Missionary's little child had scarcely breathed the tainted air when it was seized with the malady. On the 10th of October, her anxious father, fatigued with constant watching by the couch of affliction, was himself prostrated with the fever, and on the 18th he was a corpse. Mrs. M'Mullen had borne up during these days of woe with wonderful fortitude, being sustained by her unwavering faith in the goodness and wisdom of God; but at the hour which ended the life of her dear husband, she was herself smitten with the shaft of the pestilence, and followed him in a few days to the tomb. Contrary to all expectation, the orphan child survived; and, as soon as possible, was sent, under suitable care, to England. In His kind providence the God of her parents gave her a home in the family of good Dr. Adam Clarke. That fatherly man and his excellent wife brought up the little Gibraltar orphan girl as their own daughter, and had the satisfaction of seeing her rise into life well-educated, amiable and pious. She became the wife of a Methodist minister, the Rev. John Rigg, and lived to see her children the subjects of Divine blessing in providence and grace, one of her sons being the Rev. J. H. Rigg, D.D., the esteemed Principal of the Westminster Training College. She finished her course in peace at Southport, on the 3d of June, 1869, in the seventy-third year of her age.

Four years elapsed after this dark cloud had passed over the scene before another attempt was made to establish a Wesleyan Mission at Gibraltar. The call being still loud and pressing, the station was at length resumed by the appointment of the Rev. William Griffith in 1808. On his arrival the Missionary received a cordial welcome from a few sincere souls who had been anxiously looking out for him; and he entered upon his work with a zeal and diligence which gave promise of success. Without loss of time, a small piece of ground was purchased, and arrangements made for the erection of a chapel. After many difficulties had been overcome, this desirable object was accomplished, and the building was opened for Divine worship early in the year 1811. Mr. Griffith was succeeded by the Revs. Messrs. Gill, Wood, Davis, Rees, Coscombe, Dixon, Pratten, Barber, Stinson, Rule, and others; but it is to the zealous and able minister last named that Gibraltar is more particularly indebted. Dr. Rule spent the long period of ten years in connection with the station, and in earnest efforts to introduce the Gospel into Spain. At different periods previous to his appointment, serious difficulties had been thrown in the way of soldiers attending the Wesleyan Chapel. Indeed, on one occasion, as early as the 11th of July, 1808, the year before the arrival of the first Missionary, a regimental court-martial was held, by order of Lieutenant-Colonel Ramsay, for the trial of Corporals James Lamb, and Richard Russel, and Privates James Hampton, John Reeves, and John Fluccard; charged with un-soldier-like conduct, in attending a Methodist meeting, contrary to regimental orders. And, strange as it may appear, they were found GUILTY; and the sentence passed upon them was, that the two corporals were to be reduced, and all the five men were to receive FIVE HUNDRED LASHES EACH! Persecution was not often carried to these extreme lengths it is true; but various annoyances were experienced, from time to time, till Dr. Rule adopted measures to secure to British soldiers the rights of religious liberty which are enjoyed by Her Majesty's other subjects. Ultimately, all military men who declared themselves Wesleyans, were not only permitted to attend our services, but regularly paraded and marched to chapel every Sunday morning. The attendance, of course, is fluctuating; but four or five hundred men have sometimes thus been marched to the Wesleyan parade service at Gibraltar. A blessed work of grace has, moreover, been frequently experienced among the soldiers, and we have met with pious men in different parts of the world who have thanked God that ever they heard the Gospel preached by our Missionaries at the "Rock." We have also heard them speak of happy prayer-meetings in a secluded grotto in a mountain glen, well known to all praying soldiers. We have now on that station only *one Missionary, twenty church members, and two hundred and seventy-five scholars* in the Mission school; but the Gospel is faithfully preached to large congregations.

When the Wesleyan Mission to Gibraltar was first organised, it was not only with a view to the benefit of the military stationed there, but also with the hope that SPAIN and other neighbouring countries would ultimately derive considerable advantage from it. In fact, Gibraltar was considered to be the *key* to Spain, the Mediterranean, Northern Africa, and the Holy Land, in a Missionary sense, as well as in relation to political and mercantile affairs. And if this pleasing idea has not been realised to the extent that was anticipated, the failure must not be attributed to any neglect on the part of the agents of the Society; but to causes entirely beyond their control. The Missionaries stationed at Gibraltar, from time to time, have constantly kept an eye upon Spain, and have made frequent attempts to benefit the inhabitants;

but they have hitherto been, to a great extent, disappointed and thwarted in their efforts. The Spanish department of the work on the Rock, with its schools, preaching and other services in the Castelian language has been sustained with the hope that it would not only prove the means of salvation to the native inhabitants of the settlement, but also prepare the way by training suitable agents and otherwise, for an agressive movement on the Popish darkness and superstition of the interior. Nor have direct efforts for the accomplishment of this desirable object being wanting, however unsuccessful in their results

As early as 1836, Dr. Rule made arrangements for the extension of the mission to Spain; and in order to ascertain the post most eligible for occupation, he visited Cadiz, Malaga, and Granada. This led, in the course of the following year, to the appointment of a Spanish Wesleyan schoolmaster to Cadiz, who, for some time, held religious services, distributed copies of the Scriptures, and tracts, first on board the merchant ships in the harbour, and then on shore as he had opportunity. He soon met with the most determined and violent opposition from the priests and others. Dr. Rule himself went over and held a service or two, and tried to smooth the way for his agent; but this made matters worse, and the spirit of persecution increased till the Mission-school was closed by authority, when the teacher was obliged to leave Cadiz, and the work was consequently relinquished. Another attempt was made in 1838, and the Mission at Cadiz was recommenced under more favourable circumstances, when sanguine hopes were entertained of ultimate success. But the same hostility to the light and truth of the Gospel ere long manifested itself; and the opposition became so violent, that the Missionary was again obliged to abandon his post, and return to Gibraltar. In 1868 a revolution occurred in Spain, the Queen being driven from the throne, and a Provisional Government organised to make arrangements for the future. When legislating on ecclesiastical matters the Cortes decreed that Roman Catholicism should be the established religion of the State; but that free toleration should be allowed to any other professions of faith. What will result from these measures in favour of religious liberty remains to be seen; but we are free to confess, from what we have seen of the *animus* of Popery in other countries, that we are not very sanguine as to the religious future of Spain, so long as that form of error continues dominant. The Wesleyan Missionary Society has a lay-agent, well acquainted with the Spanish language, employed in the Peninsula, holding religious services, distributing tracts and collecting information as he finds opportunities, and the Committee is ready to enter any opening which may present itself for the permanent promulgation of the Gospel, so far as the friends of Missions will authorise them by their contributions.

In common with all other countries where Popery predominates, PORTUGAL also stands in need of the pure light of the Gospel. A few pious Methodists, resident at Oporto, being anxious to worship God in their own way, as well as to promote the spiritual welfare of their neighbours, built a little Wesleyan chapel in the year 1868, and a few services were held in it with manifest tokens of the Divine presence and blessing. Before long, however, a spirit of persecution was evoked, which marred the peace of the humble worshippers. The principal promoter of the enterprise was put in prison for the serious crime of preaching the Gospel. When the case was tried judgment was given in favour of the prisoner, and he was set at liberty; but the little flock of *seventeen in number* are subject to much persecution and annoynnce, whilst they wait, and hope, and pray for better days.

We must now pass over to ITALY and take a glance at the rise and progress of a work of God which, although but of yesterday, gives promise of a bright and glorious future. Italy had long been regarded as an inviting field of labour; but for many years, like all other Popish countries, it continued effectually closed against the Gospel. But, after the revolution in the civil government of the country which occurred a few years ago, a measure of religious liberty was allowed to the inhabitants, and a desire was expressed in many places for evangelical instruction, The Wesleyan Missionary Society gladly embraced the opportunity which presented itself and entered the field, by the appointment in 1860, of the

Rev. Richard Green to commence the new Mission. In the course of the following year Mr. Green was joined by the Rev. Henry J. Piggott, B.A.; and the two brethren took extensive tours to collect information, and seek the most suitable place to begin their Missionary operations. At length they fixed upon Milan for their head-quarters, and commenced their labours with sanguine hopes of success, being favoured with the assistance of Signor Bosio, an Italian evangelist, who soon afterwards joined them. Mr. Green having been obliged to return to England was succeeded, in 1863, by the Rev. T. W. S. Jones, who proved admirably adapted for the somewhat peculiar enterprise.

The blessing of God evidently attended the labours of His servants, and in a short time the work was extended to Florence, Jura, Parma, Monza, and other town and villages where preaching places, Christian schools, and book depôts were established, and the work of evangelisation vigourously carried on in all its departments. At this early period the English Missionaries gladly availed themselves of the services of Signors Lassolo, Ferretti, and Gualtieri Ravioli, and Del Mondo, native evangelists, who were providentially raised up to aid them in the good work. The brother first named was subsequently, after the usual probation, received into our Connexion as a Wesleyan Italian minister. Whether the success of the Wesleyan Mission in Italy has met the sanguine expectations of its friends and supporters or not, there can be no doubt but it has already been made the means of salvation to many; and if earnestly prosecuted, and liberally sustained by the friends of Missions at home, as it deserves to be, there is reason to believe that in time to come, the results will be much more abundant. We have now in Italy *three English Wesleyan Missionaries, nine Italian ministers, seven hundred and nine church members,* and *seven hundred and forty-three scholars* in the mission schools. The report presented by the Rev. G. T. Perks, M.A., and the Rev. W. Gibson, of Paris, who visited the respective stations in Italy, in the autumn of 1859, as a deputation from the parent society, was most encouraging.

Malta and the Mediterranean.

At an early period of the Society's history, several Mission stations were commenced at different points on the islands and shores of the MEDITERRANEAN, which seem to deserve a passing notice in a work of this kind, notwithstanding the circumstance that most of them were afterwards relinquished. We have already remarked that in former times Gibraltar was regarded, in a Missionary sense, as the key to all the countries beyond the Straits; and whilst this pleasant dream was indulged, earnest efforts were made to plant the standard of the cross in various prominent centres of the population. As early as 1824, the Rev. John Keeling was appointed to Malta, and the Rev. Charles Cook to Palestine; and the following year the Rev. Donald Macpherson was appointed to Alexandria in Egypt. In 1827, the Rev. Walter Oke Croggon was appointed to Zante; and he was afterwards joined by the Rev. James Bartholomew, with the hope of extending the work to different parts of Greece. These interesting stations, with the exception of Palestine, which was never fully entered upon, were occupied for several years, with different measures of success; but, on the whole, the results were not such as to warrant their continuance, and they were consequently given up, to the disappointment and sorrow of numerous liberal supporters of the cause who felt an interest in their success.

But, although Missions once considered important and promising were thus relinquished, we are not to conclude that no good was done during their continuance. Perhaps the number of souls that were saved through their instrumentality more than justified the expense that was incurred in their support; but the numerous claims upon the Society's funds by fields of labour more necessitous and more fruitful, were such as to render this step imperatively necessary; for we must remember the obligation to " go, not only to those who want us, but to those who want us most."

The station that was occupied by the Wesleyan Missionary Society, for the longest period in the Mediterranean, was MALTA,

MALTA.

the island where St. Paul was shipwrecked on his voyage to Rome, and the inhabitants of which showed him and his fellow-sufferers "no small kindness." This place was favoured with the labours of a Missionary for about twenty years, and was only given up in 1844, when numerous changes had taken place among the few English residents, and the military to whom his services were chiefly devoted. The natives of Malta were so completely under the influence of the Romish Priests, who strictly prohibited them from attending any Protestant religious service whatever, that, with very few exceptions, they were entirely inaccessible to the Missionary, or, perhaps, he would not have been withdrawn from the island.

It is pleasant to be able to add that Malta has recently been re-occupied by the Society as a military station. Henceforth as Methodists, sailing up the Mediterranean, come in sight of this beautiful island, they will have the pleasure of knowing that a Wesleyan Missionary is once more stationed there. At the Conference of 1869, the Rev. William S. Caldecott was appointed to minister to the Wesleyan soldiers and sailors stationed there. Under date of the 21st of April, 1869, Mr. Caldecott thus reports the promising commencement of his work: "During the first quarter we have discovered between two and three hundred declared Wesleyans in the army. I have also found in the ships of the royal navy, which have been in port, a hundred and sixty-one Wesleyans who were enrolled as such on joining their ships, and a hundred and ninety-one who, not being acquainted with the regulations, were not so enrolled. Three services are now held every Sunday. Soldiers and seamen also meet in my Bible-class, where about thirty are generally present. Our regular Society class is well attended." Surely, such a work as this, for the spiritual benefit of the sons of our people who have entered the army and navy, and are far away from home, is worthy of the cordial support of British Methodists, and it would be well if every garrison and naval port in the world were thus favoured. We number at Malta only *one Missionary* and *twenty church members;* but large congregations of soldiers and sailors assemble every Sabbath at parade service for the public worship of God, and it would be difficult to calculate the benefits which may ultimately result from the faithful preaching of the Gospel to such classes of men.

We cannot bring this chapter to a close, and take our leave of a country associated in the mind with so many touching historical recollections, without expressing our regret that the Wesleyan Missionary Society has at present no station in Rome, Greece, Egypt, Palestine, or any of the other classic Bible lands, where Popish and Mahomedan darkness and superstition reign triumphant, and where the light of the Gospel is so much required. All honour to the Scottish and American Missionaries who have toiled so long and so earnestly in those eastern regions with so little fruit; but we respectfully submit that a body like ours, which claims to be the largest Protestant Missionary Society in the world, ought not to be without its agents and representatives in a part of the globe which must always be interesting as the original home of mankind, the birth-place of Christianity, and the cradle of civilisation. May the time soon come when British Methodists shall be honoured to take their full share in the important task of disseminating the pure light of the Gospel throughout the dark benighted regions of the East.

The aggregate number of Wesleyan Ministers now labouring in Europe is *one thousand nine hundred and forty-two;* and they have under their pastoral care a church-membership amounting to *five hundred and ninety-one thousand, two hundred and twenty;* with colleges, seminaries, and schools for the training of the rising generation, which number their pupils by *hundreds of thousands.* Gratifying, as this rate of progress may appear, when viewed in connexion with the comparatively brief period which has elapsed since the commencement of the work, we must not forget that much more yet remains to be done before this highly favoured land, and the countries in our immediate vicinity, can be said entirely to belong to Christ. The Home Mission work of Methodism was never more needed than at the present time. Nor was it ever more important, whether viewed in its direct bearing on the spiritual interests of our countrymen, or in its inseparable connection with the foreign Missionary enterprise, to which the attention of the reader will next be directed.

CHAPTER II.

AMERICA.

DISCOVERY OF THE NEW WORLD—THE UNITED STATES—CANADA—HUDSON'S BAY TERRITORY—BRITISH COLUMBIA—NOVA SCOTIA—NEW BRUNSWICK—PRINCE EDWARD'S ISLAND—NEWFOUNDLAND—BERMUDAS.

ONE of the most remarkable events recorded in ancient or modern history is the discovery of the New World by the celebrated Christopher Columbus. Age after age had passed away without any definite idea having been entertained by the ancients of the existence of a vast continent and numerous islands, beyond the expansive ocean which bounded the distant horizon, as seen from the shores of Europe and of Africa, when the grand problem was solved, towards the close of the fifteenth century. After considerable study and much experience as a navigator, Columbus came to the conclusion that, in order to preserve the equilibrium of the globe in its constant revolving motions, there must be a large body of land in the western hemisphere, and the most direct course to the remote regions of the east was by sailing due west. Impressed with this conviction, his ardent mind longed for the means of exploring the distant western seas to bring his theory to the test of experience. He sought for the aid which he required in England and other countries; but he was disappointed and thwarted in every direction, till Ferdinand and Isabella, King and

Queen of Spain, became his patrons, and enabled him to take his first adventurous voyage in 1493. The undertaking was altogether so novel and romantic that it was not without difficulty that seamen were engaged to man the ship; and when they had sailed westward for about four weeks without realising the object of their search, the sailors were on the point of mutiny in their anxiety to return. Columbus promised that if they did not succeed in three days he would comply with their request, and abandon the enterprise; but early the next morning, the 12th of October, to the surprise and delight of all on board, they came in sight of land. It was an island of the Bahama group, to which they gave the name of San Salvador, and where they soon landed and became acquainted with a country and a people such as they had never seen before. Then commenced a series of incidents of a most interesting character in connection with the discovery of other islands, and the exploration of the neighbouring continent, into the particulars of which we cannot now enter, as they are not relevant to the important object we have in view.

Amongst the crowd of adventurers from all parts of Europe who followed in the wake of Columbus, after his first wonderful voyage, was an enterprising Florentine navigator, named Americus Vesputius, who directed his course northwards, and who is said to have been the first to discover the mainland of the northern continent, to which he gave his own name. From thenceforward, whether appropriately or not, the western world was known as AMERICA. In the year 1497, a famous foreign navigator, named Cabot, a Venetian by birth, but who had for some time been settled in England with his three sons, sailed from Bristol, under the auspices of Henry VII., King of Great Britain and Ireland, and traced the coast of Labrador. These enterprising voyagers made other discoveries southwards, which, being followed up by other English adventurers, resulted in the settlement by emigrants from the United Kingdom, of those extensive provinces formerly known as our American plantations. Several of these ultimately became independent of the British crown, and were formed into a

The United States.

By a reference to the map we shall see that the United States embrace nearly one-half of the continent of North America, having on the east the Atlantic Ocean, on the south Mexico and the West Indies, on the west the Pacific, and on the north the British dominion of Canada. At the same time, it must be observed that the boundaries of the Union have varied from time to time as new territories have been annexed by purchase, aggressive war on the aborigines, or otherwise. At its first formation the Republic consisted of only thirteen states; but by the means alluded to they have now increased to thirty. The population has steadily but rapidly increased in the meantime, as a mighty tide of emigration has continued to flow from Great Britain and Ireland, and the different states of continental Europe.

The extensive emigration to America, which has been going on for so many years, may be traced to various causes besides that love of change and adventure which is inherent in human nature. As population increased, from year to year, in Europe, remunerative employment, and a comfortable subsistence for industrious labourers, and artizans, and their families, became more and more difficult to acquire. Religious persecution, moreover, fell heavily upon the people in many places, and made them long for a residence in a country where they might worship God without molestation, according to the dictates of conscience. These considerations of civil and religious liberty, in connection with the flattering prospects of worldly prosperity which were held out to them, have induced tens of thousands to leave their native land, and to try to improve the social position of themselves and their posterity in the Western hemisphere. Whilst a few indolent and apathetic persons have been much disappointed and wished themselves home again, others who were characterized by industrious and energetic habits have succeeded beyond their most sanguine expectations. From whatever point of view we regard the question, it must be admitted that America possesses every necessary quality for a great and prosperous country. Its commodious harbours, majestic rivers, towering mountains, fertile plains, and abundance of timber, coal, iron, and other metals, with many other advantages which might be named, all bespeak for it a grand and glorious future.

The introduction of Methodism into America must be regarded as one of the most important events that ever occurred in its moral and religious history, and was attended by a train of providential circumstances which are worthy of notice. In the year 1760, among the emigrants who came from Ireland were a few pious persons who had been gathered into the fold of Christ in their native land, by the zealous and devoted Wesley or his fellow labourers in the Gospel. The most distinguished of these were Philip Embury and Barbara Heck, who were of Palatine descent, and who, with their friends, settled at New York. Like many other emigrants, whom we have known, they seem to have suffered considerably from religious declension during the voyage across the Atlantic, and in their struggles to establish a home in the New World; for we have no information of any religious movement among them for several years after their arrival in America. Some, indeed, have asserted that the whole party had so far wandered from God as to become addicted to the pleasures of the world, such as dancing, card-playing, and the like. However this may have been, there appears to be no doubt but that Barbara Heck, a "Mother in Israel," was the principal means of arousing them to a sense of their religious obligation, and of initiating measures which led to the organisation of the first Methodist Society on the continent of America.

According to the accounts which have been published by the most reliable American historians, a large company of the Irish emigrants were engaged in playing cards one evening in the autumn of 1766, at the residence of one of them, when Barbara Heck came in, and, burning with indignation at their sin and folly, she hastily seized the cards and threw them into the fire; and, at the same time, administered a scathing rebuke to all concerned. She then went to the house of Mr. Embury, and told him what she had seen, and what she had done, adding with great earnestness, "Philip, you must preach to us, or we shall all go to hell, and God will require our blood at your hands!" The backsliding professor was somewhat confused by this startling appeal, and he endeavoured to excuse himself saying, "How can I preach when I have neither a house to preach in, nor a congregation?" "Preach," said this noble, earnest, Christian woman, "in your own house, and to your own company;" and before she left, she elicited a promise from Mr. Embury, who had been a local preacher in Ireland, that he would endeavour once more to speak to the people in the name of the Lord. A few days afterwards he redeemed his pledge by preaching the first Methodist sermon ever delivered in America, in his own hired house, to a congregation of *five* persons. Such was the humble origin of the Methodist Episcopal Church of the United States, now the largest and most influential body of Christians on the great American continent. Well may we exclaim with the prophet, "Who hath despised the day of small things?"

Having been aroused to a sense of the responsibility of his position, and led to give himself afresh to God, Mr. Embury, encouraged by the zealous Mrs. Heck, thenceforth regularly exercised his talents which had so long lain dormant; and the Lord greatly blessed his labours. In a short time his congregation so increased, that it was found necessary to obtain a larger place of worship. Accordingly, a spacious "upper room" in Barrack-street was hired, where the people assembled in large numbers to hear the Word of God, and where a class was soon formed of twelve members. Among those who were gathered into the fold of Christ at this early period, there were three British soldiers, James Hodge, Addison Low, and John Buckley, who soon became valuable helps to Mr. Embury, labouring zealously as prayer-leaders, and exhorters, and co-operating with him in every possible way to carry on the good work. In the early part of the year 1767, it was found necessary for the infant church, in New York, still further to extend their borders; and a large room was hired in William-street, generally known as the "Rigging Loft," it having been formerly used as a marine-store room. The number of services was now increased; and preaching was commenced on week nights, as well as on the morning and evening of the Sabbath. About this time the society was strengthened by the arrival of Mr. Thomas Taylor from England, and another party of Methodist emigrants from Ireland, among whom were Messrs. Charles White and Richard Sause. Several of these being persons of more than ordinary respectability and of undoubted piety and zeal, and also possessed of considerable property, they were able to render efficient help in various ways to the rising cause of Methodism in the New World.

Shortly afterwards a little incident occurred which shows how God frequently provides the means for carrying on His work in a manner quite unexpected by His people. When the infant church at New York had been meeting together for Divine worship about three months in the "Rigging Loft," one Sabbath evening, a strange-looking military gentleman appeared amongst them. He was dressed as a British officer in full uniform, and had lost the use of one of his eyes, over which he wore a green shade. The appearance of the stranger caused some excitement among the timid worshippers, and a general enquiry was made as to his character, and what could be his object in coming to the meeting. The fears of the people soon gave way to joy and gratitude, however, on learning that the dashing military officer was a Christian brother, and a Methodist, who had been converted to God under the preaching of Mr. Wesley in Bristol about three years before. The general joy was still further increased, when it became known that he had come to reside in the country, having received the appointment of barrack-master at Albany, and that he was a zealous Local Preacher, and would be able to render valuable assistance to Mr. Embury and his associates in carrying on the good work in which they were engaged. His name was Captain Webb— a name which is deservedly associated with those of Philip Embury and Barbara Heck in the history of the planting of Methodism in America. The gallant soldier preached in his regimentals, his trusty sword lying on the desk in the meantime; and

CAPTAIN WEBB PREACHING IN THE "RIGGING LOFT," NEW YORK.

the novelty of the sight, together with the warm and earnest manner of the preacher, drew vast crowds to hear him. The Word preached was attended with "soul-converting power," and under his ministry, as well as that of the faithful Embury, multitudes were gathered into the fold of Christ. The far-famed "Rigging Loft," in which the people assembled for Divine worship, soon became too small for the rapidly-increasing congregation, and the erection of a regular Christian sanctuary was seriously contemplated.

The building of a new chapel under such circumstances, by a people so few in number, and of comparatively slender means, was a great undertaking. But they were animated by a true spirit of Christian zeal, and commenced the work with a measure of earnestness worthy of the occasion. The difficulties which they had to encounter were numerous; but in the strength of the Lord they overcame them all, and the building being at length completed, it was dedicated to the service of God on the 30th of October, 1768, when Mr. Embury preached from Hosea x, 12, just two years after his first sermon in his own hired house. Barbara Heck took a lively interest in the building of the new chapel, and it is said she whitewashed the walls with her own hands, her husband, Paul Heck being one of the trustees. This first Methodist place of worship on the continent of America, was the old chapel in John-street, on the site of which the present noble John-street Methodist Church was erected several years afterwards,—a place which we visited with feelings of peculiar interest when in New York in 1844, as it is known throughout America as the "Cradle of Methodism" on that vast continent.

Whilst Mr. Embury was as earnestly engaged in evangelical labours in New York as the claims of his worldly avocation would permit, Captain Webb was boldly proclaiming the glad tidings of salvation in other places, especially in Albany and Long Island, where numbers were brought to a saving knowledge of the truth, and prosperous societies were formed at an early period. About the same time, namely, in 1767 or 1768, Methodism was introduced into Maryland, in the south, by Robert Strawbridge, who was also a pious emigrant from Ireland, and formerly in connexion with Mr. Wesley. He had left his native land a short time before to improve his temporal circumstances; but although he seems to have failed in that object, he was nevertheless made the instrument of spiritual good to thousands. He settled at a place called Sam's Creek, in Frederick County, then a backwoods' settlement, where he immediately commenced preaching in his own dwelling-house. Numbers were soon converted, several of whom were called by the great Head of the Church to take a part with him in the good work as Exhorters and Local Preachers; and before long a "Log Meeting-house" was built at a place about a mile from Mr. Strawbridge's residence, which, being the first Methodist chapel in Maryland, ultimately became as noted in the annals of Methodism in that part of America as had been the old "Rigging Loft" in New York.

But zealous and earnest as were the labours of Philip Embury, Captain Webb, and Robert Strawbridge, and those of their noble band of helpers, all of whom had to attend to their secular affairs for the support of themselves and families, as the work expanded, the need of regular Missionaries, who should be entirely devoted to the work, was much felt. Hence, about two years after the formation of the first Society, we find the members uniting in an earnest request that Mr. Wesley would send them regular preachers from England to take the spiritual oversight of the infant church, which had been organised under such promising circumstances, and to labour for the further extension of the Redeemer's kingdom. The founder of Methodism appears to have seen at a glance the important bearing of the question, and to have resolved to do his utmost to meet the wishes of his correspondents. When the Conference, therefore, met in Leeds, on Tuesday, the 1st of August, 1769, Mr. Wesley brought before his brethren the claims of the work of God in America, and enquired who would volunteer his services to meet the emergency. It has been said by those who were present on the occasion, that at first all were silent, none of the Preachers being willing to brave the dangers of the passage, and the still more formidable discouragements identified with the work itself. Mr. Wesley was bitterly disappointed; and at five o'clock the following morning he preached before the Conference from the words, "I have nourished and brought up children, and they have rebelled against me." At the re-assembling of the Preachers the same day, it is said he again proposed the question, "Who is willing to go and assist our brethren in America?" when Richard Boardman and Joseph Pilmoor immediately volunteered. In answer to the question, "What can we do further to show our brotherly love?" it was recorded, "Let us now make a collection among ourselves." This was immediately done; and out of it fifty pounds were allotted towards the payment of the debt remaining on the chapel in New York; and twenty pounds were given to the Missionaries for their passage.

In looking at this striking incident from our present distant point of view, it is difficult to say which is most to be admired, the zeal and earnestness of Mr. Wesley, the sincere devotedness of the Missionaries themselves, the self-denying liberality of the assembled Ministers, or the wonderful providence of God, by which the whole arrangement seems to have been directed. The promptitude with which action was taken in the matter is equally remarkable. No great preparation was necessary for these simple-minded, holy men. Almost immediately after the Conference the two newly appointed Missionaries set out for the place of their destination, taking with them the £50 so nobly contributed by their brethren in aid of the infant cause in America.

But before we follow them to their new and distant sphere of labour, we must pause to notice, however briefly, a little incident connected with their departure from their native land, which was destined, in the order of Divine Providence, to exercise in after years a mighty influence over the Methodist Societies throughout the world. When on his way to Bristol, the port of embarkation, Mr. Boardman had occasion to pass through the little town of Monyash, in Derbyshire, where he spent the night, and preached in a humble Methodist cottage, from the prayer of Jabez (1 Chron. iv. 9, 10). In the congregation there was a young woman, named Mary Redfern, who was anxiously seeking the Saviour; and the message of mercy from the lips of the stranger proved a balm to her wounded spirit. Some years after this she married William Bunting, a pious Methodist layman; and in grateful remembrance of Mr. Boardman's sermon, and the blessing which she received under it, she named her first-born son Jabez Bunting—a name which afterwards became a household word in the homes of Methodism in every part of the globe.*

The two Missionaries appointed to America arrived in Philadelphia on the 24th of October, 1769, and without delay entered upon their work in the true spirit of the Gospel. Mr. Boardman hastened to New York, to strengthen the hands of Mr. Embury and Captain Webb, whose united labours the Lord had greatly blessed; and Mr. Pilmoor commenced preaching at once in the "Quaker City," where he found a Methodist Society already organised, consisting of one hundred members. A short time previous to this the number of labourers in this part of the Lord's vineyard had been increased by the arrival from Ireland of Messrs. Robert Williams and John King, two zealous Local Preachers, who did good service in the cause of Christ from the day on which they landed on the shores of America, and who ultimately became men of considerable influence in the ranks of the regular ministry. In the meantime, while the good work was rapidly advancing in New York, Albany, Long Island, Philadelphia, and other places, it was not less prosperous in Baltimore, Sam's Creek, and other parts of Maryland, where Mr. Strawbridge and his fellow labourers

---

* On Thursday, the 16th of September, 1869, just one hundred years after the occurrence of this striking little incident, a religious centenary service was held in its commemoration, in the secluded little town or village of Monyash, when an impressive and appropriate sermon was preached by the Rev. Joseph Hargraves, chairman of the Sheffield District. About 150 visitors also sat down to a social tea, which was provided on the occasion, after which a public meeting was held under the presidency of Mr. G. Bassett, when several excellent speeches were delivered by the Revs. J. S. Workman, R. Stephenson, J. Hargraves, J. Howard, and Messrs. Bassett, Jones, and others; and a collection was made in aid of the funds for the erection of a new chapel in Bakewell, the circuit town. The day was one which will long be remembered, although the weather was somewhat un-

were nobly exerting themselves in the cause of their Divine Master. Wherever the Word of God was preached by these noble bands of pioneer evangelists, it had "free course and was glorified." Hundreds of sinners were savingly converted to God; and although many of the new converts were themselves called to preach the Gospel, the number of labourers was still inadequate to meet the demands for their services, as all the preachers, with the exception of Messrs. Boardman and Pilmoor, had to pursue their worldly avocations for the support of themselves and families, and could, consequently, devote only a small portion of their time to the interests of the Church.

When the intelligence of the success of the work in America reached England, it caused much joy in the Methodist Connexion, and both preachers and people were willing to aid to the utmost of their power in the spread of the Gospel in a part of the world which was then so spiritually destitute. To supply in part the want of labourers which existed on the American continent, in 1771, Mr. Wesley sent out Messrs. Francis Asbury and Richard Wright; and in 1773 they were followed by Messrs. Thomas Rankin and George Shadfield; all men of acknowledged ability as preachers of the Gospel, and of active zeal and fidelity in the cause of Christ. Up to this period no regular Conference had been held in America, and little conventional business of any kind had been done for the systematic working of Methodism. The preachers were widely scattered through the different provinces, and appropriated their labours as circumstances seemed to require, without any particular regard to ecclesiastical rule and order. But now Mr. Rankin, who was the senior minister, took the general superintendency of the work in the place of Mr. Asbury, in accordance with the instructions of Mr. Wesley, and summoned a conference of preachers at Philadelphia, to commence on the 4th of July, 1773. At this Conference it was unanimously agreed that the founder of Methodism ought to exercise the same authority over the preachers and people in America as in England; and that, in doctrine and discipline, the Societies should be governed by the same rules in both countries. On examination it was found that the Societies in America comprised ten itinerant preachers and eleven hundred and sixty members.

From this period to the Conference of 1784, when the Methodist Societies in America were organised into a separate and distinct church, the work was prosecuted under numerous difficulties, some of which threatened its utter ruin. These arose chiefly from the revolutionary war, which commenced in 1776, and continued for about seven years without intermission. War, under any circumstances, is very unfavourable to religious progress; for when contending armies are marching and counter-marching through the country, and husbands, sons, and brothers are in the field of battle, amid carnage and death, it is almost impossible to fix the public mind upon any other subject, even when there is the utmost harmony in relation to the cause and object of the war. But one unfortunate feature of this war was that the community were divided in sentiment and feeling with reference to it; some contending earnestly for independence, and others for continued subordination to the mother-country. Thus were families and friends, ministers and people frequently found at variance with each other, by reason of their respective political opinions. It was, moreover, in some respects unfortunate for Methodism that most of the preachers were Englishmen by birth, and Loyalists in principle, as they were consequently looked upon with suspicion by the Republican party, which was rapidly gaining the ascendancy. Ultimately they all left the country and returned to England, with the exception of the zealous and self-denying Asbury, who nobly remained at his post of duty and danger, amid unspeakable trials and sufferings which time would fail to particularise.

For a considerable length of time party feeling and political jealousy ran so high that Mr. Asbury himself found it necessary to retire to the hospitable residence of Judge White, where he remained in comparative concealment for nearly twelve months. In this quiet asylum the man of God was frequently visited by Freeborn Garrettson and the other American preachers who were glad of his counsel and direction during that stormy and trying period. By these means the work of God was still carried on, but it was impeded in its progress by difficulties which would require many pages to recite in detail. Suffice it to say, that scattered and harrassed as they were the preachers were instant in season and out of season, embracing every opportunity of delivering their Lord's message to soldiers in the field and civilians at home, everywhere endeavouring to diffuse abroad a knowledge of the Saviour. The societies were kept together much better than could have been expected, and some pleasing instances occurred of the conversions of sinners to God.

At length the American colonists succeeded in establishing their independence, and peace was restored to the land. The altered state of affairs now required prompt and peculiar measures to meet the vast demand for religious instruction in the promising new-born nation. The resources at the command of the sagacious and indefatigable Wesley were again found equal to the emergency. Believing that he had the power to do so, and that such a form of church government would be best, he ordained and sent out Dr. Coke as General Superintendent or bishop, with Messrs. Whatcoat and Vasey as Presbyters, to lay the foundation of the Methodist Episcopal Church in the United States. They arrived in New York on the 3rd of November, 1784; and at the General Conference, which was convened at Christmas in the same year, the plan proposed by Mr. Wesley for the re-organisation and government of American Methodism was unanimously adopted by the preachers. On this occasion *sixty* of the *eighty-three* travelling preachers, then in the American Connexion, were present; and it was found that, notwithstanding the difficulties with which the infant church had to contend during the trying years of the revolutionary war the number of members had increased to *fourteen thousand nine hundred and eighty-six.*

It would be a very pleasing task if time and space permitted to follow the newly organised Methodist Church of the United States in the rapid progress which it made, when all political and other difficulties were removed out of the way of its full development. But were we to enter into minute particulars we should have no space for a brief account of the origin and progress of Methodism in Canada, Nova Scotia, New Brunswick, Prince Edward's Island, Cape Breton, and Newfoundland—countries which remained attached to the British crown after the declaration of American independence. For ample information respecting the progress and extent of this wonderful work of God, we may refer to the excellent works of Drs. Stevens, Dixon, and Jobson, and to the interesting memoirs of Bishop Asbury, the Revs. Messrs. Garrettson, Cartwright, Findlay, Spicer, and other zealous Missionary pioneers of the West. Suffice it to say, that wherever the Gospel was faithfully preached by Methodist ministers, a gracious influence attended the Word, sinners were convinced and converted, and multitudes were gathered into the fold of Christ. Beautiful church buildings were erected, societies formed, and schools established in almost every town and village of the Union, as rapidly as they sprang up, east, west, north, and south. New Circuits, Districts, and Conferences were organized in quick succession, as the work advanced, in every direction, and as the population flowed westward; till, in process of time, the whole country, from the Atlantic to the Pacific, and from the Gulf of Florida to the St. Lawrence, was permeated with the leaven of Christianity in the form of Methodism, to say nothing of the foreign and domestic missions which have been established in the destitute parts of the States, in India, China, Africa, and other countries. In the wide field for Christian enterprise, presented by the vast extent and rapidly increasing population of the United States, other religious bodies have nobly exerted themselves for the spiritual welfare of the people; but, for successful labour, numbers, power, and influence, none have surpassed the Methodist Episcopal Church.

In the course of years there were several off-shoots from the parent body, owing to various causes; but the largest secession was in 1844, when nearly one half of the entire community went off, and organized themselves as the " Methodist Episcopal Church South," on account of slavery, which they were determined to uphold.

Being present at the General Conference in New York that

year, we watched, with feelings of deep interest, the course of events, and listened with profound attention to the speeches which were delivered both for and against the favourite domestic institution during the debate, which lasted more than a week. As the recent civil war has terminated in the entire destruction of American slavery, and thus removed, in the order of Divine providence, the bone of contention for ever out of the way, it is hoped that the two great branches of the Methodist Episcopal Church in the United States, may be ultimately re-united, as on all general questions of doctrine and discipline they are understood to be identical.

In the autumn of 1866, the first Centenary of American Methodism was celebrated throughout the length and breadth of the country, one hundred years having passed away since the first society was formed in New York by Philip Embury, Barbara Heck, and a few other Irish emigrants. Songs of praise ascended to heaven from almost every church and every family connected with the body, for the great things which God had wrought. Princely offerings were also laid upon the altar of Christian benevolence for the various objects contemplated in the financial arrangements of the celebration. One gentleman, Daniel Drew, Esq., presented the noble sum of one hundred thousand pounds on the occasion; and the entire amount contributed to the Centenary Fund was upwards of one million sterling. But these are trifling matters compared with the spiritual results of the great movement. In the Centenary year alone the increase of church members was about one hundred and twenty-three thousand, making the total number of Methodist communicants in the United States amount to about *two millions*, with about *fourteen thousand* Ministers in the ranks of the itinerancy, and an equal number of zealous Local Preachers. Schools, seminaries, colleges, and universities have increased in equal proportion; whilst the church buildings are estimated at *twenty thousand* in number, which, allowing for those which have been superseded by larger edifices, will give an average of about one place of worship erected each day during the century—a rate of progress unparalleled, it is believed, in any other branch of the Christian Church.* Viewing the magnitude of the work of Methodism in all its phases, and its probable influence on the future of America, we cannot fail to admire with gratitude and praise the providence and grace of God so clearly manifest in every stage of its progress. And when we regard it as the legitimate fruit of the Missionary enterprise, we are lost in wonder, love, and praise, and constrained to exclaim, with adoring gratitude, " What hath God wrought ?"

The rapid progress and extensive spread of Methodism in the United States is to be attributed in a large measure to the continual influx of Wesleyan emigrants from Europe, especially from Ireland, and to the zeal and success with which they have laboured in the good work. It is believed that there are at the present time a larger number of Irish Methodists in New York than in Dublin ; and among the bravest and best of the noble band of ministers of the Methodist Episcopal church there are not a few who are the genuine sons of Green Erin, or their descendants. America owes

* The Methodist churches of the United States are generally neat and elegant ecclesiastical buildings with spires, and are easily distinguished from houses appropriated to secular purposes. But the most splendid structure of the kind ever erected in America, was the "Metropolitan Memorial Methodist Episcopal Church," built in Washington in the year 1868, by the united contributions of the members in all parts of the Union. It is in the gothic style of architecture, and constructed chiefly of brown stone. The spire is to be 220 feet high, and when finished, is to be furnished with a full chime of bells, the gift of a gentleman in Pittsburg, in memory of a beloved daughter. The windows are of stained glass, with beautiful designs, most of them being memorial presents. The pulpit is also of chaste design, constructed in part of black walnut, the panels being of olive wood from the Mount of Olives, in the Holy Land, the posts having pieces of cedar from Mount Lebanon inserted into them, whilst, on its front, is an elegantly-carved cross, wreathed with entwined ivy. The caps on each side of the reading desk, and altar rails are made of olive wood from the Mount of Olives. The church is furnished with a powerful organ, twenty feet high, and thirteen feet deep, which occupies a prominent place over the main entrance. This splendid sanctuary was dedicated to the public worship of Almighty God on Sunday, the 28th of February, 1869, when eloquent and appropriate sermons were preached by Bishop Simpson, the Rev. W. M. Punshon, M.A., and Dr. Eddy, after which a collection was made amounting to upwards of £500. General Grant, the President of the United States, who is said to be a member of the Methodist Episcopal Church, was in attendance at the opening service with his family and suite, and the concourse was very large, hundreds being unable to gain admittance.

METHODIST COLLEGE, BELFAST, IRELAND.

(The Foundation-stone was laid in 1865 by W. M'Arthur, Esq., M.P., one of the most liberal contributors, and it was opened in 1868, under the presidency of the Rev. W. Arthur, M.A. for the education of the laity, the sons of Methodist ministers, and for the training of candidates for the Wesleyan ministry).

a large debt of gratitude to Irish Methodism; and she has not been slow to acknowledge her obligation. When a deputation was sent by the Irish Conference of 1866 to the United States, consisting of W. M'Arthur, Esq. M.P., Dr. R. Scott, and the Rev. R. Wallace (the last of whom, alas! found a grave in American soil), to solicit aid towards the erection and endowment of a Methodist College in Belfast, their appeals met with a most generous response. The noble sum of one hundred thousand dollars was contributed by American Methodists towards this object, by means of which, and the substantial aid received from England added to Irish liberality, the college buildings have been erected, and an institution inaugurated, which bids fair to be a blessing to both hemispheres.

CANADA.

After the declaration of independence by the United States of America, there remained more than one half of the vast continent still attached to the British crown. The largest and most important section of British America was called CANADA, the country which next claims our attention. To prepare the way for its Missionary history, which is the principal object we have in view, it will only be necessary to make a few brief observations. In its general features the country is very similar to the United States; but being situated to the northward the climate is said to be somewhat more severe, the cold being more intense in winter, whilst the heat is equally great during the summer months. It is approached from the Atlantic by the majestic river St. Lawrence, which, in its upper course, above Quebec and Montreal, expands into a number of extensive lakes or inland seas, which give a peculiar charm to the aspect of the scenery, whilst, at the same time, they greatly facilitate commercial intercourse by means of the navigation which is constantly carried on in all kinds of vessels on their majestic waters.

Canada is said to have been discovered by the French as early as 1534; but it was not until the year 1607 that they formed their first settlement of Quebec, on the site of an Indian village called Sadacona. For several years but little progress was made in colonization, the country being almost completely covered with primeval forests, and occupied with a considerable population of native Indians. In the wars of 1759, the colony was taken by the English under General Wolfe; at which period the number of settlers amounted to about 70,000, who were chiefly of French extraction, and Roman Catholics by profession. Soon after the termination of the revolutionary war the population of Canada was considerably increased by the arrival of a large number of Loyalists, who could not brook the idea of a republican form of government, and who preferred to maintain their allegiance to England. From this source, as well as by the constant arrival of emigrants from the United Kingdom, the British element in the population has continued to preponderate; and through the enterprising spirit of the settlers, the colony has realised a cheering measure of prosperity. With the blessing of a kind and gracious Providence, and the skill and energy of the colonists, there is reason to anticipate for this important section of the British Empire still greater prosperity in the future; and more especially so from its recent union with most of the other British American provinces in a general confederacy, designated "the Dominion of Canada."

A population so widely scattered and of such a mixed character, and largely imbued with Popish ignorance and superstition, did not present a very favourable soil for the cultivation of religion and morality; and many difficulties had to be encountered in the first efforts which were made to propagate the Gospel in Canada. It is a pleasing fact, however, that in process of time every obstacle was surmounted, and a great and glorious work was inaugurated which, in its history and results, will bear a favourable comparison with that of any other land. As British emigrants arrived, either from the United States or from the mother country, they generally settled in the Upper Province, on the banks of the rivers, the margins of the lakes, and on the shores of the Bay of Quinte; but the original settlers, of French extraction, continued to occupy the Lower Province, whilst the aborigines generally retired westward. Among all these classes of people the leaven of pure Christianity has spread to a considerable extent; but the result is seen more especially in the energy, zeal, perseverance, and prosperity, both temporal and spiritual, which characterizes the British portion of the population. To bring about the advanced state of religious progress which at present exists in Canada, various agencies have been employed; but none have been more powerful or more beneficial to the country than those connected with Wesleyan Methodism, a brief history of which we have now to record.

It is believed that the first Methodist sermon ever heard in Canada was preached in Quebec in the year 1780, by a Local Preacher named Tuffey, who had just arrived from England in connection with the commissariat of the 44th Regiment. This zealous and devoted servant of God, seeing and lamenting the wickedness which prevailed among the military and the Protestant emigrants, and the Popish ignorance and superstition of the older settlers, nobly lifted up his warning voice with a view to reclaim them from the error of their ways. In this labour of love the British soldier was assisted by a few of his pious comrades, with whom he was in the habit of holding religious meetings for their mutual edification; but it does not appear that any regular Methodist Society was formed among the civilians at Quebec at this early period. At the restoration of peace, Mr. Tuffey returned to England; but several British regiments in Canada were disbanded on the spot, and the discharged soldiers had portions of land given to them on which to settle, and form their homes in the land of their adoption. Among these were some of Tuffey's comrades and converts, who retained their first love to the Saviour, and who also became the means of blessing to others.

A Christian brother belonging to this class of men was the honoured instrument in the hands of God of introducing Methodism into Upper Canada also. This was George Neal, an Irish Local Preacher of considerable power and ability. He had come to America with a cavalry regiment, in which he held the rank of major; and at the close of the war he crossed the Niagara river at Queenston, on the 7th of October, 1786, to take possession of an officer's portion of land, which had been given to him in acknowledgment of his past services in the British army. Whilst busily engaged in the labours and anxieties incident to the establishing of a new home in a strange land, Major Neal embraced every opportunity of preaching the Gospel to his fellow-settlers on the banks of the Niagara, and he was made the means of spiritual good to many, notwithstanding some opposition with which he had to contend.

Whilst George Neal was thus labouring zealously as he had opportunity among the settlers in the Niagara river district, that part of the country bordering on the Bay of Quinte continued for some time in a state of great spiritual destitution, there being no religious teacher of any denomination among the people. At length the Lord of the harvest made provision for this district also. In 1788, a pious young man named Lyons, an exhorter in the Methodist Episcopal Church, came to Canada, and commenced teaching a school at Adolphus-town. Having a zeal for the Lord, and seeing the ignorance and sin which abounded on every hand, he collected the people together on Sabbath days in different parts of the country, and conducted Divine worship as best he could, earnestly exhorting them to flee from the wrath to come. He also visited the people from house to house for the purpose of praying with and instructing every family to which he had access, and the Lord greatly blessed the labours of His servant.

In the same year came James M'Carty, a zealous Irishman from the United States, who was also made very useful in turning sinners to God. He had heard Whitfield during his last visit to America, and the Word preached had been the power of God to his salvation. Earnestly desiring to bring others to a saving knowledge of the truth, he crossed from the United States to Kingston, and proceeded to Earnes-town, where he formed the acquaintance of Robert Perry, and some other Methodists in those parts, who encouraged him to hold religious services in their log-houses. He was a man of attractive manners and address, and large numbers attended his preaching, many of the settlers in that part of the country never having heard a Gospel sermon before since they left their native land. The labours of this humble evangelist were blessed of the Lord to the salvation of many souls; but he had not been long engaged in this work when a storm of persecution arose which cost him his life. Some of the Loyalists who had retired to Canada at the close of the revolutionary war, and who were fiery politicians as well as enemies to the Gospel, looked upon the stranger with a suspicious eye, on account of his coming from the United States, and organized a powerful party to oppose his movements. Having failed to put a stop to the progress of the work, and prevent the continuance of the meetings of the Methodists by an appeal to the authorities, and by numerous petty acts of violence, they resolved to make away with the Preacher in a secret and clandestine manner. It is certain that poor M'Carty soon afterwards disappeared in a very mysterious way; and it has been asserted by persons who lived in the neighbourhood that his enemies hired a party of unprincipled Frenchmen to seize him, throw him into a boat, and take him by force to one of the desolate islands which stud the outlet of the Lake Ontario, where the rapid waters rush into the river St. Lawrence. There, they say, the Preacher was landed, and left to perish, being never heard of any more.

Other instances of violent opposition to the truth on the part of the enemies of the Cross of Christ might be given; but, as in all ages and countries, the more the Gospel was opposed the more it prospered and prevailed. Whilst Mr. Lyons was preaching as he had opportunity in the settlements on the shores of the Bay of Quinte, Major Neal was made very useful in the Niagara townships. Among those who were brought to God at the place last named, in the year 1791, was a young man named Charles Warner, who, with several of his converted neighbours, was united in a class, of which he was appointed the Leader. This is believed to have been the first Methodist Society organised in Upper Canada. It is a pleasing fact that Mr. Warner, who had settled in the township of Stamford, near the falls of Niagara, never changed the place of his residence, but continued to be a useful class-leader for more than forty years, till his peaceful death in 1833.

In our researches into the history of early Methodism in Canada, it is pleasant once more to meet with the honoured names of Philip Embury and Barbara Heck, which figure so prominently in

MRS. HECK TEACHING THE SETTLER'S CHILDREN.

connection with the commencement of the work in New York. It would appear that they, with many others of their original party, removed to Canada soon after the breaking out of the revolutionary war, and for some time they lived at Camden, near Lake Champlain, where they were the founders of another new Methodist cause. After a residence of about ten years in Lower Canada they came to the Upper Province in 1785, and settled at Augusta, in the neighbourhood of Big Creek. We find no record of the last days of Mr. Embury, but his widow was married to a godly man named John Laurance, and his son Samuel was the leader of the class which was formed at Augusta. Here Barbara Heck finished her course in peace, in the year 1804, her husband Paul having died about fourteen years previously. About twelve months afterwards their eldest son, John, died in the State of Georgia. Two other sons, Jacob and Samuel, survived their parents for many years, in whose pious footsteps they continued to tread, the one last named being a highly respectable and useful Local Preacher. The remains of Mr. and Mrs. Heck, with those of other members of the family, repose in the Blue Church grave-yard, near the place of their former residence at Augusta.

As the work of God extended its influence, both in the Upper and Lower Provinces, and Societies were organised in various places, the need of a regular ministry was urgently felt; the good men who had hitherto been the only preachers of the Gospel among the scattered settlers having to attend to their farming and other worldly avocations, which left them but little time for evangelical labours. It was therefore resolved to make application for a regular Missionary, to minister to the spiritual necessities of the people, and to seek still further to promote the extension of the Redeemer's kingdom.

The work having now taken deep root in the United States, and conferences having been organised by the Methodist Episcopal Church in different parts of the country, it was to this body that application was made in the first instance, when additional labourers were required in the Canadian provinces. The respectful request of the people met with a cordial response, and the first regular Methodist minister appointed to labour in Canada was the Rev. William Losee. He was a man of moderate talents, but of great energy and perseverance, and well adapted for the rough pioneering work which he had to do. Mr. Losee had visited Canada previous to his appointment as a Missionary, several of his relatives having settled in the country; and being wishful to join them, he volunteered his services, and was, in fact, the bearer of the petition to the New York Conference requesting a minister. The judicious Bishop Asbury and his coadjutors the more readily acquiesced in the appointment of Mr. Losee to Canada in consequence of his being a Loyalist in principle, a circumstance which would render his labours more acceptable in a British colony. The young evangelist set out for his distant sphere of labour on horseback; and, after a long and tedious journey in the depth of winter, he crossed the St. Lawrence, at Kingston, on the ice, and formed the first regular Methodist Circuit in Canada among the scattered settlers on the Bay of Quinte, in the early part of the year 1791. Divine service was now conducted by the new preacher and his assistants in log huts, or shanties, wherever an opening presented itself, and the Lord of the harvest greatly blessed the labours of His servants. Those who were convinced of their sins, or savingly converted to God, were united in classes for further instruction, three of which were formed in the short space of ten days, one at Adolphus-town, another at Earnes-town, and a third at Fredericksburgh.

Among the first converts in the extensive revival of religion which now took place was a notable young man named John Roblin, who had been a prominent person in the dancing parties and other vain amusements which were so prevalent at that period. On finding peace with God his conscience would not permit him to indulge in gaudy dress, much less to pursue the pleasures of sin, which are but for a season. He therefore went to his room and returned with his frilled shirt, saying to his mother, in the presence of the family: "Mother, as soon as you can, take off these frills from my shirt; I shall wear such no more. O, mother, the Lord has converted my soul this morning. Let us all kneel down and pray." He then, for the first time, prayed with his mother, and brother, and sisters. Soon afterwards he went to William Moore's, about a mile distant, and exhorted and prayed with the family, leaving a deep impression, which resulted in a change of heart and life in the case of several of its members.

William Moore soon became the leader of a class, and for several years bore the character of a good and useful man, whilst the somewhat eccentric but truly pious Mr. Roblin laboured successfully as a Local Preacher, and was ultimately elected as a member of the first Parliament in Upper Canada, a position which was not at all congenial to his feelings, however, and which he soon relinquished.

Numerous other instances of remarkable individual conversions might be given, but we must proceed to state the progress of the work in the aggregate. Such was the success which attended the labours of the first Missionary and his assistants, that in the following year the dwelling-houses of the settlers were found altogether too small to contain the congregations which assembled to hear the Word preached. The people, therefore, set to work, and erected the first Methodist place of worship ever built in Canada —on a piece of land generously given for the purpose by Mr. Paul Huff—at Adolphus-town, in whose cottage the meetings had previously been held. The building was a humble structure of framed timber, thirty-five feet by thirty, and was erected amid many difficulties, a comparatively poor people subscribing towards it the noble sum of £108. This little sanctuary was almost immediately followed by the erection of a similar structure for the use of the people at Earnes-town, in the eastern part of the Circuit. After about two years spent in useful labour, in the spring of 1793 Mr. Losee attended the New York Conference, held at Albany, at which he was able to report one hundred and sixty-five persons united in Church fellowship under his pastoral care in Canada. The encouraging account which he was enabled to give of the general character of the work, and of the prospects which were opening up before him, induced the Conference to appoint the Rev. Dirius Dunham to accompany him on his return, as his colleague in his interesting sphere of labour.

At this Conference Mr. Losee was ordained Deacon; and Mr. Dunham being already an elder, he was duly authorised to administer the sacraments, and to celebrate marriages, which was a great advantage to the Societies, as they had hitherto been deprived of these privileges. Methodism in Canada having now assumed the organisation and status of a regular Christian Church, at a period when there were but few agents of other religious bodies in the field, the work took deep root and greatly prospered, and the two Missionaries prosecuted their labours for some time with encouragement and success. In the following year, however, an untoward circumstance occurred, which affected the health, both mental and bodily, of Mr. Losee, the first missionary to Canada, in such a manner that he was obliged to relinquish the work and enter into business. But before long, at intervals, several more Ministers were sent from the United States, as Messrs. Coate, Coleman, Wooster, Bangs, Ryan, and others; additional Circuits were formed, and a regular District was organised, over which Mr. Dunham was appointed Presiding Elder. In after years the work was greatly extended in every direction, reaching ultimately to the scattered settlements on the Lakes Ontario and Erie, Long Point, Sam's Creek, and other places, where chapels were built, congregations gathered, Societies formed, and multitudes of sinners brought to a saving knowledge of the truth.

For several years after this systematic organisation and extension of Methodism in Canada, the work continued in connexion with the Methodist Episcopal Church, by whom the first regular Missionary had been appointed; but it was afterwards found necessary to detach it entirely from the direction and control of parties resident in the United States. And, after various vicissitudes, into the particulars of which we need not now enter, it ultimately became connected with the British Conference, with a separate organisation of its own. From the time that the States declared their independence, political party feeling ran high on the American Continent; and the Loyalists, who had found a home in Canada, looked with a jealous eye upon their republican neighbours in the States. Consequently many of the Canadian Methodists were ill at ease on being obliged to receive their supply of ministers from a body whose political views they could not always endorse, although in general harmony with it as to doctrine and discipline. For instance, when the Conference of the Methodist

Episcopal Church in 1796 ordered a general thanksgiving-day, and gave directions that, among other things, all the people should render thanks to God for the " admirable revolution obtained and established " in their country, it was not likely that Canadian Methodist Loyalists, who were dearly attached to the British Government, should relish the sentiment or comply with the order. The influence of true religion, however, for a length of time helped all parties to overcome numerous difficulties, and the good work continued to extend and prosper, till the breaking out of the war between England and the United States in 1812, when many of the American preachers left their stations, to return to their own country, and everything was thrown into confusion.

Under these circumstances the attention of the Canadian Methodists was turned to England, from whence they earnestly requested to be supplied with Ministers. The Wesleyan Missionary Committee in London readily responded to this natural desire of British colonists, and they would, no doubt, have thought of doing something for Canada before had not their resources been so heavily taxed with the support of their extensive Missions in the West Indies and other places. They were, moreover, the less concerned about Canada so long as the stations there could be supplied with Missionaries from the United States, and tolerable harmony was preserved in carrying on the work. But the case was altered now, and it seemed absolutely necessary to interfere, and to supply preachers for the destitute settlers from the British Conference. The first Missionary thus appointed was the Rev. John Strong, who was stationed in Quebec in 1814; and in subsequent years he was followed by the Revs. Messrs. Williams, Pope, Booth, Binning, Crosscombe, Johnston, Lusher, Wood, and others, who laboured with success, and whose memory is still cherished with much affection by a few surviving aged members.

At the same time, a number of American preachers, who regarded Canada as their adopted country, remained in their circuits during the war, and continued afterwards to prosecute their labours with acceptance and success. With these brethren and their work the English Missionaries had no wish to interfere; but when difficulties afterwards arose, it was mutually agreed that the newly-arrived Ministers should confine their labours to Lower Canada, whilst those from the United States should prosecute their work within the limits of the Upper Province. Under this arrangement Methodism in Canada continued to advance with amazing rapidity; large numbers being added to the Church every year; and commodious places of worship being erected in every town and village of importance. In 1824, political reasons already alluded to rendered it necessary for the Ministers in Upper Canada to form themselves into a separate Conference, to be independent of the control of the Methodist Episcopal Church in the United States. Amid all these changes the work of God steadily advanced with the rapidly increasing population of the colony; and wherever there was a small company of settlers located there was almost sure to be a Methodist chapel, and a Society either in connexion with American or English Missionaries.

Ultimately, however, through the wise and judicious intervention of Dr. Alder, who was sent out to represent the English Missionary Committee and Conference, a union was effected of the whole body of Methodists in Canada, including ministers and people, with a few inconsiderable exceptions, under a new organisation, called the "Canadian Conference in connexion with the British Conference;" the discipline of which it in the main adopted, being already identical with it in the more important matters of Christian doctrine. After this arrangement the cause was still more prosperous, and the Methodists of Canada have now become the most numerous, powerful and influential body of Christians in the country, numbering *five hundred and forty-five Ministers, and fifty-seven thousand seven hundred and sixty-four church members*, with a corresponding number of places of worship; many of which for magnitude, beauty and elegance, equal or surpass our first-rate chapels in England. Nor has the training of the rising generation been neglected by the Canadian Methodist Conference. Schools, seminaries, colleges and universities have been provided on an ample scale; and if the reader could but see Methodism as it exists in Montreal, Toronto, Kingston, Hamilton, London, and other large cities and towns in Canada, he would be convinced that it is not surpassed in any part of the world.

In no portion of the British empire is greater attention paid to the organization and management of Sabbath-schools, than in the dominion of Canada. Annual "conventions" are held in various parts of the country, to take into consideration the best means of carrying on this important part of Christian labour. On these occa-

ROBERT RAIKES.

sions the speakers may be heard expatiating in terms of glowing eloquence on the institution as it exists in the "mother country," and on the character and career of the celebrated Robert Raikes, its honoured founder. From this and other pleasing circumstances which might be mentioned, as the zeal manifested in the circulation of the sacred Scriptures, and the genuine Missionary spirit which generally animates professing Christians, we have good reason to anticipate for this part of the western hemisphere still greater religious prosperity in time to come.

Hitherto our notices of Methodism in Canada have been confined to the work as it has been carried on among the colonists, and we must now call attention to a few remarks on the aborigines and the efforts which have been made to evangelise them. When the pale-faced strangers first landed on the continent of North America, the country was in many places densely populated by a race of native Indians, divided into various tribes, and speaking different languages. These simple children of the forest generally retired westward, as the European settlers advanced to take posession of their ancient hunting grounds. Great advantage was frequently taken of their ignorance, and when the formality of a bargain was gone through, they were often induced to sell their lands for merely a nominal sum; Long Island having been purchased, it is said, for a pair of spectacles! In other instances they were driven off without ceremony, and left to find a home where they could. At the same time their numbers rapidly decreased; partly by the wars which were frequently carried on among themselves or with the colonists, and partly by the introduction of small-pox and other European diseases, and especially by the fatal "fire-water," in the form of whisky, rum, gin, and brandy, which the whites brought among them. Notwithstanding this unhappy state of things, the true friends of religion and humanity both in England and America, have always looked upon the poor Indians with feelings of compassion, and of late years much has been done to promote their social and religious improvement.

When the scattered remnants of several native tribes were collected and located on lands reserved for them by Government in Upper Canada, the Wesleyan Missionary Society readily came forward to take their share in the important but difficult work of seeking to raise them in the scale of being. Missionaries were appointed, preaching commenced, schools established, and societies organised, as openings presented themselves, among the various tribes of Indians at their respective locations. But the most important and prosperous stations were formed with the Mohawks on the Grand River, and the Six Nations and other tribes at New Credit, Muncy, St. Clair, Rama, Alnwick, Mud

Lake, and in a few other localities. At these places a great and good work was effected. Hundreds of poor Indians were savingly converted to God, and taught the arts of civilised life, whilst their children were trained up in the Mission schools; and, in some instances the Holy Scriptures were translated into their native tongue. It is a rich treat to visit one of those Christian Indian villages, and to behold the wonderful change which has been effected both in the temporal and spiritual condition of the people, by the power of the Gospel. Thoroughly weaned from the wandering habits to which they were addicted in their uncivilised state, when they subsisted by hunting and fishing, the natives may now be seen decently clothed, occupying comfortable cottages, cultivating the ground, and following useful trades which they have been taught by the Missionaries. And if we spend a Sabbath on the Station, and witness the appearance of the congregation, and the fervour of their devotion, we shall be forcibly reminded of the declaration of the Apostle, that " Godliness is profitable unto all things, having the promise of the life that now is, and of that which is to come."

In this humble but important department of Christian labour, the Rev. William Case, the father and founder of the Indian Wesleyan Missions, and other zealous Missionaries were long and usefully engaged. Three of the most prominent of the early converts were Peter Jones, Peter Jacobs, and John Sundays, young Indian chiefs, who were called of God to preach the Gospel to their fellow-countrymen, and made very useful in winning souls for Christ. They each of them paid a visit to England at different times; and, by their godly simplicity and religious earnestness, they greatly interested the friends of Missions at public meetings and on other occasions, and clearly proved that the red men of the American wilderness have souls as susceptible of Divine influence as those of their pale-faced brethren of Europe. More than *one thousand* converted Indians are now united in church fellowship on the respective Wesleyan Stations in Canada, with a proportionate number of scholars in the Mission schools; and it is hoped that in time to come the number will be greatly increased.

HUDSON'S BAY TERRITORY.

HUDSON'S BAY was so called in honour of Captain Henry Hudson, by whom it was discovered in 1610; and the vast territory to which it is the principal entrance, extending one thousand four hundred miles in length, and three hundred and fifty in breadth, was secured to a mercantile company about sixty years afterwards, for the purpose of carrying on trade with the scattered tribes of Indians inhabiting those cold and dreary regions; a number of forts and stations were established to which the natives annually resort to exchange their furs for blankets, ammunition, and other necessaries. In the course of years, a considerable population, both of half-castes, and aboriginal, was concentrated at those places, the spiritual destitution of which attracted the notice of the Wesleyan Missionary Society; and, in 1840, a Mission was organized for their benefit. The Committee was encouraged to engage in this benevolent enterprise by the liberal offers of assistance which were made to them by the Hudson's Bay Company. Such was the anxiety of that honourable association for the propagation of Scriptural truth among their agents and servants, as well as among the native Indian tribes within their territory, that they agreed to provide for the Missionaries the Wesleyan Committee might send, whether married or single, board and lodging, interpreters, servants, and means of conveyance from place to place, free of expense to the Society. In addition to this generous offer, the Governor and Committee contributed £100 towards the outfit and passage of the first party of Missionaries.

With this influential and substantial patronage, and with the promise of continued liberal support, the Mission was commenced, although the Committee was well aware of the difficult and arduous nature of the undertaking. The first Missionaries to the Hudson's Bay Territory were the Revs. Messrs. Barnley, Mason, and Rundle, who embarked at Liverpool for their distant field of labour, in the month of March, 1840. On reaching the place of their destination, they were joined by the Revs. Messrs. Evans and

Hurlburt from Canada, together with Peter Jacobs, Assistant-Missionary, and Henry Steinhaur, schoolmaster and interpreter. The two brethren last named were converted Indians of the Ojibway tribe, whose services it was thought would be very useful, from the similarity of their language to that of the natives farther north. The Missionaries arrived in safety at their destination, and were kindly received by the agents of the Honourable Company. They arranged their plans of operation according to their best judgment; and commenced their labours at Norway House, Lake Winnipeg, Edmonton, Moose Factory, and other places, with pleasing prospects of success. Places of worship were erected, Christian schools established, the Scriptures translated into the native language of the people, and the Gospel of Christ was faithfully preached to hundreds and thousands of poor Indians, many of whom, it is believed, were in process of time savingly converted to God.

The Missionaries by whom this Mission was commenced, and the honoured brethren by whom they were succeeded in after years, frequently prosecuted their pious labours under circumstances of peculiar privation and trial. They have often had occasion to travel hundreds and even thousands of miles, by land and by water, over ice and snow, encamping night after night on the cold ground, exposed to hardships and dangers unknown to those who remain at home, surrounded by the blessings and comforts of civilised life. The Rev. George M'Dougall, the present General Superintendent of the Hudson's Bay Mission, visited Canada in 1867; and before he reached the end of his weary journey, and found himself on the verge of civilisation once more, he had travelled a distance of one thousand miles, and slept eighty-seven nights on the plains, frequently in the vicinity of hostile Indian tribes. But amid all the perils and discomforts of Missionary life in the bleak north-western wilds of the American continent, the Lord has graciously preserved His servants, and a glorious work has been accomplished through their instrumentality. Notwithstanding the wandering habits of the people and their reluctance to settle down in any fixed locality, several Christian villages have been formed at the respective stations of the Society, in the neighbourhood of which the ground is cultivated, and the natives are instructed in the various arts of civilised life. And, what is better still, a large number of Indians have been taught to read the Word of God for themselves, and brought to a saving knowledge of the truth as it is in Jesus, *six hundred and ninety-seven* of whom are now united in Church fellowship, under the pastoral care of *seven* zealous Missionaries.

This important branch of the foreign work is now under the direction of the Canadian Conference, although still aided by the Wesleyan Missionary Society in England. It has recently been reinforced by the appointment of two additional Missionaries; and a new station has been formed at Red River, which promises to be a great blessing to the people of that neighbourhood. Should the proposed arrangement be carried out for the addition of the extensive territory of the Hudson's Bay Company to the dominion of Canada, it is highly probable that the result will be such an increase of population, by means of emigration, to these north-western regions as will open a wide and extensive field of missionary labour. May a kind and gracious Providence direct and control the future destiny of this important section of the British empire!

BRITISH COLUMBIA.

Beyond the territory of the Hudson's Bay Company, and bordering on the Pacific Ocean, there is an extensive region of North America called BRITISH COLUMBIA, which in its soil, climate, and physical aspect resembles other northern parts of the great continent. This country was colonized in 1858, owing chiefly to the discovery of extensive gold fields in the interior. Vancouver Island in the Pacific, a few miles from the continent was incorporated with it, and was considered the most convenient place for the seat of Government. In common with all new settlements; British Columbia has had to struggle with numerous difficulties; but there is reason to hope that in due time they will all be surmounted and the colony will prosper. If the grand theory of a railway on British ground, through Nova Scotia, Canada, and British Columbia, connecting the Atlantic with the Pacific, and forming a short route to China and the East, should be practically worked out, it is impossible to say what would be the destinies of these countries, especially as an ample supply of coal has recently been discovered. In the meantime it is the duty of the Christian Church to extend the blessings of the Gospel as far as possible to the perishing sons of men in all their wanderings.

As population rapidly flowed into British Columbia from all parts of the world after the gold discoveries, it seemed very desirable that something should be done to supply the spiritual wants of the emigrants, as well as to Christianize the aborigines. It was this circumstance that attracted the notice, and excited the sympathy of the Methodist people of Canada, several emigrants having gone from thence to the land of gold beyond the Rocky Mountains. The Canadian Conference at length resolved to organize a Mission to the new colony; and when the case was laid before the Wesleyan Missionary Committee in London, they generously voted a grant of £500 in aid of the commencement of the enterprise. There was no lack of agents to engage in the arduous and hazardous undertaking. Such was the enthusiasm which prevailed among the Ministers in Canada, that fourteen volunteers presented themselves as willing to go to British Columbia. From these, four devoted brethren were selected for the service, namely, the Revs. Messrs. White, Robson, and Browning, with the Rev. Dr. Evans at their head as General Superintendent.

They set out for their distant field of labour in the month of December, 1858, followed by the prayers and best wishes of a large circle of genuine friends and supporters. By the good providence of God, the Missionaries and their families were preserved in health and safety during a journey by land and by sea of more than six thousand miles, performed in the winter season, and they arrived at their destination in the spring of 1856. They met with a friendly reception at Victoria, Vancouver's Island, from his

88 HISTORY OF WESLEYAN MISSIONS.

Excellency Governor Douglas, and the other officers of Government and the people generally, and were kindly allowed the use of the

METHODIST CHURCH, VICTORIA, VANCOUVER'S ISLAND.

Court House for their religious services, till more permanent arrangements could be made. In the course of the following year, a beautiful Methodist church was built in the capital of the colony, at a cost of £2,000, in which Dr. Evans ministered to a respectable and attentive congregation, whilst his brethren established themselves at the most central places on the Fraser River. For some time the Missionaries in the interior preached in the open air; but ere long places of worship and Ministers' residences were erected at New Westminster, Fort Hope, Nanairno and other settlements; and Class-meetings, Sunday-schools, and Temperance Societies were established, as opportunities presented themselves, for the benefit of the gold-diggers and other adventurers. If, from the fluctuating state of the population in British Columbia, and other untoward circumstances, the aggregate amount of success has not been so great as the Missionaries desired or their friends anticipated, it is a pleasing fact that their labours have not been in vain in the Lord. Many a poor wandering emigrant has been gathered into the fold of Christ, through the instrumentality of this Mission, whilst something has been done towards Christianizing the native Indians, who are said to be numerous in some parts of the country. Thus the foundation of a great and good work has been laid which may be followed by important results in time to come. The number of Missionaries employed in the British Columbia District is *seven*, and *one hundred and forty-three* persons are united in Church fellowship on the respective stations, *six* of whom are converted Indians. The little one may yet become a thousand, and the small one a strong nation. May the Lord hasten it in His time!

Nova Scotia.

We must now return to the other side of that portion of the American continent which still belongs to the British Crown, and consider the missionary history of several interesting colonies which are situated on the borders of the Atlantic. The first which claims attention is Nova Scotia, concerning which a few preliminary remarks may be necessary. This country, including Cape Breton, comprises an extensive peninsula two hundred and thirty-five miles long, and about forty-four broad. It has several lakes and a vast number of small rivers. The climate, though healthy, is somewhat severe; the cold during four months in winter, being sometimes intense, with heavy fogs beclouding the atmosphere. The soil is in many places thin and sterile; but it contains some tracts of land not inferior to the best portions of New England. Since this part of the American continent was first settled by the French, previous to their forming any establishment in Canada, it has changed its rulers more than once, and it was not till the Peace of Utrecht that it was finally confirmed to England. From this period a stream of emigration began to flow from the United Kingdom to these western shores, in the course of which we may trace the origin of Wesleyan Methodism.

The honoured name of William Black must ever stand inseparably connected with the important event alluded to. Mr. Black was a warm-hearted Yorkshireman, who emigrated, whilst yet a youth, with his father and family to Nova Scotia, in 1775. They settled at Amherst, where they found a few godly people from England who had preceded them. There being no one to preach the Gospel, these pious emigrants held occasional religious meetings among themselves for their mutual edification. Amongst others who attended these services came William Black, who was soon brought to a saving knowledge of the truth. Being a young man of more than ordinary ability, and of remarkable earnestness and zeal in the cause of God, the new convert was made useful to others from the time that he began to serve the Lord; and ere long he was called to be a preacher of the Gospel to a people who were literally hungering for the bread of life. By his pious, self-denying labours, Mr. Black earned for himself the title of the "Apostle of Methodism in Nova Scotia," and for more than half a century he continued to exercise his acceptable and powerful ministry in the eastern provinces of British North America, to the spiritual benefit of vast numbers of the settlers.

Whilst a good work was going on at Amherst, through the instrumentality of Mr. Black, and others who had been raised up to call sinners to repentance, the population of Nova Scotia, in common with that of other British American provinces, was considerably increased by the arrival of a large number of emigrant Loyalists from the United States, who, on the declaration of independence, preferred to live anywhere rather than submit to a Republican form of government. The venerable Mr. R. Barry, of Liverpool, N.S., was one of the number, and he has preserved some interesting recollections of this early period in a valuable manuscript document, which has been placed at our disposal, and from which we are permitted to quote. He says:—" On the 7th and 8th of May, 1783, sixteen sail of ships arrived at Port Roseway from New York with emigrants, among whom were ten or twelve white members of the Methodist Society, and a few blacks. Soon after we had drawn our town lots, landed our goods, and pitched our soldiers' tents furnished by Government for our temporary accommodation in the woods, we were visited by the Rev. William Black and Captain Dean, of Liverpool. This early visit to our new settlement was truly welcome; but being unexpected, we were not prepared to accommodate our friends as we could have wished. Such as we had, however, we cheerfully placed at their disposal. I resigned my tent and bed for their use and sat up all night outside, with some discomfort, as heavy rain came on. The next day preaching was announced, and there being no house of any kind as yet erected, a table was placed in the street, opposite my lot, on which Mr. Black delivered the first sermon that was preached in the settlement. Opposition was offered by some who had dined together and had made too free with the wine; but the congregation so closely hemmed in the preacher, that no evil was allowed to be done to him, beyond a short interruption."

After Mr. Black and Captain Dean had returned to Liverpool, the Methodist settlers held their class-meetings and other religious services as best they could; but, feeling the want of a Gospel ministry, Mr. Barry, who had commenced teaching a school, made application to Mr. Wesley for help. The founder of Methodism replied as follows, dated Epworth, July 3rd, 1784:—" I know your brother well, and was at his house the last time I was at Portsmouth, as probably I shall be again in autumn, before I return to London. The work of God, among the blacks in your neighbourhood, is a wonderful instance of the power of God, and the little town they have built is, I suppose, the only town of negroes which has been built in America, nay, perhaps in any part of the world, except only in Africa. I doubt not but some of them can read: when, therefore, we send a preacher to Nova Scotia, we will send some books to be distributed among them, and they never need want books while I live. It will be well to give them all the assistance you can in every possible way. We purpose considering fully at the Conference what we can do to help our brethren abroad—not only those that are settled in the southern provinces of America, but those that are in Nova Scotia and Newfoundland also. Indeed, it is an invariable rule with me not to require any one to go over to America; nay, I scruple even to advise them to it. I shall only propose it at the Conference, and then of those who shall freely offer themselves, we shall select such as we believe will most adorn the Gospel. In teaching school you have an opportunity of doing much good, if you consider that you are called of God to teach those you are entrusted with, not only to read and write, but to fear and serve Him. Indeed, in order to this, you will have need of much courage as well as much prudence and patience; and it may be long before you see the fruit of your labour; but, in due time, you shall reap if you faint not. I wish you would, from time to time, send an account of the progress of the work of God, and of anything remarkable that occurs to your affectionate brother, John Wesley."

Previous to the receipt of this letter, Mr. Barry had succeeded in building a log house, in which he set apart a room for the class-meeting and other religious services; and to edify his friends and neighbours he read to them Mr. Wesley's sermons when they met together. Concerning these exercises, he says, "Blessed be God, we enjoyed times of refreshing from His divine presence." In the fall of the year another fleet of ships with emigrants arrived from New York, in one of which Mr. John Mann, a Local Preacher, and his family came passengers. This was a valuable acquisition to the infant cause at Shelburne; and Mr. Barry cheerfully gave up a part of his log house for the use of Mr. Mann and his family. Before winter improved arrangements were made for the public services. One of the leaders had erected a large building for the purpose of carrying on his business as a coppersmith, which, not being used for this purpose, was converted into a preaching-house, and large congregations assembled to hear the Word of God.

In 1784, Mr. Mann having removed to Liverpool, Bishop Asbury, at the request of Mr. Wesley, and in response to the application of Mr. Black, who attended the Conference held at Baltimore, sent two Preachers from the United States to Nova Scotia, namely, the Revs. Freeborn Garrettson and James O. Cromwell, who were alternately appointed for Shelburne, and the good cause prospered much under their ministry. Mr. Garrettson was remarkably popular and useful. He commenced preaching in the open air, at a place called "the Cove," a thickly-settled part of the town, where much good was done. He also frequently visited the negro settlement, called Birchtown, alluded to by Mr. Wesley. It was situated about eleven miles from Shelburne; and contained a considerable population of blacks, two hundred of whom had been brought to a saving knowledge of the truth, and were united in Church fellowship. There was a good work among this simple-minded people till a preacher, named Marrant, of their own complexion, was sent to minister to them by Lady Huntingdon, who, by a display of gown and bands, and the introduction of strange doctrine, turned their heads, if not their hearts, from the simplicity of the Gospel. Most of them were soon afterwards removed to Sierra Leone in Western Africa, to which place they carried with them their characteristic peculiarities. Mr. Garrettson also extended his visits to a destitute settlement called Barrington, about twenty miles from Shelburne, where a preaching house was built and a good work commenced. In 1788, a Missionary, named James Wray, was sent from England to Nova Scotia, whose ministry was rendered a great blessing during the short time that he laboured there. He preached alternately at Shelburne, Birchtown, Cape Negro, and Barrington, till he was appointed to the West Indies, where he soon fell a sacrifice to the climate.

The venerable John Wesley kept up a regular correspondence with the Missionaries and leading friends in Nova Scotia. In his last letter to Mr. Barry, dated London, January 4th, 1790, he says:—"As a town of negroes in America was almost unprecedented I was struck to hear of a Society there. It is worthy of your particular care. I am glad our Preachers visit them regularly. It is no wonder that all religious societies by turns ebb and flow, particularly in an age of revolution; there must be time before things can settle into order. One great point will be for our Preachers to live in the strictest harmony. Love as brethren. Beware of prejudice against each other. Open your hearts to one another without disguise or reserve. If you unite with one force nothing will stand against you. The world and the devil must fall under your feet."

Subsequently to the appointment of Messrs. Garrettson and Cromwell, already mentioned, several other Preachers were sent from the United States. One of these, the Rev. William Jessop, was made a special blessing both in the Shelburne Circuit and in Halifax, where he took an active part in the erection of the first Wesleyan chapel, as well as in gathering a congregation. During a second period of labour in Nova Scotia, this zealous Missionary exerted himself beyond his strength, frequently travelling on foot through deep snows between Shelburne and Barrington, until his health entirely failed, when he returned to his native land to die. About this time Mr. James Mann, then keeping a school in Liverpool, was prevailed upon by Mr. Garrettson to come to his assistance. He accordingly gave himself entirely to the work of the ministry, and became a popular and useful preacher, especially in the Shelburne Circuit. He frequently expressed his wish, in the language of the poet,

> My body with my charge lay down,
> And cease at once to work and live;"

which in his case was literally fulfilled, for after labouring faithfully for many years, on a Christmas day he preached, administered the sacrament of the Lord's Supper, married and baptized several persons, then complained of a slight pain, and in the afternoon expired in the arms of a friend. The remains of the dear Missionary were drawn on a sledge over deep snow a distance of thirty miles, from Cape Negro to Shelburne, where they were interred in the chapel under the pulpit, the funeral service being performed bythe Rev. R. H. Crane, who was several years afterwards the friend and fellow labourer of the writer, and who presented him with an autograph letter of Mr. Wesley, addressed to Mr. Mann, which he highly values.*

It would be very agreeable to extend still further records, from documents in our possession and from personal recollection, of interesting incidents connected with the planting of Methodism in Nova Scotia; but other sections of the great Mission field have equal demands upon our space. It may, therefore, suffice to remark that when Messrs. Garrettson and Cromwell had returned to the United States, the work was mainly dependent upon the zealous and laborious Mr. Black, Messrs. James and John Mann, and other Preachers raised up on the spot, with such Missionaries as could be obtained from England from time to time, through the kind intervention of Mr. Wesley and Dr. Coke. At an early period

---

* As this letter of the founder of Methodism, written precisely two years before his lamented death, is so characteristic, and throws some light on the early history of the Nova Scotia Mission, we here give a copy of it *verbatim*:—

"MY DEAR BROTHER,   "London, Feb. 27, 1789.

"When I consented to spare three of our Preachers for America, I supposed two of them would have been stationed in the Islands, and one in the North; but I suppose Dr. Coke found so great a call for Preachers in the South, that he believed it advisable to leave them all there. It is not strange that a work of God, which is lively at first, should afterwards decay. It *must* do so, if those who are partakers of the grace of God do not take care to improve it. For 'from him that hath not, shall be taken away what he assuredly hath.' We have need to be the more urgent with all who have received the grace of God, that they may not receive it in vain.—I am your affectionate friend and brother,

"*Mr. James Mann.*   "J. WESLEY.

"March 2nd.

"P.S.—Alas, my brother! one just come from Halifax informs me that they made objection to James Wray, that he is an Englishman! O American gratitude, Lord, I appeal to Thee!   "J. W."

of its history the Mission was favoured with the labours of the Revs. Messrs. Averd, Pope, Crane, Shenstone, Temple, and other faithful Missionaries who extended the work to Halifax, Liverpool, Yarmouth, Windsor, and other important centres of population, to the great advantage of all classes of the community. In every town and village of importance, and in many rural districts, commodious Wesleyan chapels have been erected, congregations gathered, circuits formed, churches organized, and schools established; and Methodism has taken deep root among a people, many of whom are poor in their worldly circumstances, but rich in faith and good works.

In the year 1829 the Missionaries extended their labours to CAPE BRETON, an island separated from the peninsula by a narrow channel, and possessing a considerable population. The Rev. Matthew Cranswick was the first Missionary appointed to this distant station, and his zealous labours, with those of the excellent ministers who succeeded him, resulted in the establishment of a work of God, which has continued to prosper to the present time, and which in its main features resembles that which is carried on so successfully on the mainland. In various parts of the province gracious revivals of religion have frequently taken place, and multitudes of people have been gathered into the fold of the Redeemer. In Nova Scotia and Cape Breton we have now *fifty-three Ministers, five thousand four hundred and eighty church members*, and *five thousand one hundred and thirty-three scholars* in the Sabbath and day schools.

NEW BRUNSWICK

In scenery, soil, climate, and physical aspect, NEW BRUNSWICK resembles Nova Scotia, of which province it originally formed a part. It therefore needs no particular description, and we may proceed at once to consider its Missionary history, which we shall find very interesting. The first Wesleyan Missionary sent to New Brunswick, was the Rev. A. J. Bishop, a native of Jersey, who, during the time that he laboured there, was made abundantly useful in winning souls for Christ. He arrived in the city of St. John, the capital of the colony, on the 24th of September, 1791, and was received with gratitude and joy by a few pious people who had previously gone out from the mother country as emigrants; and who earnestly desired a faithful Gospel ministry for their own benefit, and that of their long-neglected neighbours. They soon procured a suitable place for preaching, and the Missionary commenced his labours with an encouraging prospect of success. From the very first a gracious influence attended the preaching of the Word; and sinners were converted, and believers edified. There is reason to believe that in the short space of six months upwards of two hundred people were brought to a saving knowledge of the truth, and induced to cast in their lot with the people of God.

Mr. Bishop did not confine his labours to the city, but visited various settlements on the banks of the St. John's river, at the mouth of which the city stands; and he soon formed an extensive circuit, round which he itinerated, at stated periods, to the great advantage of a scattered and spiritually destitute population. Everywhere the faithful preaching of the Gospel was attended with soul-saving power; and the Missionary rejoiced to see the fruit of his labour. Several of the new converts were black and coloured persons of African descent, and others were European settlers, or refugees from the United States. The society in St. John's soon numbered eighty members, and the congregation increased so rapidly, that it was necessary to procure a larger place of worship. Just at that time an unoccupied church was offered for sale, with pulpit, pews, and galleries complete. This was at once purchased by the Methodists, and the good work proceeded in the most delightful manner, "the Lord adding to the church daily such as were saved."

The success which attended the Wesleyan Mission in New Brunswick, at this early period, rendering assistance very desirable, the zealous and devoted Mr. Black, of Nova Scotia, at the invitation of Mr. Bishop, hastened across the Bay of Fundy, on a visit to St. John's, to share in the labours and triumphs of his happy brother, and to supply the pulpit in the city whilst he visited some of the country stations. This well-meant arrangement was, however, thwarted by the enemy. When far away in the interior, Mr. Bishop heard, with regret, that, in consequence of the interference of some evil-disposed person in authority, a stop had been put to Mr. Black's preaching, because he had not obtained the Governor's license, and that he had been obliged to return to his own station in Nova Scotia before he had rendered the full amount of service which he intended. The lonely Missionary was consequently left to pursue his arduous work without any aid beyond such as was raised up on the spot as the result of his own labour.

Mr. Bishop had scarcely completed two years of happy and successful labour when he was appointed to the Island of Grenada, in the West Indies, in consequence of his knowledge of the French language giving him peculiar adaptation for that station. There he soon finished his course, and entered into the joy of his Lord. In the meantime the good work continued to advance in New Brunswick. The Rev. Messrs. Marsden, M'Coll, Crosscombe, Bell, Lewis, and other faithful Missionaries were appointed in succession to this interesting field of labour; and their zealous efforts to bring sinners to Christ, and to extend the interests of the Redeemer's kingdom throughout the province were owned and blessed by the great Head of the Church. Regular circuits were formed, chapels built, and societies organised, not only in St. John's, but in Fredericton, Sackville, Annapolis, Maramichi, Bathurst, and other towns, villages, hamlets, and rural districts on the banks of the river, and in other parts of the country. Nor has the education of the rising generation been neglected. Sabbath and day schools have been provided in various places, and the Wesleyan Academy, at Sackville, will bear a favourable comparison with the superior seminaries of any country.

Notwithstanding the numerous difficulties which have been experienced from the rigour of the climate, the comparative poverty of the inhabitants, and the scattered character of the population, it is a pleasing fact, that there are now, in connexion with the Wesleyan church in the Province of New Brunswick, *forty-six Ministers, four thousand seven hundred and twelve church members*, and *four thousand seven hundred and twenty-eight scholars* in the Sabbath and day schools. It is, moreover, worthy of notice that the Governor himself, the Hon. L. A. Wilmot, is a zealous Methodist, a Class Leader, Trustee, and Sunday-school Superintendent,—the first resident in the colony who has been raised to that high position by the suffrages of the people.

Prince Edward's Island.

In the southern part of the Gulf of St. Lawrence, between New Brunswick and Cape Breton, there appears on the map, a long straggling and irregular shaped tract of land marked "Prince Edward's Island," which next claims our attention. It is said to be sixty miles long, and thirty broad, with a soil comparatively fertile, and watered by numerous rivers. In its climate, productions, and population, it resembles other parts of British North America, and was brought under the dominion of England in 1745. In common with the neighbouring provinces, Prince Edward's Island received a considerable accession to its population at the close of the revolutionary war, soon after which the spiritual destitution of the people attracted the attention of the zealous and devoted Dr. Coke; but a delay of several years occurred before a Wesleyan Missionary could be sent to labour among them.

The first Missionary appointed to Prince Edward's Island was the Rev. James Bulpit, a zealous English Preacher, well adapted for the foreign work. He embarked at Poole, on the 9th of April, 1807, and arrived in Quebec on the 8th of June, having preached eighteen times on board-ship during the passage. The Missionary was detained a month in the capital of Canada; and, finding no minister there at the time, he was usefully employed in preaching, in a large dwelling-house, to a most friendly people.

At length the way was opened for proceeding to the place of his destination, and on the 20th of July he landed at Mary Harbour, where he found about fifty people, most of whom were from Jersey, where they had heard the Gospel from the lips of Methodist preachers. These simple-hearted settlers surrounded the Missionary, and welcomed his arrival with tears of joy, whilst he at once arranged to improve the occasion by preaching to them a sermon on the goodness of God. Mr. Bulpit then proceeded to Charlotte Town, the capital of the island, where he commenced his evangelical labours under very favourable circumstances. He experienced no kind of opposition, but everybody appeared disposed to favour the enterprise in which he was engaged. The Governor kindly allowed the Missionary the use of the court-house for his services, till more permanent arrangements could be made. The only Episcopalian minister in the country was very friendly; and, with his family, attended the meetings of the Methodists, his son becoming a member of the first class that was formed for the religious instruction of inquirers.

Thus was the Missionary encouraged to persevere in the work of the Lord, and the cause gradually advanced and expanded more and more. In the course of a few years, a new chapel and minister's residence were erected by the people at Charlotte Town; preaching was commenced at Fullerton's Marsh, Murray's Harbour, Cherry Valley, Tyron River, Bedeque, and other places; and, both in town and country, sinners were savingly converted to God, and prosperous Societies established. At some of these places the faith and patience of the Missionary were at first severely tried however, not only by the stolid indifference manifested by many of the settlers to their religious interests, but also by the antinomian sentiments which some of them had imbibed. But in a short time every difficulty gave way before the persevering diligence and zealous efforts of the servant of God, and the Word of the Lord had "free course, and was glorified." On the removal of Mr. Bulpit to another sphere of labour, he was succeeded by the Rev. Messrs. Hick, Strong, Fishpool, Snowball, and other faithful ministers, who nobly followed up the good beginning which had been made; so that, by the blessing of God upon the zealous labours of His servants, the work has been greatly extended, and we have now in Prince Edward's Island *nine Ministers, one thousand one hundred and sixty-four church members*, and *one thousand six hundred and fifteen scholars* in the Sabbath and day schools.

NEWFOUNDLAND.

The next place to pass under review is NEWFOUNDLAND, a large island on the east coast of North America, three hundred and fifty miles long and three hundred broad. It was discovered by Sebastian Cabot in 1496; but no settlement was formed on it till many years afterwards. After numerous disputes with the French, who first attempted to colonise the country, it was ceded to the English in 1713, and has ever since remained in our possession. The interior of the island is in most places either sterile, mountainous, or woody, and very few localities are said to be adapted for agricultural purposes. The climate is, moreover, severely cold in winter, the snow frequently covering the ground for several months in succession. The settlements of the British are chiefly confined to the harbours, the country near Placentia, and along the bays eastward towards Cape Race, and thence to Cape Bonavista.

The principal occupation of the inhabitants of Newfoundland is that of fishing; and in the season, which begins in May and ends in September, the place is resorted to by tens of thousands of people from different countries, to catch, dry, and cure the codfish, which is taken in large quantities on the extensive banks to the south-east of the island. Towards the latter part of the last century the spiritual destitution of the scattered inhabitants of the colony and of the visitors during the fishing season, attracted the notice of the friends of Missions in England; and about the year 1765, the Rev. L. Coughlan was ordained and sent out as a Missionary by the "Society for the Propagation of Christian Knowledge," at the recommendation of Mr. Wesley, who had been instrumental in his spiritual enlightenment, and with whom he kept up a friendly correspondence during the seven years that he laboured in the island. Although this devoted servant of Christ was not in connection with the Wesleyan Conference, he avowed himself a Methodist, and was made the means of salvation to many precious souls. One of his early converts, Pierre Le Sueur from Jersey, who had settled in Newfoundland, was made the honoured instrument in the hands of God, of conveying the light of Divine truth to his native land, to which he returned a few years afterwards,—an event which led to the introduction of Methodism into the Channel Islands.

When Mr. Coughlan had gathered into the fold of Christ a number of earnest converts to the faith of the Gospel, and was proceeding in his work with evident tokens of the Divine blessing, a spirit of persecution was evoked which seriously interfered with his usefulness for a time; but out of all the Lord delivered His servant, and caused the wrath of man to praise Him. At length Mr. Coughlan's health failed, and he returned to England, when, after some unavoidable delay, the vacancy was supplied by the appointment of the Rev. John M'Geary, a regular Methodist Preacher, who was sent out by Mr. Wesley in 1790. On examining the state of the work, the newly appointed Missionary found that it had declined very much since the departure of Mr. Coughlan. Some of the converts had been called to their eternal rest, and others had gone back to the world. Only fifteen members of Society were still found adhering to their religious profession, so that the work had to be re-organised and commenced almost anew. Mr. M'Geary laboured chiefly in Carbonear, which was at that time one of the principal settlements of the colony; but the results of his efforts were for a while so unsatisfactory that he was seriously thinking of abandoning his station, when he received a friendly visit from the Rev. William Black, from Nova Scotia. This event infused new life into the heart of the lonely Missionary, and was attended with circumstances of the greatest importance to the infant Mission.

This timely visit of Mr. Black to Newfoundland, in 1791, was not only very encouraging to the Missionary, but it was attended with a gracious revival of religion, in the course of which a number of sinners were savingly converted to God. The zealous stranger preached with soul-saving power at Carbonear, Conception Bay, and other settlements. At the place last named it is believed that not less than two hundred persons were brought to a saving knowledge of the truth during his stay; and the time he spent in the colony on this occasion is said to have been "the most useful and interesting period of his life." Having assisted Mr. M'Geary in re-organizing the Society, securing church property, and in applying to Mr. Wesley for additional labourers, Mr. Black returned to his own station in Nova Scotia. Concerning his departure, he says, "I think I never had so affecting a parting with any people before. It was hard work to tear myself away from them. I was nearly an hour shaking hands with the members, some twice and thrice over, and even then we hardly knew how to part; but I at last rushed from among them, and left them weeping as for an only son."

From this time the work of God continued to prosper in Newfoundland. Additional labourers were sent out from England, regular Circuits formed, new chapels built in various places, and promising Societies organised in St. John's, Harbour Grace, Bonavista, Conception Bay, and other settlements, in addition to Carbonear, where the work was first commenced. In many of these places the people were perfectly destitute of the means of religious instruction, till the Missionaries came among them, and the results of their self-denying labours will only be known in the last great day. In process of time, the dreary coast of Labrador was visited by the Missionaries during the summer months from year to year, and many a poor wanderer was pointed to the Saviour, who might otherwise have been left to perish in his sins. The Missionaries who laboured in Newfoundland at this early period, after the removal of Mr. M'Geary, were the Revs. Messrs. Bulpit, Rimington, Ellis, M'Dowell, Lewis, Busby, Hickson, Walsh, Cubitt, Pickavant, Knight, Haigh, Corlett, Bate, Wilson, Smithies, and others in more recent times. To the zeal and diligence of several of those devoted servants of Christ we can testify from personal knowledge; and if space permitted, it would be pleasant and profitable to follow them in their zealous and self-denying labours, amid storms and tempests and chilling cold, such as are unknown to those who dwell in temperate climes; to say nothing of other privations and dangers to which they were exposed. It is gratifying to be able to add in conclusion that the Lord of the harvest has greatly blessed the united labours of His servants in Newfoundland, and that there are now in connection with the Wesleyan Church in the island, *twenty-one Ministers, three thousand two hundred and forty-seven church members*, and *two thousand seven hundred and forty-five scholars* in the Sabbath and day schools

BERMUDAS.

Before we finish our survey of the Mission Stations, which come under the general head of America, we must take a glance at the BERMUDAS. In their climate, scenery, productions and the character of the inhabitants, the Bermudas very much resemble some of the West India islands; but in some other respects they appear more closely allied to America, with the Missions of which they have been for some time connected in their ecclesiastical organisation. Hence the propriety of giving a brief account of them here, in connection with a brief sketch of the origin and progress of the Wesleyan Mission commenced there several years ago.

The Bermudas are a group of islands, said to be more than three hundred in number; but only five of them are inhabited, the rest being mere rocky islets jutting out from the sea, and separated from each other by the foaming surf or narrow channels of water. As may be seen by a reference to the map, they are situated in the wide Atlantic Ocean, more than five hundred miles from Charleston on the American Continent, in latitude 32° north, and longitude 64° west. They were discovered by Juan Bermudas, a Spaniard, in 1527; but not inhabited till 1609, when Sir George Somers was cast away upon them, and they have belonged to Great Britain ever since. The soil is generally fertile, producing sugar, coffee, arrowroot, and vegetables, and fruits of various kinds. They abound in cedar-wood, with which a number of small vessels are built. The population is estimated at ten thousand, one-half of which are whites, and the other black and coloured persons.

The first Wesleyan Missionary to the Bermudas was the Rev. John Stephenson, who was sent there by the British Conference, at the recommendation of Dr. Coke, in 1799. The zealous Doctor had received a letter the year before, from an officer on board a man-of-war at that station, respectfully urging him to the measure, in consequence of the spiritual destitution and moral degradation of the inhabitants. Mr. Stephenson had no sooner landed on the shores of the Bermudas, than he proved by painful experience the truth of the accounts which had reached England as to the "moral degradation of the people." From the very first he was bitterly persecuted by the whites, in consequence of the deeply-rooted prejudice which existed among them against all efforts to benefit or elevate the poor slaves, or free persons of colour. The most determined efforts were made to silence the newly arrived Missionary—efforts which, alas! succeeded but too well; for he had not exercised his ministry long when he was apprehended, tried, and condemned, and, by an undue stretch of power on the part of the authorities, sentenced to six months' imprisonment, to be fined £50, and to pay all expenses. At the close of his six months' imprisonment, during which he was graciously supported by the presence of God, the Missionary was compelled to leave the colony, and the Mission was relinquished. Thus did the enemies of the cross of Christ triumph for a time over the well-meant efforts of the Wesleyan Missionary Society to carry the glad tidings of salvation to a people that were literally "led captive by the devil at his will;" and who stood in great need of their evangelical labours, although they saw it not.

After this interruption the Wesleyan Mission to the Bermudas was suspended for about eight years, at the end of which period, the hostility of the people to the Gospel having somewhat abated, the Rev. Joshua Marsden was sent from Nova Scotia to occupy the vacant station. He arrived at the place of his destination in the month of May, 1808, and went on shore a perfect stranger; but he soon found out the only person in the colony who professed to be a Methodist, all the rest who were brought to God during the short period of Mr. Stephenson's ministry having died, re-

NEW WESLEYAN CHAPEL, HAMILTON, BERMUDA.

This beautiful place of worship may serve as a specimen of a number of similar buildings which, from year to year, are being erected on our foreign stations, some in entirely new localities and others in the place of the humble structures which were built in the infancy of the Mission. The architect of the new chapel at Bermuda, as well as that of Honduras, and the "Fletcher Memorial College Buildings," in Switzerland, and some others, was E. Hoole, Esq., of London, son of Dr. Hoole, the senior Secretary of the Wesleyan Missionary Society; and the designs are a credit to his genius and skill as well as to his benevolence, for he has in several instances supplied the plans gratuitously as his contribution to the enterprise.

moved, or fallen away. He had, however, a letter of introduction to the Governor, which proved of considerable service to him; and after some delay and hesitancy on the part of the Chief Judge and Attorney-General, who were consulted by His Excellency as to the bearing of the law on the question, he was permitted to open his commission to the inhabitants, who were still to a considerable extent destitute of the means of religious instruction. Mr. Marsden was a man of a mild and genial disposition, and a poetical genius withal, and soon gained the good-will of the people. He was, moreover, zealous and earnest in the cause of his Divine Master, and left no means untried to win souls to Christ. From the very beginning the blessing of God rested upon his labours, and sinners in considerable numbers were brought to a saving knowledge of the truth. As the work extended from island to island, places of worship were erected in St. George's, Hamilton, Somerset, and other towns and villages; and the Mission assumed a position of respectability and usefulness which it has continued to maintain to the present day. Mr. Marsden laboured in the Bermudas with acceptance and success for about four years, and was succeeded by the Revs. Messrs. Dunbar, Wilson, Rayner, Sutcliffe, Dowson, Moore, and others in more recent times, who nobly followed up the good beginning which had been made, and who are still remembered with much affection by some of the old people. Bermuda had, moreover, the honour of giving to Methodism, as the fruit of Missionary labour, the Rev. Edward Frazer, a young man of colour, and himself once a slave, but made free by the truth, and raised to the dignity of the Christian ministry, in which office he has proved a credit to our Church, and been made instrumental in the conversion of many of his sable brethren.

In the year 1844 we had an opportunity of visiting the beautiful islands of Bermuda, and of beholding for ourselves some of the results of the Wesleyan Mission in that country. We preached to large congregations in Hamilton and St. George's, and received a very favourable impression of the intelligence and piety of the people. We also went on a British man-of-war in company with the Rev. W. E. Shenstone, the resident minister, and met a Methodist class for the renewal of quarterly tickets. It consisted of eighteen members, whose Christian experience was clear and satisfactory, and whose reputation for diligence, sobriety, and steady courage, was cheerfully attested by the officers under whom they served. We have now in connexion with our Bermudas Mission, *three Missionaries, four hundred and fifty-seven church members*, and *fifty-eight scholars* in the mission schools.

In further illustration of the growth and expansion of Methodism in North America, it may be briefly added that, in the year 1855, the late Rev. Dr. Beecham was commissioned by the British Conference to proceed to Nova Scotia to make arrangements for the formation of the districts of the Eastern Provinces, including Newfoundland and the Bermudas, into a distinct Connexion. The object of this deputation was carried out in a manner satisfactory to all parties concerned; and the first Session of the Conference of Eastern British America was held at Halifax, under the able and judicious presidency of the Rev. Doctor, in the month of July. Since this period the good work has continued to prosper, the poorer Circuits and Stations being still aided by grants from the Wesleyan Missionary Committee in London. The total number of Ministers in connexion with this Conference is now *one hundred and thirty-two;* and they have under their pastoral care *fifteen thousand and eight church members*, with *fourteen thousand six hundred and seventy-nine scholars* in the Sabbath and day schools. Viewing these results in connection with the statistics of the Canadian Conference and those of the Methodist Episcopal Church in the United States, we are constrained to thank God for what He has done, through the instrumentality of Wesleyan Missions, on the American continent during the past century, and to pray that still greater results may follow in time to come.

CHAPTER III.

THE WEST INDIES

DESCRIPTION OF THE ISLANDS—THE ANTIGUA DISTRICT—THE ST. VINCENT'S DISTRICT—DEMERARA—JAMAICA—HONDURAS—THE BAHAMAS—HAYTI.

THE West India Islands are situated in that part of the Atlantic Ocean which forms itself into a deep and extensive bay between the vast continents of North and South America. They were discovered at different times by the enterprising Columbus, towards the close of the fifteenth century; and were most of them inhabited by savage tribes of natives, whom the Spaniards called "Indians," or "Caribs," evidently of different races or descent. These unfortunate aborigines were too independent to submit to the slavery which their cruel conquerors would have imposed upon them. They were, moreover, unfitted by nature, and their previous habits of life, to endure that severe toil and drudgery to which they were required to submit. By degrees they were almost entirely extirpated; rapidly passing away under the cruel treatment of their oppressors. Their places were soon supplied by negro slaves, who had been torn from their homes in Africa, and doomed to a life of perpetual toil and hopeless bondage. The mass of the population in the West Indies at present consists of the descendants of these people, now happily made free, and rapidly rising in the scale of being.

But if we would have a correct view of the West Indies as a scene of Missionary labour, we must now look at the islands somewhat more minutely, and regard not only their locality and the character of the population, but also their nationality, scenery, and productions. By the fortunes of war and other changes, the islands forming the Archipelago of the West have fallen into the hands of various European powers. At the present time the English colonies are, Jamaica, Antigua, Dominica, Montserrat, Nevis, St. Christopher's, Barbuda, Anguilla, St. Lucia, the Virgin Islands, the Bahamas, Honduras, Demerara, Barbadoes, St. Vincent's, Grenada, Tobago, and Trinidad. The French islands are, Martinique, Guadaloupe, Marie Galante, and St. Martin's in part. The Spanish colonies are Cuba and Porto Rico. The Dutch have St. Eustatius, Saba, and St. Martin's in part. There are belonging to the Danes, St. Thomas's, St. John's, and St. Croix; and the Swedes claim St. Bartholomew's; whilst Hayti has become a republic of free blacks, and coloured persons, who cast off the French yoke in 1803.

These islands and continental settlements, which usually pass under the general name of the West Indies, possess, in their climate, scenery, soil, and productions, several features in common with each other, whilst at the same time each place has a history of its own, and something peculiar to itself. But it is unnecessary here to enter into minute details with respect to the physical aspect and civil history of the sunny isles of the West, as sufficient on these points for our purpose will turn up in connection with each place as it passes in review before us. We may, therefore, proceed without further preliminary observations, to the main object which we have in view, namely, to trace the rise, progress, and present state of Wesleyan Missions in this interesting field of labour.

The Antigua District.

The introduction of Methodism to the West Indies may be traced directly to the blessing of God on Mr. Wesley's preaching in England. That holy and blessed man mentions, in his journal, under the date of the 17th of January, 1758, that he preached at Wandsworth in the house of Nathaniel Gilbert, Esq., a lawyer, and the Speaker of the House of Assembly in Antigua, who was staying there for the benefit of his health. He states also that two of his negro servants and a mulatto were present, and appeared much affected under the sermon. Mr. Gilbert heard Mr. Wesley preach repeatedly afterwards during his sojourn in England, and there is reason to believe that both he and some of the members of his household were brought to a saving knowledge of the truth; for two of his slaves were baptized by Mr. Wesley,—one of whom he declares to be " the first regenerated African that he had ever seen,—and the planter himself ever afterwards became identified with the despised people of God.

On his return to Antigua, Mr. Gilbert confessed to his friends and neighbours what a treasure he had found; and commenced at once to hold meetings for the religious instruction of his own people, and those of the surrounding estates. From his high connexions and position in life, this strange proceeding brought upon this man of God the ridicule and sneers of the ungodly; but these he regarded not. At first he confined himself in the meetings which he held to the reading of sermons and the singing of hymns; but he soon found himself doing the work of an evangelist as an exhorter and catechist, and leading classes composed of those who were willing to flee from the wrath to come. In these exercises he was assisted and encouraged by some members of his family, who had been made the happy partakers of the like precious faith, and by the founder of Methodism himself, with whom he kept up a constant correspondence. By these pious efforts Mr. Gilbert was made the means of salvation to a considerable number of negroes and others; and he ceased not to labour for the benefit of his fellowmen in every possible way till he was called to his reward in heaven.

There was no one qualified to take Mr. Gilbert's place when he was removed by death; but the Society which he had formed was kept from desolation by the faithful labours of two pious negro slaves named Mary Alley and Sophia Campbell. Whether these sable converts were the two domestics whom Mr. Wesley baptized in England, we have been unable to ascertain; but it is evident that they were unwearied in their efforts to do good, by holding prayer meetings and other religious services among their fellow negroes almost every evening, till the Lord of the harvest provided more efficient help. This was brought about in a manner quite unexpected by the evident interposition of Divine Providence. Additional shipwrights being required for his Majesty's service in Antigua, in 1778, John Baxter, a Methodist Local Preacher was sent from the royal dockyard at Chatham. He found the remnants of Mr. Gilbert's society still kept together by the two pious female leaders already mentioned, and immediately began to preach to them. The results were most encouraging; and to meet the urgent demands for religious instruction, he soon extended his labours to various parts of the island, exerting himself to the utmost of his power for the spiritual welfare of the people, whilst at the same time he had to labour at his worldly calling for his daily bread.

As the work expanded, application was repeatedly made to Mr. Wesley and Dr. Coke for Missionaries for the West Indies, but at that early period Methodism was doing a great Missionary work at home and in America, where every available labourer was required to assist in reclaiming deeply degraded populations, only just emerging from the darkness of ages. Consequently Mr. Baxter was left to toil alone with his sable charge in the island of Antigua. He had thus laboured with untiring zeal for eight years, and had under his care a Society of one thousand five hundred and sixty-nine members, all blacks except ten, when help was sent by an interposition of Divine Providence which has scarcely a parallel in the history of Missions. About five o'clock on the morning of Christmas Day, 1786, when the lonely preacher was plodding his way along the streets of St. John's, in order to conduct Divine service in the rude chapel which he had built chiefly with his own hands, he was unexpectedly met by a party of strangers, the arrival of whom was destined to mark a new era in the religious history of Antigua and of the whole of the West Indies. The principal person in the group, which consisted of four weather-beaten travellers who had just landed from a half-wrecked vessel in the harbour, was a little clerical-looking gentleman, who inquired for Mr. Baxter, and whose eyes sparkled with joy when he found he was speaking to the man himself, and understood where he was going at that early hour. This was Dr. Coke, with Messrs. Hammett, Warrener, and Clarke, three Missionaries, with whom he had embarked at Gravesend for Nova Scotia, just three months before, and who had been thus mysteriously driven by the violence of the tempest to the West Indies under the guidance of Him whom "wind and seas obey." The Missionaries at once saw the hand of God in this remarkable dispensation of His Providence; and they went directly to the chapel to render thanks to their heavenly Father for their merciful preservation. Dr. Coke immediately ascended the pulpit, and preached with his wonted zeal and energy to a large and attentive congregation. The loving heart of the zealous little Doctor overflowed with emotion as he gazed upon the upturned faces of a thousand negroes, anxiously listening to the Word of life; and he no doubt felt, as he had never done before, the force of his own favourite text, "Ethiopia shall soon stretch out her hands unto God." He was, moreover, struck with the neat and cleanly appearance of the congregation, as it clearly showed the beneficial influence of the Gospel in a temporal point of view.

It was now arranged that Mr. Warrener should continue in Antigua, and that the other brethren should be stationed in those islands where their labours appeared to be most urgently required; several of the other West India Colonies having already made earnest applications for Missionaries. During the two weeks that he remained in St. John's, Dr. Coke preached twice a day to crowded congregations, besides two or three times in the country; and on the 5th of January, 1787, he embarked, in company with Messrs. Baxter, Hammett, and Clarke, on a tour of observation among the islands. They visited in succession Dominica, St. Vincent's, Nevis, St. Christopher's, and St. Eustatius, collecting information, and embracing every opportunity which presented itself of preaching to the people. In every island there appeared to be openings for Missionaries, with the exception of the one last named; but as only two preachers were disengaged, they were stationed in the most important colonies, Mr. Hammett being appointed to St. Christopher's, and Mr. Clarke to St. Vincent's. Having made the best arrangement in his power to meet the present emergency, Dr. Coke embarked for America on the 10th of February, promising that on his return to England he would do his best to send more Missionaries to strengthen the hands of the brethren.

As the work advanced from year to year, new stations were occupied, and the number of labourers was considerably increased, till almost every colony was brought under the influence of the Gospel. The nature and progress of the enterprise will be best understood by a succinct and systematic account of the respective islands and circuits comprised in the ANTIGUA DISTRICT.

ANTIGUA itself is not the most important island in the West Indies, but it is deserving of prominent and further notice, as the cradle of Methodism in the Antilles, and also because it possesses many features of special interest in a Missionary point of view. It was discovered by Columbus in the course of his second voyage, but it was not till the year 1529 that a small French settlement was formed on the island. Three years afterwards it was taken by the English, and formally confirmed to us by treaty in 1668. The land being generally low, the scenery is not so grand and romantic as that of some other islands; it is, moreover, liable to a scarcity of water, which militates against it as a place of residence. The soil is generally fertile, however, and it is celebrated as a sugar colony. As a Wesleyan Mission station, Antigua has been one of the most prosperous in the West Indies, according to the extent of the population, which is estimated at thirty-eight thousand. When additional Missionaries were supplied to occupy the ground, after the favourable commencement already noticed, the work of God greatly prospered, out-stations being ultimately formed at English Harbour, Parham, Bolans, Sion Hill, Freetown, and other places, in addition to the head quarters in St. John's, the capital of the colony, where the work commenced. The chapels in some of these places are substantial and elegant buildings, especially that in St. John's, which was erected in 1844, under the superintendency of the Rev. Jesse Pilcher. The island has recently been divided into two circuits, which unitedly employ *five Missionaries*, and number *one thousand nine hundred and fifty church members*, with *one thousand one hundred and eight scholars* in the Mission Schools.

DOMINICA is a romantic, mountainous, rugged island, twenty-nine miles long and sixteen broad, with a population of about twenty-two thousand. The interior of the country is still covered with forests of timber; but there are many fertile valleys, watered with numerous streams, and well adapted for cultivation. In former years coffee and cotton were cultivated to a considerable extent; but sugar is now the principal article of produce. As already stated, Dr. Coke called at Dominica in the course of his first voyage of observation in 1787, and preached to the people with much acceptance; but nothing more was done at that period. About two years afterwards he visited the island a second time, accompanied by the Rev. William M'Cornock, whom he left to commence the Mission. The zealous Missionary had only laboured a few months, however, when he was called away by death, being the first Wesleyan Missionary who fell in the West Indies, or in any other part of the foreign field. After this afflictive bereavement the infant church was left without a pastor for several years. In 1793 Dr. Coke once more visited Dominica; and being much affected by the destitute condition of the people, the following year he sent the Rev. John Cook to recommence the Mission. Mr. Cook was succeeded by Messrs. Dumbleton, Taylor, Bocock, Shipley, and others, several of whom fell a sacrifice to the climate, which is generally admitted to be one of the most unhealthy in the West Indies. But notwithstanding the difficulties arising from this circumstance, and from the prevalence of Popish error, the Mission has been favoured with a cheering measure of prosperity. Chapels have been built and societies formed, not only in Roseau, the capital of the colony, but also in Lasoye, Prince Rupert's, and other villages and rural districts. We have now in Dominica *two Missionaries, five hundred and eighty-three church members*, and *four hundred scholars* in the Mission schools.

MONTSERRAT is the next island to be noticed. It is only twelve miles long and seven broad, and is said to have received its present name from its rugged, mountainous aspect. The population was once estimated at fifty thousand, but it has dwindled down in the course of years to about one half that number, chiefly by emigration to Trinidad, Demerara, and other prosperous colonies, where better prospects of success presented themselves to the inhabitants. Dr. Coke was unable to commence a Mission there when he visited the neighbouring islands; but he makes mention, in his journal in 1793, of a class of twelve members, who were regularly met by a pious coloured Leader. It was not till the year 1820 that a Mission was regularly organised in Montserrat. The first Missionary was the Rev. John Maddock, who was called away by death in the midst of his labours a few months after his arrival in the island. He was succeeded by the Rev. Charles Janion and others, who laboured with much success, both in town and country, forming stations and building chapels, at Bethel, Salem, and Cavalla, as well as in Plymouth, the capital of the colony. It is a pleasing fact that although the importance of the Mission has in a measure declined with the decrease of population, Methodism has taken deep root in the country, and we have still in the island *one Missionary, four hundred and fifty-five church members*, and *four hundred and fifty-four scholars* in the Mission schools.

NEVIS is another beautiful little island, which appears on the approach of the voyager like a conical mountain rising out of the sea. It is only eight miles long and five broad; but, being well watered and fertile, it was formerly very productive in sugar, ginger, and the usual fruits and provisions of the tropics. It could once boast of a population of thirty thousand; but by reverse of circumstances, emigration, and the desolating effects of cholera in 1853, it has been reduced to less than one-third that number. Nevis is separated from St. Kitt's, at its south-eastern end, by a narrow channel only three miles broad; and it was originally settled by a party of Englishmen, under Sir Thomas Warner. Dr. Coke first visited this lovely little isle on the 19th of January, 1787; and in the course of the following year a Mission station was regularly organised by the Rev. William Hammett, who came from St. Kitt's to preach to the negroes, at the invitation of a Mr. Brazier. This gentleman, together with the Messrs. Nisbett, supported the cause most nobly for many years; and from the beginning the work was favoured with uninterrupted prosperity. At an early period we find the names of Messrs. Kingston, Brownell, Taylor, Turner, Isham, Woolley, Morgan, Hurst, Mortier, and other worthies associated with this station; and by the blessing of God upon their earnest labours in succession, the work was firmly established, not only in Charleston, the capital, but also at Gingerland, Combermere, and other places. We have now, in connexion with this station, *one Missionary, one thousand four hundred and twenty-one church members*, and *six hundred and fifty-one scholars* in the Mission schools.

St. Christopher's was discovered by Columbus in 1498, and for some reason, not explained, he gave to it his own christian name. The island is of a peculiar shape, having the form of an outstretched leg. The soil is very fertile, and produces large crops of sugar. The population is estimated at twenty-three thousand. In 1787 the Rev. W. Hammett was left in this island by Dr. Coke, as already mentioned, and he commenced the Mission under the most encouraging circumstances. The Lord of the harvest greatly blessed the labours of His servant; and on revisiting the colony in 1789, the zealous Doctor was delighted to find seven hundred members in the Society. Mr. Hammett was succeeded by the Revs. Messrs. Harper, Andrews, Truscott, Brownell, and others; and this soon became one of the most prosperous and important Missions in the West Indies. Spacious and substantial chapels have been erected and stations formed, not only in Basseterre, the capital, but also at Old Road, Sandy Point, Half-way-Tree, and other towns and villages, which give ample employment to *four Missionaries*, who have under their pastoral care *two thousand eight hundred and ninety-three church members*, with *one thousand three hundred and nineteen scholars* in the Mission schools.

ST. EUSTATIUS is a pleasant little island, presenting the appearance of a conical mountain, with a rugged, rocky summit, and gently sloping sides, which are adorned with plantations of sugarcane and yam grounds. Dr. Coke earnestly desired to establish a Mission in this island; but the attempt was met with the most determined resistance on the part of the Dutch Governor Rennolds, and other civil authorities of the colony. It was not till the year 1811 that the preaching of the Missionaries was permitted, when the Rev. M. C. Dixon commenced the Mission under the most favourable circumstances, all opposition having entirely ceased. From the very first the special blessing of God attended the enterprise, sinners being converted under the faithful preaching of the word, and the church built up on the true foundation. The Dutch, having no religious establishment of their own upon the island, now encourage the Wesleyan Mission, and help to support it by an annual grant from the public funds. The station has *one Missionary*, and *two hundred and fifty-five church members*, with *one hundred and ten scholars* in the Mission schools.

ST. BARTHOLOMEW'S is the only island belonging to Sweden in the West Indies. It has a good harbour, but the soil is comparatively poor and the scenery uninviting. The Wesleyan Mission in this colony was commenced by the Rev. William Turton, in the year 1796, under the most encouraging circumstances. The Governor at first granted the Missionary the use of the national church; but, as it was not available for evening services, a commodious chapel was erected, and the blessing of God rested upon the labours of His servant. Mr. Turton was succeeded by the Revs. Messrs. Dobson, Whitworth, White, Gilgrass, Felvus, and other zealous Missionaries; and, notwithstanding the reduction in the population by emigration to other islands, we have still in St. Bartholomew's *one Missionary*, *ninety-five church members*, and *sixty-four scholars* in the Mission schools.

ST. MARTIN'S is an interesting little island belonging to the Dutch and French conjointly; but the Protestant portion of the population of both colonies is entirely dependent upon the ministrations of the Wesleyan Missionaries for religious instruction. It may be stated, to their credit, that the public functionaries, and the people generally, attend the public worship of God with remarkable regularity; and of late years both the Emperor of the French and the King of Holland have contributed liberally towards the support of the Wesleyan Ministry in their respective possessions. The Mission was commenced in 1819 by the Rev. Jonathan Rayner, who was called away by death soon after the work was begun. He was succeeded by other zealous Missionaries, however, whose labours were crowned with success. The station has only part of the services of a Missionary, with about *three hundred church members* under his pastoral care, and *two hundred scholars* in the Mission schools.

ANGUILLA, or Snake Island, so called from its peculiar serpentine form, is thirty miles long and seven broad. It is generally flat, and destitute of mountains or rivers. The soil is deep, but of a chalky nature, and not well adapted for tropical produce, although some sugar and cotton, as well as provisions, are cultivated. The chief staple for exportation is salt, which is manufactured and shipped to America and other places in large quantities. The Gospel was first preached in this island by a converted native, himself the fruit of Missionary labour, and he was afterwards called to the office of the Christian ministry. When the Mission had been regularly organised, a resident Missionary occupied the station; but of late years, from the smallness of the population and the pressing demands of more important stations, it has shared the labours of a Minister with St. Martin's. There are, however, nearly *four hundred persons* united in church fellowship on the station, with a goodly number of children in the Mission schools.

TORTOLA is the largest and most important of a group called the "Virgin Islands." They are celebrated for the excellency and great variety of the fish which is caught on their shores; and in some of them mines of copper, black lead, arsenic, and even gold and silver were formerly worked to advantage. The population of Tortola and the adjacent islets was in a fearful state of spiritual darkness when Dr. Coke first landed there in 1789; but a wonderful change was speedily effected by the regenerating influence of the Gospel. The Rev. William Hammett was charged with the duty of commencing the Mission; and by the blessing of God upon his labours, many were brought to a saving knowledge of

METHOD OF GOLD AND SILVER WASHING.

the truth. He was succeeded by the Revs. Messrs. Owen, M'Kean, Turner, Murdock, Brownell, and others, and the results of their zealous labours have been very encouraging. Tortola is the head of the circuit, where the ministers reside, and they extend their labours to West End, East End, Spanish Town, and other places, where commodious chapels have been built and Societies formed, as well as in Road Town, the capital of the colony. *Two Mis-*

sionaries are employed in this circuit, and they have *one thousand six hundred and sixty church members* under their pastoral care, with *three hundred and two scholars* in the Mission schools.

Since the commencement of Wesleyan Missions in the Antigua District, about eighty-three years ago, many interesting and affecting incidents have occurred in connection with the work on the respective stations which have now passed under review, on which it might be profitable briefly to dwell; but we must hasten to visit other fields of labour which have yet to be surveyed. We cannot take our leave of this District, however, without a brief notice of one of the most afflictive dispensations of Divine Providence that ever occurred in connection with the Missionary enterprise. We allude to the loss of the *Maria* mail-boat. It was in the month of February, 1825, that the Rev. Mr. and Mrs. White, with their three children and a servant; the Rev. Mr. and Mrs. Truscott, with one child and servant; and the Rev. Mr. and Mrs. Jones, and the Rev. Messrs. Hillier and Oke, were returning in the *Maria* mail-boat to Antigua from St. Kitts, where they had been to the Annual District Meeting. They had almost completed their voyage, when they were overtaken by a fearful storm during the night, which drove the vessel upon a reef of rocks, where she was dashed to pieces in a few hours. Some of the party were immediately plunged into a watery grave, whilst others survived for a time, and clung to portions of the wreck for two or three days and nights, exposed to indescribable sufferings; but, ultimately, all on board perished, with the exception of Mrs. Jones, who was spared, as by a miracle, to tell the mournful tale. How dark and mysterious was the dispensation of Divine Providence by which thirteen persons, connected with the Mission, besides the captain and the crew of the vessel, were thus suddenly hurried out of time into eternity! But the Lord doeth all things well, and " what we know not now, we shall know hereafter."

THE ST. VINCENT'S DISTRICT.

It is with feelings of sincere pleasure that we now call the attention of the reader to the ST. VINCENT'S DISTRICT. It is not only a section of the Mission field, which possesses many features of peculiar interest, but it was the scene of our personal labours, and in connection with several of its principal stations we spent fourteen very happy years, in earnest efforts to instruct and elevate the sable sons and daughters of Ham. Notwithstanding the resemblance which exists between some of the Windward Islands to

GRU-GRU AND PALMIST TREES.

those in the Leeward group, the best view will be obtained of the nature and claims of the Mission work in this part of the West Indies by taking a glance at each island separately as before.

St. Vincent's is a rugged, mountainous, and romantic island, rising in the centre, in the form of a cone, to the height of three or four thousand feet above the level of the sea. The interior is still covered with forest trees and brush-wood; but some of its fertile valleys and the plains along the shores are well cultivated and very productive, being watered by numerous streams. Having been neglected for a length of time during the early period of West India colonization, this island became the place of refuge, and the principal stronghold of, the oppressed native Indians or Caribs, with whom fearful wars were waged by the colonists for many years. At length they were subdued and scattered, and their place was supplied with negro slaves, only a very small remnant of the aboriginal tribes remaining when we laboured there. The Wesleyan Mission in St. Vincent's was commenced by the Rev. Mr. Clarke, whom Dr. Coke left in the island on the occasion of his first visit, as already stated. He was afterwards joined by the Rev. Messrs. Gamble and Werrill, whilst Mr. Baxter, from Antigua, who had now devoted himself entirely to Missionary work, was appointed to labour among the Caribs at Grand Sable. For some time the work was generally very prosperous, except that among the Caribs, which failed of its object. Then came a storm of persecution which has seldom been surpassed for violence. One of the Missionaries was imprisoned, the chapels were closed, and the progress of the Gospel was seriously retarded by persecuting enactments passed by the local legislature. An appeal having been made to the British Government, religious liberty was, at length, restored to the land; and every hindrance being removed out of the way, the word of the Lord had free course, ran, and was glorified. From Kingstown, the capital, the work extended to Layou, Barrouallie, and Chateaubellair to leeward, and to Calliaqua, Calder, Biabou, Union, Georgetown, and other places on the windward part of the island. At all these places commodious chapels were ultimately erected, and prosperous societies formed; and the whole island became encircled with a chain of Wesleyan Mission Stations, by means of which about one half of the entire population, estimated at thirty thousand, was brought under religious instruction. In its best days the St. Vincent's Mission exhibited a grand specimen of the triumphs of the Gospel; and, although many changes have taken place since the era of emancipation, when ministers of other denominations eagerly pressed into the field, the work having become comparatively pleasant and easy, the three Circuits into which the island is divided still employ *six Missionaries*, who have *three thousand three hundred and twenty-one church members* under their pastoral care, with *one thousand four hundred and sixteen scholars* in the Mission schools.

GRENADA is the next island which claims attention. It has an interesting civil history of its own, into the particulars of which we cannot now enter. From its having originally been a French colony, most of the negro inhabitants formerly spoke a strange *patois*—a mixture of European and African dialects. They were, moreover, to a considerable extent, under the influence of a curious combination of Popish and Pagan superstitions. These circumstances rendered it somewhat difficult to introduce the Gospel among them. The attempt was made, however, in the name and strength of the Lord. The first Wesleyan Missionary appointed to labour in Grenada was the Rev. A. Bishop, a man of untiring zeal and devotedness to his work; but his day was short. He had only laboured about six months in the island when he fell a sacrifice to the climate. He was succeeded by the Rev. Messrs. Pattinson, Sturgeon, Dixon, Lill, Shrewsbury, Goy, and others, who were made the honoured instruments in the hands of God in bringing multitudes of sinners to a knowledge of the truth. In process of time the work extended from St. George's, the capital, to Woburn, Constantine, La Bay, and other places, including the island of Carricou. At most of these places chapels were ultimately built, societies formed, and schools established, affording to the people the means of religious instruction, of which they must otherwise have remained destitute. Considering the peculiar difficulties of this Mission, the success which has attended the efforts which have been put forth is very gratifying. We have now in Grenada *two Missionaries, six hundred and sixty-eight church members,* and *six hundred and nine scholars* in the Mission schools.

TRINIDAD is a large and fertile island, eighty miles long and thirty broad, bordering on the continent of South America, being only separated by the Gulf of Paria from the Spanish Main. The colony originally belonged to Spain, and from the foreign element which pervaded the masses of the population, and from the prevalence of Roman Catholicism, it did not present a favourable soil for the propagation of Protestant Christianity at an early period. But of late years a tide of emigration has been flowing from the Windward Islands, which has supplied more favourable materials for Missionary operations, and the result has been, with the Divine blessing, a large ingathering of precious souls into the fold of Christ. The Wesleyan Mission to Trinidad originated in a visit, on his own private affairs, of the Rev. T. Talboys from St. Vincent's, in 1809. Finding a favourable opening for usefulness, the Missionary preached as he had opportunity during his stay in Port of Spain; and the results were so satisfactory that an earnest request was made for the continuance of his labours. This led to a series of services, which were made a blessing to many; till, ultimately, the Committee in London sanctioned the arrangement, and Mr. Talboys was authorised to remain and organise the Mission. The work had not advanced far when it was retarded for a time by a storm of persecution which burst upon the infant station, but by a kind Providence it was overruled for good. Mr. Talboys was succeeded by the Rev. Messrs. Blackburn and Pool, and all went on well for a time, till, to conciliate the Papists, the Governor thought proper to require all Christian teachers to sign a certain document, binding them not to give utterance to anything which would interfere with the dogmas of Roman Catholicism. This the Wesleyan Missionaries conscientiously refused to do, and the chapel was consequently shut up for twelve months. An appeal to the Imperial Government brought the desired relief, and when every restriction was removed, the Mission was re-organised, and a substantial chapel built in Port of Spain by the Rev. S. P. Woolley, who was appointed to re-commence the Mission, and who continued to labour there for several years with acceptance and success. On his removal to another station he was succeeded by the Rev. Messrs. Edmondson, Stephenson, Fletcher, Fidler, Wood, Beard, and others, and the work was ultimately extended

WESLEYAN CHAPEL AND MISSION PREMISES, PORT OF SPAIN, TRINIDAD IN 1841.

to Diego Martin, Carenage, Couva, Claxton's Bay, San Fernando, Woodford Dale, and other places, with much advantage to the people. The success which has been realised on this station is such as to excite to gratitude, and to encourage persevering efforts in hope of still greater good. We have now in Trinidad *three Missionaries, six hundred and sixty-eight church members*, and *one hundred and seventy-six scholars* in the Mission schools, with *a Catechist*, who devotes his labours entirely to the Coolie emigrants who have been brought to the island from the East Indies.

BARBADOES has sometimes been called "Little England," and in many places it presents to the view of the British traveller scenes which strikingly remind him of his native land. Being to the windward of all the rest, it is generally the first is land thatis seen by persons on board a vessel coming from Europe to the West Indies. It appears above the horizon like a huge turtle floating on the surface of the water. The aspect of the country is not mountainous, like most of the other islands, but gently undulating; and every available acre of land having been brought under cultivation, it has generally sustained a very large population. It is now estimated at one hundred and thirty thousand. The Wesleyan Mission to Barbadoes was commenced by the Rev. B. Pearce, whom Dr. Coke left there on his first visit in 1788, and who was greatly encouraged in his evangelical efforts by a few pious soldiers whom he found there, who had been for some time in the habit of holding religious meetings for their mutual edification. It was in the hired room of these men that the zealous Doctor preached on the evening of the day on which he arrived, and from the attention of the people the success of the Mission seemed hopeful. Mr. Pearce was succeeded by the Rev. Messrs. Kingston, Lumb, Bishop, Graham, and other devoted Missionaries; but for several years the cause was less prosperous in Barbadoes than in most of the other islands. At length, however, in 1822, under the earnest ministry of the Rev. W. J. Shrewsbury, there appeared signs of improvement. But no sooner did the work of God begin to revive, than the enemy came in like a flood. A storm of persecution burst forth, such as had seldom been witnessed in any country. It culminated in the entire demolition of the chapel and Mission-house in Bridgetown, and the banishment of the Missionary from the island. During the dark night which followed these acts of violence and enmity to the Gospel, the timid flock who had lost their shepherd were kept together by the vigilant care and zealous efforts of Mrs. A. Gill, a pious coloured female Leader, who was truly a "mother in Israel." In 1826 the Mission was re-commenced by the Rev. Moses Rayner, who erected a commodious chapel in James-street, on the site of the sanctuary destroyed by the ruthless mob. Henceforth the Mission was carried on in peace; a tide of almost unparalleled prosperity set in, and Barbadoes ultimately became one of our most important stations in the West Indies. Two spacious chapels have been erected in Bridgetown, the capital, and several others in different parts of the country, especially at Speight's Town Providence, Ebenezer, and St. George's, to which place the cause was extended at an early period. In the three Circuits into which the island is now divided, *six Missionaries* are usefully employed, and they have *two thousand six hundred and ninety-four church members* under their pastoral care, with *two thousand and twenty scholars* in the Mission schools.

TOBAGO is the last station to be noticed in connection with the St. Vincent's district. The island is thirty-three miles long and nine broad. It is situated within about fifty miles of Trinidad and the Spanish Main, and, on a clear day, the distant blue mountains of the continent can be distinctly seen from Scarborough, the capital. The soil is generally fertile, but with a population of only fourteen thousand, it is not surprising that a considerable portion of the country continues in its original wilderness state, covered with dense jungle and forest trees. Although Tobago is not one of the most important British colonies in the West Indies, it has an interesting missionary history, to which we can but briefly advert. Repeated visits of observation had been made to the island by Missionaries of our Society, when in 1817 arrangements were made for its permanent occupation as a Mission station. The Rev. J. Rayner was the first Wesleyan Missionary appointed to Tobago, but a few months after his arrival his dear wife sickened and died, and being left with a little infant he was obliged to remove to another station. Mr. Rayner was succeeded by the Rev. Messrs. Smedly, Larcum, Nelson, Stephenson, Powell, Wood, Blackwell, and others, who laboured with varied measures of success in the service of their Divine Master. But it was during the years immediately succeeding the era of the glorious emancipation that the most remarkable revival of religion was realized on this station, through the instrumentality of the Rev. Messrs. Ranyell, Bickford, and Hurd, who, in succession, had charge of the circuit at that period. In Scarborough, at Mount St. George, Mason Hall, Courland, and other places, chapels have been built, societies formed, and schools established, to the unspeakable advantage of multitudes of people who were previously in a state of extreme spiritual destitution. We have now in Tobago *two Missionaries, nine hundred and thirty-one church members*, and *five hundred and fifty-five scholars* in the Mission schools.

In connection with our Missionary work in the St. Vincent's District, many interesting incidents have occurred at different times which would require many pages to narrate; but the one most worthy of notice was a very remarkable interposition of Divine Providence which the writer himself experienced when he and a native were saved, as by a miracle, from impending destruction. It was on the 5th of August, 1846, when sailing in an open boat, with two negroes, on the placid waters of the Gulf of Paria, which separates the Island of Trinidad from the Spanish Main, that we were overtaken with a fearful thunder-storm. We were on our return from a Missionary visit to the Couva station, when the heavens gathered blackness, the lightning flashed, and the thunder roared in fearful peals, whilst the sea was lashed into tempestuous waves by the fury of the storm. When the hurricane was at its height, and the foaming billows and the lowering clouds seemed mingled in one confused mass around us, in a moment, in the twinkling of an eye, the electric fluid struck the frail bark in which we sailed, and shivered it to pieces beneath our feet. One of the men was struck dead in an instant and never moved or breathed again, whilst the other was paralysed, and we all went down together into the mighty deep. By a remarkable providence the survivors, both of whom could swim, regained the wreck of the boat when it arose to the surface of the water, to which they clung by a desperate effort, till seen and rescued by a passing sloop some time afterwards when the storm cleared away. After being out at sea another night we were mercifully restored to our homes and friends, who received us with gratitude and joy, as if we had been raised from the dead. But many tears were shed for the "one who was not," and on the following Sabbath the writer endeavoured to improve the affecting event by preaching from the words of the Psalmist, "I will sing of mercy and of judgment: unto Thee, O Lord, will I sing."

On another occasion the writer, with his wife and several brethren, suffered shipwreck in this District, when the Missionary schooner *Hadie* was dashed to pieces on the coral reef whilst sailing out of Calliaqua harbour in the Island of St. Vincent. In that instance there was much damage and loss of property, as all we had was on board; but there was no imminent danger to life, a number of boats immediately coming out to take us from the wreck. The next day we procured another vessel, and proceeded on our voyage to the District Meeting, truly thankful to the Almighty for His preserving goodness when "in perils in the sea."

DEMERARA.

The next section of the Mission field which is to pass under review may require a few brief geographical and historical observations, in order to place the matter in a clear light before the mind of the reader. DEMERARA has been described as an *island* in parliamentary speeches, and in popular histories of Methodism; but this is a mistake which should be guarded against by all who take an interest in the missionary enterprise. Demerara, Essequibo, and Berbice, are British settlements on the continent of South America, and were formerly governed as separate colonies; but since the year 1831 they have been united in one government under the general name of the Province of British Guiana. The name first mentioned, however, is still frequently employed by way of accommodation to designate this part of the British Empire, and it is generally called the Colony of Demerara. It is considered to belong to the West Indies, not only from its proximity to the islands so designated, but more especially from its identity with them in climate, population, and produce.

The entire province has a line of coast about three hundred miles long, with a width of country not well defined, but extending a considerable distance inland. The soil is uncommonly rich and fertile; but the general aspect of the country is low and swampy. Indeed, in some places the coast is below the level of the sea; and, as the tide rises to an unusual height in this part of the world, the land is only kept from inundation by the construction of extensive dykes, with sluices to let the water off when the tide is down. Travelling is rendered very difficult and unpleasant in wet weather by the muddy state of the roads; but of late years a railway has been constructed to a distance of about thirty miles along the coast, which is a great convenience.

The city of Georgetown, the capital of the province, occupies an extensive plain in latitude 6° north and longitude 58° 25' west, at the mouth of the river Demerara, from which the colony takes its name. It consists of several wide streets laid out at right angles; and the dwelling houses generally stand apart from each other in their own garden grounds, which are, in many instances, adorned with flowers and shrubs, giving quite a lively and rural aspect to the scene. Most of the buildings are framed of the hard wood of the colony, and when well finished, and neatly painted, they are both handsome and durable. Of late years, however, a few good houses have been built of brick and finished with stucco, the most substantial and elegant of which is the structure known as the "Guiana Public Buildings," which stands in the centre of Georgetown, and would be an ornament to any city in Europe.

It was not till the year 1815 that the Wesleyan Missionary

Society succeeded in establishing a Mission in Demerara; a previous attempt, in 1805, having been frustrated by the expulsion of the Missionary, the Rev. J. Hawkshaw, from the colony. Neither was it without difficulty and much opposition that the Rev. T. Talboys commenced the work, aided as he was by Messrs. Claxton and Powell, two pious men of colour who had come from Nevis several years before, and were themselves the fruit of Missionary labour in that island. Mr. Talboys was succeeded by the Rev. John Mortier, a man of quiet zeal and an amiable disposition, who continued to labour in the colony for many years with acceptance and success. On the 1st and 2nd of November, 1821, both the Missionaries then labouring in the colony, the Rev. Messrs. Bellamy and Ames, were cut down by fever in a few hours, and the station was left without a minister, when the Rev. W. J. Shrewsbury hastened down from Barbadoes, with his wonted promptitude, to fill the vacancy till a supply of men could be sent from England. In process of time opposition began to decline, the Missionaries were favoured to labour with tolerable health and comfort, and the zealous efforts of the Rev. Messrs. Mortier, Cheeswright, Edmondson, Rayner, Vigis, Hornabrook, Ranyell, and others, in succession, were crowned with a cheering measure of success. Two excellent chapels were erected in Georgetown—one at Werken-Rust and the other at Kingston; and hundreds of sinners were savingly converted to God, and gathered into the fold of Christ. A still more remarkable revival of religion was experienced in Georgetown, in 1868, when upwards of one thousand new members were received into church fellowship in the short space of six months. For numbers, respectability, intelligence, and general efficiency, our Mission in Georgetown would compare favourably with that of any other country, and it has been made a great blessing to all classes of the community.

When the work was fully established in the city, the Missionaries extended their labours to Mahaica, an ancient village on the west coast, about twenty-five miles from Georgetown, on the banks of a navigable creek, and central to a large number of populous sugar estates. Here a resident minister was ultimately stationed, a commodious chapel erected, and a large number of people united in church fellowship. From this important and central point the work was extended still further down the coast to Mahaicony, Perth, Virginia, Stanleyville, and other places in the Mahaica circuit, where religious instruction was much required. At a subsequent period, a Missionary was appointed to Victoria and Golden Grove, new villages which were formed soon after the era of the emancipation, about mid-way between Georgetown and Mahaica. These places, together with Friendship, Buxton, and Ann's Grove, form an interesting circuit, where a good work has been carried on for several years, among the emancipated slaves who settled there.

Essequibo is the name given to a circuit formerly known as Abrim Zuil, on what is called the Arabian coast, to the west of the Essequibo river. This Mission was commenced by the Rev. R. Hornabrook in the year 1836, and has exerted a very beneficial influence in that part of the country. Out-stations were ultimately established at Zorg, Queen's Town, Ebenezer, Anna Regina, Daniel's Town, and more recently in the island of Wakenaam. At some of those places chapels have been built, societies formed, and schools established; and at others strenuous efforts are being made to supply what is wanted to give permanence to the work. In the wide field which presents itself to view in this part of the colony, there is reason to hope for still greater progress in years to come.

Berbice is comparatively a new station, having only had the advantage of a resident minister for a few years. Our services were imperatively called for in that place, so remote from our other stations in British Guiana, by the circumstance of a considerable number of our people having removed thither from the Leeward Islands, to say nothing of the dense population in general which required additional means of religious instruction. Several respectable persons of Dutch descent having no pastor of their own were, moreover, anxious to have a Wesleyan ministry, and generously offered the free use of the Dutch Reformed Church and parsonage, with substantial pecuniary aid besides, for the support of the work. Under these circumstances the Mission was commenced in 1847, and more fully organised in 1853; the Rev. John Wood, jun. being the first Missionary appointed to the station. He was succeeded by the Rev. Messrs. Padgham, Banfield, and Dickson, whose labours were made a great blessing to the people. Out-stations have been formed at Smith Town, Stanley Town, and Cumberland, and a good work is in progress throughout the circuit.

In addition to the spheres of labour already described, and the various kinds of instrumentality alluded to, a new department of Missionary labour has recently been entered upon in this district, which deserves a passing notice. To supply the lack of agricultural labourers occasioned by the emancipation of the negro slaves in 1838, many of whom became mechanics and shopmen, a large number of Coolies have been brought over from the East Indies, from time to time, and for their special benefit a Mission has been formed. The Rev. H. V. P. Bronkhurst, Assistant Missionary, is at present the agent employed among them. Being himself a native of India, he is able to preach to these poor Hindus the Gospel of Christ in their own language; and he has already been the honoured instrument in the hands of God in bringing several of them into the fold of Christ. A school has also been established for the instruction of Coolie children, and it is hoped that in future a rich harvest will be reaped from this interesting department of Christian labour.

A very gratifying measure of success has attended the labours of the Wesleyan Missionary Society on the respective stations in British Guiana. We have now in connection with the Demerara District *twelve Missionaries, four thousand two hundred and sixty-seven church members,* and *three thousand eight hundred and fifteen scholars* in the Mission schools. It is pleasing to be able to add that for many years past the principal stations have been entirely self-supporting, and the people have contributed liberally towards the funds of the parent society to help to send the Gospel to other lands.

JAMAICA.

The largest and most important island in the West Indies belonging to the British crown is JAMAICA. It is said to be one hundred and fifty miles long and fifty broad. The general aspect of the country is rugged and mountainous, but it abounds with fertile valleys, and almost every part of it is covered with perpetual verdure. It is, moreover, watered with numerous streams, which flow towards the ocean in every direction, which circumstance seems to justify the name given to it by the aborigines, which signifies in their language, "the Land of Springs." The island was discovered by Columbus in the course of his third voyage to the new world, in 1494; but it was not settled by the Spaniards till 1503, soon after which they commenced their cruel work of exterminating the native Indians. In the wars of 1655, the colony was taken by the English, since which time it has continued to be a part of the British empire. For civil and ecclesiastical purposes the island was divided into three counties, Middlesex, Surrey, and Cornwall; these were again divided into parishes. A church was ultimately erected in every parish; but we are informed on good authority that when there was a priest for every parish, which was not always the case, the church was seldom opened, except on occasions of marriages and funerals. Sunday was the day devoted to the public market and parties of pleasure. It is doubted whether, previous to 1789, the Sabbath ever dawned on Jamaica which witnessed five hundred persons assembled in all the places of worship put together, out of a population of nearly four hundred thousand. The idea of imparting religious instruction to the negro slaves scarcely seems to have entered into the mind of any one; and, with few exceptions, all classes were sunk to the deepest depth of moral degradation. The Sabbath being the principal market day, the negroes assembled in the towns and villages, for the purposes of petty trade and worldly amusements rather than to worship God.

When the zealous and devoted Dr. Coke had succeeded in establishing Methodist Missions in several of the smaller islands of the West Indies, he hastened to Jamaica on a tour of observation to see what could be done for a place and a people such as we have described.

He landed at Kingston on the 19th of January, 1789, and preached four times in the city during his brief stay, though not without some opposition and disturbance at two or three of the services which he held. The noise and interruption proceeded not from the poor negroes, however, but from a few intoxicated white men, who boasted of their respectability, but who were not ashamed to mock the man of God whilst faithfully warning sinners to flee from the wrath to come. These trifles the noble-minded Doctor regarded not; but proceeded with his work, rejoicing that the common people heard him gladly, and that the way was being opened for the introduction of the Gospel where it was very much required. Indeed, with few exceptions, all classes of the community showed him the greatest possible respect. "In no place," he writes, "did I ever receive greater civilities; four or five families of property having opened to me their houses and evidently their hearts also, and assured me that any missionaries we may send shall be welcome to everything their houses afford." Having delivered his message and made his observations, the pioneer evangelist embarked at Port Royal for America on the 24th of February, and proceeded, with his wonted alacrity and zeal, to visit other fields of hallowed labour.

The impression made upon the Doctor's mind by this hasty visit appears to have been on the whole, favourable; for immediately on his return to England he sent out the Rev. William Hammett, as the first missionary to Jamaica. He arrived in the month of August, and his first efforts to evangelise the people being successful, he was encouraged to purchase and fit up as a place of worship, an old building that was offered to him for the purpose. In the beginning of the year 1791, the Rev. William Brazier was sent to assist Mr. Hammett; and shortly afterwards Dr. Coke arrived on his second visit to the island, in company with the Rev. T. Worrell, another Missionary. After remaining for a few days at Montego Bay, where they landed, and where the Doctor preached several times, they rode over the mountains to Kingston, a distance of one hundred and twenty miles, and had a fine opportunity of seeing the country, with which they were much pleased. Having inspected the state of the work, and preached several times in the city, Dr. Coke embarked for America, taking with him Mr. Hammett, to recruit his impaired health in a colder climate. In the month of August Mr. Brazier followed them, having also suffered from the excessive heat. The only remaining Missionary, Mr. Worrell, over exerted himself, was seized with a fever, which baffled medical skill, and died happy in God on the 15th of November. Thus early fell the first of a long list of Missionaries, who were called to rest from their labours in Jamaica, and the Society was left without a pastor.

The intelligence of this sad bereavement no sooner reached England than help was sent, and about five months afterwards, in the month of May, 1792, the hearts of the people were gladdened by the arrival of the Rev. William Fish, who soon succeeded in reorganising the Mission. About the end of the year, Dr. Coke paid his third and last visit to Jamaica; and after spending a few days, during which he was "in labours more abundant," preaching, travelling, and endeavouring to strengthen the hands of the Missionary, he embarked for England, and Mr. Fish was left to pursue his useful labours alone. In after years the Jamaica Mission was strengthened by the appointment of the Rev. Messrs. Alexander, Fowler, Bradnack, Wiggins, Johnston, Shipman, Duncan, and a host of other brave and zealous ministers of Christ, who successively laboured and patiently suffered in the cause of their Divine Master. A cheering measure of success attended the Word preached from the very first, and a goodly number of the sable sons and daughters of Ham were brought to a saving knowledge of the truth.

But we generally find that when God works Satan also makes himself busy. In tracing the history of the Wesleyan Mission in

Jamaica, in the earlier stages of its progress, we find it marked by scenes of persecution such as scarcely have a parallel in any other country. Many of the planters, and the whites generally, were living in a fearful state of immorality and sin, and they no sooner saw that the successful labours of the Missionaries would probably interfere with the gratification of their unbridled passions, than they vented all their wrath against them. And then there was the vexed question of negro slavery, with which they feared the free promulgation of the Gospel might interfere. These circumstances, in connection with the innate depravity of the human heart and its natural opposition to the truth of God, gave rise to a systematic course of hostility to Missions in Jamaica, which continued for several years, in various forms and with different degrees of violence, which it would be tedious and unprofitable to attempt to detail. Sometimes laws were passed by the local legislature, prohibiting the preaching of the Missionaries without a license, which the magistrate might decline to give at pleasure. Then for the alleged violation of the law the Missionaries were cast into prison, where they suffered indescribable miseries. Again, they were assailed by ruthless mobs, and insulted in the most shameful manner. Some of the chapels were closed for years together, and others were entirely demolished by the enemies of the Gospel. The faith, and patience, and Christian courage of the Missionaries was often severely tested during these days of darkness; but the Lord Jehovah was the support and strength of His servants. In due time the dark cloud passed over, persecuting acts were disallowed by the Imperial Government, enemies to the Mission were removed out of the way by the hand of God, and religious liberty was restored to the land.

Through all those years of labour and of conflict the cause of God continued to advance in Jamaica, and when every hindrance was removed out of the way of its progress, the Word of the Lord had free course, ran, and was glorified. It is truly delightful to contemplate the success which has attended this important Mission. The good work has spread from Kingston, where it was first commenced, to Spanish Town, Morant Bay, Grateful Hill, Falmouth,

St. Ann's Bay, Bath, Clarendon, Manchioneal, and other places, far away into the interior of the island. The whole country has been divided into Circuits and Stations, and in every town and village of any consequence, and in many of the rural districts, commodious chapels have been built, Societies formed, and schools established. At different periods gracious revivals of religion have, moreover, been experienced, when multitudes of sinners have been converted, and gathered into the fold of the Redeemer.

WESLEYAN MISSION HOUSE, ST. ANN'S, JAMAICA.

The improvement in the social and moral condition of the people is also truly gratifying, and a change has passed over the whole aspect of the population which it is most pleasing to contemplate. Notwithstanding the adverse circumstances with which the Jamaica Mission has had to contend in common with the work in several of the other West India colonies, it is a delightful fact that we have now in connection with our respective Stations in this island, *twenty-six Missionaries, fourteen thousand two hundred and four church members*, and *six thousand six hundred and sixty-two scholars* in the Mission schools.

HONDURAS.

HONDURAS is a British settlement on the southern part of the continent of North America, in the province of Yucatan, which, from its climate, character, and position, is generally classed with the West Indies. The town of Belize, the capital of the colony, is situated in latitude 17° 25′ north and longitude 88° 30′ west; and the territory claimed as belonging to the settlement embraces an area of about 62,750 square miles. The sea-coast is generally flat and swampy, and the water along the shore is studded with numerous low and verdant islands. On advancing some distance into the interior, the country rises into lofty mountains, covered with dense forests, interspersed with rivers and lagoons, by means of which access is gained to the valuable timber, especially logwood and mahogany, of which the principal trade of the settlement consists. The population comprises a strange mixture of Europeans, Spanish Creoles, Negroes, and Indians; and all classes were in a fearfully degraded state before Christian Missionaries were sent among them.

The Wesleyan Mission to Honduras was commenced in 1825. The Rev. Thomas Wilkinson was the first Missionary sent out, and he entered upon his work in the town of Belize, and among the scattered settlements of the wood-cutters on the banks of the rivers, in the true missionary spirit; but in the course of a few months after his arrival he fell a sacrifice to the climate, which is generally admitted to be more trying to the European constitution than most of the West India islands. The next Missionary to Honduras was the Rev. Thomas Johnston, who was also called to rest from his labours before the close of the first year of his appointment. Other zealous Missionaries followed, who, by the good providence of God, were spared to labour for a longer period, and from whose unwearied efforts the foundation of a good work was laid which has continued to advance with steadiness, if not with rapidity, to the present time. All classes of the community have been benefitted by the establishment, and seem grateful for the opportunities which are afforded them of Divine worship and religious instruction.

A substantial Wesleyan chapel was erected at Belize at an early period of the Mission, which a few years ago was destroyed by fire; but it has since been replaced by a more commodious and elegant structure. Here the congregation is large and respectable, and in 1868 a gracious revival of religion took place, in the course of which many were added to the Lord. Of late years the good work has been extended to Freetown, Ruatan, Corosal, and other places, which have now become important stations. To supply as far as possible the spiritual necessities of all classes of this mixed population, preaching and teaching are carried on in English, Spanish, and Maya. Into the language last named, which is used by a considerable tribe of Indians, portions of the Holy Scriptures and other books have been translated, and it is hoped that access will thus be obtained to native populations which have not yet been brought under the influence of the Gospel.

In the year 1829 a Mission was attempted to the wandering Indians inhabiting the Mosquito Shore, in Honduras Bay. The Rev. James Pilley was the Missionary appointed to this new and arduous station. He persevered in his zealous efforts for some time; but the difficulties were so numerous, and the prospect so discouraging, that the undertaking was ultimately relinquished, other openings of a more promising character requiring the attention of the Society. The Honduras Mission was formerly attached to Jamaica, but a few years ago it was organised into a separate District, and it has become an important and interesting portion of the Mission field, having *four Missionaries, nine hundred and twenty-four church members,* and *nine hundred and twenty-nine scholars* in the Mission schools.

The Bahamas.

The Bahamas are a singular group of islands extending in the form of a crescent, a distance of about six hundred miles from the Matanilla reef to Turk's Island. New Providence is the most important island of the group, and the seat of government for the whole; but it is the one named San Salvador, that is celebrated as the land first seen by Columbus, on the 12th of October, 1492, when on his first voyage of discovery to the New World. The Bahamas were then densely peopled by a race of Indians, who were soon shipped off to work the mines of Mexico and Peru,

SAN SALVADOR.

when the Spaniards began their search for gold. In 1629 New Providence was settled by the English, the natives having become entirely extinct. About twelve years afterwards the Spaniards drove the English settlers from the island, and murdered the Governor, besides committing many other acts of cruelty. In 1666 the English made another attempt to colonise the Bahamas;

but the French and Spaniards again expelled them and destroyed their plantations. After many other changes, and the fearful depredations of pirates, the Bahama Islands were finally ceded to the British by treaty in 1783, since which period they have remained in our possession.

From the favourable character of the climate and other circumstances, a larger portion of the inhabitants are whites in these islands than in any other of the West India colonies. But, according to undoubted testimony, all classes were in an awful state of spiritual destitution at the beginning of the present century, when they first attracted the notice of the friends of Missions. The Rev. William Turton, himself a native of the West Indies, and the fruit of Missionary labour, had the honour of being the first Wesleyan Missionary appointed to New Providence in the year 1803. He afterwards extended his labours to other islands as openings presented themselves, being assisted in his important enterprise by the Rev. Messrs. Rutledge, Dowson, Ward, Moor, and others, who were sent out from England at different periods. By the blessing of God upon the persevering efforts of His servants, a great and good work was inaugurated throughout the district. The people listened to the Word preached with gratitude and joy, and it became the means of salvation to many in almost every inhabited island of the group. The work was extended to Eleuthera, Harbour Island, Abaco, Turks' Island, and other places, each of which became the head of a Circuit and a centre of light and influence to all around. In every island, settlement, town, and village of any consequence chapels were built, societies organised, and schools established; and a wonderful reformation was effected among all classes of the inhabitants.

The respective stations in the Bahamas were ultimately formed into a regular Wesleyan District, of which Mr. Turton was the honoured chairman for many years, till he was called to his reward in 1818. The Rev. Messrs. Crofts, Haigh, Whitehouse, Corlett, Cheesbrough, Bleby, and others, were in succession charged with the general superintendency of the work, and a pleasing measure of success has been realised. From the scattered character and isolated position of many of the inhabitants, not to mention their general poverty, Methodism has proved to be a system admirably adapted to meet the spiritual wants of the Bahamas, and the establishment of Wesleyan Missions among them has been attended with the most blessed results. When a fearful hurricane swept over the islands in 1867, destroying the dwellings of the people and laying waste their sanctuaries, the friends of Missions in England came forward most liberally to their aid, and the waste places of Zion were soon repaired, and the hearts of the humble worshippers filled with gratitude and joy. We have now in connection with the Wesleyan Missions in the Bahama District *eight Missionaries, three thousand eight hundred and seventy-two church members*, and *two thousand six hundred and twenty-seven scholars* in the Mission schools.

HAYTI.

HAYTI is the name now generally given to that portion of the island of St. Domingo or Hispaniola which is occupied by a republic of black and coloured people, who cast off the yoke of slavery and of the French Government together, and declared their independence in 1803. The soil, climate, produce, and general aspect of the country are similar in their main features to other parts of the West Indies; we may, therefore, confine our remarks chiefly to the inhabitants and the means which have been adopted to promote their moral elevation. This little native commonwealth, exhibiting as it does the capability of the negro race, possesses many points of interest to the genuine philanthropist; but we are most concerned in the origin and progress of Christian Missions.

In the year 1817, the Wesleyan Missionary Society sent out two Missionaries, the Revs. John Brown and James Catts, to commence a Mission in Hayti. They were kindly received, both by the Government authorities and the people; and for some time they laboured with acceptance and success. After awhile, however, when their efforts to evangelise the inhabitants were beginning to produce a powerful impression, a spirit of persecution was excited by the Romish priests, which resulted in the passing of laws entirely subversive of religious liberty; and the following year the Missionaries were obliged to leave the country. But although left as sheep without a shepherd, the converted natives would not return to the thraldom of Popery. They were insulted and oppressed in every possible manner; but they endured persecution with a patience and steadfastness worthy of the best days of the Christian Church. As they had opportunity they continued to meet together for prayer and praise; and they kept up a constant correspondence with their banished Pastors, informing them of their proceedings, and of the course of public events, indulging the hope that brighter days would dawn upon them.

At length the way seemed to open for an effort to re-establish the Mission; and in 1835 the Rev. John Tindall was appointed to Hayti, in conjunction with Mr. St. Denis Bauduy, a converted native, who had been, up to this time, instrumental in keeping the people together, and who was now called to the honourable office of assistant Missionary. There being now no longer any violent opposition to Methodism, the work was prosecuted for a time with cheering prospects of success. In the course of the following year the Rev. James Sharracks was sent out to strengthen the hands of the brethren; but he was soon called away by death. Other zealous Missionaries were appointed from time to time, and their united labours resulted in the conversion of many souls to God, notwithstanding the antagonistic influence constantly exercised by the Romish priests and their adherents. As the work grew and expanded, various parts of the country were visited by the Missionaries, and their assistants; and promising stations were ultimately established in Jérémie, Cayes, Cape Haitien, Levgane, and other towns and villages of the republic, in addition to Port-au-Prince, the capital.

For many years the Rev. Mark B. Bird has been the honoured superintendent of this difficult Mission, and in prosperity and adversity he has clung to his post of duty, with a courage and moral heroism worthy of the highest commendation. In consequence of the instability of the Government, the intolerance of

Popery, and the trying character of the climate, there have often been stations without Missionaries, and the work has been generally prosecuted amid numerous difficulties, and with frequent fluctuations. In the month of November, 1869, one half of the city of Port-au-Prince was burnt down, during the prevalence of a civil war. This calamity involved the entire destruction of the Wes-

WESLEYAN CHAPEL, PORT-AU-PRINCE, HAYTI.
(*Destroyed by fire in 1869.*)

leyan Mission premises, consisting of a substantial chapel, school-house, and minister's residence, which had been erected at an expense of about £4,000. With commendable zeal and diligence the afflicted members of the church procured a quantity of boards with which they constructed a temporary place of worship; but the progress of the Mission has been seriously retarded.

Although Hayti was formed into a separate District several years ago, it has, through the adverse circumstances to which we have alluded, once more been reduced to a single station, and we have now in connection with it only *one Missionary, two hundred and ten church members,* and *seventy-two scholars* in the Mission school.

Although we would not attach undue importance to mere statistics, knowing that they cannot always be regarded as a sure index of the state and prospects of the work of God; yet, taking them for what they are worth, it is pleasing to contemplate, by their light and aid, the progress which has been made in our Mission work in this important part of the great field up to the present time. There are now in connection with the respective Wesleyan circuits and districts in the West Indies *eighty-five Missionaries, forty-one thousand six hundred church members,* and *twenty thousand scholars* in the Mission schools. But these numbers represent only a small portion of the good which has been done by the agency of the Wesleyan Missionary Society in the sunny isles of the west. An influence has been exercised, and spiritual results have been achieved, which can never be tabulated on earth, and which will only be fully known in heaven. Happy are those who take any part, be it ever so humble, in labouring to diffuse a knowledge of salvation among the dark benighted nations of the earth. "They that be wise shall shine as the brightness of the firmament; and they that turn many to righteousness as stars for ever and ever."

In bringing to a close this brief historical sketch of the origin and progress of Wesleyan Missions in the West Indies, perhaps the reader may be interested by a few observations in reference to the impression produced on the writer's own mind as to the character and claims of the work during the period of his personal labours in that country. We look back with feelings of gratitude and joy to the happy years we spent in the West Indies, from 1834 to 1847 inclusive, when the poor negroes were just emerging from their long night of slavery, passing through their transition state of apprenticeship, and entering upon the enjoyment of full and unrestricted freedom. Our appointments were to Demerara,

Barbadoes, St. Vincent's, Grenada, and Trinidad in succession, and on almost every station, being associated with earnest, zealous, loving colleagues, we were permitted to realise a pleasing measure of success. Indeed, in some instances we were favoured with showers of blessing, and large ingatherings of precious souls into the fold of Christ, to say nothing of the gradual improvement of the people in knowledge, civilisation, and social position, which invariably accompanies the reception of the Gospel. At the period to which we refer, much of the attention of the Missionaries had to be given to the building of chapels, the establishment of schools, the organisation of friendly societies, and other comparatively secular works, in addition to the faithful preaching of the Gospel, to prepare for the approaching emancipation. These exercises involved much care and anxiety, as well as physical and mental toil; but we had an immediate and rich reward in seeing the blessed results of our labours, and in witnessing manifold proofs of the affection and gratitude of a loving people.

The most important event which occurred during the period of our personal labours in the West Indies, was the glorious emancipation of the negro slaves. We had long waited, and laboured, and prayed, in anticipation of the happy day; but when it came it seemed to take us by surprise, and a mental effort appeared necessary to realise the fact that it was even so. The conduct of the people themselves on the occasion, especially those who made a profession of religion, was everything that we could desire. They received the boon of freedom as from heaven. The last night of their bondage found most of them assembled in their respective places of worship on their bended knees before God, holding a solemn watchnight service. And when the clock struck twelve, which was the death knell of slavery, they rose to their feet, and with joyful hearts sung, "Praise God from whom all blessings flow." Then might be seen husbands and wives, parents and children, and friends and relatives, fondly embracing each other, and with overflowing hearts and eyes rejoicing that they had lived to see the day of freedom come. It was with strange emotions that they repaired to their homes, and in the domestic circle tried to realise the fact that they themselves and their children were their own.

The beneficial effects of this great and glorious change in the civil condition of the people was at once apparent in their proceedings and circumstances. Being no longer under the control of others, they could go to the house of God on the Sabbath, and at other times without restraint; and there was, consequently, a large increase in the attendance on public worship. New chapels had now to be erected and old ones enlarged on almost every station; and it was with difficulty that accommodation could be provided for the crowds who flocked to the sanctuary. A gracious influence, moreover, attended the preaching of the Word, and every week, if not every day, witnessed numerous accessions to the Church of Christ, and in one circuit where we laboured one thousand new members were received into church fellowship in the course of twelve months.

In view of this rapid extension of the work we are aware that the real friends of Missions have been somewhat dubious as to the genuine piety and religious steadfastness of our West India converts. But even in this respect we should guard against coming to a too hasty conclusion. So far as we have had experience true religion is the same all the world over. The Gospel of our Lord Jesus Christ is the same now as it was in the days of the Apostles: it is "the power of God unto salvation to every one that believeth." When the heart is brought under the renewing influence of Divine grace, the daily walk and conversation will be upright and consistent. With regard to steadiness and perseverance in the way to heaven, much will depend upon natural temperament, previous habits, and the position and circumstances in which professors of religion are placed. Our people in the West Indies are naturally impulsive, lively, and animated. They do everything with hearty earnestness, and from the impulse of the moment, rather than from calm deliberation. Hence it is not surprising, when we consider their want of education in former times, and the peculiar temptations to which our converts were often exposed, that we should have been occasionally tried by instances of religious instability. Our native churches were, moreover, sometimes very large, and it was extremely difficult fully to meet the demands for pastoral oversight. We had charge of one circuit with nearly four thousand members, and, although associated with three excellent colleagues, we found it no easy task to overtake the pressing claims of our work in all its departments. But making due allowance for these things, we are deliberately of opinion that, for consistent piety and zeal in the cause of Christ, the members of our churches in the West Indies will compare favourably with those of any other country. And we are quite sure that in some other respects they excel and might be imitated with advantage by their fair sisters and brethren in other lands.

Our people in the West Indies are remarkable for their affection and respect for their ministers; and they regard no sacrifice too great to make to promote their comfort, whilst at the same time they cheerfully submit to church discipline when wisely exercised. They, moreover, manifest an ardent love for God's house, the services of which they attend with a punctuality and decorum of manner worthy of the highest commendation. In the higher departments of religious experience and Christian benevolence, we have met with instances of devotedness to God, fervour in prayer, zeal in the cause of Christ, and spontaneous liberality, which have excited our admiration and made us wish that professing Christians in other lands would " go and do likewise." Whilst listening to the simple and touching testimonies of the people to the regenerating, sanctifying, and sustaining power of Divine grace, as given in our class-meetings and lovefeasts, we have often thought that if the friends of Missions at home could see and hear for themselves, they would be delighted beyond measure, and in time to come be more than ever earnest in their efforts to send the Gospel of Christ to the perishing heathen in every part of the world. We have also seen the religion of our people in the West Indies tested in seasons of persecution, trial, affliction, and in the hour of death; and we have been led to praise the Lord with a heart overflowing with gratitude for the blessed results of the Missionary enterprise among the sable sons and daughters of Ham in the lands of their exile.

It has been insinuated, and even asserted, that, however emotional and sensitive to religious impressions the black and coloured population on our Mission stations may be, the negro race are, mentally, much inferior to every other nation of men; and that, in fact, they lack those endowments of mind which belong to rational intelligent creatures, being only animals a little above the baboon or gorilla. These sceptical notions, which it was hoped had passed away with a bygone age, have recently been revived by speakers and writers belonging to an association called the "Anthropological Society." In view of our own experience, as stated above, we have never considered such slanderous insinuations deserving of serious notice, insomuch as the characters of the men from whom they emanated seemed to render them perfectly harmless.

Perhaps the best refutation of the attacks which have been made upon the negro race by the enemies of freedom, was given by a black man himself, who asked permission to speak at one of their own meetings. A gentleman had been expatiating, very learnedly as he thought, on the manifest improbability of the negro belonging to the human family, from the fact of his curly hair, the thickness of his skull, and his shuffling gait, when an intelligent negro youth, who had come to England to study at one of our colleges, stood up, and, with the permission of the chairman, spoke substantially as follows: "The gentleman who has just addressed the meeting thinks that I and my brethren of the negro race are not men because we have curly hair, our craniums are thick, and we have a shuffling gait when we walk. I have lately been down in Dorsetshire, where I observed the farm labourers have a shuffling gait; and I thought that my countrymen, who generally walk much better, might be tempted to laugh at them for their awkwardness, if they saw them; but I do not think they would doubt their humanity on that account. And as to our curly hair, I think that need be no disparagement to us, as I have known persons of fairer complexions try to make theirs curl without success. With regard to the thickness of our skulls, I may observe that I suppose that our Almighty and all-wise Creator knew what He was doing when He made us so. Our home is in a very hot and sultry climate, where the fiery rays of the sun have great power, and where the inner region of the cranium no doubt requires such a defence. If, by any mistake in our conformation, we had been made with skulls as thin as the learned gentleman who last spoke, our brains, under the influence of the heat, would perhaps become as thin and addled as his appears to be, judging from the foolish and unphilosophical statement which he has made; and then it might have been reasonably doubted whether we were men worth listening to." The young negro resumed his seat, amid thundering applause; and, for once at least, it appeared to be the general opinion that the black was as clever as the white man.

We may further observe on this subject that the negro children in our Mission schools display remarkable aptitude for learning; and we have known a degree of efficiency attained by them, under favourable circumstances, which we have never seen surpassed in any country. We remember an instance in which Lord Harris, the Governor of Trinidad, expressed his admiration and surprise at the advanced state of our Mission school in Port of Spain, when he honoured us with a visit; the specimens of writing, and the exercises in arithmetic, grammar, geography and history were very creditable; and all the pupils were black or coloured children. Whilst the people generally, in every position in life, display an average share of good, sound, common sense, we occasionally meet with remarkable instances of native genius and mental superiority. In the West Indies we can point to Christian ministers, physicians, lawyers, magistrates, legislators, philosophers, mechanics, of African descent, who perform their respective duties with as much efficiency and dignity as persons of any other race, although some of them have had but slender means of raising themselves to their present honourable position.

Nor are there wanting among the lower classes instances of wit and humour which are frequently very amusing. On one occasion a Missionary's wife, who had just arrived from England, was talking with our negro servant girl, and wishing to tease her, said of something which she held in her hand, "O, it will do very well! it is only for black people." Matty looked up, and said to the white lady, " No, ma'am, anything will not do for black people, because black and white are all the same." " How do you know that black and white are all the same?" asked the Missionary's wife. " Because," answered the negro girl, " I read in my Testament that ' God hath made of one blood all nations of men to dwell on all the face of the earth.' " " Thn," remarked Mrs. D——, " do you think the blood of white people and the blood of black people is the same?" " Yes," responded Matty, " the blood is the same; it is only the skin that is different." Holding out a penknife, which she happened to have in her hand, Mrs. D—— said, playfully, " Do you really think so? Let us each cut a finger and see!" " Yes, ma'am," archly replied Matty, " if you will cut yours first!" This was a climax which the stranger hardly expected; and, highly amused at such a display of negro wit, she came running to relate to us the little incident.

After many years of varied experience and extensive observation, we are disposed to look with favour on the natural abilities and general character of the people of the West Indies as a whole. We are aware that the enemies of freedom, and of the negro race, have sometimes pronounced the experiment of emancipation to be a failure; but this only displays an amount of ignorance at which we may well afford to smile. Let anyone who was personally cognisant of the degradation, the wretchedness, and the miseries of slavery, inspect the villages, dwellings, dress, and entire social condition of the rural population of the West Indies at the present time, and especially let them worship with the natives in some of their beautiful chapels, and mark their appearance and demeanour in the house of God, and they will be convinced that emancipation is not a failure, but a grand success, and an unspeakable blessing.

Many reasons might be assigned for the depression of the commercial and religious interest of the West Indies, over which we have had to mourn for some time past, without reflecting upon emancipation. Some of these reasons, if fairly examined, would point in a direction the very opposite; but we forbear. Planters and merchants, and legislators are learning wisdom; and the labouring classes in the " sunny isles of the west" have brighter prospects, both temporal and spiritual, than they have had in former years. Already the clouds are dispersing, and the light of prosperity is beginning to shine forth. The deeply-rooted prejudices of a bygone age are rapidly passing away. Man is no longer regarded with reference to his complexion; but according to his moral worth and intellectual endowments. Many of the sable sons of Ham have been elevated to positions of respectability and honour, by their persevering efforts, combined with the benign influence of Christian missions; and the population of the West Indies generally is rapidly improving, notwithstanding the numerous difficulties which in times past have tended to impede its progress. In the present state and future prospects of the work in this interesting part of the mission field we see cause for gratitude and joy. Agricultural and commercial affairs look more hopeful; and showers of blessing are descending on the heritage of the Lord. Let the friends of religion, of freedom, and of the negro race, liberally and zealously sustain this department of the Missionary enterprise a little longer, and they will secure for the West Indies, a bright, a happy, and a prosperous future.

CHAPTER IV.

WESTERN AFRICA.

CHARACTER OF THE COUNTRY—HABITS OF THE PEOPLE—SIERRA LEONE
—THE GAMBIA—THE GOLD COAST.

THAT part of the Mission field which is next to pass under review is possessed of more than ordinary interest to the Christian philanthropist and the friends of freedom, as the original home of countless multitudes of people who have, from time to time, been dragged into hopeless slavery in distant lands. With a view to a clear understanding of the nature and results of the efforts made at different periods to counteract the evils which have so long oppressed the negro race, and to elevate them in the scale of being, we may first call attention to the position and character of the country in which the people live, and the circumstances in which they were found when they first attracted the notice of Europeans.

The term Western Africa is generally applied to that part of the vast continent which lies between the Great Desert on the north, the Equator on the south, the Atlantic on the west, and the river Niger on the east; embracing the regions of the Senegal, Gambia, Sierra Leone, Liberia, Guinea, and the island of Fernando Po. When we consider the great extent of this portion of the globe, embracing, as it does, not less than a million square miles, we are not surprised to find that the topographical aspect and general appearance of different localities vary considerably. In some places we meet with arid, sandy deserts, where not a blade of grass, or a drop of water is to be found for scores of miles, and where caravans of merchants and their slaves suffer much from various causes, but chiefly from thirst. Again we meet with extensive tracts of fertile land, teeming with vegetation, and abounding with extensive forests of valuable timber. These more favourable districts are generally situated on the banks of the numerous rivers and tributary creeks, with which the country abounds. They sometimes present the appearance of verdant grassy plains, having a gently undulating surface, reminding one of an English park or meadow, with here and there a beautiful hill or rocky towering mountain of considerable altitude. With the exception of Cape Verd, however, the neighbourhood of Sierra Leone, the Cameroons, and a few other localities, the land on the coast is generally level. It is not till we proceed a considerable distance into the interior that we meet with elevations worthy of the name of mountains. The districts bordering on the rivers, creeks, and lagoons are, moreover, frequently low and swampy, and covered with a dense jungle of mangroves which strike their numerous roots into the muddy soil and derive nourishment from the rising and falling tidal waves. The respective settlements in those places are consequently unhealthy for all classes of people, but especially for Europeans. Formerly the chief productions of the country were slaves, gold, ivory, and beeswax; but since the suppression of the slave trade, palm oil has become the most important and valuable item of export.

The idea has been entertained by some that the extreme unhealthiness of the climate of Western Africa is owing mainly to the excessive heat that generally prevails. This is a misapprehension, however, and the matter requires a little explanation. The air is certainly very hot, especially at that season of the year when the land breeze prevails, and the *harmattan* winds blow across the extensive sandy deserts in the interior; but it is not to this circumstance that we attribute its unhealthiness. It may rather be ascribed to the impure state of the atmosphere occasioned by the exhalations from the numerous swamps which everywhere abound in the lowlands, especially in the vicinity of the rivers and creeks. For nine months in the year we have no rain; but during the remaining three months it pours down. Then the rivers overflow their banks, the surrounding country becomes inundated; and, when the rains are over, large bodies of water remain in the swampy regions, to stagnate beneath the fiery rays of a

THE MANGROVE TREE.

tropical sun. These being in many places impregnated with large masses of animal and vegetable matter in a state of putrefaction, the fatal marsh miasma is generated; and, being borne across the country on the wings of the wind, it carries with it the seeds of a peculiar type of fever which is always attended with danger, and frequently with death. As the land becomes more generally cleared and cultivated in the neighbourhood of the European settlements and Mission stations, it is hoped that the climate will become more healthy. Indeed, it is pleasing to observe that of late years some improvement has taken place in this respect.

But, however interesting the physical aspect and general character of the country may appear, in a Missionary point of view, the habits and condition of the people are still more so. To these we now invite the attention of the reader. The coast districts of Western Africa are inhabited by numerous tribes of natives, speaking different languages or dialects; but they all belong to the negro race. Those which are best known to Europeans are the Mandingoes, Jolloffs, Foolas, Moors, Fellatas, Yarribans, Ashantis, Fantis, and Dahomans. Whilst these, with several minor tribes which might be mentioned, have their own peculiarities, they possess many features of character in common with each other, a few remarks upon which may serve to give a sufficiently correct idea of the whole negro race in their own country.

The negroes of Western Africa, especially those who have never been subject to slavery, are generally tall and athletic in person, with woolly hair, and of complexion varying somewhat from a shining jet black to a dark bronze colour. Their clothing is next to nothing while young and when engaged in the ordinary avocations of life; but on state occasions the men dress in long robes, wide trousers, turbans, and sandals; and the women envelope themselves in oblong cloths of native manufacture called *pangs*, with a head-dress of handkerchiefs, so folded as to assume the shape of a sugar-loaf. They are all fond of ornaments, and wear numerous ear-rings, bracelets, anklets, and greegrees, with strings of beads round their necks and waists. They live in huts formed of clay or wattled work of bamboo canes, of different forms, according to circumstances or the fashion of their respective tribes. Some are square and tolerably comfortable, according to European ideas; but most of them are built of a circular shape, very much resembling the form of a bee-hive, with a low entrance, and without any windows. Their furniture consists of a large iron pot, in which they cook their food, a wooden bowl or two, a mortar and pestle, in which they beat their *cus-cus*, and a few mats, of which they make their beds when they go to sleep. For food they make use of rice and native corn, which they grow in large quantities, and prepare in various ways, according to their respective tastes, with the addition of other vegetables, or sour milk occasionally for a change. Animal food is but seldom used by the natives generally. Their wants are very few, and easily supplied; so that in their uncivilised state they live an indolent kind of life, taking little thought for the morrow.

The form of government adopted by the native tribes of Western Africa is almost invariably despotic; for, although they recognise certain laws and usages, and have pompous pleadings, in cases of litigation, on the *bentang*, or under the *palaver tree*, it is well known that the will of the king or chief is the real law by which the matter must be ultimately decided. The entire population was, no doubt, originally Pagan, but now a rude kind of Mohammedanism is professed by a portion of many of the tribes, especially the Mandingoes and Jolloffs. But, whatever distinction may exist nominally, there is but little difference to be observed between them. They are all intensely superstitious, and the Mohammedan *greegree* and the Pagan *fetish* are scarcely to be distinguished from each other, either in their mode of preparation or in the idolatrous regard which is paid to them. If possible, the Pagan portion of the population is even more degraded than the Mohammedan, for they pay homage to little wooden images, to serpents, crocodiles, monkeys, and other animals; to the spirits of their deceased chiefs, and even to the devil himself.

To persons who live in a land of Gospel light and liberty it may seem strange that any portion of the human family should be so degraded as to pay Divine homage to creeping reptiles and wicked spirits; but it is, nevertheless, a fact. Having no Bibles and no Christian teachers, the people are destitute of the true knowledge of God; and, to allay the feelings of fear and dread of which they are frequently the subjects, they have recourse to these superstitious practices, of which we who go out as Missionaries are often the mournful witnesses. The natives of Western Africa are trained to the most servile subjection to their chiefs. Whilst they live they pay them the most profound deference and respect; and after death they believe their departed spirits return to the earth and dwell in these serpents and crocodiles, which they worship. Consequently in some instances they feed them and take care of them like domestic animals, and offer sacrifices to them in times of trouble. At a place on the coast called Dix Cove, a few years

JU-JU-HOUSE, OR TEMPLE OF SCULLS.

ago, a huge crocodile constantly received Divine honours. It was kept in a large pond near the fort, and any person going on shore there might have had a sight of it, at the expense of a white fowl and a bottle of rum. The heathen priest, or fetish-man, took the fowl and spirits, and proceeded to the pond, making a peculiar whistling noise with his mouth, on which the crocodile came forth and received the fowl as his share of the present, whilst the priest appropriated the liquor to himself. On one occasion two gentlemen were exposed to considerable risk on paying a visit to this place; for the fowl having escaped from the fetish-man into the bush, the crocodile made towards them, and pursued them so closely in their flight that, had not a dog crossed their path, on which the animal made his repast, one of them would most probably have fallen a victim to his rapacity. The natives, moreover, believe in the existence of a great wicked spirit who controls all the rest, whom they worship, and to whom they offer sacrifices to appease his wrath, and, as they say, to cultivate friendship with him that he may do them no harm. Thus all the homage of the heathen, to whatever object it is paid, is the result of fear and dread, and not of love or affection for their deities; and the disgusting forms which their worship assumes remind us of the Apostle's description of the heathens of his time: "Professing themselves to be wise they became fools, and changed the glory of the incorruptible God into an image made like to corruptible man, and to birds, and four-footed beasts, and creeping things."

The moral degradation of the people is further illustrated by the prevalence of war, slavery, and human sacrifices, to which our references must necessarily be very brief, although some districts have been almost depopulated thereby. These vices are intimately associated, and the fearful extent to which they have prevailed in Western Africa reflects no credit upon Europe, with its high pretensions to civilization. We are free to admit that a mild kind of domestic slavery may have existed in that country from ancient times; but the slave trade, properly so called, with all its atrocities, is the offspring of the white man's cupidity, and would never have existed if European nations had not embarked in it. To supply the sugar plantations in the West Indies with labourers, when the poor hapless aborigines had nearly all been swept away by the cruel treatment of their oppressors, vessels were sent to the Western Coast of Africa to transport the unsuspecting negroes to a land of hopeless bondage. Sometimes they were purchased from the petty chiefs for a few trinkets, and at other times they were kidnapped and carried off by stealth. At length the demand created a constant supply of slaves from the interior, to obtain which a strange kind of warfare was organised, which had for its special object the capturing and enslaving of the natives. The slave-hunters would attack a peaceful village in the dead of the night, set fire to the huts, and capture or kill the hapless people as they attempted to escape from the flames. All that were thus taken were marched off to the coast like cattle driven to the market. Thus were hundreds of thousands of poor negroes every year dragged from their homes and doomed to a life of perpetual bondage, till at length England interposed, relinquished the traffic herself, and laboured hard to induce other nations to do the same. Already France, Holland, and the United States have followed the noble example; and it is to be hoped that, ere long, Spain, Portugal, and the Brazils will follow, and that slavery will cease throughout the whole world. Then may we hope, with the blessing of God upon the efforts put forth to promote legitimate commerce and Christian civilisation, Africa will be regenerated, and take her place among the enlightened nations of the earth.

But perhaps the most revolting feature in the character of the native tribes of Africa is their delight in human sacrifices. And this is intimately associated with the crimes already mentioned, inasmuch as captives or criminals are generally the victims immolated. On the death of a chief or other distinguished person of rank, it is customary in many places to decapitate a considerable number of slaves and to drench the grave with human gore. This is done from a strange notion that their demon gods delight in blood, and that the spirits of those who are thus put to death will attend the departed chiefs and minister to them in another world. Thus the number of victims offered at the funeral is in proportion to the dignity and rank of the deceased, and frequently amounts to several hundreds, or even thousands. The prevalence of this abominable practice has of late years been checked somewhat by the proximity of mission stations to some of the principal scenes of superstition and blood, but it is believed that hundreds and thousands of natives are thus immolated every year. So true is it that the dark places of the earth are full of the habitations of cruelty.

Most of the superstitious rites and ceremonies of the negroes

METHOD OF COLLECTING COCOA-NUTS AND PALM WINE.

are celebrated under the influence of intoxicating drink, which they use to an extent almost incredible. Ardent spirits, or the "fire water" of the white man, has been most frequently called into requisition on these occasions of late years. But when this pernicious liquid fails, palm wine is made use of, which is a powerful intoxicant when it has passed through the process of fermentation. This is collected in the most ingenious manner by perforating the palm tree near the top, when the juice flows freely into calabashes prepared for the purpose of receiving it; and every morning the natives may be seen ascending the trees by means of hoops to bring down the precious treasure. On occasions of festivity, and especially at funerals, scenes of revelry and debauchery are witnessed which defy description, and which are little less than "hell upon earth."

It is with a measure of relief to our feelings that we now turn aside from these revolting scenes, to consider the means which have been employed to promote the elevation and civilisation of the native tribes of Western Africa, so fearfully depraved, and the results which have followed the philanthropic efforts of the friends of the negro race on their behalf, especially so far as the Wesleyan Missionary Society is concerned.

SIERRA LEONE.

The first British settlement formed on the Western Coast of Africa, the avowed objects of which were the suppression of the slave trade, the encouragement of legitimate commerce, and the moral and religious improvement of the natives, received the name of SIERRA LEONE, from a river so called, on the southern bank of which the first town, appropriately named Freetown, was built, in latitude 8° 30' north, and longitude 10° 11' west. To this place a large number of slaves captured by British men-of-war have been brought from time to time, for the purpose of settling them upon lands set apart for their use, so that the population consists chiefly of liberated Africans, brought from different parts of the continent, and speaking different languages or dialects. The entire population of the colony is estimated at fifty thousand, occupying a number of villages scattered over an extensive tract of country, which has been secured for them by the British Government. These people soon become industrious, learn to speak broken English, and attend to the instructions given them, and a good work has been carried on among them by several Christian agencies for many years, and the results are on the whole very encouraging. The capacity of the negro race to receive instruction, and the perfect adaptation of the Gospel to meet their case, and to raise them in the scale of being, have been proved beyond the possibility of successful contradiction. It only requires that the grand remedy for the woes of Africa be applied on a scale commensurate with the wants of this vast continent, and there can be no question as to the final issue.

As early as the year 1769, the venerable Dr. Coke, the father of Methodist Missions, devised a scheme for the civilisation of the Foolas, in the neighbourhood of Sierra Leone. This undertaking, which originated in motives so purely benevolent, proved an entire failure, chiefly from want of adaptation in the agents employed, and perhaps partly from the mistaken views which were entertained at that early period on what may be called the true philosophy of Christian civilisation. The persons sent forth by the good Doctor on this important mission were a company of mechanics, with a surgeon at their head, who were intended to teach the wandering Foolas the arts of civilised life. On arriving in the colony they became discontented, and were soon dispersed. Some died of fever, others absconded, and the rest returned home, without having ever reached the scene of their intended labours in the interior of the country.

This experiment, together with other similar failures, led the friends of missions to see that mere plans of secular civilisation were not likely to prepare the way for the introduction of the Gospel to barbarous native tribes, as had been supposed. Christian people in England at length became convinced that the faithful preaching of the truth itself, together with the establishment of schools for the training up of the rising generation in the knowledge and love of God, were the surest means of promoting genuine civilisation among the heathen, whilst at the same time they have a tendency at once to prepare the people for another world. Hence it is pleasing to observe that the next effort that was made by the Wesleyan Missionary Society for the benefit of Western Africa was based upon the true evangelical foundation, the excellence of which has since been proved on an ample scale.

In the year 1811, the Rev. George Warren and three school teachers were sent out to Sierra Leone for the purpose of preaching the Gospel and of training the rising generation in the way they should go. They opened their commission under the most promising circumstances, and were favoured by the great Head of the Church with almost immediate fruit of their labours. On the arrival of this, the first real missionary party of Wesleyan labourers in the colony, on the 12th of November, they found about a hundred persons who were in the habit of meeting together for religious worship, and who called themselves Methodists. These were chiefly free blacks from Nova Scotia, who had received the Gospel at the hands of the missionaries there, and who had thus brought with them to the land of their forefathers a knowledge of the good news of salvation. They had already built a chapel, in which they held their meetings for exhortation and prayer, and, wishing to be favoured with a regular Gospel ministry, they had written repeatedly to England for a missionary, and now they rejoiced to see the fulfilment of their desires.* The

* Of this party of free negroes from Nova Scotia, eleven hundred in number, who landed at Sierra Leone from fifteen vessels on the 28th of March, 1792, only three now remain, and they are far advanced in years. Of those who have passed away several lived to a good old age. As specimens of African longevity the following may be quoted from a list of recent deaths: Moses Newman, aged 82, Phœbe Bragger, 87, Peggy Macauley, 92, Abraham Newman, 93, Ann Edmonds, 103, Mimey Johnson, 105. The names of these and other pious settlers from America are deservedly held in grateful remembrance by the Methodist people of Sierra Leone; for, notwithstanding some eccentricities of character, they gave strength and permanence to the cause of Christian truth on that part of the benighted coast of Africa, at an early period of the Mission.

ministry of Mr. Warren was greatly blessed to the good of these simple-hearted people, and to that of many others also, for the afflictions through which the liberated Africans had passed, in being torn away from their homes into slavery, before they were rescued from their oppressors by British cruisers, seemed to have humbled their minds and prepared them in some degree for the reception of the Gospel. The missionary career of Mr. Warren, so auspiciously begun, was of short duration, however. He was suddenly stricken with fever, and finished his course of useful labour on the 23rd of July, 1812, about eight months after his arrival in the colony, being the first of a large number of Wesleyan Missionaries who have fallen a sacrifice to the climate of Western Africa.

A gloomy period of more than two years elapsed before a suitable missionary was found for the vacant station. At length the Rev. William Davies and his wife were sent out, and they arrived safely at Sierra Leone on the 13th of February, 1815. The following rainy season was very unhealthy, and among those who were carried off by fever was the Captain of the *Wilding*, the vessel by which Mr. and Mrs. Davis had sailed to Africa; but the missionary and his wife passed through their " seasoning fever" favourably, and pursued their useful labours for some time with gratitude and joy. Towards the close of the year, however, they were both prostrated by fever at the same time; and on the 15th of December, ten months after she arrived in the colony, Mrs. Davis breathed her last. On the morning of the day on which she expired, Mr. Davis, being ill himself, " crawled to see her," and was much affected by the change which had passed upon her once rosy but now emaciated frame. In answer to the question, " Is Jesus precious ?" she, with a faint voice and a gentle pressure of the hand, said, " Yes, yes!" soon after which her redeemed and sanctified spirit passed away, to be for ever with the Lord. This was the first of a long list of female labourers who have fallen in Western Africa, and the touching and appropriate motto on her tombstone is, " NOT LOST, BUT GONE BEFORE !"

The lonely and bereaved Missionary, on recovering from his illness, was soon at his post of duty, endeavouring to point the sable sons and daughters of Ham to the "Lamb of God that taketh away the sins of the world;" and the blessing of the Almighty rested upon his labours. Mr. Davis was spared to prosecute his beloved work with success during the following year, and on the 26th of December, 1816, he had the pleasure of receiving the Rev. Samuel and Mrs. Brown, who were sent out by the parent society to his aid, or to relieve him if necessary. Mrs. Brown had only lived in Africa seven months and two days when she also was cut down by fever in the prime of life, on the 28th of July, 1817. The two Missionaries, thus bereaved, toiled on together in the work of their Divine Master, encouraged by His presence and blessing till the end of the year; but repeated attacks of fever rendered it necessary for Mr. Davis to embark for England, and Mr. Brown was ultimately left entirely alone on the station.

The next reinforcement of labourers consisted of the Rev. Messrs. Baker and Gillison, two single young men, who were sent out to relieve Mr. Brown, who, in consequence of the failure of health and the loss of his wife, needed a change. The new missionaries landed in Sierra Leone on the morning of February the 14th, 1819. It was the holy Sabbath day, and they proceeded at once from the ship to the chapel, where they opened their commission without delay, one of them preaching in the morning and the other in the evening, to crowded and delighted congregations. Mr. Brown embarked for England soon afterwards; but before his departure he thus gives expression to his feelings in a letter to the Missionary Committee, alluding to the success which had attended his labours, one hundred new members having been added to the society during the year:—"I have sown in tears but now we reap in joy. Thank God! this is an ample recompense for every sigh, every tear, every shaking ague, every burning fever, every bereavement, and every restless and sleepless night I have had to endure since I came to Africa. This makes me very reluctant to leave. I feel willing to spend and be spent for the welfare of the Church and for the honour of my adorable Redeemer."*

The brethren Baker and Gillison had not laboured together long before they realised the truth of that saying of the Master, "Then two shall be in the field: the one shall be taken and the other left." Mr. Gillison had only been in Africa about six months when he fell a sacrifice to the climate. He died happy in the Lord, on the 10th of August, 1819. Mr. Baker was himself ill at the time, but as soon as he was a little better he preached the funeral sermon of his dear departed brother, and then proceeded with his work in the name and strength of the Lord. In the course of the following year a gracious outpouring of the Holy Spirit was experienced in Sierra Leone; and as the result of the revival, upwards of two hundred new members were added to the society, making the total number at that time four hundred and seventy. In reference to the genuineness of this work Mr. Baker says, "I do not hesitate to say of nearly all those who have been added, I have no more doubt of their conversion than I have of my own. The work has produced a general reformation."

In the latter part of 1820 the Rev. John and Mrs. Huddleston embarked for Sierra Leone and landed safely in Freetown on the 8th of November. They were much pleased with the cordial reception which they received, as well as with the prosperous state of the mission. Early in the following year they were joined by the Rev. George Lane, on whose arrival from England Mr. Baker proceeded to St. Mary's, on the River Gambia, to take part in the commencement of a new mission there, according to the appointment of Conference. Messrs. Huddleston and Lane had laboured together in harmony and love for a few months when

* This noble-minded and zealous Missionary afterwards laboured in the West Indies, and in England for nearly forty years: and in the evening of life, when he had retired as a supernumerary, he felt it upon his heart to revisit the scenes of his early labours and sufferings, and in 1857 he actually went out to Sierra Leone of his own accord. There he spent three years, assisting the Missionaries in their work as his strength would permit; and then returned to Liverpool, where he died in peace, on the 5th of October, 1861—a noble instance of true devotedness to the great missionary enterprise.

the latter was also called to the Gambia to supply the place of a deceased Missionary. He returned to Sierra Leone, however, in the course of the following year, but never fully recovered from the effects of an attack of fever which he had at St. Mary's. He died in peace at Freetown on the 16th of April, 1823. The loss of Mr. Lane was severely felt by Mr. and Mrs. Huddleston, as well as by the members of the society and other friends; but, painful as this bereavement was, it was soon followed by another mysterious dispensation of Divine Providence equally trying. Scarcely had three months passed away when Mr. Huddleston himself was called to his reward in heaven. He died of yellow fever, on the 20th of July, 1823, having laboured successfully in Western Africa for nearly three years, with little interruption from sickness till the time that he was attacked with the fatal malady. Mrs. Huddleston embarked for England soon after the death of her husband, and the members of the Wesleyan Society at Sierra Leone were once more left without a pastor.

No sooner was it known in England, however, that Missionaries were required for Western Africa than two devoted servants of God, the Rev. Messrs. Piggot and Harte, voluntarily offered themselves for the post of danger and of honour which had become vacant by the death of Mr. Huddleston. The new Missionaries landed at Sierra Leone on the 19th of March, 1824, where they were received as the angels of God, and commenced their evangelical labours in excellent health and spirits. But, although strongly attached to each other, they were destined in the order of Divine Providence soon to be separated. Mr. Harte sickened and died of the "country fever" on the 18th of December, after a sojourn in Africa of only nine months, and his bereaved colleague was left to proceed with his work alone.

On the 20th of May, 1826, the Rev. Samuel and Mrs. Dawson landed at Sierra Leone on their way to the Gambia, their appointed station; but before an opportunity offered for proceeding to that place they were both seized with the African fever, and Mrs. Dawson died on the 1st of August, only two months and five days after their arrival. Mr. Dawson himself was mercifully raised from the brink of the grave, and after labouring at Sierra Leone for some time he proceeded to his station at the Gambia with a heavy heart, but fully resolved to spend and be spent in the service of God. He was accompanied by his friend Mr. Piggot, who now returned to England by that route, having been relieved by the arrival at Sierra Leone of the Rev. Messrs. Courties and May, on the 28th of November, 1826.

These two brethren pursued their beloved work for about two years without much interruption from sickness, preaching the Gospel of Christ in the respective towns and villages of the colony with great success. The term of their appointment having at length expired, the Rev. Messrs. Munro and Peck were sent out to relieve them, and the hope was entertained that they would reach England in safety, and be long spared to labour in other parts of the mission field. But, alas! it was otherwise ordained by Him whose wisdom is unsearchable and whose ways are past finding out. The two new Missionaries arrived at Sierra Leone on the 16th of November, 1828, and the first intelligence which they received from the pilot before they landed was that Mr. May had died of fever on the 4th of October, whilst in the midst of the preparations for his expected voyage to England. Mr. Courties had been also frequently prostrated by fever; and when he embarked for Europe he was so weak that his newly-arrived brethren had to support him to the boat which was to convey him to the ship. The captain seemed confident, however, that he would rally when he got out to sea. But it was not so. The poor Missionary became weaker and weaker, and finished his course three days after the vessel left the coast of Africa. His body was committed to a watery grave in "sure and certain hope of a glorious resurrection to eternal life through our Lord Jesus Christ," in the last great day, when the "sea shall give up the dead that are therein." The Lord, no doubt, in mercy took His servant from the evil to come, for the ship in which he had embarked never reached her destined port, but was totally wrecked six days after his death, when everything on board was lost, the captain and crew saving their lives with great difficulty.

From the apparent adaptation of Messrs. Munro and Peck to the work in which they were engaged, it was hoped that they might endure the climate, and be spared for many years to come; but they were both of them cut down by an epidemic fever before they had been eight months in the country. Mr. Peck died on the 3rd and Mr. Munro on the 8th of July, 1829. The intelligence of this afflicting and mysterious dispensation of Divine Providence was communicated to the committee in London by the missionaries of the Church Society, who paid the kindest attention to their brethren of the Wesleyan Mission in their last illness and in their dying hours. The Methodist Societies and congregations in Sierra Leone were thus once more left without a missionary to minister to them the word of life.

The sudden and unexpected removal of Messrs. Munro and Peck so soon after the lamented deaths of Messrs. May and Courties produced a deep and gloomy impression, not only upon the minds of their personal friends and relatives, but upon the minds of the friends of missions in general. Some went so far as to question the propriety of continuing to send European missionaries to a country so unfriendly to health. It is a pleasing fact, however, that although the committee sent to Western Africa only such young men as freely offered their services, they had never long to wait for volunteers to fill up the vacancies which so frequently occurred. No sooner had the intelligence reached England of the painful bereavement which the Sierra Leone Mission had suffered than a personal friend of the late Mr. Peck nobly offered himself as his successor. This was the Rev. John Keightley, who embarked for Africa before the end of the year, and who landed at Freetown on the 27th of January, 1830. On the 18th of March in the following year he was joined by the Rev. William Ritchie. These honoured and devoted Missionaries laboured successfully at Sierra Leone for upwards of two years, and they both lived to return home and to serve the Church efficiently in the West Indies and in England for many years afterwards.

Before leaving Sierra Leone in the early part of 1833, Mr. Ritchie had the pleasure of receiving the Rev. Edward Maer, who had been sent out to relieve him; and towards the close of the same year Mr. Maer was joined by the Rev. Isaac Clarke. These two brethren laboured together very earnestly and successfully for a while, extending their visits to several villages which had not been reached by former Missionaries. Their labours were soon interrupted, however; for Mr. Clarke, whose lungs were supposed to be affected before he left home, never recovered from the effect of his seasoning fever, but died in peace of pulmonary consumption, on the 4th of November, 1834, about twelve months after he arrived in the colony. The Rev. Benjamin Crosby had embarked for Africa before the intelligence of Mr. Clarke's death had reached England, and on his arrival in Sierra Leone he united with Mr. Maer in the work of the mission with all his heart. These two faithful Ministers of Christ did good service in Western Africa, but they never saw their native land again. Mr. Maer, having continued at Sierra Leone longer than the appointed time, embarked for England on a visit, fully intending to return to the coast when his health was restored; but he died at sea three days after leaving the shores of Africa, on the 27th of March, 1837, and Mr. Crosby finished his course of useful labour at Sierra Leone on the 24th of the following month.

In the meantime, the Rev. William Sanders was sent out to strengthen the mission. He arrived in Freetown on the 4th of December, 1835; and, having laboured with success for more than two years, he was spared to return to England early in 1838, and to be afterwards usefully employed in the home work. The Rev. James and Mrs. Patterson were also sent out in the following year, and landed in Sierra Leone on the 10th of October, 1836; but Mr. Patterson was cut down by fever on the 21st of May, 1837, before he had been in the colony eight months, and his bereaved widow soon afterwards returned to England. This year was remarkably unhealthy on the whole line of coast, the yellow fever being very prevalent, and the Wesleyan Missionary Society lost by death on their respective stations six missionaries, and two excellent wives of missionaries, in less than six months.

But notwithstanding the arduous and hazardous nature of the

onterprise, there was no lack of labourers. Before Mr. Sanders left Sierra Leone he had the pleasure of receiving the Rev. Thomas and Mrs. Dove and the Rev. Henry Badger, who arrived at Freetown on the 19th of November, 1837. Mr. and Mrs. Dove had previously spent three years at the Gambia, and were considered in some measure inured to the climate; but, notwithstanding this advantage, Mrs. Dove was cut down by fever on the 7th of June, 1840. Messrs. Dove and Badger continued to prosecute their useful labours for four years, and were spared to return to England together in the month of May, 1842, other brethren having been sent out to relieve them. This interval, however, had not been a period of uninterrupted health to the Mission families. The Rev. Thomas Edwards, who arrived at Sierra Leone on the 15th of December, 1838, had been brought to the verge of the grave by illness, and obliged to return to England in June, 1840. The Rev. Henry Fleet, who landed in Freetown on the 7th of January, 1839, finished his course on the 30th of May following, having lost his beloved wife by death on board the ship three days before he reached the shores of Africa. The Rev. David Jehu, who arrived at Sierra Leone on the 23rd of December, 1839, had been called away by death on the 2nd of July, 1840. Thus severely was the mission afflicted from year to year at this early period of its history.

It is pleasing, however, to observe that some assistance was at length afforded by native assistant Missionaries, who were raised up to take a part in the work, and that for several years after the date last mentioned the European missionaries and their families endured the climate with less suffering from sickness and bereavement than formerly. The Rev. Messrs. Raston and Annear arrived at Sierra Leone in January, 1842, and both were mercifully spared to return to England for a season, Mr. Annear in May, 1843, and Mr. Raston in February, 1845. The Rev. William A. and Mrs. Quick, and the Rev. Richard Amos, went out in February, 1843, and the entire party were spared to return home in due time, Mr. and Mrs. Quick in May, 1844, and Mr. Amos in September, 1845. The Rev. Messrs. Dove and Badger, with their excellent wives, went out again to Sierra Leone, where they arrived in July, 1843. Mr. and Mrs. Dove were spared to return to England in May, 1846, Mr. Dove having been connected with the Missions in Western Africa for nearly thirteen years. Mrs. Badger was called away by death on the 28th of January, 1844; but Mr. Badger continued his useful labours some time longer, notwithstanding his painful bereavement, and was favoured to return to England in May, 1848. On the 1st of December, 1845, the Mission at Sierra Leone was reinforced by the arrival of the Rev. Thomas and Mrs. Raston and the Rev. Messrs. Wayte and Griffiths, after a perilous passage from England. Mrs. Raston was cut down by fever on the 27th of December, after a residence in Africa of only twenty-six days, and Mr. Wayte finished his course a few weeks afterwards, on the 16th of January, 1846. Mr. Raston returned to England in March, 1847, and Mr. Griffiths followed him in the month of September in the same year, having been relieved by the arrival of other Missionaries. On the 7th of December, 1846, the Rev. Richard and Mrs. Wrench and the Rev. John Lewis arrived at Sierra Leone; but Mr. and Mrs. Wrench returned home in June, 1847, on account of the failure of their health. Mr. Lewis continued his useful labours for more than three years, and was spared to return to England in May, 1850.

In the course of our brief and hasty sketch of the numerous bereavements and changes to which the Sierra Leone Mission was subject on account of the trying nature of the climate, it is pleasing to note a few instances of remarkable preservation and devotedness to the work. In illustration of this, we may cite the case of Mr. Raston, who, with Mrs. Raston and Messrs. Hart and Purslow, landed in Freetown for the third time on the 8th of December, 1847. Mr. Purslow's race was soon run, however. He died triumphantly happy in God, on the 2nd of October, 1848; but the rest of the party were spared to return to England, after fulfilling their appointed period of service in Western Africa. In 1849 the Rev. Walter P. Garry, a native of the West Indies, having finished his studies in the Richmond College, was sent out as a missionary to Sierra Leone, where he laboured successfully for three years, with tolerable health and comfort, before he returned to his own country.

The next party sent out to Sierra Leone consisted of the Rev. James and Mrs. Edney, and Messrs. Gilbert and Fletcher, towards the close of 1850, all of whom were spared to labour for several years, and on their return were appointed to stations in the West Indies, where Mr. and Mrs. Edney had previously been usefully employed. For a few years, about this period, the sickness and mortality among the Missionaries on the Western Coast of Africa was much less than formerly. Several native ministers had, moreover, been raised up, who rendered efficient service by labouring among their fellow-countrymen on some of the stations, so that fewer European Missionaries were required. In 1852 the Rev. Lionel D. Reay was appointed to Sierra Leone, and in 1854 he was joined by the Rev. Messrs. Teal and Dillon, all of whom were spared to return to England after labouring in Africa for more than three years. This was not the case, however, with the Rev. William Barrowclough, who died of fever at Freetown on the 3rd of April, 1856, three months after his arrival on the coast.

In 1857 the Rev. John and Mrs. Weatherston were appointed to Sierra Leone; but Mrs. Weatherston soon sank under the influence of the climate, and her bereaved husband afterwards returned home. The Rev. Messrs. Champness and Coe were sent out in the interim towards the end of 1858, and were both spared to return to their native land. In 1859 the Rev. John and Mrs. Bridgart, who had laboured for several years with much acceptance and success at the Gambia, proceeded, by direction of the Committee, from that station to Sierra Leone. There they were soon joined by the Rev. James J. and Mrs. Wray and Mr. Hulbert, from England, and thus the mission was once more efficiently reinforced. But this noble band of labourers were soon broken by sickness and death. Mrs. Bridgart and Mr. Hulbert were both removed after short periods of illness to their eternal rest, whilst Mr. and Mrs. Wray were obliged to return to England on account of the failure of their health. Mr. Bridgart also embarked for Europe after his painful bereavement; but his health and constitution were so completely shattered by what he had passed through on the coast, that he sank before the voyage was completed, and he never saw his native land again. The number of labourers were thus reduced when the Rev. Messrs. Berry and Blanchard arrived in Sierra Leone, in the month of January, 1860, both of whom were spared to return to England in due time. These excellent brethren were joined by the Rev. James W. Berrie on the 10th of November, 1861, who returned home in 1865, the Rev. Joseph Hall having gone out in the interim to strengthen the mission. The brother last named was also favoured to return in safety to his native land, and to be usefully employed in the home work.

The Sierra Leone District having been left without a General Superintendent for several years, since the removal of the Rev. James Edney, the vacancy was filled in 1864 by the appointment of the Rev. Benjamin Tregaskis, who nobly volunteered his services for Western Africa, after labouring in the West Indies for nearly thirty years. Under the judicious direction of this devoted missionary the work is now carried on by the Rev. Messrs. Waite and Fletcher, from England, and six native Ministers—namely, the Rev. Messrs. Knight, Maude, King, Marke, Thorpe, and May—who have been raised up on the spot as the fruit of missionary labours, and trained for this holy service chiefly in the colony.

This brief historical sketch of the Sierra Leone Mission has been hitherto confined chiefly to a mournful record of the numerous bereavements and afflictions which have tended to retard the progress of the work of God, with the hope of engaging the sympathy and the prayers of the reader on behalf of those who are so frequently exposed to danger from the pestilence that walketh in darkness. But it must be remembered that there is a brighter side to the subject. Many devoted missionaries, and the heroic wives of missionaries, have fallen a sacrifice to the climate, it is true; but they have not laboured in vain, nor spent their strength for naught. Important circuits and out-stations have been formed, congregations gathered, schools established, and churches organised, not only in Freetown, the capital of the colony, but also in Gloucester, Regent, Wellington, Kissy, York,

Kent, Russell, Wilberforce, Hamilton, and other villages. In connection with these stations we have now *nine Missionaries, four thousand nine hundred and fifty-two church members*, and *three thousand one hundred and seventy-four scholars* in the Mission schools. For the training of native agents there is also a seminary of a higher character, which may with propriety be designated a Theological Institution, at King Tom's Point, near Freetown, which bids fair to be an important auxiliary to the good work. In view of these encouraging results of missionary labour at Sierra Leone, notwithstanding the difficulties with which we have had to contend, we may well "Thank God, and take courage."

The Gambia.

The next Mission which was established by the Wesleyan Missionary Society on the Western Coast of Africa was on the River Gambia; and it is with feelings of peculiar interest that the writer calls attention to this station, inasmuch as it was the scene of his earliest missionary labours nearly forty years ago. Many of the observations which have been made with reference to the character of the country, scenery, climate, productions, and the habits of the people will apply to this part of the coast in common with the rest. Our description of the place as introductory to the history of the Mission will therefore be necessarily brief.

The Gambia is one of the noblest rivers of Africa, and may be fairly classed with the Niger and the Senegal with regard to the facilities which it affords for direct and easy access to the interior of the country. It varies in width from three miles to one, and it is navigable for small vessels to a distance of five hundred miles from the sea. It takes its rise in the northern extremity of the Kong Mountains, and after watering a beautiful and fertile country, through which it winds its serpentine course for about a thousand miles, it empties itself into the Atlantic Ocean to the south of Cape Verd, in latitude 13° 30' north, and longitude 15° 0' west. The principal native tribes occupying this part of the continent are the Jolloffs, Mandingoes, and Foolas, some of whom remain in their original Pagan state, whilst others have embraced the religious dogmas of the False Prophet. A number of liberated Africans of various tribes have, however, of late years been located on the different settlements of the Gambia, so that the population has now become of a very mixed character. Previous to the introduction of the Gospel among them all classes were deeply degraded and totally destitute of the true knowledge of God.

In the year 1816, an English settlement was formed on the Island of St. Mary, near the mouth of the river, on the same principle as that at Sierra Leone, for the suppression of the slave trade and the encouragement of legitimate commerce. The principal town was called Bathurst, after a noble earl of that name, and, being chiefly built on the margin of the water, it presented a beautiful appearance from the shipping in the harbour. Nothing was done, however, for the religious instruction of the people till 1821, when the Wesleyan Missionary Society commenced its labours. The first Missionary sent out from England was the Rev. John Morgan, who was soon afterwards joined by the Rev. John Baker, from Sierra Leone. The two zealous pioneers were somewhat perplexed as to which would be the best locality to commence their labours. At length they fixed upon a place called Mandanaree, on the mainland, in the kingdom of Combo, about eight miles from the British settlement at St. Mary's. In the true missionary spirit, they commenced to fell the trees and clear the ground which they had obtained from the native chief, and to build a rude house in which to reside, with a large room for their religious services. This they accomplished in a few weeks with the help of the natives, but they soon discovered to their sorrow that they had selected a very unhealthy place for the station, as they were both attacked with fever at an early period of their labours. The natives, moreover, who were of the Mandingo tribe, and rigid Mahommedans, would not attend to their instructions, and they were very much discouraged. The difficulties with which they had to contend, from the character of the climate and the indifference of the people, were so numerous that at length they resolved to remove from Mandanaree to St.

Mary's, where they could obtain medical aid in sickness, and where the people appeared more willing to attend to their ministrations. Here the missionaries had occasionally preached ever since their arrival in the country, and from this time forward St. Mary's became the head-quarters of the Gambia Mission.

The advantages of this change of station were soon manifest, and from the very first the blessing of God rested upon the labours of the missionaries at St. Mary's. Several of the natives were brought to a saving knowledge of the truth at an early period through the faithful preaching of the Gospel. These were chiefly of the Jolloff tribe, who had come with the English merchants from the island of Goree, and an interesting class of hopeful converts was soon formed, whilst at the same time a school was established for the instruction of the children. Before the end of the first year, however, the health of Mr. Baker having completely failed, he removed to the West Indies by direction of the Missionary Committee, and the Rev. William Bell was sent out from England to take his place. He arrived at St. Mary's on the 28th of January, 1822, but although he appeared well adapted for the work his course was soon run. He was cut down by fever on the 15th of March, forty-six days after his arrival, the first of a long list of devoted labourers who have since fallen a sacrifice to the climate, in connection with the Gambia Mission.

Mr. Morgan was thus once more left at St. Mary's alone, and he toiled on as best he could till the brethren at Sierra Leone, being aware of his circumstances, sent the Rev. George Lane to his assistance. This arrangement, though well meant, was not of much advantage to the Gambia station, as the amiable young missionary was soon entirely disabled from active duty by affliction, and was obliged to return to Sierra Leone, where he shortly afterwards rested from his labours as already mentioned. On hearing of the loss which the Mission at the Gambia had sustained, the Committee sent out the Rev. Robert and Mrs. Hawkins, who arrived at St. Mary's on the 14th of April, 1824. The Mission was now put on a more permanent footing, a substantial stone building

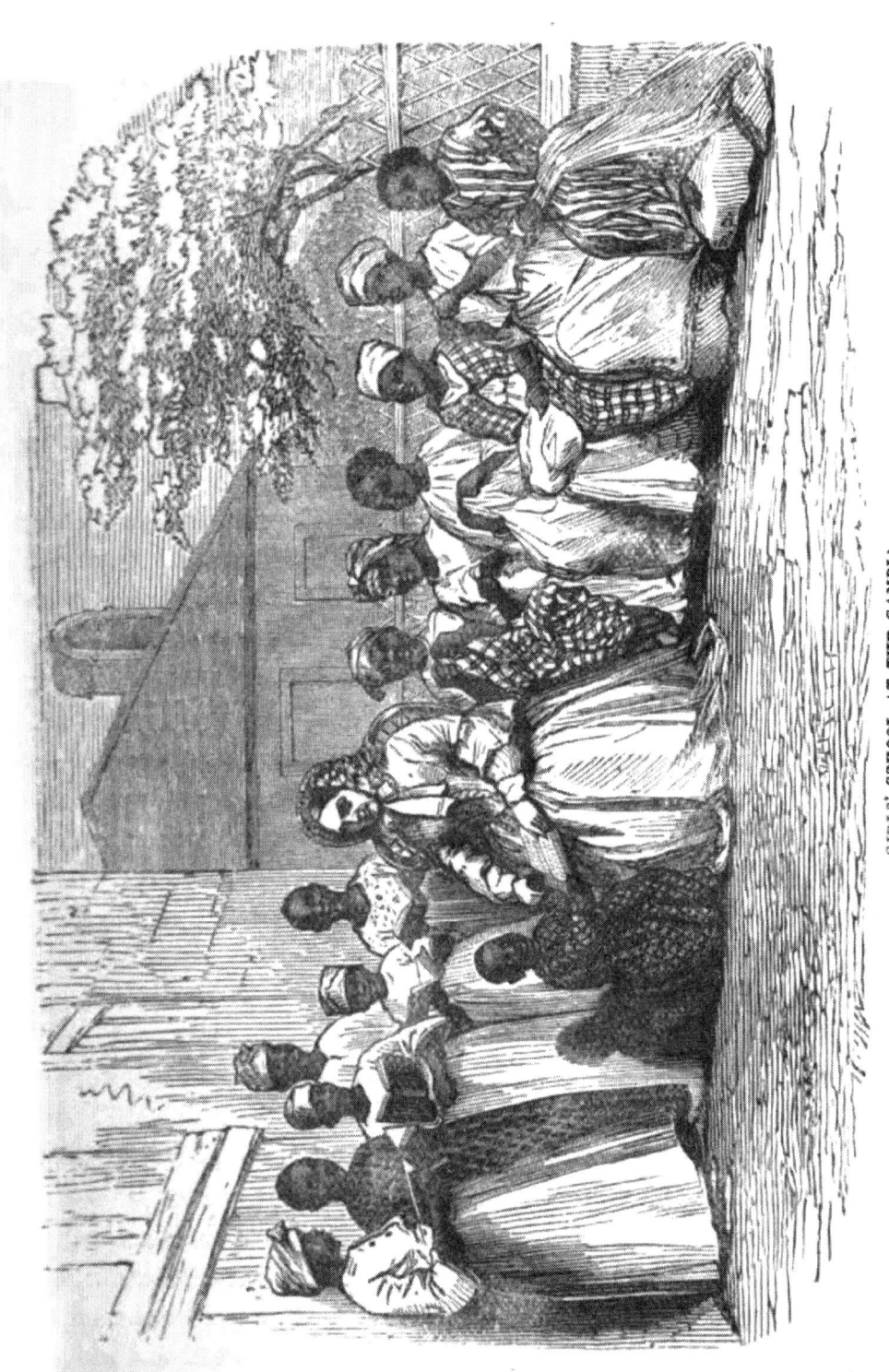

GIRLS' SCHOOL AT THE GAMBIA.

being erected for its use, with a large room for the school and religious services on the ground floor, and accommodation for the residence of the mission family above. In the early part of the year 1825, Mr. Morgan, having had repeated attacks of fever which incapacitated him for further service, embarked for England; and as soon as Mr. and Mrs. Hawkins had passed through their "seasoning," they proceeded very happily with their work, and the blessing of God rested upon their labours. The girls in the mission school had now the advantage of being instructed by a white lady, a privilege which they highly appreciated, and it was a novel and beautiful sight to see the missionary's wife surrounded by her African school girls, receiving their first lessons in reading and sewing.

Mr. and Mrs. Hawkins did good service for the Mission at the Gambia, and were spared to return to England in the month of May, 1827, having been relieved by the Rev. Samuel Dawson, who had just lost his wife at Sierra Leone, as already stated. Mr. Dawson laboured under considerable disadvantage in consequence of his painful bereavement, there being now no one to attend to the girls in the mission school, and to exercise that influence among the people which belongs peculiarly to the missionary's wife. He did his best, however, under the circumstances, and was spared to return home in the latter part of the year 1828, having been relieved by the arrival, on the 18th of November, of the Rev. Richard and Mrs. Marshall. The station being once more favoured with the zealous efforts and genial influence of a Christian lady, as well as with the ministrations of a missionary apparently well adapted for the work, a cheering measure of prosperity was realised both in the school and the higher departments of spiritual labour. But, like many others engaged in the same blessed work, these devoted servants of Christ soon finished their course of useful labour. After toiling successfully for about a year and nine months, Mr. Marshall was suddenly cut down by malignant fever on the 19th of August, 1830. Two days after her afflictive bereavement Mrs. Marshall embarked for England with her infant son and an African nurse. She arrived in Bristol in a state of great mental and bodily suffering, and being seized with convulsions, she expired about forty-eight hours after she landed, and before she had an opportunity of seeing any of her relatives or friends, who resided in the north. Thus was the Gambia station left without a missionary, and the settlement without a minister of any denomination.

It was at this eventful period of its history that the writer became personally connected with this interesting mission. When the African nurse arrived at the Mission House in London with the orphan child of the late Mr. and Mrs. Marshall, they were at once surrounded by a number of missionary candidates, who listened with feelings of deep emotion to the tale of sorrow which the negro girl related of her country, and the sad bereavement which the Mission had been called to experience. Feeling his heart strangely drawn towards Western Africa under these circumstances, the writer was induced to make that voluntary offer of his services which the Committee required, and being forthwith appointed to the Gambia, he and his dear wife embarked for Africa early in the year 1831, to occupy the vacant station. We arrived at St. Mary's on Thursday, the 10th of March, where we met with a most cordial and affectionate reception from the few native converts who had been gathered into the fold of Christ through the instrumentality of our devoted predecessors, and commenced our labours with cheering hopes of success. Everything was very strange at first, but we soon became accustomed to the place and the people, and we were very happy in our work. Immediately after our arrival we directed our attention to the reorganisation of the mission school, which had been given up since the death of Mr. and Mrs. Marshall, and we soon had a large number of negro children under instruction. In this important department of Christian labour we were very much encouraged, being favoured to see a goodly number of our pupils brought under the influence of religion as well as advanced to a respectable position as to general knowledge. At the same time a gracious influence frequently rested upon the congregations, both at our English and native services, and through the faithful preaching of the Gospel we had reason to believe that many were brought to a saving knowledge of the truth.

Among our early native converts at the Gambia were two or three intelligent young men who were called of God to point their fellow-countrymen to the Saviour of sinners. This circumstance encouraged us to entertain the hope that we might be able, with God's blessing, to make an aggressive movement on the dark benighted interior, and plant the standard of the cross in the regions beyond. Although the writer was the only missionary or minister of any denomination in the country, and his wife the only European female, an attempt was made in the name and strength of the Lord to extend the Mission to the upper regions of the Gambia. Before the commencement of the rainy season we embarked on our first voyage up the mighty river. We sailed in a small sloop, and called at numerous native towns and villages on either hand, with the hope of being able to shed a few rays of heavenly light on the surrounding gloom, through our intercourse with the natives. After about a week spent in ascending the river we reached Macarthy's Island, the place of our destination. There we spent two Sabbaths and the intervening days in preaching, teaching, visiting, and collecting information with a view to future operations; and such was the impression made upon the minds of the people, many of whom had never before heard the glad tidings of salvation, that they entreated us to remain and instruct them still further in the things belonging to their peace. Indeed they were unwilling that we should leave them till we promised, if spared, to visit them again, and, if possible, establish a mission station for their benefit. We then returned to St. Mary's, and were thankful to find that all had gone on well during our absence.

We did not forget our promise to the poor neglected people in the interior, but soon afterwards a circumstance occurred which delayed its fulfilment for a length of time. This was the breaking out of war between a powerful tribe of Mandingoes and the British settlement where we lived, into the particulars of which we need not here enter, although it seriously affected our mission work. The war raged for five months, during which the usual intercourse with the interior was interrupted, and travelling became impracticable. As soon as peace was restored to the land, however, and the country was once more open, we commenced our second voyage up the Gambia. On this occasion we took with us a native teacher, and the requisite materials for the commencement of a mission station on a humble scale. On reaching Macarthy's Island, we were received by the people with the liveliest demonstrations of gratitude and joy, and commenced operations at once. We secured a piece of land and erected the first Christian sanctuary and school-house ever built in that country. We then collected a number of little wild naked children together, partially clothed them, as best we could, and attempted to organise the first mission school. It was an experiment somewhat novel and amusing, but by patience and perseverance we succeeded better than we expected. We then returned to our own station at St. Mary's, leaving a native teacher in charge of the infant work at Macarthy's.

After the lapse of twelve months we paid a third visit to the interior, having repeatedly heard in the interim from the native teacher of the progress of the good work. On our arrival at Macarthy's Island on this occasion, we witnessed a scene which more than compensated for all the toil and privations through which we had been called to pass in our efforts to commence this station. We had not only the pleasure of preaching to a congregation of devout worshippers, much improved in their personal appearance by the civilising influence of the Gospel, but we had the satisfaction of finding that several had been brought to a saving knowledge of the truth. The mission school also exhibited evident proofs of progress. A number of children, who twelve months before did not know one letter from another, could now read easy lessons from the New Testament. Several children and adults were received into the Church by baptism, whilst parties were united in holy matrimony who had but recently been recovered from heathen darkness, and the Sacrament of the Lord's Supper was administered to a goodly number of devout communicants. Altogether it was a glorious sight, and we returned to St. Mary's truly thankful to God that we had been permitted to commence a station in the far-distant interior of Africa, which thenceforward proved to be a centre of light and holy influence to the surrounding country.

In the meantime the good work at St. Mary's was favoured with a cheering measure of prosperity. But being at length much broken in health by repeated attacks of fever, and the period of our appointment having been fulfilled, the writer and his dear wife were glad to welcome to the shores of Africa the parties sent out to relieve them, and they returned to their native land truly grateful to Almighty God for His preserving goodness in that land of sickness and of death; and having both been spared for so many years since to labour in other parts of the mission field, whilst so many have fallen, it will be no matter of surprise to the reader that we should now look back on the scenes of our earlier labours with gratitude and joy, and continue to watch the progress of the Mission at the Gambia with feelings of peculiar interest.

Some time before we left St. Mary's, we had the pleasure of receiving, on the 23rd of April, 1833, the Rev. William and Mrs. Fox, and the Rev. Thomas and Mrs. Dove, a noble band of zealous and devoted labourers. Mr. and Mrs. Fox were sent out to take our place at St. Mary's, and Mr. and Mrs. Dove were appointed to the new station at Macarthy's, where it was hoped that the wandering tribe of Foolas might be induced to settle and be brought under the influence of the Gospel, as well as the Mandingoes and liberated Africans, some of whom had already been converted to the truth of Christianity.

From this period the Gambia Mission branched out into two important divisions, each of which has a separate history of somewhat mournful interest, although sometimes linked together by dint of circumstances. To prevent confusion, we shall first trace the course of events at the new station at Macarthy's Island, and then return to consider the progress of the work at St. Mary's.

Soon after his arrival at Macarthy's, Mr. Dove commenced the erection of a substantial stone building, to answer the double purpose of a mission-house and chapel; and subsequently other

WESLEYAN MISSION PREMISES AT MACARTHY'S ISLAND, RIVER GAMBIA, 1835.

(These premises, when completed, received the name of the "Lindo Institution," in honour of the late Dr. Lindo of Southampton, one of the most zealous and liberal supporters of the Foola Mission. A superior school was attached for the training of the sons of native chiefs, which was made a blessing to several African youths who were entrusted to the care of the Missionaries).

buildings were added for the educational department of the work, towards the cost of which a benevolent gentleman in England contributed the noble sum of £1,000. After labouring successfully for about three years, Mr. and Mrs. Dove embarked for Europe, and were succeeded at Macarthy's by Mr. Fox, who now returned to the Gambia after a short visit to England for the benefit of his health, accompanied by the Rev. R. M. MacBriar, whose special mission was to reduce the Mandingo and Foola languages to a grammatical form, and, if possible, to translate portions of Scripture into those tongues. Mr. MacBriar found the climate of Western Africa very unfavourable to literary pursuits, and soon returned to England, taking with him an intelligent native, by whose assistance he compiled and published a Mandingo grammar and a translation of a portion of the New Testament. In the meantime, Mr. Fox addressed himself to the general work of the Mission with his wonted zeal and energy, and, having left his wife in England on account of the delicate state of her health, and having moreover been joined in November, 1837, by the Rev. William and Mrs. Swallow, who were sent out to reinforce the Mission, he felt at liberty to take several interesting journeys of observation into the more remote interior, with the hope of extending the work still farther in that direction.

But, strong and robust as was the health of Mr. Fox generally, is arduous labours and the trying nature of the climate of the Gambia at length made a serious impression upon it, and he found it necessary to return to England in the month of June, 1839. In the meantime Mr. and Mrs. Swallow removed to St. Mary's, and were succeeded at Macarthy's Island by the Rev. W. S. F. and Mrs. Moss, who arrived on the 30th of November, 1838. In less than two months afterwards, however, on the 22nd of January, 1839, Mrs. Moss was cut down by fever, and her bereaved husband ere long removed to St. Mary's, and in the following year returned to England. The vacancy thus occasioned was supplied by the appointment of the Rev. William and Mrs. James, who arrived at Macarthy's Island in the month of May, 1840. But the labours of this amiable and worthy couple were soon terminated; for Mr.

James fell a sacrifice to the climate on the 1st of July, before he had been three months on the station, and his bereaved widow embarked for England a few weeks afterwards, having received substantial tokens of sympathy from the missionaries and other European gentlemen at St. Mary's.

The next missionary to Macarthy's Island was the Rev. William Swallow, who nobly returned to the Gambia with Mrs. Swallow, after a visit to England for the benefit of their health, and arrived at their destination in January, 1841. These devoted servants of Christ bore up under the influence of the climate with commendable courage and perseverance; but they suffered much from affliction, and were obliged repeatedly to seek relief by temporary visits to Cape Verd Islands and Goree. At length they were bereaved of a dear child; and on the 28th of January, 1843, Mrs. Swallow was called to rest from her toils and sufferings, and to enter into the joy of her Lord. Her bereaved husband soon afterwards embarked for England, with his own health much shattered by repeated attacks of fever, the Rev. Samuel Symons having been sent out to reinforce the Mission, and especially to superintend the educational department of the work. Mr. Symons had laboured for two years with acceptance and success, when he also fell a sacrifice to the climate on the 20th of January, 1844. In consequence of the sickness and mortality with which the mission families were visited, the Rev. Benjamin Chapman having been obliged to return to England on account of severe illness, the Rev. George Parsonson was left alone for some time, the only European missionary at the Gambia, and was obliged to leave his own station at Macarthy's and come down the river to take the superintendency of the work at St. Mary's. The vacancy at Macarthy's Island was filled by the appointment of the Rev. Robert Lean, in 1847; but in less than four months after his arrival he was called to rest from his labours. He died very happy in God on the 23rd of March, 1848.

Since this period it has been deemed advisable to supply the station at Macarthy's with native ministers, to act under the direction of the European missionary at St. Mary's. These have been brought chiefly from Sierra Leone, where they had been favoured with special training for the work; and, by their piety, zeal, and intelligence, they have given general satisfaction, and been made very useful. The Revs. Joseph May, Charles Knight, Philip Wilson, James Hero and York F. Clement, themselves the fruit of missionary labour, and some of them originally rescued from the horrors of slavery, have in succession occupied this station, and a great and good work has been carried on from year to year. The benevolent intention to benefit the Foola tribe especially, by the Mission at Macarthy's Island, has not been realised to any great extent; but hundreds, if not thousands, of liberated Africans settled there, and a few Mandingoes have been brought to a saving knowledge of the truth through its instrumentality, many of whom have safely passed to a brighter and a better world above, whilst others who still survive exemplify the beauty of religion by a holy walk and conversation. Much has also been done, notwithstanding many hindrances, in the promotion of education and civilisation, and all classes of the population have realised the manifold blessings of Christianity. We have now in connection with the Macarthy's Island station *one Missionary, one hundred and forty-nine church members*, and *one hundred and thirty-one scholars* in the Mission schools.

We must now return to the principal station at St. Mary's, and trace the course of events subsequent to the date last mentioned. Cheering as was the success of the Mission during the period of the writer's personal connection with it, the progress of the good work was still more remarkable in after years. It is a melancholy fact, however, that the history of this station is marked by similar affecting vicissitudes to those which have characterised our other Missions in Western Africa. During Mr. and Mrs. Fox's first period of service at St. Mary's, the congregations so far increased as to render necessary the erection of a new chapel at Bathurst, the principal town on the island, after the opening of which, in July, 1835, they embarked for England, having been relieved by the arrival, a few months before, of the Rev. Henry and Mrs. Wilkinson. In the year 1837, a fearful epidemic visited the country in the form of yellow fever, and swept off one half of the European population. One of those who fell at an early period of this awful visitation was the devoted missionary Mr. Wilkinson. He died happy in God on the 24th of August, having preached on the previous Sabbath from that striking text, "So teach us to number our days as to apply our hearts unto wisdom."

The Rev. Thomas Wall was immediately sent from England to supply the vacancy thus occasioned at St. Mary's. He arrived on the 26th of November, but, like that of many others, his course was soon run. He was cut down by fever on the 24th of August, 1838, and the station was for a time supplied by Mr. and Mrs. Swallow, from Macarthy's; but they had already suffered so much from fever that they were obliged soon afterwards to return to England. The next missionary appointed to St. Mary's was the Rev. J. E. Peard, who, with Mrs. Peard, embarked for the Gambia on the 23rd of November, 1838. This devoted couple were destined in the order of Providence never to set their feet on mission ground, for the *Columbine*, in which they sailed—the same vessel in which the writer and his wife returned from Western Africa a few years before—was overtaken by a severe storm in the English Channel, and driven upon the Chesil Bank, near Weymouth, where she became a total wreck, and every person on board perished in the waves. The bodies of the dear missionary and his wife were washed on shore some time afterwards, and buried in the Portland chapel yard, where a neat stone was erected to their memory, on which the writer has since gazed with feelings of mournful interest.

The Rev. James and Mrs. Parkinson were sent out to the Gambia towards the close of the same year. They arrived at St. Mary's on the 13th of September, 1838; but before they had been nine months in the colony they were both cut down by fever, under circumstances peculiarly painful and affecting. Mr. Parkinson finished his brief but active course of service on the 8th of September, 1839; and his dear wife followed him to the better country four days afterwards, having never been made acquainted with her sad bereavement, for fear the painful intelligence would be more than she could bear. A tender infant was left, which was sent to England soon afterwards, with the hope that its life might be saved; but it died on the passage, and so escaped from a world of sin and suffering to join the society of its sanctified parents in heaven.

The Rev. William Fox now returned to the Gambia after a visit to England, accompanied by Mrs. Fox and their little son, as well as by the Rev. William English. The missionary last named soon afterwards proceeded to the West Indies by order of the Committee, in consequence of the failure of his health and other untoward circumstances; and ere long his colleague was called to pass through the deep waters of affliction and bereavement. On the 17th of September, 1840, Mrs. Fox sank under a severe attack of malignant fever, four days after giving birth to a daughter, their infant son having been called away by death only a week before. Thus was the poor missionary left a lonely widower, with the care of a new-born infant on his hands. The little orphan was sent to England soon afterwards, in charge of Mr. Moss, who was obliged to return home early in the year 1841, having himself been bereaved of his beloved partner at Macarthy's Island. Mr. Fox nobly continued at his post of duty some time longer, and only returned to England finally in the month of May, 1843, after spending ten years in connection with the Gambia Mission.

The next missionaries appointed to the Gambia were the Revs. Mathew Godman and George Parsonson, who arrived there on the 5th of May, 1843. Mr. Parsonson proceeded at once to Macarthy's Island, according to appointment, and Mr. Godman took charge of the station at St. Mary's, where he laboured successfully for nearly three years, and was spared to return to England with his afflicted wife, who passed away to her reward in heaven soon after they landed on the shores of their native country. In the meantime the Society suffered a great loss by the death of Mr. Lynn, a trained teacher, who had gone out to take charge of the Mission School at Bathurst. Mr. Parsonson being now the only missionary remaining at the Gambia, as already mentioned, came down to St. Mary's till the arrival of the Rev. Messrs. Meadows and Lean on the 8th of December, 1847, when he also embarked for England, Mrs. Parsonson having been obliged to return some time before in consequence of illness.

Notwithstanding these repeated interruptions, the good work continued to advance among the people, and the respective stations on the Gambia appearing to require the supervision of a Missionary of some standing and experience, the Rev. Henry Badger was appointed as General Superintendent of the District. He arrived at St. Mary's from Sierra Leone, with Mrs. Badger, on the 21st of February, 1849, and was joined, the following year, by the Rev. Mr. Hirst from England. Mr. Badger having lost his devoted wife by death, returned home towards the close of 1852; and Mr. Meadows, who now returned from a visit to Europe, was appointed his successor as General Superintendent at the Conference of the following year. This zealous Missionary was soon afterwards joined by the Rev. John Bridgart, who was sent out to fill a vacancy, and the two brethren were permitted to labour together for some time, with little interruption from sickness, and with a pleasing measure of success. At length the health of Mr. Meadows gave way under the trying influence of the climate, and he returned to England in 1856. The Rev. A. J. Gurney was now sent out to supply the vacancy, and he arrived at St. Mary's in the month of November the same year. In a short time afterwards, Mr. Bridgart was compelled by sickness to embark for Europe; but having recruited his health, he returned to the Gambia with Mrs. Bridgart in November, 1857. The Rev. R. Cooper had arrived at St. Mary's somewhat earlier to supply the place of Mr. Gurney, who was removed to the Gold Coast, to fill an important vacancy there. The next Missionary sent from England was the Rev. J. H. Peet, who was appointed to succeed Mr. Bridgart on his removal to Sierra Leone in December, 1859.

For several years about this period the Missionaries were favoured to prosecute their useful labours with less interruption from sickness than formerly, till Mr. Cooper was suddenly smitten with fever, and finished his course on the 18th of August, 1859.

For some time Mr. Peet continued to labour alone at St. Mary's, till the arrival of the Rev. R. Daw, who was sent out to his assistance in the month of November, 1860. Both of these brethren were spared to return to England, after completing their allotted period of service at the Gambia; and the next Missionary appointed to St. Mary's was the Rev. Arthur A. Southerns, who was sent out in the year 1862, and who was also favoured to return home after labouring efficiently for two years, being relieved by the Rev. V. Tyas in 1864. Mr. Tyas endured the climate much better than many others, and being assisted by the Rev. Y. F. Clement, native assistant Missionary, he continued at his post of duty for more than four years, and did not return to England till 1869, when he was succeeded by the Rev. Henry J. Quilter, who embarked for St. Mary's on the 24th of October.

Although our observations in this brief historical sketch have been confined chiefly to the afflictions and bereavements which the Missionaries and their families have been called to experience in this trying climate, that the reader may fully comprehend the claims which they have upon his sympathy and prayers, it is a pleasing fact that during all those years of trial a blessed work was in progress at St. Mary's. From the head quarters of the Mission at Bathurst the light of Divine truth went forth to Soldier's Town, Jollar Town, Melville, and other villages on the small island of St. Mary; and also to Barra Point, and other places on the mainland, where out-stations were formed, chapels built, and schools established. We have now in connection with our station at St. Mary's *two Missionaries, five hundred and nine church members,* and *four hundred and eighty-nine scholars* in the Mission schools.

The Gold Coast.

That part of Western Africa called Guinea and the GOLD COAST is situated to the eastward of the Gambia and Sierra Leone, and stretches away towards the Bight of Benin. In its general features, appearance, climate, and productions, the country is very similar to other parts of the extensive Western Coast, and therefore needs no particular description here. With regard to the population, it may be sufficient to observe that it is to a considerable extent of the same mixed character as that which is found to prevail in other localities. It consists of a vast number of petty kingdoms or tribes, who live with a kind of independent government under their respective kings or chiefs. The principal of these are the Ashantis, Fantis, Dahomans, and Yarabans, all of whom are avowed pagans, Mahomedanism having made little impression upon this part of the vast continent.

It was not till a comparatively recent period that the Wesleyan Missionary Society was able to commence its labours on the Gold Coast, and the early history of the Mission was so clearly marked by the special providence of God that it is worthy of particular notice. A few native youths had learned to read the Bible at the Government school at Cape Coast Castle, the principal English settlement in those parts, and their minds became so deeply impressed with the contents of the Sacred Volume that they formed themselves into a little society for the more careful reading and study of the Holy Scriptures. As their supply of the precious volume was very limited, they agreed to send to England for a number of copies of the New Testament. They accordingly made their case known to Captain Potter, the master of a merchant vessel from Bristol, who happened to be there in the year 1834. The heart of this noble-minded Christian man was so interested in favour of these intelligent African youths, that, on his return to England, he not only secured the necessary supply of the Scriptures, but he also called at the Wesleyan Mission House in London, and generously offered to take out a Missionary to Cape Coast, free of expense to the Society, engaging, at the same time, to bring him home again, if the attempt to introduce the Gospel to this part of the Coast of Africa should prove a failure.

Believing that Divine Providence was opening the way before them, the Committee readily accepted this generous offer, and the Rev. Joseph Dunwell was appointed to commence the Mission on the Gold Coast. He sailed with Captain Potter on his return to Africa, and landed in safety at Cape Coast Castle on the 1st of

January, 1835. The zealous young Missionary was received with marked kindness by His Excellency Governor M'Lean, and with feelings of rapture by the native youths who were so anxious to be more fully instructed in a knowledge of God's Holy Word. He opened his commission to preach the Gospel in Africa under the most encouraging circumstances; and both at Cape Coast, and in other parts of Guinea which he visited, his labours were attended with evident tokens of the Divine presence and blessing. His career of useful labour, like that of many others on this pestilential coast, was, however, very short. He was attacked with fever of such a malignant type that it baffled the power of medical skill, and he died in peace on the 24th of June, before he had been six months in the country,—the first of a long list who fell in the holy conflict here also.

Some time after the lamented death of Mr. Dunwell, two other Missionaries and their wives, the Rev. George O. and Mrs. Wrigley, and the Rev. Peter and Mrs. Harrop, were sent out by the Committee to occupy the vacant station; the party first named arriving at Cape Coast on the 15th of September, 1836, and the others on the 15th of January, 1837. They commenced their work in good health and spirits, and laboured with much success during the short time they were permitted to live; but, within the short space of fifteen months, the whole of this noble band were numbered with the silent dead, having been cut down by fever in rapid succession. Indeed, both Mr. and Mrs. Harrop died in about three weeks after their arrival. They finished their course and were called to their reward in the following order:—Mrs. Harrop on the 5th of February, Mr. Harrop and Mrs. Wrigley on the 8th of February, and Mr. Wrigley on the 16th of November, 1837. We may imagine the feelings of the poor afflicted and bereaved Missionary, Mr. Wrigley, the last survivor of the four, when he was called to close the eyes of his beloved wife and those of his dear colleague in the same hour, and that within three days of the death of the first victim of the fatal malady with which they were seized. In writing to the Missionary Committee shortly afterwards, he says, "Life, indeed, in my circumstances, has no charms; nor could I support myself beneath the weight of such a stroke, were it not for the hope of ere long joining the glorified spirit of my devoted partner, and, in the meantime, of following up those victories of the Cross of our Immanuel, which together we have been enabled to achieve to His glory, since we arrived on these inhospitable shores." This hope of meeting in heaven the glorified spirits of the dear departed was soon realised; but the members of the infant church in the wilderness were once more left as "sheep having no shepherd."

The next Missionary sent out to the Gold Coast was the Rev. T. B. Freeman, who arrived at Cape Coast Castle, with his devoted and newly married wife, on the 3rd of January, 1838. The course of Mrs. Freeman was soon run however. She was seized with fever soon after she landed, and died on the 20th of February, within seven weeks of her arrival. On the 13th of January, 1840, the Rev. Josiah and Mrs. Mycock, and the Rev. Robert Brooking, arrived at Cape Coast to reinforce the Mission, and to enable Mr. Freeman to visit England. This party were all mercifully spared to return home after fulfilling different periods of service in Africa. Early in the year 1841, Mr. Freeman with Mrs. Freeman (second) returned to the Gold Coast, accompanied by the Rev. Thompson and Mrs. Hesk, and the Rev. Samuel A. and Mrs. Shipman, and the Rev. Messrs. Watson, Thackuray and Walden. They arrived at Cape Coast Castle on the 1st of February, and entered upon their work in good spirits. This was a large and valuable accession to the number of labourers in the Gold Coast District, but the ranks were soom thinned again by sickness and death. Mrs. Freeman died on the 25th of August following, and Mrs. Hesk three days afterwards. Two of the brethren of the party were also called to rest from their labours soon after their arrival, Mr. Thackuray on the 4th of May, and Mr. Walden on the 29th of July. Thus four out of the nine died within seven months of the date of their landing on the shores of Africa; and the fifth, Mr. Shipman, finished his course on the 22nd of February, 1843, after labouring with success for two years. Mr. Hesk and Mrs. Shipman returned to England almost immediately after their respective bereavements, and Mr. Watson was also spared to return home after fulfilling his appointed period of service in Western Africa.

In the month of January, 1842, the Mission on the Gold Coast was reinforced by the arrival from England of the Rev. William Allen, who was spared to return home after labouring efficiently for more than two years. This was not the case, however, with the Rev. Messrs. Wyatt and Rowlands, who arrived a few weeks afterwards. Mr. Wyatt fell a sacrifice to the climate on the 6th of April, when he had only been about three months in the country, and Mr. Rowlands was called away by death on the 10th of July, after a residence of about six months. The next Mission party sent out to Cape Coast consisted of the Rev. Benjamin and Mrs. Watkins, and the Rev. George Chapman, who reached their destination on the 23rd of January, 1843. Mrs. Watkins only lived thirty-nine days after her arrival, being called away on the 1st of March, after a short but painful illness. About thirteen months afterwards she was followed to the better country by her beloved husband, who finished his short course of useful labour on the 7th of February, 1844. Mr. Chapman was spared to return to England, and was afterwards usefully employed for many years as a Missionary in Southern Africa.

These painful bereavements rendered a fresh supply of Missionaries necessary, and the Rev. Samuel and Mrs. Annear, who had previously laboured at Sierra Leone, and the Revs. John Martin and Timothy T. Greaves were next sent out. They arrived at Cape Coast on the 12th of December, 1843. Mr. and Mrs. Annear and Mr. Martin were spared to return home in due time, and favoured to render useful service in other parts of the Lord's vineyard; but Mr. Greaves fell a sacrifice to the climate on the 14th of July, 1844, about seven months after his arrival. On the 20th of March, 1844, the Rev. Robert Brooking landed at Cape Coast the second time, accompanied by Mrs. Brooking. They were both mercifully spared to return to England in due time, and were afterwards usefully employed in Canada and in the Hudson's Bay Territory.

On the 23rd of June, 1845, the Rev. T. B. Freeman returned to the Gold Coast for the third time, accompanied by the Rev. Henry Wharton, a native of the West Indies, and himself the fruit of Missionary labour. Mr. Wharton had been brought to a saving knowledge of the truth, and trained for the Christian ministry on one of the stations occupied by the writer, and he was much delighted when his pupil and colleague nobly offered himself as a Missionary to the land of his forefathers. Being well adapted for the work, both mentally and physically, this zealous servant of the Lord has fully justified the anticipations of his friends in his appointment to Western Africa, where he has laboured successfully for more than twenty-five years. About this time also several native assistant Missionaries were raised up in the Gold Coast District to take a part in the good work. These accessions to the ranks of earnest labourers in this interesting but trying part of the Lord's vineyard were hailed with gratitude and joy by the friends of Missions, inasmuch as they exhibited fruit of the most desirable kind, and at the same time gave ground of hope that in future there would consequently be less exposure of European life in carrying on the work.

It was still necessary, however, to send a considerable number of Missionaries from England to supply the various stations which had been commenced in different parts of the country, and on the 30th of December, 1845, the Rev. William Allen arrived at Cape Coast, for the second time, accompanied by Mrs. Allen and the Rev. Messrs. Findlay and Addison. These were all spared to return to England after labouring successfully for two or three years, with the exception of Mr. Findlay, who was cut down by fever in the midst of his useful labours on the 10th of March, 1846, about eight months after his arrival. The next party of Missionaries sent out consisted of the Revs. John Thomas, John Harrop, and Charles Hilliard, who arrived at Cape Coast Castle on the 7th of January, 1847. They proceeded to their respective stations, and after fulfilling their appointed period of service in Western Africa, they were all spared to return to England, and were afterwards usefully employed in other parts of the Lord's vineyard.

In the month of March, 1849, the Rev. F. Hart arrived at Cape Coast, and towards the close of the following year he was joined by the Rev. Messrs. Gardener and Richards. Messrs. Hart and Richards were obliged to return to England at an early period on account of the failure of their health; but Mr. Gardener continued to labour on different stations in the Gold Coast District, with great acceptance and efficiency, for the long period of nine years, and after his return to England he was usefully employed in the home work.

In consequence of the increased number of native agents employed, and some improvement in the sanitary condition of the country, no additional Missionaries were required for some time after the date last mentioned, till, in 1856, the Rev. William and Mrs. West were sent out to take the general oversight of the work. These devoted servants of Christ had previously laboured for several years in the West Indies, and were well adapted for the work in Western Africa. They landed at Cape Coast on the 18th of November, and in the following year they were joined by the Rev. Alexander J. Gurney, from the Gambia. In the interim, the circumstances of the Gold Coast District appearing to require such a measure, the Missionary Committee in London sent out the Rev. Daniel West, as a special deputation, to examine into the state of the work; and, had he lived to report, in person, the result of his observations, the benefit to the Mission in future would, no doubt, have been considerable; but, in the order of Divine Providence, he was not permitted to see his native land again. He was seized with malignant fever, and died at the Gambia, where he had called on his homeward passage on the 24th of February, 1857.

The next Missionary sent out to Cape Coast was the Rev. W. H. Milward, in the year 1859; but he was soon obliged to return to England on account of the failure of his health. Mr. and Mrs. West and Mr. Gurney also returned the same year, having more than completed the term of their appointment. After these departures there was not one European Missionary remaining in the Gold Coast District. The labourers on all the stations were natives of Western Africa, themselves the fruits of our Missions planted there, with the exception of Mr. Wharton from the West Indies, who was charged with the management of the financial and other important matters connected with the general supervision of the work till the return of Mr. West the following year.

But pleasing as was the circumstance just mentioned in some respects, experience soon proved that, if the work was to be efficiently prosecuted, a supply of European Missionaries must be immediately provided. Hence, towards the close of the year 1860, the Rev. Thomas and Mrs. Champness, who had previously laboured at Sierra Leone, and the Rev. Messrs. Morris and Sharp, were sent out to the Gold Coast District. Mr. Morris was soon obliged to return to England, however, and was succeeded by the Rev. Alfred Taylor, who arrived at Cape Coast on the 18th of January, 1862, accompanied by the Rev. William West, who now went out to Western Africa as General Superintendent for the second time. In the year 1863 the Gold Coast District was further reinforced by the appointment of the Rev. Messrs. Davies, Gardiner, and Sykes, Mr. Champness having been obliged to return home on account of the failure of his health and the loss of his beloved wife, who died at Abbeokuta a few months before. Mr. Sykes was spared to return to England, after a long and honourable period of service in Western Africa, and has since been usefully employed in the home work.

The number of Missionaries in this part of the wide field having been reduced by the return to England of Messrs. Gardiner, Taylor, and Sharp, the Rev. Messrs. Richmond, Robinson, and Cuthbert, were sent out in 1864; but Mr. Cuthbert was cut down by fever at Lagos soon after his arrival. Messrs. Richmond and Robinson both suffered much from fever, but they were spared to return to England, with their health much shattered, after a short period of service on the coast. The Mission also suffered a serious loss about this time in the death of the Rev. Edward Bickersteth, an excellent and useful native minister. In 1866 Messrs. Taylor and Sharp, with their excellent wives, and the Rev. M. Grimmer returned to the coast, and for awhile resumed their beloved work, till sickness again compelled them to leave the coast. In 1868 the Rev. W.

West visited England once more; and during his stay in this country the writer had some very pleasant Christian intercourse with him as a worthy Missionary brother. As no suitable minister could be found to take his place as General Superintendent, Mr. West nobly volunteered to go out to the Gold Coast once more. He sailed on the 24th of January, 1869, accompanied by the Rev. Thomas R. Picott; the Rev. Joseph Rhodes having embarked for Lagos a few weeks before. Notwithstanding his willingness still further to serve the Mission cause in Western Africa, the debilitated state of Mr. West's health obliged him to return to England after the lapse of a few months; and on the 24th of October, the Rev. Matthew and Mrs. Grimmer embarked for Cape Coast, and the Rev. Thomas P. Spencer for Lagos. Mr. Grimmer, having previously laboured in the Gold Coast District with acceptance and success, now returned to Western Africa as Mr. West's successor in the general superintendency, with the advantage of considerable Missionary experience, and an acquaintance with the peculiarity of the climate, by which he was more fully adapted for his important position.

We have thus endeavoured to present the reader with a brief and consecutive account of the Gold Coast Mission, with special reference to the numerous bereavements and afflictions which have, from time to time, been experienced, after the plan adopted in treating of the work in other parts of Western Africa. A clearer view may thus be obtained of the manifold difficulties which attend the enterprise arising from the unhealthy character of the climate, to say nothing of those which spring from the heathen darkness and superstition which everywhere prevail. It is earnestly hoped that this will lead to an increase of sympathy and a larger amount of practical interest in the Missionaries and their work. At the same time, it is with sincere gratitude to Almighty God that we are able to record the pleasing fact that, amid all these difficulties, a blessed work has been in progress from year to year in the Gold Coast District. Important circuits and out-stations have been formed not only at Cape Coast Town, the head-quarters of the Mission, but at Dix Cove, Elmina,

Anamabu, Domonasi, James Town (Akrah), Winnibah, Lagos, Badagry, Whydah, Abbeokuta, and other places along the coast and far away into the interior. For some time Kumasi, the blood-stained capital of Ashanti, was occupied by the Missionaries, and the Gospel was faithfully preached to the King and his people, who delight in human sacrifices; and it is hoped that ere long the wars which have kept the country in a state of constant commotion will cease, and a way be opened for the proclamation of the Gospel of peace throughout the length and breadth of the land. At all these stations Christian congregations have been gathered, places of worship erected, Mission schools established, and a large amount of real spiritual good effected in the conversion of souls to God, to say nothing of the temporal advantages of civilisation and social improvement which invariably follow the introduction of Christianity. In connection with the Gold Coast District the Wesleyan Missionary Society has now *twelve Missionaries*, six of whom are native Africans, *two thousand one hundred and twenty-four church members*, and *one thousand three hundred and fifty-eight scholars* in the Mission schools.

Before we take leave of our important Missions on the western coast of Africa, we may with propriety glance at their aggregate result, not forgetting the peculiar circumstance under which they have been prosecuted from the unhealthy character of the climate. In the course of fifty years sixty-three Wesleyan Missionaries, and the wives of Missionaries, have fallen a sacrifice to the climate on our different stations in Western Africa, or have died at sea when proceeding to or from their respective appointments; and yet there is no lack of labourers. As one falls another, being baptized with the true Missionary spirit, volunteers to occupy his place, and so the good work is still carried on. Knowing the interest that is generally felt in such matters, we have dwelt more particularly upon the bereavements and afflictions which the Missionaries and their families have experienced than we should otherwise have done; and we consider those who thus go forth, with their lives in their hands, are worthy of the sympathy, the prayers, and the support of the friends of the Missions. At the same time, we wish

CHRISTIAN WOMEN OF WESTERN AFRICA.

it to be distinctly remembered that, in Western Africa, the work itself, irrespective of the hazardous nature of the climate, is of a most interesting character. The people are so simple-hearted, confiding, and affectionate, that they are easily led to the Saviour; and through God's blessing upon the faithful preaching of the Gospel, tens of thousands have been gathered into the fold of Christ, many of whom have landed in a brighter and better world above, whilst others are pressing on in the way to Zion. It is a pleasing sight to behold the change which has passed upon the natives, both males and females, in their appearance, dress, and manners, since they received the Gospel. Formerly they appeared in public almost in a state of nudity, without shame, and presented to the view of the Missionary a spectacle of the most revolting character; but now they are sensitive in their feelings, and appear in the house of God on the Sabbath and other occasions, neatly clothed in the native style, with an occasional mixture of European fashion. Nor are the direct spiritual results of the Mission less remarkable and gratifying, a rich blessing having attended the faithful preaching of the Word. We have now on our respective stations, on the Western Coast of Africa, *twenty-four Missionaries*, and about *eight thousand church members*, and *four thousand scholars* receiving instruction in the Mission schools.

We cannot close this chapter more appropriately than in the language of the Rev. Melville B. Cox, the first Methodist Missionary sent from America to the Coast of Africa. He landed at the Gambia during the residence of the writer there, in 1832, spent a few weeks with us very pleasantly, proceeded to Liberia, and in about three months he sickened and died. Before he left his native shores he said to a friend, "I go to that land of sickness and death; but if I die, you must come and write my epitaph." It was asked, "What shall I write?" "Write," said the devoted Missionary, "THOUGH A THOUSAND FALL, LET NOT AFRICA BE FORGOTTEN!"

CHAPTER V.
SOUTHERN AFRICA.

HISTORICAL NOTICES—NATIVE TRIBES—CAPE OF GOOD HOPE DISTRICT—GRAHAM'S TOWN DISTRICT—QUEEN'S TOWN DISTRICT—BECHUANA DISTRICT—NATAL DISTRICT.

SOUTHERN AFRICA may be said to comprise the whole of that portion of the great continent which lies to the south of the equator. It is bounded on the east by the Indian Ocean, on the west by the Atlantic, on the north by the unexplored regions of the interior, and on the south by the stormy waters of the ocean which wash the immediate shores of the Cape of Good Hope. In a country of such vast extent, being about two thousand miles in length and nearly the same in breadth, we necessarily find great diversity of scenery, soil, and climate. There are some striking features, however, which appear to apply pretty generally to the whole of this extensive and interesting portion of the globe. Everything which presents itself to our view on the continent of Africa is on a grand and gigantic scale. There is nothing little or insignificant in the topography of the country. Every scene in nature corresponds with the magnitude of the vast continent on which it is found. The mountains generally rise to a high altitude, and frequently stretch away in apparently interminable chains as far as the eye can reach, till they are lost in the dim distance. The valleys, the rivers, the lakes, and the deserts are equally imposing in their general aspect. Although Southern Africa abounds with large tracts of desert, rocky, barren land entirely unfit for cultivation, and affording but scanty pasturage for domestic cattle or wild animals in the most favourable seasons, there are here and there fertile valleys with a productive soil which would amply repay the labour of the husbandman. The produce of the country consists of timber, corn, wool, wine, aloes, dried fruits, hides, horns, skins, tallow, ivory, ostrich feathers, copper ore, and diamonds, for exportation, besides the ordinary necessaries of life for home consumption. On the whole, the climate is said to be healthy, although the heat during the summer months is somewhat oppressive to Europeans.

The discovery of Southern Africa is by general consent awarded to Bartholomew Diaz, a native of Portugal, who flourished in the latter part of the fourteenth century. The enterprising navigator having been commissioned by his sovereign, John II., to seek for a maritime passage to India, embarked on his perilous voyage in the year 1486. After tracing upwards of two thousand miles of the unknown western coast of the great continent, he proceeded southward till he came in sight of the bold promontory, since designated "Table Mountain," which is the terminating point of Africa in that direction. Here he was overtaken by a violent tempest, which for the time obstructed his further progress; and, having named the peninsula which he had discovered "The Cape of Storms," he returned to his own country, supposing he had reached the utmost practical limits of navigation in the southern hemisphere. The King of Portugal, however, was more sanguine in his views; and, anticipating still further success, he changed the name of the great southern promontory discovered by Diaz to that of "The Cape of Good Hope." He, moreover, commissioned the navigator to proceed on a second voyage of discovery with a view to explore the unknown regions beyond; but on this occasion Diaz met with still greater disasters, and ultimately perished in a storm, and found a watery grave not far from the place where he was obliged to relinquish his first enterprise.

About ten years afterwards, the celebrated navigator Gama was employed in the service of his enterprising sovereign, Emanuel II., when he succeeded in doubling the Cape; and, on his return, reported the result to the king, who immediately despatched other ships for the purpose of examining more minutely a place which appeared to be of great importance in its relation to India. On reaching the Cape the vessels anchored in Table Bay, near Robin Island, and the sailors lowered their boats and went on shore, where they found a barren country, inhabited by wandering tribes of Hottentots, who were living in a state of extreme barbarism.

Although the Cape of Good Hope was thus discovered by the Portuguese, it does not appear that they established any permanent settlement there, but merely used it as a convenient place of call and refreshment for their ships, when on their way to and from India. It seems also to have been used by the English for the same purpose, inscriptions, evidently by our countrymen, having been found on trees and rocks with the respective dates of 1604, 1620 and 1622. The Dutch were wiser in their generation; and in the year 1652, they took formal possession of this part of Southern Africa, and formed a settlement where Cape Town now stands, with a strong fortress, called "The Castle," to secure themselves against the attacks of the savage natives. In 1795, when the powers of Europe were at war with each other, the Cape of Good Hope was captured by the British under Sir James Craig; and in the month of May, 1797, Lord Macartney arrived from England to take charge of the Government. In 1802, the colony was restored to the Dutch at the Peace of Amiens; but on the breaking out of war again in 1806, it was retaken by the English, under Sir David Baird. Since this period it has continued in our possession, and the colony has gradually advanced to its present state of prosperity.

If we would obtain a correct view of Southern Africa as a field of Missionary labour, we should make ourselves acquainted with the map of the country and carefully trace its various divisions, mountains, rivers, and the localities of important places. There we should see the relative position of the Cape Colony, British Kaffraria, the Colony of Natal, the Orange Free State, the Transvaal Republic, Kaffirland, Griqualand, Basutuland, Zululand, Bushmanland, Namaqualand, Damaraland, and Ovampoland. In addition to these countries which have been explored and described by Missionaries and travellers, there are other and extensive regions, stretching away into the vast interior of the continent, which are as yet comparatively unknown; but to which it is hoped the Gospel of Christ will be ultimately carried by the messengers of the churches.

That portion of the great continent now under review, and which is known by the general name of Southern Africa, is inhabited by people of various nations and tribes, of different shades of complexion, and speaking a great variety of languages or dialects. Some of these may be regarded as aborigines, properly so-called; whilst many more have come from distant regions, settled in the country, and adopted it as their home. Perhaps the *Hottentots* have the best claim to the title of original inhabitants. They were a numerous race of people when the country first became known to Europeans; and, although their number has greatly decreased of late years, by amalgamation with other tribes and otherwise, those who still remain, especially the poor despised Bushmen, have strong claims upon our sympathy and benevolence, as they are a people deeply degraded by vice and oppression. When we hear or read of Namaquas, Korannas, Griquas, and other coloured or mixed races of people in Southern Africa, we must bear in mind that they are all of Hottentot descent. The *Kaffirs* are a bold, daring, independent, and warlike people, never having been enslaved and oppressed like the poor Hottentots. They are supposed to have come originally from the north, and to have driven the comparatively weak and timid aborigines towards the Cape. They live in different tribes under the government of separate chiefs, and are known as the Amakossas, Amampondas, Amazulus, &c. The Bechuanas, Damaras, and other tribes, although speaking different languages, must all be referred, in our opinion, to a Kaffir origin. There are also a number of *Negroes*, properly so-called, living in Southern Africa. Most of these have been brought originally from the eastern or western coasts, where they were rescued from slave ships by British cruisers. They are known by the general name of Liberated Africans, and are a useful and industrious class of labourers. There is also in the colony a considerable population of *Malays*,—the descendants of slaves brought by the Dutch settlers from Java many years ago,—who are generally a quiet and industrious class of mechanics, shopkeepers, and domestic servants, notwithstanding their rigid Mohammedanism. In addition to these various tribes and classes of men, we have in Southern Africa the usual variety of European colonists, as Dutch, English, Scotch, Irish, French, German, and others.

For many years after the commencement of European colonisation in Southern Africa little or nothing was done for the spiritual benefit of the people. The Dutch gave great prominence to the forms of religion among themselves, as colonists; but the natives, or heathens, as they always called them, were regarded as outcasts from God's covenant, and were enslaved and severely oppressed in various ways, not being allowed even to enter their places of worship. It was not till a comparatively recent period that the Dutch Reformed Church awoke up to a recognition of the spiritual claims of the aborigines, and of coloured people in general. Although they are still too frequently excluded from their regular sanctuaries, of late years Missions and schools have been established for their benefit in several places. The Moravians had the honour of being first in the field as Missionaries to the Hottentots and Kaffirs. Their first station in Southern Africa was commenced at Genadendal by the Rev. George Schmidt, who went out in 1737; and they have now seven or eight other similar establishments in different parts of the country, which have served as so many asylums for the oppressed in times of trouble, as well as places of religious instruction for the poor neglected natives.

The London Missionary Society also commenced its labours in Southern Africa at an early period. The eccentric, but zealous Dr. Vanderkemp, their first Missionary, went out in 1799; but it was not till several years afterwards that he and his colleagues gained a permanent footing in the country by the establishment of their first station at Bethelsdorp, near Algoa Bay, and by the introduction of the Gospel to other localities. The agents of this respectable and useful Society now occupy a considerable number of stations both within and beyond the colonial boundary, and their labours have been attended with a cheering measure of success. In this wide field of Christian enterprise the Church of England, the Church of Scotland, the Dutch Reformed Church, and the Rhenish, Berlin, Hamburg, and French Protestant Missionary Societies also employ a number of zealous labourers; and, as a general rule, the Missionaries of the respective institutions labour together in much harmony and love, there being no occasion for jealousy, as there is ample room and abundant work for all. We now call the attention of the reader to the origin and progress of Wesleyan Missions in this part of the world, classifying them according to the ecclesiastical arrangements of the church to which they belong.

Cape of Good Hope District.

It was not until the year 1814 that the Wesleyan Missionary Society was in a position to take its share in the evangelisation of Southern Africa, when the Rev. John M'Kenny was sent out as the first Missionary. He arrived, with Mrs. M'Kenny, in Cape Town on the 7th of August; but, such was the jealousy of the Government authorities at that early period, that the Missionary was not allowed to open his commission, or to preach in the colony, although he produced credentials of the most satisfactory character. All that he could do, under the circumstances, was to hold private meetings for conversation and prayer, with a few pious soldiers and others who had hailed his arrival with gratitude and joy, and patiently to await the result of his representations to the Missionary Committee in London. Before the difficulties in the way of the establishment of the Mission could be removed, Mr. M'Kenny was instructed to proceed to Ceylon, where he was afterwards made very useful in the service of his Divine Master.

The Society in England was not disposed, however, to relinquish its efforts for the spiritual welfare of the degraded tribes of

CAPE TOWN AND TABLE MOUNTAIN.

Southern Africa in consequence of the comparative failure of its first experiment, and next appointed the Rev. Barnabas Shaw to attempt the commencement of a Wesleyan Mission in the Cape Colony. He landed in Cape Town, with Mrs. Shaw, on the 14th of April, 1815; but, on presenting his credentials to the Governor, he met with no better success than his predecessor. His Excellency declined to give the Missionary permission to preach in Cape Town, on the ground that the English and Dutch colonists were provided with ministers, whilst the owners of slaves were unwilling to have them religiously instructed. But Mr. Shaw was of too ardent a temperament to brook delay, and he ventured to take the matter into his own hand. He naïvely says, " Having been refused the sanction of the Governor, I was resolved what to do, and commenced without it on the following Sabbath. My congregations at first were chiefly composed of pious soldiers; and it was in a room hired by them that I first preached Christ and Him crucified in South Africa."

Although it would appear that the Government authorities took no notice for the time being of this infringement of their regulations, yet the spirit of prejudice against Missionary efforts prevailed among the colonists to such an extent, that Mr. Shaw was much discouraged, as he saw little prospect of good in Cape Town. Under these circumstances he longed for an opening to preach the Gospel to the heathen in the far distant interior, where he might labour to win souls for Christ without being subject to the annoyances and hinderances which he experienced in the colony. At length an opportunity was afforded of engaging in an enterprise on which his heart had long been fixed. The Rev. Mr. Schmelen, of the London Society, arrived in Cape Town from Great Namaqualand on a visit, and he made such representations of the openings for Missionary labour in that country, that Mr. and Mrs. Shaw resolved to accompany him on his return, according to his kind invitation. A waggon and a span of oxen, with stores, and all other requisites, were accordingly purchased, and every other necessary preparation for their long journey was made; and on the 6th of September, 1815, the Missionaries, with their families and attendants, took their departure, being accompanied for some distance by a few friends from Cape Town.

The Missionary party had pursued their toilsome journey for nearly a month, and had crossed the Elephant River, when, on the 4th of October, by a remarkable providence, Mr. Shaw found an opening for a suitable sphere of labour. He actually met with the chief of Little Namaqualand, accompanied by four men, on his way to Cape Town, to seek for a Christian teacher, being aware of the advantages which other tribes had realised by the reception of the Gospel. Having heard his affecting story, and being deeply impressed with the fact that the finger of God was pointing in the direction in which he ought to go, the Missionary agreed to accompany the chief to his mountain home, and to take up his abode with him and his people, whilst Mr. Schmelen continued his journey to his own station in Great Namaqualand. About three weeks afterwards, on the 23rd, Mr. and Mrs. Shaw, with the chief and his party, reached Lily Fountain, on Khamiesberg, the principal home of the tribe of Little Namaquas; and the foundation of an interesting Mission was laid, which, from that day to this, has continued to exercise a most beneficial influence on all around.

As the waggon ascended the mountain, and long before it reached the chief's "great place," the Missionary was met by a party of more than twenty natives, mounted on oxen, and riding at full gallop. They had heard the good news, and came to welcome their teacher to the country, and especially to have a "good look" at *Juffrouw*, the Missionary's wife, whom they surveyed with feelings of reverence and awe, never having seen a real white lady before. On reaching the end of their journey, and outspanning for the night, a council was held by the chief and his head men respecting the arrival of the Missionary, when they all entreated Mr. and Mrs. Shaw to remain with them, promising to assist in every possible way in the establishment of the Mission. The Missionary, therefore, immediately opened his commission by proclaiming to the wondering natives, the glad tidings of salvation in the open air, and by teaching both old and young, as he had opportunity, the elements of religion, and the use of letters, by means of which they might ultimately be able to read for themselves the Book of God. It was trying work, and required much patience; but labour, prayer, faith, perseverance, were eventually rewarded with a pleasing measure of success. Not only did a number of children and young people learn to read with tolerable facility, but the hearts of several were brought under the influence of Divine grace, and a native church was formed of living, faithful members, who were a credit to their religious profession. At the same time the civilising influences of Christianity were brought to bear upon the people; and, from year to year, their temporal condition was materially improved, so that they experienced the truth of the Apostle's declaration, "Godliness is profitable unto all things, having the promise of the life that now is, and of that which is to come."

Whilst the Missionary was thus endeavouring to instruct the people, he had to labour hard at intervals to build a house to live in, and a humble sanctuary for the public worship of Jehovah. In the accomplishment of these undertakings many difficulties had to be overcome. The people, although willing to assist, had never been accustomed to continuous labour, and some ludicrous scenes were witnessed in the progress of the work. When the buildings were ready for the roofs, no trees fit for timber could be found within a day's journey of the station; but when they arrived at the place, the Missionary produced for the first time his cross-cut saw, himself working at one end and a Namaqua at the other, great was the joy of the people on beholding the result; and they could scarcely be restrained from cutting more timber than was required, from their delight to witness the performance of the instrument as one tree after another fell to the ground.

Nor were their delight and surprise the less on seeing the first plough set to work, which the Missionary had made chiefly with his own hands. The old chief stood upon a hill for some time in mute astonishment. At length he called to his councillors, at a short distance, saying, "Come and see this strange thing which Mynheer has brought. Look how it tears up the ground with its iron mouth! If it goes on so all the day, it will do more work than ten wives!" Hitherto the work of tilling the ground had been left to the women and slaves; but the introduction of the Gospel into the country was destined to mark a new era in agricultural pursuits as well as in the moral condition of the people. Mr. Shaw had taken with him to Africa a few garden seeds, the rapid growth of which amused the natives very much; but when they saw the use to which the lettuce and other salads were appropriated, they laughed heartily, saying, "If the Missionary and his wife can eat grass, they need never starve!" These and many other amusing incidents the writer has often heard Mr. Shaw relate with characteristic humour when associated with him in Missionary labours in the same country in after years.

The friends of Missions in England were delighted to hear of the success which attended these efforts to establish the first Wesleyan station in Southern Africa. There was, moreover, a charm about Mr. Shaw's simple and touching communications as they appeared in the "Missionary Notices," from month to month, which had a powerful tendency to awaken and sustain a deep and lively interest in the Missionary enterprise. At that early period, the claims of the Friendly and Fiji Islands, and other interesting fields of Missionary labour which have since occupied such a prominent place in the public mind, had scarcely been heard of, and the attention of the British churches was, to a considerable extent, fixed on Africa. Hence the peculiar interest with which intelligence from the newly-established Mission was received; and the names of Barnabas Shaw and his Namaqua station became household words in many a Methodist family in the United Kingdom, who cheerfully contributed of their substance to support the work, as the Lord had prospered them.

When the Mission was fully organised, Mr. Shaw required assistance, and the Rev. Edward Edwards was sent out from England to join him. He arrrived in Cape Town in the early part of 1818, and, as there was no waggon to convey him and his baggage to the scene of his future labours, he performed the journey to Khamiesberg, a distance of nearly four hundred miles, on horseback—a feat which gave good promise that he was made of the true Missionary metal, which was amply verified in after years.* Arrangements were now made for the extension to various out-stations in the Underveldt and in Bushmanland, as well as for repeated visits to Cape Town for supplies, which appear to have been unavoidable at that early period. In the month of July, 1819, the Mission in Namaqualand was further reinforced by the arrival at Khamiesberg of the Rev. John and Mrs. Archbell, who soon afterwards proceeded to a place called Reed Fountain, to commence a new station. This enterprise not answering the expectation of the Missionaries, Mr. Archbell made an experimental journey of several hundred miles to the northward, travelling through Great Namaqualand, and part of Damaraland to Walvich Bay. Mr. Shaw also paid a visit to his friend, Mr. Schmelen, at Bethany, in Great Namaqualand; and, although the way did not open at that time for the establishment of permanent stations in those remote regions, much valuable information was collected in reference to a part of the continent hitherto unexplored by Europeans.

Before we advert further to other scenes of Missionary labour in Southern Africa, it may be best to trace the subsequent history of the first station that was established at Lily Fountain on Khamiesberg. Under the judicious management of the Rev. Messrs. Edwards, Haddy, Jackson, Bailie, Parsonson and Godman, in succession, after the removal of Mr. Shaw, the good work continued to prosper in all its departments, notwithstanding numerous difficulties which have tended to impede its progress. When the

---

* The Rev. E. Edwards was spared to labour as a Missionary in Southern Africa for upwards of half a century; and, by his amiable disposition, simple piety, and untiring zeal, he not only did good service in the cause of his Divine Master, but endeared himself to his ministerial brethren and the people generally. During ten happy years the writer was associated with him in Missionary labours, and always found him the same cautious, humble, and devoted servant of Christ. In 1867 a religious service was held at Stellenbosch, where Mr. Edwards had laboured the longest, to celebrate the jubilee of his arrival in Africa, when a touching address and testimonial were presented to him, by his brethren, and flock. On the 6th of April in the following year, he finished his course with joy at Mowbray, amid the lamentations of many who had profited by his ministry, in the seventy-sixth year of his age.

old chief died it was thought desirable not to appoint a successor, but to let the government of the tribe devolve upon a number of councillors, especially as the institution lands were now included within the colonial boundary, and the people consequently amenable to British law. The community consists of about one thousand persons, occupying a large tract of land reserved for their use by the Colonial Government, some portions of which they cultivate, whilst the rest is left for the pasturage of their cattle. This territory was secured to the people through the intervention of the writer in 1855, by a regular diagram and grant signed by the Governor General, Sir George Cathcart. From the peculiarity of the climate, the whole body of the people with their stock have to remove from their mountain home into the lowlands, called the Underveldt, during the winter months. In these temporary emigrations they are accompanied by the Missionary and his family, who take up their abode for the time being at a secondary station, called Bethel, where a rude dwelling-house and chapel have been erected for their accommodation. In times of drought the people are moreover widely dispersed, to find grass and water for their stock, on which they mainly depend for subsistence; and, when the crops fail, they are frequently hard pressed for want of food for themselves, and fodder for their cattle.

When the Mission was first commenced, scarcely any of the natives understood either Dutch or English, and the Missionary had to preach through the medium of an interpreter; but now all the services are conducted in the Dutch language, which is generally understood both by old and young, whilst a few are gradually becoming acquainted with English. Such have been some of the drawbacks to the progress of religious knowledge and civilisation. Considerable advancement has, nevertheless, been made, and the Little Namaquas belonging to Lily Fountain Missionary Institution afford a fine specimen of the benefits conferred by Christianity on the natives of Southern Africa. With this fact the writer was deeply impressed on two occasions when he visited the station, during the time that he was in charge of the Cape of Good Hope District, nearly forty years after the commencement of the work by the venerable Barnabas Shaw. A brief account of these visits may form an appropriate sequel to that of this interesting Mission already given.

The first visit of the writer to Little Namaqualand was in the month of July, 1858, in company with his friend Mr. James Morris. After a toilsome journey through the wilderness, we arrived at Bethel on Friday, the 14th, and were glad to find that the resident Missionary, the Rev. J. A. Bailie, and the people of the station had already removed to the Underveldt for the winter months. Saturday was spent in conversing with Mr. Bailie and a few of the head men on various matters pertaining to the religious and temporal interests of the institution, the result of which was very satisfactory. Towards evening a number of natives arrived at the station from distant places, some in waggons, and others on horseback, to pay their respects to "oud Mynheer," as they were pleased to call the general superintendent, and to be ready for the services of the Sabbath. At an early hour on Sunday morning we were awoke by the singing of the natives, who had already assembled in the adjoining chapel to hold their usual prayer-meeting. We immediately arose, and joined them in their devotions. The prayers were offered partly in Dutch and partly in Namaqua; and, although we could not understand all that was said, their supplications were apparently so fervent and so sincere, that we felt it good to be there. At ten o'clock the writer preached to an attentive congregation of about two hundred Namaquas, Mr. Bailie kindly interpreting. There was an evident manifestation of Divine influence, and it was a season long to be remembered.

At the close of this service the writer read to the congregation a beautiful, simple, and affectionate letter, of which he was the bearer, from their old friend and minister, the venerable Barnabas Shaw. The following is the substance in a free translation: "My dear friends, many years have passed since I was at Khamiesberg. In this time many of my friends have been removed; and I hope they rest with Christ in heaven. You and I are following them, and I hope to get safe home. Let us continue to watch and pray, and so shall we obtain help and support from our Saviour and

Redeemer. It will be thirty-seven years on the fourth of next October since I met the chief, old Gert Links, old Adam, Jan Willem, and Peter Links, near Rimhoogte, Elephant's River. How good and gracious the Lord has been to us all these years! 'What shall we render unto the Lord for all His benefits?' Let us give our hearts more fully to Jesus Christ, and cleave to Him. He will never leave us. He will never forsake us. You old people, walk uprightly before the young ones, and pray for them continually. You young men and women, hearken to the aged, and help them in all things. But I must conclude by praying that 'the grace of our Lord Jesus Christ, and the love of God, and the fellowship of the Holy Ghost may be with you all.' I hope to see many men, women, and children of Namaqualand in heaven."

When this letter was handed to old Gert Links in the name and on behalf of the rest of the people, with the charge to read it to them again and again, tears stood in his eyes; and, with a heart evidently full of emotion, the old man uttered a sentence or two, which, when translated, were in substance as follows:—"Yes, sir, we do not forget our old teachers; but we love them still. When Mr. Shaw first came among us with the Gospel, he brought us a treasure more precious than gold." In the evening we held a service in English for the benefit of the Mission family, and on the following day resumed our journey to visit the still more remote stations beyond the great Orange River. On our return to the Cape we passed over Khamiesberg; but being in the depth of winter everything wore a cheerless aspect. We were overtaken by a snow-storm on the top of the mountain, in which we lost one of our horses and were glad to escape to the plains below on our homeward journey, where we found a milder climate.

The second visit of the writer to Khamiesberg was in the month of October, 1855, and under more favourable circumstances for thoroughly examining the state of the institution. The Missionary and the people at Lily Fountain, the principal station, had just completed the erection of a beautiful new chapel, to the opening services of which they had cordially invited their General

Superintendent. This commodious sanctuary, capable of accommodating six hundred people, built of stone, in the Gothic style of architecture, had cost about £1,000, and yet it had been erected by the united efforts and contributions of the people, without any foreign aid, with the exception of the gift of the pulpit by a few friends in Cape Town. It is a striking monument of the genius, zeal, and liberality of both the Missionary and his flock, as well as a tangible proof of the progress of religion and civilisation among a people whom the Gospel has raised from a state of the deepest moral degradation. The new chapel was filled with a congregation of deeply attentive and well-dressed natives, and at the first of the opening services the collection amounted to £16 4s. 0d., although money is but little used in that country. *One hundred and eighty-four persons were found united in church fellowship*, and *three hundred scholars* were attending the Mission schools. In a meeting which was afterwards held for Christian counsel, some of the aged members bore honourable testimony to the regenerating power of Divine grace, as realised in their own experience, as well as to the beneficial effects of the Gospel generally on the whole community. Abundant evidences also appeared of material progress and improvement in the temporal affairs of the people. About seven hundred acres of land had been brought under cultivation, and the natives belonging to the institution owned about one hundred ploughs, thirty waggons, two thousand five hundred horned cattle, four hundred horses, and seven thousand sheep and goats. The good work of civilisation and religious instruction has also been extended to Norap, Kaauewgoed Vlekte, Roodebergs Kloof, and other out-stations, with much advantage to the people.

Before we leave the western coast of Southern Africa we must briefly notice the labours of the Wesleyan Missionary Society in the more remote regions of Great Namaqualand, beyond the Orange River. The agents of the London Missionary Society having been withdrawn from that part of the continent, the country was left without any means of religious instruction for several years, and war and tumult prevailed in every part of the land. Notwithstanding the unsettled state of the native tribes, accounts were brought to Khamiesberg at different times, that, in some places, the people were willing to receive Missionaries, and our brethren there were anxious to extend to them the blessings of the Gospel; but, for awhile, the means were wanting.

At length, in the year 1825, the way for the extension of the work to Great Namaqualand seemed to open. The Rev. William Threlfall, who had just arrived at Khamiesberg for the benefit of his health, after an unsuccessful attempt to establish a Mission at Delagoa Bay, offered to take a journey of observation; and about the end of June he left Lily Fountain, with the permission of his Superintendent, Rev. B. Shaw, accompanied by Jacob Links and Johannes Jager, two native teachers. They were mounted on oxen, after the fashion of the country, and travelled without molestation till they had got two or three days' journey beyond the Orange River. At this point they came in contact with troublesome wandering tribes of Bushmen. Although they had with them a few goods for barter, they suffered much for want of food, the people being unfriendly and unwilling to supply them. They obtained a guide at a certain Bushman village; but he and his companions formed a plot for the destruction of the whole Mission party, that they might take possession of their effects. The following night, while Mr. Threlfall and his companions were sleeping under a bush, as usual, without the slightest apprehension of danger, their foes came upon them, and murdered them in cold blood. And, although the principal culprit was afterwards apprehended, tried, condemned, and executed for his crime, the sad disaster cast a gloom over the Mission cause, and put an end, for the time being, to any further attempts to establish a Mission to the north of the Orange River.

On the 11th of August, 1826, however, the chief of the tribe called Bundlezwarts, with ten of his people, arrived at the Mission Station at Khamiesberg from the Warm Bath, having come to request that a Missionary might be sent to his country; but the Rev. R. Haddy being alone on the institution at the time, was unable to comply with his request. The chief afterwards visited Cape Town with the same object in view; but, the Missionaries being few in number, he was obliged to wait a little longer without a teacher.

At length, in the year 1832, the way seemed to open once more, and the Rev. E. Cook was appointed to commence the new Mission in Great Namaqualand. He took up his residence with the Bundlezwarts at the Warm Bath, now called "Nisbett Bath," in honour of Josiah Nisbett, Esq., of the Madras Civil Service, by whose benevolent contributions the Mission was materially aided in its commencement. Mr. Cook laboured with success for several years in Great Namaqualand, and at length died in his travelling waggon, happy in God, on the banks of the Orange River, on the 7th of March, 1848, when on his way to the Cape for the benefit of his health. The work so auspiciously begun by this devoted Missionary was nobly carried on by the Rev. Messrs. Ridsdale, Bailie, Tindall, Ridgill, Thomas, and Priestley, who were appointed to labour there in succession; and at different periods gracious revivals of religion were experienced, hundreds of poor sinners being gathered into the fold of Christ, and made happy in the pardoning love of God.

It must be admitted, however, that the work was, on the whole, very fluctuating, owing chiefly to the migratory habits of the people, rendered necessary by the frequent occurrence of droughts and the sterile character of the country over which they roam to find pasturage for their cattle, and the impossibility of cultivating any portion of the soil for their subsistence. Supplies of corn for the use of the Mission families had to be brought from Khamiesberg, a distance of two hundred miles. These circumstances have always been a great drawback to the progress of the work of God, and have materially retarded the advancement of religious instruction and civilisation among the people in this part of the Mission field.

In addition to the work among the Bundlezwarts at Nisbett Bath, a station was established at Bleijdeverwacht,—afterwards called Hoole's Fountain, in honour of our senior Missionary Secretary,—for the benefit of Africaner's tribe. This place is beautifully situated, the village being on the margin of a periodical river, and surrounded by bold and romantic scenery. Although seventy-five miles distant from the principal station, Hoole's Fountain was for many years regularly visited by the Missionaries with good effect for the spiritual interests of the people, till a large number of them removed to Damaraland along with their chief Jonker, when the population was considerably reduced, and the station rendered less important.

In the year 1858, when on a tour of inspection to ascertain the state of all the interior stations in the Cape of Good Hope District, the writer crossed the Orange River and proceeded to Nisbett Bath, where he found the Rev. Joseph Tindall and his gifted son usefully employed in the work of the Mission. There had been a long drought in the country, and the people were scattered in various directions to find grass for their cattle, and consequently the station appeared to great disadvantage. A tolerable congregation assembled, however, on the Sabbath, and marked attention was paid to the word preached. Although not so far advanced in civilisation and religious knowledge as the people at Khamiesberg, the condition of the natives clearly showed how much they had been benefited by the reception of the Gospel, and it presented a striking contrast to that of those who were still involved in heathen darkness. Accompanied by the Rev. Henry Tindall and Mr. James Morris, the writer visited Hoole's Fountain, and although one hundred men and ten waggons had just left the station on their annual hunting expedition to supply themselves with meat for the winter season, we had a considerable gathering of people at our religious services, especially of old men, women, and children.

A meeting which was held with the people of Hoole's Fountain on this occasion, at their encampment in the open field, will never be forgotten. The natives assembled after sunset around the evening camp-fire, which was constantly supplied with bundles of faggots that had been collected during the day for the purpose by the school children. We had singing, prayer, and speaking, in three different languages, that all might understand. As the blaze of the fire, which was kept up to give light rather than warmth,

SOUTHERN AFRICA.

SCHOOL'S FOUNTAIN MISSION STATION, GREAT NAMAQUALAND, 1855.

occasionally cast its lurid glare on the sable countenances of the people by which it was encircled, now radiant with Christian intelligence and joy, it was almost impossible to refrain from expressions of gratitude to God for what the Gospel had done for them. This feeling was further enhanced by the noble testimony of some of the old men, as to the great change which had taken place since the Missionaries came among them, before which the different tribes often met in deadly conflict not far from the place where we were assembled; but now they were united in Christian harmony, love, and peace. We found in connection with our stations in Great Namaqualand *two hundred and fifty-nine church members*, and about *four hundred scholars* attending the Mission schools during the most favourable seasons of the year.

But we cannot quit this interesting country without a passing glance at a still more distant field of labour. When Jonker Africaner had removed from Bleijdeverwacht to Damaraland, with a number of his people, and desired the services of a Missionary, the way seemed to open for the introduction of the Gospel to the regions beyond; and in 1842, Mr. Cook paid his first visit to that country. This led to the appointment, some time afterwards, of the Rev. Messrs. Haddy and Tindall, who established stations at places which they called Concordiaville, Elephant Fountain, and Wesley Vale; and they laboured for some time with pleasing prospects of success. Afterwards, however, they had reason to be discouraged by the restless, wandering and warlike propensities of the people, and the difficulties connected with obtaining supplies of stores from the colony for the support of themselves and their families. In the meantime a number of German Missionaries connected with the Rhenish Society had established themselves in various places in Great Namaqualand and Damaraland; and it was ultimately thought best to withdraw our men and transfer our Stations on the South Western coast of Africa beyond the Orange River to the Germans; who, having few Missions elsewhere, seemed in a better position than our Society to supply them with an adequate amount of labour. Whilst this arrangement might convey to the minds of some the idea of entire failure in this department of Missionary enterprise, we view it in quite another light, and sincerely trust that it will one day appear that the labour spent on those remote regions of Southern Africa by the Wesleyan Missionary Society was not in vain in the Lord.

We must now call the attention of the reader to the progress of the work in the capital of the Cape Colony. Although the first Wesleyan Missionaries to Southern Africa found ample scope for their labours in Namaqualand, when prohibited from exercising their vocation in Cape Town, and had reason to acknowledge the providence of God in all their ways, they did not lose sight of the claims of the metropolis, or relinquish the hope that they might some day be able to form a Station there as the basis of operation for the extension of the work in other directions. When the brethren in the interior had occasion to visit Cape Town for supplies, they gladly availed themselves of every opportunity of doing good; and by their counsels and prayers the few persons who claimed to belong to the Wesleyan body were kept united in heart and affection, in hope of better days to come.

At length, in the early part of 1820, former prejudices having in a measure passed away, the Rev. E, Edwards proceeded from Namaqualand to Cape Town, to attempt the commencement of a Mission Station, by direction of his superintendent, the Rev. Barnabas Shaw. Wishing to commence on a sure footing, Mr. Edwards waited on his Honour the acting Governor, who cheerfully gave the necessary permission to preach and instruct the slave population of the town and neighbourhood. The first services were held in an upper room in Plein-street; but after a few weeks, the congregation having greatly increased, a large unoccupied wine store in Barrack-street was hired and fitted up with pulpit, pews, and benches as a place of worship, and the work of the Mission was regularly inaugurated.

In this humble sanctuary the Gospel was faithfully preached, both in Dutch and English, and the Missionary frequently visited the slaves under Table Mountain, where they were accustomed to assemble together for the purpose of dancing and other amusements; some of whom were persuaded to attend the chapel and Sunday-school. Soon after the opening of this, the first Methodist place of worship in Cape Town, the Rev. William Shaw arrived in Simon's Bay, in the emigrant ship "Aurora," on his way to the Eastern Province. He went on shore and hastened to Cape Town, where he arrived just in time to preach his first sermon in Africa, from that beautiful text, "Who, when he came, and had seen the grace of God, was glad, and exhorted them all, that with purpose of heart they would cleave unto the Lord" (Acts xi. 23). On the following day Mr. Edwards accompanied Mr. Shaw on board his ship, when he was introduced to his excellent wife; and, having commended them to the providence and grace of God, he returned to his interesting sphere of labour.

Mr. Edwards was succeeded in Cape Town by Mr. B. Shaw, who was soon afterwards joined by the Rev. T. L. Hodgson from England. More suitable premises were now purchased and fitted up as a permanent place of worship, the old wine store having become too small for the congregation; and the work was carried on upon a scale more in accordance with the importance of the Station than was practicable in the first humble beginning. In 1830, the former places of worship, each of which had answered its purpose for the time being, were superseded by the present commodious Chapel in Burg-street, where an English congregation assembles for Divine worship every Sabbath and on week evenings, which, for respectability, intelligence, and devout attention to the Word preached, would compare favourably with our average town congregations at home.

Seven years afterwards a new chapel was erected for the native congregations in Sydney-street under the most auspicious circumstances. At the opening services the Rev. Messrs. Barnabas Shaw and William Shaw * both preached to large and attentive congre-

---

* The Revs. Barnabas Shaw and William Shaw were not brothers, as erroneously stated in some books published in America and elsewhere. They had no natural relationship, but were simply two highly honoured pioneer Wesleyan Mission-

gations, the honoured Missionary last-named having again called at the Cape when on his way from England (where he had been on a visit) to his own station in the Eastern Province. In 1857, whilst the writer was labouring in Cape Town, a third chapel was erected in Hope-street, on the south side of the city, and nearly a mile distant from either of the others. These places of worship are generally well attended, and in connection with each there is a prosperous Sunday-school, as well as another in Loop-street; the whole being formed into a "Union," which is worked with exemplary zeal and diligence by the friends of education in the Cape Town Circuits. At Sydney-street and Hope-street we have also excellent day-schools connected with our Mission, which provide religious and secular instruction to many who would otherwise be destitute of them. And yet there is room for expansion and aggression in Cape Town, with its population of thirty thousand, one-fifth of whom are rigid Mohammedans.

We must now leave the city, and take a tour into the country, that we may see what is going on at our respective Mission stations in the rural districts. About four miles from Cape Town stand the beautiful suburban villages of Mowbray and Rondebosch, with their dwellings scattered along each side of the road, at a considerable distance from each other, embowered in trees, gardens, and vineyards. The neat little gothic Wesleyan chapel which may be seen a short distance from the road to the right was built by the late Rev. T. L. Hodgson, in the year 1845, and has been made a great blessing both to the English and native population. Here

---

aries in Southern Africa, for several years contemporary with each other,—the scene of Barnabas Shaw's labours being the Cape of Good Hope, and Namaqualand, to the westward; and that of William Shaw, Kafirland, and the southeastern coast of the vast continent. The writer was for several years happily associated with Barnabas Shaw in the Mission field, and can therefore testify to his many excellent qualities. After labouring for more than forty years in the cause which he so dearly loved, he died, in the faith and hope of the Gospel, at Rondebosch on the 21st of January, 1857. William Shaw, having returned to England and entered the home work, was elected President of the Conference in 1867, and is still spared to witness the prosperity of Mission stations which he planted fifty years ago in the days of his youthful vigour.

also a Mission day-school is in active operation. This station is endeared to the writer as the scene of his personal labours and residence for several years. Two miles further we come to Claremont, a scattered village in many respects similar to Rondebosch, where the Wesleyan chapel may be seen to the left. It was built in the year 1859, on a lot of land generously presented to the Society by J. A. Stegman, Esq., with a view chiefly to benefit a large native Mohammedan population concentrated in that neighbourhood. Whether we proceed by the railway, or by the common road, we pass Newlands, a scattered rural hamlet to the right under the spur of Table Mountain. A neat little chapel was erected there in 1858, after we had preached in the open air under some oak trees for about three years, and been favoured to see some fruit to our labours.

The beautiful village of Wynberg, so celebrated as a sanatorium for visitors from India and other places, is eight miles from Cape Town. The elegant Wesleyan chapel built in the Italian style of architecture, with its tower complete, was the munificent gift to the Society of J. M. Maynard, Esq., and was erected in 1851. Two miles further we come to Diep River, an important out-station of the Wynberg Circuit. The commodious chapel on the right near to the road was erected by the Rev. R. Haddy in 1840, to meet the wants of a considerable, though somewhat scattered, native population residing on the surrounding flats, to whom the preaching and the instruction imparted in the day-school have been made a great blessing.

Proceeding along the public road we soon come in sight of the sea at the head of False Bay, having crossed the entire peninsula; and passing through the villages of Muzenburgh and Kalk Bay, where the Missionaries have occasionally preached, but where no permanent stations have been established, we see in the distance Simon's Town, with the Wesleyan chapel standing on a hill above most of the dwelling-houses, with its modest spire pointing towards heaven, to which the Gospel preached there has been the means of leading many a poor wanderer. This Station is twenty-two miles from the city, and, with Elsey's River over the hills, as an outpost, forms an important and interesting sphere of Missionary labour. There are a number of English residents at Simon's Town connected with her Majesty's naval dock-yard, and in other official positions, besides the native population, who have been largely benefitted by our Mission, and who, according to their ability, are liberal supporters of the cause.

WESLEYAN CHAPEL, WYNBERG, CAPE OF GOOD HOPE.
Presented to the Society by James Mortimer Maynard, Esq. in 1851.

Stellenbosch is another picturesque village situated in a fertile valley about twenty-eight miles from Cape Town by railway, or by the common road in another direction. The Wesleyan Missionaries extended their labours to this neighbourhood several years ago;

and in 1840 the present commodious chapel was erected, chiefly for the accommodation of the large population of coloured people labouring on the adjacent farms and vineyards, who flocked to hear the Word of God; and many of whom have been gathered into the fold of Christ through the instrumentality of this Society. An important out-station has been established at Raithby, which, together with a little village called Sandfleet, makes the Stellenbosch circuit a useful and interesting sphere of Missionary labour. Two day-schools are in active operation, and provide religious and secular instruction to a large number of native children who would otherwise be uncared for.

The next place which claims our notice is Somerset (West), a pleasant spot on the high road from Cape Town to the eastern frontier, at a distance of thirty-one miles from the city. The good work was commenced there in 1834, when an old wine-store was purchased and converted into a school-room and place of worship. In 1861 this humble sanctuary was superseded by the present elegant and commodious chapel, the erection of which, amid many difficulties, reflects great credit on the untiring zeal and energy of the Rev. Richard Ridgill, who was for many years the resident Missionary there. Neat little chapels have also been erected at the out-stations of Terrington Grove and the Strand, both of which are included in the Somerset (West) circuit, and have exercised a very beneficial influence on the surrounding neighbourhood. The supply of these places with a stated Gospel Ministry, and the efficient conducting of the three Mission day-schools connected with them, afford ample employment for the Missionary and his teachers.

Robertson is comparatively a new station, situated in a central position in the midst of a dense population, about one hundred miles from Cape Town. It was commenced by the Rev. Henry Tindall in 1859, by whose zealous efforts a large congregation has been collected, a prosperous native church formed, and an elegant new chapel erected. Important out-stations have been established at the villages of Lady Gray, Montague, and Newmanville, which, together with Robertson, form an extensive and interesting circuit.

WESLEYAN CHAPEL, SOMERSET (WEST), CAPE OF GOOD HOPE.

Two Mission day-schools are also in active operation for the training up of the rising generation. The Missionary is ably assisted in supplying the respective stations with the means of grace, and in carrying on the good work by a few devoted local preachers and native teachers, and through their united and zealous efforts many precious souls have been won for Christ. A promising commencement was also made at Swellendam, an ancient colonial town still more distant from the capital; but after the work had been carried on with encouraging results for a few years, the chapel and Mission premises were destroyed by fire. This happened at a time when the state of the Society's funds did not warrant the re-erection of the buildings, and the Station was relinquished, much to the disappointment of the people, and the regret both of the Rev. William Barber, the resident Missionary, and the Rev. Samuel Hardey, the writer's worthy successor as General Superintendent of the Cape of Good Hope District.

Before we proceed to explore other parts of Southern Africa, and to trace the leading events of their Missionary history, the writer may be permitted to say, that he looks back with heartfelt gratitude to God on the ten years which he spent in connection with Mission work at the Cape of Good Hope. From the commencement of the enterprise Methodism has had to contend with many difficulties in this part of the wide field, owing to the ignorance and prejudice of the people in times past. The Dutch portion of the population, which largely preponderates in the western province, have never been very favourable to the cause of Missions, and in some instances, in former years, have manifested open hostility to it. The work has, nevertheless, taken deep root, and on some of the stations it has advanced to a pleasing state of prosperity. Of late years the cause has been crippled by embarrassing measures of retrenchment, rendered necessary, it is said, by the state of the Society's funds; but if the liberality of British Christians will enable the Missionary Committee to sustain the work in a state of tolerable efficiency a little longer, we have no doubt but it will prosper more and more, and ere long become entirely self-supporting. Our people at the Cape of Good Hope are proverbially large-hearted and liberal; contributing to the Mission Fund, besides what they give for local objects, about £500 a year. The spiritual results of the Mission are, moreover, such as to excite in our hearts the liveliest feelings of gratitude and praise to God. In connection with the respective stations in the Cape of Good Hope District we have now *nine Missionaries, one thousand three hundred and three Church members,* and *two thousand three hundred and eleven scholars* in the Mission schools.

Graham's Town District.

METHODISM was introduced into the Eastern Province of the Cape Colony under more favourable circumstances than those we have already had to notice, inasmuch as it formed a considerable element in the original settlement of the country. In the year 1820, a plan having been formed by the British Government to send out about four thousand emigrants, to occupy a large tract of country called Albany to the north of Algoa Bay, the Rev. William Shaw, with Mrs. Shaw, embarked with a party of Wesleyans, Mr. Shaw having been appointed as their chaplain or minister, according to previous arrangements. On arriving at the land of their adoption, and during the first portion of their African experience, the British settlers had many difficulties to contend with, arising chiefly from unpropitious seasons, the failure of their crops, and the labour and exposure which invariably attend the first efforts of the emigrant to break up the fallow ground and establish a home for himself and his family in the wilderness. In all their trials and privations the people found their faithful pastor ready to sympathise with them, and to aid them in every way to the utmost of his power, whilst he was ever intent on supplying their souls with the "bread of life." Thus were the first two or three years of Mr. Shaw's ministerial life in Southern Africa spent in itinerating, visiting, and preaching to the settlers at their respective locations in Upper and Lower Albany, pretty much after the style of a Methodist travelling preacher in

England in olden times; and he was favoured to realise a pleasing measure of success.

From the first arrival of Mr. Shaw and his party of Wesleyan emigrants on the shores of Africa, the miserable and degraded state of the natives with whom they came in contact, both Kaffirs and Hottentots, attracted their notice and excited their sympathy. Nor did they fail to exert themselves to promote their spiritual and social welfare as they had opportunity. But, at the same time, the religious interest of the colonists occupied a large portion of the time and attention of the minister who came out with them, and who was located in their midst. And here it may be necessary to offer a remark on the principle adopted by the Wesleyan Missionary Society in carrying on their Colonial and Foreign Missions. Whilst other religious associations think it best to confine their attention to the aborigines of the countries where they labour, our Missionaries invariably seek to promote the welfare of all classes of the community, irrespective of language, complexion, or condition; and they are especially careful not to neglect their fellow-countrymen whom they find in foreign lands, knowing that when *they* are brought to a saving knowledge of the truth, they generally prove both able and willing to render important aid in extending the Gospel to the degraded native tribes around them. This is the principle which has been acted upon from the beginning in Southern Africa, and, indeed, on all our foreign stations. Hence has arisen the mixed character of our work in many places; for, although we endeavour to classify and arrange our labours as much as possible in distinct compartments, it often occurs that the same Missionary has to minister and teach in two or three different languages. The carrying out of the principle here indicated, and the unavoidable intermingling of different departments of our work on the same station, renders it almost impossible to discuss the colonial and native branches of our Mission separately; but we shall do our best to present the reader with a clear and intelligible view of what is being done by the agency of the Wesleyan Missionary Society for the benefit of the community generally in South Eastern Africa, commencing with the Colonial circuits.

GRAHAM'S TOWN itself first claims our attention, as it is the capital of the Eastern Province and the head of the District. From an inconsiderable village it has, in the course of half a century, risen to the position of an important colonial city, with a population of about ten thousand, and contains buildings and mercantile establishments which reflect much credit on the zeal and energy of the British settlers and their descendants, by whom it is chiefly inhabited. The first Methodist sermon ever heard in Graham's Town was preached by the Rev. W. Shaw, in the house of Serjeant Major Lucas, who, together with a few other pious military men, who had been savingly converted to God in Cape Town, gave the Missionary a hearty welcome, and aided him in his important work to the utmost of their power. The preaching room having soon become too small for the congregation, on the 5th of December, 1821, the foundation-stone of the first chapel was laid, and the building was completed in due time, notwithstanding numerous and pressing difficulties. Such was the progress of the good work that in the course of a few years this humble structure was first enlarged, and then succeeded by the erection of the second chapel. In 1850 the third Wesleyan sanctuary was built in Graham's Town, and received the name of "Commemoration Chapel," in memory of the arrival of the first British settlers. This is said to be the most elegant place of worship in the colony, and it is attended by an English congregation of remarkable zeal, intelligence, and respectability. At the same time an important work is carried on among the natives, who assemble in the old chapel, which is now entirely appropriated to their use, and to whom the Missionaries preach in two different languages. Out-stations have also been formed at West-hill, Fort England, and other places in the Graham's Town circuits, and the results have been very encouraging. Mission schools have likewise been established for the religious and general instruction of the children of all classes of the community.

SALEM also became an important Station at an early period, the foundation stone of the first chapel having been laid there on the 1st of January, 1822. When the sanctuary was finished it was a great convenience and comfort to the settlers, who were located in considerable numbers in this neighbourhood, and it became the spiritual birthplace of many precious souls. A large and prosperous educational establishment was conducted for many years in connection with our Mission at Salem, which, together with the

WESLEYAN MISSION STATION, FARMERFIELD, SOUTHERN AFRICA.

neighbouring native institution at Farmerfield, afforded ample scope for the labours of the Missionaries and teachers who were stationed there from time to time. At the village of Bathurst, and among the farms and scattered hamlets of Lower Albany, Methodism was early planted, and chapels erected for the benefit of both

Europeans and natives; and the work has continued to grow and expand from year to year to the present time. Fort Beaufort, Seymour, and Alice, unitedly, form an important circuit; but the work has fluctuated according to circumstances, the repeated Kaffir wars having proved a serious hindrance to its stability in former times.

Heald Town, so called in honour of the respected senior treasurer of the Wesleyan Missionary Society, has for many years been an important station. From its central position it was selected as the best locality for a native industrial school, which was established and conducted for some time under the auspices of Government. The object of this institution was to train a number of native youths in a knowledge of religion and of the arts of civilised life; and so long as the experiment was continued the results were satisfactory. But when the Government grant was withdrawn the spacious buildings which had been erected were converted into an institution for the higher object of training native Teachers and Missionaries. In its new character, the establishment bids fair to prove a great blessing to the stations generally, as it has been formed for the purpose of preparing native agents for the whole District. Whilst the students are diligently pursuing their studies during the greatest portion of each day, both they and the Missionaries under whose care they are placed are usefully employed, as they have opportunity, in preaching the Gospel, and in other pastoral duties among the native Fingoes, a large number of whom are located in the neighbourhood. During the usual vacations they visit distant stations in small parties to hold special meetings, and gracious revivals of religion have sometimes resulted from their zealous labours.

As the work of the Mission was gradually extended to the places already named, and to others which have yet to pass under review, the necessity of more labourers to cultivate the ever-widening field was keenly felt. For some time the noble pioneer Missionary, Mr. Shaw, was aided by a number of zealous local preachers, some of whom had come from England, and others had been raised up on the spot. But these worthy Christian brethren had to attend to their respective secular callings; and in the course of time, with the exception of two or three who gave themselves wholly to the work, they became widely scattered through the colony, to provide homes for themselves and families. Hence the gratitude and joy which were experienced on the arrival of Missionaries from England. Mr. Shaw was first joined by the Rev. Messrs. Kay, Threlfall, and Young; and a few years afterwards by the Rev. Messrs. Palmer, Boyce, Cameron, J. Edwards, W. J. Davis, and others; and the work rapidly extended to various parts of the Eastern Province, as well as to Kaffirland. It would be a very pleasant task to enter more minutely into the history of this important and interesting Mission; but the claims of other sections of the wide field upon our space necessarily confine us to a brief outline of the progress of the work, and a hasty glance at the principal stations.

Port Elizabeth, formerly known as Algoa Bay, is worthy of special notice. No other town in Southern Africa has risen more rapidly than this; and, being the principal seaport of the province, it now rivals, if it does not surpass, Graham's Town itself, both as to population and importance. On the arrival of the British settlers in 1820, it was a mere landing-place or fishing village, hemmed in by barren sand hills; but now it presents the appearance of a respectable and well-built town of eight thousand inhabitants. At an early period Divine service was conducted in a large room fitted up for the purpose; but in the year 1840, a substantial Wesleyan chapel was erected for the use of the settlers; and more recently still, a place of worship was provided for the accommodation of sailors in the harbour as well as for the natives generally, who were for a long time neglected by our Missionaries at the Bay, in consequence of a real or alleged compact with another religious body that they were to take care of them. As the Fingoes collected there in large numbers for the sake of employment among the shipping in the harbour, it was found that there was ample work for all; and our Society now takes its proper position, both in the English and native departments of Christian labour, with great advantage to all classes of the community.

At a distance of about eight miles from Port Elizabeth, stands the pleasant rural village of Uitenhage, with its gardens, orchards, and vineyards. We have long had a station there; and, although the population is comparatively small, it has recently been favoured with a resident Missionary, as a sphere of usefulness seems to present itself among the natives employed at the large wool-washing establishments in the neighbourhood. Higher up in the country we have important stations at Cradock, Somerset (East), Peddie, and Newton Dale. In connection with some of these places extensive circuits have been formed, in which the Missionaries itinerate among the isolated farms and villages, preach to settlers and natives as they have opportunity, superintend the schools which have been established, and exert themselves in every possible way for the benefit of a scattered population, who are, in many instances, entirely dependent on them for religious instruction. The journeys taken by these laborious servants of God sometimes extend to a distance of scores or even hundreds of miles, involving an absence from their homes and families of several days or weeks, and much danger and personal discomfort in crossing rivers, deserts, and mountains, in the prosecution of their noble enterprise. They are worthy of the sympathy, the prayers, and the support of all Christian people who stay at home and are happily exempt from the privations and trials to which the Missionaries are exposed.

KING WILLIAM'S TOWN is the capital of British Kaffraria, an extensive territory, which has been recently annexed to the Cape Colony, and East London is the seaport. At both these places we have interesting stations; and, although the work has been repeatedly interrupted by Kaffir wars, it has now arrived at a pleasing state of prosperity, the land having for several years past enjoyed the blessings of peace. A commodious chapel was erected a few years ago at King William's Town, which is attended by an intelligent and respectable congregation of colonists, whilst the spiritual interests of the natives residing in the neighbourhood are duly attended to. A school chapel has also been recently built at the German village; and the out-station of Berkley is regularly visited by the Missionary and his assistants. The Mission schools at these places are said to be in healthy and vigorous operation, and the aspect of the work generally, in British Kaffraria, is of the most hopeful and encouraging character.

Mount Coke and the native station of Annshaw are also included in the Graham's Town District, although geographically related to Kaffirland. The place first named has been selected as the most suitable locality for the Mission press, as it is central to all our stations in South Eastern Africa. From this important printing establishment, so long and so ably superintended by the Rev. J. W. Appleyard, have issued countless numbers of school books, portions of Scripture, and other publications in English, Dutch, Kaffir, and the Susutu languages, to the great advantage of the work in all its departments. The Annshaw Circuit is very populous and extensive. It comprises sixty villages and eighty preaching places; and at the respective stations and outposts one hundred and two class meetings are held every week. In connection with the respective Circuits and Stations of the Graham's Town District there are now *twenty-four Missionaries, four thousand eight hundred and nine Church members* and *five thousand and eleven scholars* in the Mission schools.

Queen's Town District.

The Mission Stations comprised in the Queen's Town District are chiefly in Kaffirland; and, with the exception of Queen's Town itself, where a number of Europeans reside, as in other colonial towns, the work is carried on among the natives entirely, and is not of that mixed character which we have described as necessary where British settlers are located in considerable numbers. That a correct view may be obtained of the nature and extent of this work, we shall now endeavour to give a brief but connected narrative of the origin, progress, and present state of our Mission in Kaffirland.

Although the Rev. William Shaw went out to South Eastern Africa with a party of British settlers, many of whom professed to be Wesleyans, and was appointed to labour specially for their benefit, we are not surprised that the degraded state of the native tribes in the neighbourhood of their locations soon attracted his attention, and excited his sympathy; for every true minister of the Gospel is necessarily inspired by the missionary spirit. At an early period Mr. Shaw formed the noble design of attempting to introduce the Gospel into Kaffirland, so soon as the necessary help should arrive from home, and, if possible, to form a chain of stations to connect the Cape Colony with Natal. The Mission in Albany having at length been reinforced by the arrival from England of the Rev. S. Kay, Mr. Shaw left the station in charge of his colleague, and removed to Kaffirland with his family in the month of November, 1823. Having fixed upon a suitable locality for a Mission village in the territory of the paramount chief Gaika, and near to the residence of a subordinate chief named Pato, he proceeded to establish the *first* station, which was called Wesleyville, in honour of the founder of Methodism. Many changes have taken place since this humble commencement of the good work; but Wesleyville has continued to be a centre of light and influence amid the surrounding darkness, and has no doubt been the spiritual birth-place of many precious souls.

In the year 1825 the *second* station in Kaffirland was formed by Mr. Kay, who proceeded up the country, on the arrival of another supply of Missionaries from England. The new establishment received the appropriate name of Mount Coke, in honour of the father of Methodist Missions. This station has also had to pass through various vicissitudes, and to be removed to a better site, the first place selected having proved unsuitable for the purposes of the Mission. At an early period it rose to a pleasing state of prosperity under the judicious management of the Rev. Samuel Young; and after it had been desolated by a Kaffir

MOUNT COKE WESLEYAN MISSION STATION, 1864.

war, it was re-commenced by the Rev. William Impey. The accompanying engraving gives an accurate view of its appearance in 1854.

The *third* Wesleyan Mission station in Kaffirland was commenced in 1827, with the chief Hintza and his tribe, by the Rev. W. J. Shrewsbury. The establishment was called Butterworth, in memory of an honoured Treasurer of the Society, long since called to his reward in heaven. This station has been repeatedly destroyed in successive Kaffir wars; but it has always been rebuilt afterwards, sometimes at the expense of the Kaffirs themselves, and has proved a great blessing to the people. Since the land has enjoyed the blessings of peace, the work has expanded into several branches, and a number of interesting out-stations have been formed which unitedly constitute an important native circuit. This extensive sphere of labour comprises thirty-four preaching places, and gives ample employment to the Missionary and eleven local preachers, who have been raised up by the providence and grace of God to take a part in the work.

In 1829 another step in advance was taken in the commencement, by the Rev. William Shepstone, of the *fourth* Kaffir station, called Morley, in honour of a respected General Secretary of the Society. This Mission was established for the special benefit of a somewhat remarkable tribe of people under a chief called Dapa. From their comparatively light complexion and sharp features, as well as from the traditions preserved among them, they appear to have descended from a number of Europeans cast away upon the shores of Kaffirland many years before. A circumstance so remarkable did not come to light without exciting much interest and inquiry at the time; but it was never cleared up in all its details, and in some of its particulars it remains involved in considerable mystery up to the present period. After the most careful research, however, there appeared to be little doubt but that the mother of the chief Dapa was a white woman, probably one of the few survivors of the ship "*Grosvenor*," from India, which was wrecked on the coast in the year 1745. She was said to have rejoiced in the name of Betsy; but of what country she was a native could never be ascertained.

The chief was wont to boast of his relation to the white men, and was kind to the Missionaries.

In the establishment of the station with this singular people Mr. Shepstone was assisted by Mr. Robinson, a pious young Englishman, who was unfortunately killed by the sudden fall of a tree which he was felling for timber for the Mission buildings. This afflictive incident cast a gloom over the undertaking for a length of time; but it was ultimately brought to a satisfactory issue, and the labours of the Missionaries were made a great blessing to this large tribe of people. In 1865 it was found necessary to remove this station to another site, the former place having proved very unhealthy. New Morley is situated on an elevated ridge in the centre of a fertile valley, with a splendid prospect in every direction; and, what is better still, it is a home for the oppressed and afflicted, and a centre of evangelical light to thousands of once degraded natives, many of whom have already been brought to a saving knowledge of the truth through its instrumentality.

The *fifth* Mission station in Kaffirland was commenced in the year 1830, by the Rev. Richard Haddy, and was called Clarkebury, in honour of the learned divine and commentator. It is a remarkable circumstance that the only two European labourers who have fallen by the hands of native marauders in this country were both of them connected with this station. The first was Mr. Rawlins, an assistant, who was killed by a horde of Fitcani, near Clarkebury, and the other was the Rev. J. S. Thomas, who was stabbed by a party of Kaffirs who were making an attack on the cattle kraal. Notwithstanding these and other adverse circumstances which for a time tended to impede the progress of the good work at this station, it has gradually advanced to a pleasing state of prosperity. Several important out-stations have also been formed in various directions; and at twenty different places in this circuit the Gospel is faithfully preached by the Missionaries and their assistants in the native language of the people.

The *sixth* Kaffir station was established about the same time as Clarkebury, in the country of the Amampondos, under the great chief Faku, by the Rev. W. B. Boyce, who had just arrived from England, and who, with his devoted wife, is still held in affectionate remembrance by a few of the old people in Kaffirland. He gave it the name of Buntingville, in honour of a distinguished minister of the Methodist connexion, and one of the founders of the Wesleyan Missionary Society, whose memory will never be suffered to die. Although this station is the most remote and isolated of any on the list, it is the only one that has never been desolated by war; all the rest which we have named have been laid waste at one time or another, and some of them repeatedly. The site of Buntingville has been changed to secure agricultural and other advantages, but it continues to answer the purposes of its first formation, and has proved a great blessing to the surrounding country.

Two other interesting stations have grown out of Buntingville, one of which is called Shawbury, in honour of the General Superintendent for the time being, whose memory is still kept green in the land of his earliest labours; and the other received the name of Palmerton in affectionate remembrance of a beloved Missionary who was called to his reward in heaven many years ago. These are situated on the borders of the colony of Natal, and thus complete the "chain of stations" on which the zealous pioneer Missionary set his heart when he first penetrated the wilds of Kaffirland. The Christian traveller may now prosecute his journey from Graham's Town to Natal in safety, and receive a welcome greeting and the rites of hospitality at many a smiling Mission station in the wilderness through which he is obliged to pass, which was not the case in former times.

On returning from our extensive but hasty Missionary tour along the line of stations which were first formed in Kaffirland, it would be very pleasant if we had the opportunity of doing so, to turn aside, and look upon the devoted brethren who occupy other stations further inland, which in course of time have grown out of those already named,—as Osborn and Mount Arthur, so called in honour of two highly-esteemed General Secretaries of the Society; and Lesseyton, Queenstown, Kamastone, and some others of more recent origin. At the place last named we should probably find the venerable William Shepstone, once the pioneer Missionary in the most remote part of Kaffirland, and now the honoured General Superintendent of the District, and who is still spared to water the good seed of the kingdom which he and others sowed in early life. It is the less necessary to enter into minute particulars with reference to these stations, inasmuch as they closely resemble those already described both in their general character and modes of action for the good of the people. We may with propriety close this brief account of our Missions in Kaffirland with a few remarks on the habits and superstitions of the natives.

The Kaffirs have, properly speaking, no religious system of their own, and consequently no forms of worship, except in some instances, when a vague and indefinite homage is paid to the memory of departed chiefs and heroes, whose spirits they think still live. They are, moreover, extremely superstitious. They believe in lucky and unlucky days, and in the power of witchcraft. These vain delusions are fostered and kept alive by the craft and ingenuity of a certain class of men known as witch-doctors and rain-makers.

All misfortunes, diseases, and deaths among men and cattle are attributed to the influence of witchcraft. When any untoward circumstance occurs to persons of rank, the first question asked is, "Who is the witch?" And as the person implicated is always liable to have his property confiscated, or, in Kaffir phrase, to be "eaten up," the wily doctor is sure to fix upon some one possessed of wealth. At the command of the chief a summons is issued to the suspected parties, a grand meeting is convened, and various rites and ceremonies are performed with a view to " smell out " the culprit. When the declaration is made by the witch-doctor implicating some one present, the unhappy victim is at once seized and subjected to the most revolting cruelty, to make him or her confess the crime, and divulge all the particulars as to where the bewitching matter has been concealed, &c. Sometimes the suspected witch is bound with cords, besmeared with grease, and placed upon an ant-hill, to be tormented by the insects; at other

BURNING OF A KAFFIR SUSPECTED OF WITCHCRAFT.

times hot stones are applied to the feet and other sensitive parts of the body, producing the most excruciating pain, and thousands have been put to death by burning at the stake, strangulation, and in various other ways, under this appalling system of superstition. So true is it that "the dark places of the earth are full of the habitations of cruelty." Scores of well authenticated instances which have come under the personal notice of the Missionaries might be given in illustration of the degraded condition of the poor Kaffirs, but it is more pleasant to dwell upon the all-sufficient remedy provided in the glorious Gospel of the blessed God.

Every Mission station in Kaffirland is an asylum for the oppressed and afflicted, as well as a school of Christ, in which may be learned the lessons of His love; and every Missionary is a friend of the persecuted outcast. Often has the life of the poor doomed victim been spared at the intercession of the man of God; and many a time has the homeless fugitive found shelter in the "city of refuge." It is a pleasing fact that Christian schools for the instruction of the rising generation have been established in connection with each station, where many have been taught to read the Word of God for themselves. And it is still more pleasing to contemplate that a large number of precious immortal souls have been won to Christ by the faithful preaching of His Gospel. This has been the case more or less from the beginning, but in the year 1866 a religious revival occurred on a scale which had never before been witnessed, and which it is believed resulted in the salvation of thousands of poor heathens. This, we trust, is only the precursor of still greater good, as the machinery of our Mission work on every station is in active operation, and both Ministers and people appear to be labouring for and expecting spiritual prosperity. There are now in connection with the Queen's Town District *twelve missionaries, two thousand seven hundred and sixty Church members*, and *one thousand nine hundred and sixty-eight scholars* in the Mission schools.

Bechuana District.

Far away in the interior of Southern Africa, between Kaffraria and Namaqualand, is situated the BECHUANA COUNTRY, which is inhabited by an interesting people, for whom something has been done by the Wesleyan Missionary Society with a view to raise them from the state of moral degradation in which they were found when they first attracted the notice of Europeans.

It was in the year 1822 that the first attempt was made to plant the standard of the Cross in that distant region; and, although it partly failed in the commencement, in consequence of the sickness of the Missionaries and the unsettled state of the country, it was afterwards renewed with more favourable results. As soon as the health of the Rev. S. Broadbent was, in a measure, re-established, he nobly offered to return to the scene of his former labours, and the Rev. T. L. Hodgson proceeded from Cape Town to accompany him. They were afterwards joined by the Rev. J. Archbell, and, for a time, by the Rev. E. Edwards also. These devoted servants of Christ explored the country in various directions, but especially to the eastward, with the hope of finding a suitable locality for a permanent station. At length Messrs. Hodgson and Broadbent, after having been repeatedly thwarted in their plans by the prevailing wars among the natives, were enabled to commence a promising station at a place called Makwasse, in the upper region of the Vaal River, with the Baralong tribe of Bechuanas. It was not long, however, before the Missionaries and their people were driven away and scattered in various directions by a powerful and hostile tribe called the Matabele, who made war upon the country from the north. But as soon as an opportunity was afforded they rallied again, and finally settled at a place called Thaba Unchu, to the north of the Orange River. Here the Baralongs, with a few remnants of other scattered tribes who joined them from time to time, have become a comparatively prosperous and happy people, through the instrumentality of the faithful Missionaries who have laboured among them for many years. In connection with this station a large chapel has been erected, and a town has gradually grown up, which now contains a population of ten thousand,—probably the largest assemblage of natives in one spot in any part of Southern Africa, affording, together with Plaatberg and other stations in the neighbourhood, a fine field of Missionary labour.

In addition to the places already named, where a good work has been carried on for many years among the Korannas, Newlanders, Baralongs, and other tribes of Bechuanas, several other stations have been formed in this district for the religious instruction of mixed populations of different tribes and languages. One of these is Colesberg, a prosperous little town with a mixed population of English, Dutch, and coloured people, for whose benefit the Missionary preaches in two or three different languages. We have there a good English chapel, with a respectable congregation; but a new place of worship for the natives is much required. Meetings are held in several houses in the town, and earnest efforts are made to extend the blessings of the Gospel to the natives on the surrounding farms, of whom there are about one thousand within a moderate distance.

Burgher's Dorp in many respects resembles Colesberg. The English congregation has not yet got a chapel, however, and the Missionary is obliged to preach to them in the public school-room. The services are generally well attended, and there is a prospect of still greater good. By the help of several native preachers who have been raised up in this neighbourhood, as the fruit of Missionary labour, eight services are conducted every Sabbath in the town and at the neighbouring farms and villages. Wittebergen, or the "White Mountains," is a purely native station, having a dense population of Fingoes settled on a tract of land reserved for their use by the colonial government. To these and to a number of Basutus located in the same neighbourhood, the Missionary and his assistants faithfully preach the Gospel in their own tongues respectively, itinerating among the surrounding kraals with the most pleasing results. Bensonville, so called in memory of a celebrated Methodist commentator and divine, differs little in its general features from the station last named. In addition to the principal chapel there are six other preaching places, where services are held in the Dutch, Sisutu, and Kaffir languages; and it is hoped that the result of these zealous efforts, in connection with the instruction given in the Mission schools, will be to raise the people to a higher state of civilisation, as well as to secure the salvation of many souls, a considerable number of native converts having already been brought into the fold of Christ.

We have also an interesting station at Bloemfontein, the capital of the Dutch republic known as the Orange Free State. This is a town of considerable importance, with a mixed population of Dutch, English, and natives. To meet the wants of these a Missionary was appointed to labour there a few years ago, and a promising commencement has been made. In 1867 a commodious new chapel was erected, to seat two hundred persons, at a cost of £1,200, nearly the whole of which was raised on the spot. The native chapel is said to be well attended, and the work is progressing in a satisfactory manner. Fauresmith is another similar town in the Free State. Encouraged by the Government authorities, who have rendered substantial assistance, a Wesleyan Missionary has been stationed there also; and although the number of church members is at present small, three English and ten native services are held weekly, which cannot fail to be productive of much spiritual good to the people. For some time past the work has been retarded by the unsettled state of the country, consequent upon the war which has existed between the Free State and the Basutos; but, as peace is once more restored to the land, it is hoped that the work of evangelisation will proceed without interruption among all classes of people.

We have now in connection with the Bechuana District *eight Missionaries, one thousand and thirty-one Church members*, and *one thousand eight hundred and eighty-six scholars* in the Mission schools.

Natal District.

The next step in advance in the establishment of Wesleyan Missions in Southern Africa was to the territory of NATAL, on the eastern coast of the peninsula, and the most distant of the British possessions in that direction, now organised into a regular colony. Successful Missions having been established with the Amampondos in Kaffirland, on the south, and with the Bechuanas and Korannas, in Basutoland, on the West, it is not surprising that the Missionaries should have felt a strong desire to extend the blessings of the Gospel to the numerous and powerful tribe called the Amazulu, inhabiting the Natal territory and the country northward.

Difficulties connected with the state of the society's funds, and the prevalence of war in the interior, for sometime retarded the commencement of the work, however, and it was not until the year 1841 that a beginning was made. By this time, a party of English traders had settled at Port Natal, and were proceeding, in their way, to inaugurate a system of colonisation. Almost simultaneously with this movement, a powerful body of Dutch emigrants entered the upper part of the country from the westward, and laid claim to the whole land, by right of conquest. The English, the Dutch, and the native populations were consequently thrown into a state of great excitement, and a serious collision appeared inevitable, when the Governor of the Cape Colony sent a detachment of British troops to preserve order in the country. The military expedition marched overland through Kaffraria to Natal, and were accompanied by the Rev. J. Archbell as a messenger of peace, and the first Christian Missionary to that distant region.

It would be foreign to our purpose to enter into a narrative of the exciting incidents which occurred before the country was permanently settled by the English, and a regular form of colonial government established. It may be sufficient to say that the Missionary found ample employment in preaching to the English, Dutch, and native inhabitants, the glorious Gospel of the blessed God, and was regarded by the people as the "friend of all, and the enemy of none," till peace and harmony were restored to the land, when permanent Mission stations were established in different places, as openings presented themselves. To meet the pressing demands for religious instruction in the new colony, reinforcements of Missionaries were sent, from time to time, from the Cape, including the Rev. Messrs. Allison, Holden, Davis, Pearse, Cameron, and others. These were joined or succeeded by the Rev. Messrs. Spensely, Gaskin, Blencowe, Pilcher, and other zealous labourers from England; and it is a pleasing fact that two devoted young Missionaries, the Rev. Messrs. J. Jackson, junr., and J. R. Cameron, the sons of Wesleyan Ministers, have been raised up in the colony to take a part in the good work. By the united and zealous efforts of these honoured and devoted servants of God, aided by a noble band of local preachers and native teachers, a number of important stations have been established.

At Durban, which is situated at Port Natal, where the work was first commenced, a commodious Chapel was erected in the year 1858, in which a respectable, and intelligent congregation regularly assembles for Divine worship. A goodly number of the colonists have been united in church fellowship, and are zealously engaged in the service of God. The native department of the work, which is carried on in the old chapel and school-room, is also said to be in a prosperous state. Several interesting out-stations have been formed, and religious services are regularly held in five chapels and eighteen other preaching places in the circuit, with very encouraging results, a gracious revival of religion having been recently experienced.

Maritzburg is the capital of the colony, and is situated about ninety miles inland from the Port. Our Mission work is of a mixed character here also, and is carried on in the same way as at Durban. The new English chapel which was erected a few years ago, is an ornament to the town, and is attended by a large and respectable congregation. The Gospel is also faithfully preached to the natives in their own tongue, both in the town and at the neighbouring locations; and a goodly number have been gathered into the fold of Christ. From Maritzburg, the work has been extended to York, George Town, Prospect, Malton, Foxhill, Camperdown, Moor River, and other places, situated at distances varying from five to fifty-five miles from the capital. In this extensive circuit, the Missionaries and their assistants travel and labour with a self-denying zeal and earnestness worthy of the highest commendation.

Ladysmith is situated in the still more remote interior of the country, and is central to a large but widely scattered population of English settlers, who would be left entirely destitute of the means of grace, if they had not the services of our Missionary. In five small towns or villages in this circuit, preaching has been established; and at six other places, chiefly isolated farms, small congregations have been collected, and the people cheerfully come from ten to forty miles to hear a Gospel sermon. The results of these widely extended labours, it is hoped, will be seen after many days.

At Verulam and Umhali, the work is carried on both in English and in Kaffir; whilst at Edendale, Kwangubeni, Indaleni, and Inanda, it is conducted chiefly for the benefit of the natives. It is unnecessary to enter into a minute description of each of these stations, as they very much resemble each other, and some of those also which have been already described, and the modes of operation are similar at every place. Divine service is conducted and the Gospel faithfully preached in the vernacular language of the people, and Mission schools are established for the training of the rising generation. It is gratifying to be able to state that a pleasing measure of success has attended the labours of the Missionaries and their assistants, notwithstanding the difficulties with which they have had to contend, partly from the injurious influence of Dr. Colenso's teaching, and partly from the deeply degraded state of the natives, which are said to number upwards of one hundred thousand in the colony.

We must not omit to notice, however briefly, another branch of Missionary labour in Natal, which, although differing in its nature from that which has been already described, has nevertheless some peculiar features of interest. We allude to our Mission to the *Indian coolies* settled there. To meet the alleged demand for continuous labour on the sugar, coffee, and other estates, several shiploads of coolies were imported to the colony a few years ago, to the number of 6,500. These were collected from almost every town of our Indian empire, and spoke no fewer than ten different languages. To provide in some measure for the religious instruction of this mixed multitude of foreigners, the Rev. Ralph Stott, a returned Missionary from India, was appointed to labour among them in 1861. He has since been joined by his son, the Rev. S. H. Stott, as it was thought there was an ample field of labour for two Missionaries. They are constantly engaged in itinerating among the estates where the coolies are located, preaching to them in their own tongues Christ and Him crucified at eighty different places, the extremes of which are one hundred miles apart. This work is only in its infancy, but the fruit which has already appeared warrants the hope of a richer harvest in time to come.

But whilst our Mission work in Natal is of the mixed character we have described, it must be remembered that its prime object is the evangelisation of the native Zulus, a tribe of Kaffirs, in their natural state savage and warlike, but remarkably shrewd and observant. A few years ago a party of them were taken to England by a Mr. C—— for the purpose of public exhibition in their war dances and other savage exploits. If the experiment failed to remunerate the silly projector of the enterprise, it gave the party of natives an opportunity of seeing and forming their opinion of the "white man's country," of which they were not slow to avail themselves. When the survivors returned to Natal, —for we are sorry to state that some of them died in this strange land,—they were immediately surrounded by crowds of their countrymen asking for news from the other side of the "great salt water." A set time having been appointed for a hearing in the presence of the chief of the tribe to which they belonged, and a large concourse being assembled to hear what their friends had seen in England, a young man of their company stood up to speak on behalf of himself and his companions. The following is a literal translation of the principal points in his address, which may perhaps be interesting to the reader. After telling of the voyage, and how frightened and sea-sick they were on board the ship, he said:—

"In the third moon we saw England. Then we were told we were in the mouth of a river, and soon after that London was before us. Those who knew London saw it; our eyes, however, saw nothing but a cloud of smoke, then houses, and presently poles standing out of the water, like reeds in a marsh, and these were the mast of the London ships. We went in among them, and our ship stood still, and we found ourselves in London, the great place of the English. The place is very large. We never saw the end of it. We tried hard to find it, but we could not. We ascended a high building like a pole (the Monument), to see where it ended, but our sight was filled with houses and streets and people. We heard that many people born and grown old there never saw the end of it, and we said, 'If such is the case, why should we, who are strangers, look for it?' We gave it up. The people are so many that they tread on one another. All day and night the streets are crowded. We thought that some great thing had happened, and said, 'Let us wait till the people have passed on,' but they never did pass. The surface of the earth is too small for the people, and some live under the earth, and even under the water (alluding to the shops in the Thames Tunnel).

"When we left London, we travelled in a fine waggon drawn by another waggon, but how I never could understand. I could only make out that the first waggon is like a large kettle on wheels, full of water, with a fire under it to make it boil. But before it boils other waggons loaded are tied on behind it, for the moment it does boil it runs away on its own road, and if it were to boil without the waggons being fastened to it I do not know where it would go to. We saw a number of oxen, but the oxen in England do not draw the waggons, but they ride in them, and are drawn along all altogether by the big thing with the boiling water in it. We saw many other strange things more than we can tell you of. We saw men ascend into the skies, and go higher than the eagle. The men did not go up

FOUR OF THE WIVES OF SANDILLI, A KAFFIR CHIEF.

with wings, but in a basket. The basket was tied to a large round bag, filled with smoke. It looked like a large calabash, with the mouth downwards, and the basket hung beneath. In this two people sat, and when the bag was let go it went up with them. I looked at it till my eyes were tired, and it became smaller than a bird. They took up sand with them and poured it on the people beneath, and some fell on us. We likewise saw dogs carrying letters, and monkeys firing off guns. We saw a horse dancing to a drum, and when he had finished, he made a bow to the people who were looking at him. We saw elephants, sea-cows, tigers, and crocodiles living in houses, and snakes handled by human hands. We saw men standing on their heads and walking on their hands for money, and we paid our own money to see them do it." After a minute and intelligent account of an interview with the Queen with which they were honoured, and a description of her palace, guards, and equipage, the young Kaffir concluded his address amid loud applause and clapping of hands. The young people were delighted, but the old men were somewhat incredulous, and shook their heads in mute astonishment, declaring that they could believe almost everything that their countryman had said, except the account which he had given of oxen riding in waggons instead of drawing them.

Such are the people among whom we labour in South-Eastern Africa. They are not deficient in mental capacity; but in their natural state both men and women are deeply degraded, and it is a pleasing fact that many of them have been brought to a saving knowledge of the truth. We have now in the Natal District *seventeen Missionaries, one thousand five hundred and eighty-one Church members*, and *one thousand five hundred and sixty-seven scholars* in the Mission schools.

Before we take our leave of this interesting sphere of Missionary labour, we may just glance at the aggregate statistical results of the past half century, so far as they can be tabulated. We have now in connection with our respective stations and districts in Southern Africa *seventy Missionaries* preaching the Gospel in the vernacular tongues of the people to whom they minister; *eleven thousand five hundred and twenty-four Church members*, of different nations and tribes of people; and *twelve thousand three hundred and forty-three scholars* receiving instruction in the Mission schools.

It is a pleasing fact, moreover, that the Holy Scriptures, hymn-books, catechisms, and other religious publications have been translated into five or six different languages, by the Missionaries, for the use of the natives. Some of these languages had never been written when the Missionaries undertook the arduous task of reducing them to a grammatical form. To the Rev. W. B. Boyce, now one of the General Secretaries of the Wesleyan Missionary Society, belongs the honour of compiling the first Kaffir Grammar, and of unravelling the intricacies of one of the most difficult languages of Southern Africa. By his unwearied and successful efforts, and those of other zealous Missionaries, the way has been in a measure prepared for the noble band of labourers who have succeeded them in this interesting field of Missionary enterprise. May the success of the future be not only as the past, but much more abundant.

CHAPTER VI.

AUSTRALIA.

PRELIMINARY OBSERVATIONS—NEW SOUTH WALES—QUEENSLAND—VIC-
TORIA—SOUTH AUSTRALIA—WESTERN AUSTRALIA—TASMANIA.

AUSTRALIA has justly been described as the largest island in the world, being nearly equal in extent to the whole of Europe. It is estimated at two thousand four hundred miles in length and twelve hundred in breadth. Notwithstanding the rapid advance of colonial enterprise, and the numerous extensive journeys which have been taken of late years, the interior of the country still remains, to a considerable extent, unexplored. So far as it has come under the notice of Europeans, the land in many places appears admirably adapted for grazing purposes, and extensive sheep-walks and cattle-farms have been established in various districts. Where agricultural experiments have been tried, the soil has been found capable of producing grain, provisions, and fruits of different kinds, with the usual variety of articles which generally flourish in semi-tropical countries. The principal items of export are wool, hides, tallow, and of late years, gold. The climate, although very warm during the summer months, is said to be, on the whole, healthy and well adapted to the constitution of Europeans.

It is generally admitted that this great island continent, if so it may be designated, was discovered by the Portuguese in the early part of the sixteenth century; but the first regular exploration of its shores was on its western coast, by a Dutch navigator, named Dirk Harto, in the year 1616. It was again visited by the Dutch three or four years afterwards, when the coast about Swan River was discovered. The southern coast was explored by the Dutch in 1627, as were also the northern shores at a later period, when an order was issued by the States'-General that the territory should be called "New Holland." The whole of the eastern coast was discovered by our countryman, Captain Cook, in 1770, and was called by him "New South Wales." Both these names are now, however, merged in the general designation of "Australia," or the "South Land," with which we may conveniently class the island of Tasmania, which was discovered about the same time. As colonisation advanced, Australia was divided into separate provinces or colonies, which divisions, with their respective civil and Methodistic ecclesiastical organisations, will more clearly appear as we proceed.

The first British settlement in the Southern hemisphere was formed in New South Wales, towards the close of the last century, on the separation of the North-American provinces from England. It was established for the avowed purpose of "ridding the mother country, from time to time, of the yearly increasing number of prisoners, who were accumulating in the jails, of affording a proper place for the punishment of criminals, and of forming a free colony out of the materials which the reformed prisoners would supply, in addition to the families of free emigrants who might be induced to settle in that country." With these objects in view, the British Government fitted out a small fleet, with two years' provisions on board, for upwards of one thousand persons, who embarked for the new colony, seven hundred and fifty of whom were convicts. This fleet sailed into Port Jackson under the command of Captain Phillip, the Governor, on the 26th of June, 1788. As soon as they had landed, the emigrants, both bond and free, were busily employed in felling the forest trees, and clearing the ground along the margin of the bay and up the slopes, on which the splendid town of Sydney now stands. There they pitched their tents and organised the first English colony in the Southern World, which has an interesting general history of its own into the minute particulars of which we cannot now enter. Neither must we make any observations at present on the convict system, so intimately connected with the origin of the settlement, as we wish to pass on

NATIVE CONTESTS.

as quickly as possible to the main object which we have in view —the history of the Missionary enterprise for the benefit of the Aborigines and the settlers. But to prepare the way for this, it is necessary to take a hasty glance at the progress of events for some time after the arrival of the English fleet in Port Jackson.

The pale-faced strangers had not been long on shore when the dark and savage natives came down upon them in a considerable body, and assumed quite a warlike attitude, as if they intended to drive them from their hunting-grounds back again into the sea, from which they appeared so strangely to have emerged. Hostilities at once commenced; but in return for a shower of arrows, the natives received a volley of musket-balls, the mysterious effects of which sent them scampering off into the depth of the forest, from which they were afterwards seen to venture only occasionally, and that in small straggling parties. On further investigation, however, it was found that the Aborigines were by no means numerous, considering the extent of the country; that they wandered about from one encampment to another without any certain dwelling-place, and that they were the most degraded specimens of humanity that had ever been found in any country. We are sorry to be obliged to admit that the natives of Australia have often met with unkind and even cruel treatment at the hands of the settlers, that their number has been gradually decreasing from year to year, and that very little has been done to promote their civilisation. The decrease in the number of the Aborigines became more perceptible when they became addicted to the use of ardent spirits, introduced among them by the European settlers, and when they had learned the use of firearms, which they freely employed in the destruction of each other. Perhaps it ought to be stated also that bitter disappointment, if not entire failure, has been the result of the few well-meant efforts which have been made by the Wesleyans, Moravians, and others to reclaim and Christianise these poor outcasts, so that the Missionary enterprise in Australia has been conducted chiefly for the benefit of European settlers and their descendants, both bond and free.

But notwithstanding this circumstance, from the character and influence of the convict system, and the demoralised state of all classes of the community for a length of time after the commencement of the new colony, there was a loud call and an imperative necessity for evangelical labour. We shall now proceed to relate under what circumstances the Wesleyan Missionary Society was induced to enter this important field of labour, and what have been the character and results of its operations in different parts of Australia, taking a view of each colony or province separately.

New South Wales.

In connection with the convict stations and free settlements which were first established in New South Wales, two or three Episcopal chaplains and a few schoolmasters were appointed by Government to attend to the religious instruction of the people; but, as the population increased, these were found to be quite insufficient to meet the spiritual necessities of the community. Two of the early teachers thus employed, namely Messrs. Bowden and Hosking, had been Wesleyan schoolmasters in London, and feeling the want of the means of grace to which they had been accustomed at home, they organised a Methodist class, the first meeting of which was held in Sydney on the 6th of March, 1812. There were present the two schoolmasters already mentioned and their wives, two senior girls from the school, two soldiers, and four other persons, making twelve in all. Such was the humble beginning of Methodism in Australia. "Who hath despised the day of small things?" But these few disciples of Christ were not satisfied with merely endeavouring to secure the salvation of their own souls; they felt deeply concerned for the spiritual welfare of others; and, believing that Methodism, as a system, was well adapted to meet the wants of the people, they wrote to England earnestly requesting that a Wesleyan minister might be sent out to them.

A brief extract from this communication, which was published in the *Methodist Magazine* at the time, may serve to throw some light on the state of society in Australia at that period. They say: "There are probably twenty thousand souls in this colony of New South Wales, natives of the British Isles and their descendants. From the description of persons sent here much good cannot be expected. The higher ranks of these, who were formerly convicts, are, in general, either entirely occupied in amassing wealth or rioting in sensuality. The lower orders are indeed the filth and offscouring of the earth in point of wickedness. Long accustomed to idleness and wickedness of every kind, here they indulge their vicious inclinations without a blush. Drunkenness, adultery, Sabbath breaking, and blasphemy, are no longer considered as indecencies. All those ties of moral order, and feelings of propriety, which bind society together, are not only relaxed, but almost extinct. This is the general character of the convicts, high and low; and, excepting the civil and military departments of Government, there is no other difference than that which wealth naturally creates in the means which it affords for greater indulgence in vice.... At first there was but one family of Wesleyans, now we have nineteen persons meeting in class. We call upon you in our own behalf; leave us not forsaken in this benighted land. We call upon you in behalf of our children; let them not be left to perish for lack of knowledge. We call upon you in behalf of those who have neither opportunity nor inclination to speak for themselves; leave them not in their blood. We call upon you in the name of the outcasts of society, landing daily on our shores; administer to them that Word which may make their exile a blessing. Send *us* that Gospel which you have received of the Lord to preach to every creature. Send amongst us one of yourselves, and many shall rise up and call you blessed."

The Committee in London regarded this appeal as the call of Providence; and, although the funds of the Society were hardly adequate to such an undertaking, in view of the claims of existing Missions, they nevertheless began to look out for a suitable Missionary, with the hope that their friends would stand by them and provide the necessary funds for the support of the enterprise. They had not long to wait; for whenever God has a work to do, He is sure to find suitable instruments to do it. The person who was raised up by Divine providence as the pioneer Missionary to the Southern World was the Rev. Samuel Leigh, a man wonderfully adapted both by nature and grace for the important work to which he was called, as we shall see in the course of our narrative. He was endowed with a robust constitution, a cheerful disposition, and remarkable energy of character. Mr. Leigh had been designed for another sphere of labour, and had left his native home in Staffordshire, taken an affectionate leave of an aged mother and a dying sister, whom he was never to see again in this world, and came up to London at the call of the Committee for embarkation; but no sooner did the emergency of the case require a change in his destination, than he cheerfully submitted to the new appointment.

Mr. Leigh embarked for Australia in the ship "Hebe," on the 28th of February, 1815, and after a tedious and stormy passage of more than five months, he arrived at Sydney in safety on the 10th of August. Immediately on his landing, Mr. Leigh proceeded to the residence of one of the parties who had so earnestly requested the appointment of a Wesleyan Missionary; but, although there was no lack of courtesy, his reception was not of that hearty and enthusiastic character which has sometimes marked the arrival of a messenger of mercy in a foreign land. Fears were expressed as to the legal difficulties which might exist with regard to the exercise of his ministry in the colony of New South Wales. And on looking over the Missionary's baggage, the gentleman who received him said, "It does not appear that you have brought any household furniture: in our application to the Committtee we particularly requested them to send furniture for a *house*." "The Committee understood you," said Mr. Leigh, "to apply for furniture for a *horse*, and I have brought a second-hand military saddle and bridle complete, and all other requisites." From the indistinctness of the handwriting, the Missionary Secretaries had substituted the word "horse" for house; hence the ludicrous mistake, which is only one of many we have known to occur from the want of clear and legible writing on the part of those who have to transact important public business.

On the day after his arrival Mr. Leigh waited on his Excellency the Governor, to pay his respects, according to custom, and to show his credentials. Here again he met with a rebuff; and it was not till after a lengthened conversation, in the course of which the object and aim of the Missionary were clearly set forth, that the objections of his Excellency were overcome. At length he said, "If those be your objects, they are certainly of the first importance; and if you will endeavour to compass them by the means you have now specified, I cannot but wish you all the success which you can reasonably expect or desire. Call at the Surveyor-General's office, present my compliments, and say, that I wish him to afford you every facility in his power in travelling from one township to another." At the close of this interview, the Governor advanced towards Mr. Leigh, and shook hands with him in the most cordial and friendly manner.

With his feelings somewhat relieved by the favourable turn which his affairs had taken, the Missionary returned to his humble lodgings to render thanks to his Heavenly Father, and to consider what steps it would be best to take next in order to succeed in the benevolent object which he had in view. His prospects were still far from bright, and it is doubtful whether a Mission was ever commenced in any part of the world under more discouraging circumstances than that to our own unfortunate countrymen and their descendants in Australia. With few exceptions the colony of New South Wales was a vast community of convicts, with wandering tribes of savage natives on its borders; and the graphic description which the Apostle Paul gives of the Gentiles of his time has been aptly quoted as illustrative of the character of these miserable outcasts:—" Being filled with all unrighteousness, fornication, wickedness, covetousness, maliciousness; full of envy, murder, debate, deceit, malignity; whisperers, backbiters, haters of God, despiteful, proud, boasters, inventors of evil things, disobedient to parents, without understanding, covenant-breakers, without natural affection, implacable, unmerciful." The free settlers and squatters were widely scattered over a large section of the country, and being entirely destitute of the means of religious instruction, their moral condition was only a few degrees above that of the convict population. Up to the time of the arrival of the first Wesleyan Missionary in the country, the Government had been busily occupied in erecting jails, barracks, and other public buildings necessary for the civil, military, and convict establishments; but very little had been done for the religious and moral improvement of the people. In fact, the whole aspect of affairs, the state of society, the mode of government, the discipline adopted in the management of the convicts, and the temper and spirit of everything and everybody appeared cold, cruel, and repulsive in the extreme, and the Missionary felt that he had indeed come to a strange place. But, in view of all these things, he was not disposed to yield to discouragement.

Having secured the countenance and protection of the Colonial Government, Mr. Leigh began to arrange his plans for a vigorous and systematic attack upon the mass of ignorance and immorality by which he was surrounded. In the true spirit of the "early Methodist Preachers," he mapped out for himself an extensive circuit, in which to itinerate, for the purpose of making known to all classes of the community the good news of salvation. Beginning at Sydney, the capital of the colony, where he fixed his head-quarters, and took care to make strong his basis of operations, he extended his labours to Paramatta, Windsor, Liverpool, Castlereagh, Prospect, Concord, Bulkham Hills, Castle Hill, Kissing Point, and other places. And, notwithstanding the unpromising aspect of affairs at first, and the numerous difficulties which had to be encountered, the Missionary was favoured to witness a measure of success far beyond his most sanguine expectations. Never was the wonderful transforming power of the Gospel more gloriously displayed than in the incidents connected with the early history of our Australian Mission. Men who had dispised parental authority at home, who had disregarded truth and honesty, who had passed through the discipline of the prison and the treadmill, and finished their convict life in the chain gang, trembled like Felix under the faithful preaching of the Gospel, gave their hearts to God, became consistent members of the Church of Christ, and exemplified the beauty of religion by a holy walk and conversation. It would be a pleasing and interesting task, if time and space permitted, to follow the enterprising Missionary, Mr. Leigh, and his fellow-labourers and successors, in their sufferings, toils, and triumphs, as detailed in their communications to the Society at home from year to year. We shall have frequent occasion to mark the wonderful providence and grace of God, and the rapid and extensive progress of the good work in the colony of New South Wales; but all we can do at present is to give a few leading facts illustrative of the character and results of the Mission.

On his arrival in the colony, Mr. Leigh found that the few Wesleyans who had sent to England for a Missionary had hired a house for their meetings in a low depraved part of Sydney, known as "The Rocks." Having removed the partition walls of the building, and fitted up the interior as a place of worship, he commenced his labours by preaching in this place every Sunday morning at six o'clock, and also at the same hour in the evening, to a strange motley congregation of emigrants, soldiers, and convicts. He likewise re-organised a Sabbath-school, the establishment of which had been attempted before his arrival, and paid special attention to the instruction of the rising generation, the children of the settlers being in danger of growing up in the practice of every vice from the evil examples which were daily set before them. In both these departments of Christian labour the Missionary was favoured with a cheering measure of success, and some of his earliest converts, together with two or three who had been previously brought to a saving knowledge of the truth, became valuable fellow-labourers in the work of the Lord.

One of the principal of these devoted men who rendered such important aid in the commencement of the Mission is worthy of special notice: this was Sergeant James Scott, who was converted to God, and joined the Wesleyan Church in the West Indies. The 46th Regiment, to which he belonged, had been ordered some time before to proceed to New South Wales, where he distinguished himself by the able and conscientious discharge of his duties as a non-commissioned officer. Having fulfilled his appointed period of service, he retired from the army, settled in Sydney, and became a zealous local preacher, and in other respects a valuable helper of the first Missionary appointed to labour there. With a view to bring the influence of the Gospel to bear upon other parts of the town besides the notorious district called "The Rocks," where the work was commenced, Mr. Scott opened his own house for preaching; and, in the ardour of his zeal, he purchased a property in Prince-street, part of which was fitted up as a Mission-house for the residence of the minister, and the other appropriated as the site of a new chapel when the enlargement of the work should require additional accommodation. The place of worship ultimately erected on this site was built at the sole expense of this devoted servant of the Lord.

When the cause was well-established in the capital of the colony, Mr. Leigh turned his attention to the country districts. His first journey into the interior was attended with some incidents which are worthy of record. He mounted his horse and set off on a tour of observation to the Castlereagh settlement. At the close of the first day's ride, he called at the house of a settler, to whom he had a letter of introduction, and respectfully solicited accommodation for himself and his horse for the night; but, to his surprise, he met with a rude repulse, and was told of a person named John Lees, who lived about two miles further on, who would probably entertain him. He rode along with a heavy heart, and on arriving at the wooden hut of the said John Lees, he knocked at the door with the end of his whip, and called out, "Will you receive a Wesleyan Missionary?" The door opened, and out came a little, stiff, ruddy lad, who laid hold of the bridle with one hand, and the stirrup with the other, and said, "Get off, sir. My father will be glad to see you."

Mr. Leigh dismounted and entered the hut. He was astonished to find a number of persons sitting round a three-legged table in the most orderly manner. Directing the attention of the stranger to some books that lay on the table, old Mr. Lees said, "We were just going to have family worship. Perhaps you will have the goodness to take that duty off my hands." "With pleasure," said Mr. Leigh; and, taking up the Bible, he opened it at Isaiah xxxv: "The wilderness and the solitary place shall be glad for them; and the desert shall rejoice, and blossom as the rose." Here he was obliged to pause and allow the tears to flow, until he could again command the power of utterance. He then proceeded with the second verse: "It shall blossom abundantly, and rejoice even with joy and singing: the glory of Lebanon shall be given unto it, the excellency of Carmel and Sharon; they shall see the glory of the Lord, and the excellency of our God." But he could proceed no further. Five minutes before he had felt himself a stranger in a strange land, enclosed in the woods of Australia at a late hour, and without a home; now he was in Bethel; while the verses which he had read opened to his view the moral renovation of the world. He was quite overcome, as were also the people; and their united prayers were presented in broken accents, but with sincere gratitude, to God for His goodness. When they rose from their knees, the farmer crossed the floor, and seizing Mr. Leigh's hand, gave him a hearty greeting, saying, "We have been praying for three years that God would send us a Missionary; and now you are come, we are right glad to see you. We had not even heard of your arrival in the colony." After supper they retired to rest exclaiming, "We have seen strange things to-day!"

The history of John Lees, as related by himself afterwards, is a very remarkable one. He was formerly a soldier in the British Army, and, after the corps to which he belonged was disbanded, the Government granted him a small allotment of land, with some other aid, to commence the settler's life. He married and soon had a rising family. After a few years of hard work, several acres of tall trees were felled by his own axe, and the timber burnt off. His live stock increased, and he began to thrive. But his former propensity for strong drink, checked for a while by industry, again developed itself and grew upon him, till he bore all the marks of a reckless, confirmed drunkard. To satisfy his constant craving for the drink, one useful article went after another, till part of his land, and all his live stock, were gone *except one pig*, now fat and ready for the knife. The unhappy man was contemplating the sale of his *last pig*, to pay off a debt which he had contracted for spirituous liquors, when a circumstance occurred which changed the whole course of his future life, and perhaps affected his destiny in the world to come.

While in bed one night, and in a sound sleep, the mind of John

Lees wandered to his usual place of conviviality. In his dream he thought he was in the act of grasping the spirit bottle to fill another glass, when, to his terror, he observed a snake rising out of the bottle with expanded jaws, and striking its fangs in all directions; its deadly eye, flashing fire, was fixed upon him, and occasioned a convulsive horror which awoke him. He thanked God that it was only a dream; yet the impression it made upon his mind could never be obliterated. He regarded the whole scene as indicating the inseparable connection between intemperance and suffering and death. The more he reflected upon it, the more deeply was he convinced of his guilt and danger. He relinquished his drinking habits forthwith, sought and obtained the pardoning mercy of God, and became a new man in Christ Jesus. Henceforth he was a consistent Christian, prospered in business, received the Missionaries into his house, was made instrumental in the conversion of several of his neighbours, and, when a congregation was gathered, of his own accord, and at his own expense, he built a little chapel, and generously presented it to the Society, free from debt. This little Wesleyan sanctuary, the first that was ever built in the colony of New South Wales, was dedicated to the service of God by Mr. Leigh, on the 7th October, 1817, when he preached from that appropriate text, " The Lord hath done great things for us, whereof we are glad."

But to return to Mr. Leigh and his first tour into the interior of New South Wales, we may observe that on the following morning, having commended the household to God in prayer, he mounted his horse to resume his journey. As no guide could be procured, Mr. Lees directed the Missionary, as well as he could, saying, " If Providence has brought you across the sea to this country to convert men, you may depend upon it you will not be left to perish in the woods of Australia. You will have a difficult journey, I can tell you, for the bush is close, and the distance cannot be less than forty miles. I will show you the direction in which the place lies to which you are going. Put your trust in God, and make the best of your way to it." The Missionary soon found that there was no exaggeration in the settler's statement either as to the length or the difficulty of the journey. He carried a good axe, and was frequently obliged to alight and cut a passage for himself and his horse through the closely compacted underwood.

Whilst the horse on which Mr. Leigh was mounted was forcing his head and shoulders through the dense coppice that obstructed his progress, he suddenly started, and falling back almost on his haunches, stood trembling, as if he would drop upon the ground. His rider struck him, but he would not move. He then descended from the saddle, and took the bridle in his hand to lead him forward. Turning his eye to the right, he observed the foliage moving, and heard a rustling noise. Instantly a large snake, nine or ten feet long, made his appearance, and deliberately crossed the path in front of the Missioniary and his horse, within a few feet of the spot where they stood. In passing, it threw off an effluvia which induced sickness and vomiting. The bite of the snake would no doubt have proved fatal to man or horse in a few hours, but providentially it evinced no disposition to molest them. Mr. Leigh continued his journey, and shaping his course by the descending sun, and marking the trees along the whole line of his progress, for his own safety in case of being lost, and for the guidance of others who might follow, he reached the settlement to which he was going at a late hour, much fatigued, but thankful to God for His preserving goodness. Having accomplished the object of his visit, he was favoured to return home in peace and safety.

The next journey of the enterprising Missionary was to Paramatta, a rising town and convict establishment, about fifteen miles from Sydney. Here he became acquainted with the Rev. Samuel Marsden, the senior of the four chaplains appointed by Government to minister to the troops and convicts, a man of sterling worth and genuine piety, whose name is honourably identified with the early history of Missions in the Southern World. In early life, Mr. Marsden had himself been a member of the Wesleyan Society in the town of Leeds, his native place; and he still cherished a kindly feeling towards a body of people to whom he acknowledged himself much indebted. Hence the clergyman gave the Missionary a cordial welcome to his station, where there was ample work for all. One of Mr. Leigh's first converts at Paramatta was a John W——, a convict, whose change of character attracted the notice of all who knew him, and whose subsequent history is worthy of a passing remark. On obtaining his freedom, John commenced running a light one-horse cart between Paramatta and Sydney, for the conveyance of passengers and parcels; and such were his steadiness and perseverance, that his humble vehicle soon gave place to a four-horse stage-coach, the first of the kind ever used in Australia. This conveyance John drove for many years, strictly prohibiting all swearing and profane conversation among his passengers; and such was his success that he acquired considerable property, brought up a large family in respectability and comfort, and in his old age he had the pleasure of seeing one of his sons called to the ministry of that Gospel which had been made the power of God to his own salvation.

Mr. Leigh also formed an out-station at Windsor, where he rented a rude shed, in which he preached for a length of time, till the cause was well established, when a neat little chapel was erected. Other places were visited as opportunities presented themselves: and wherever the Missionary went, he was favoured to see a measure of prosperity which gladdened his heart, and encouraged him to go forward in the name of the Lord. Mr. Leigh had soon a regularly organised circuit of one hundred and fifty miles in extent, which occupied him ten days to travel; and in order to give to each place a sermon, even at long intervals, he was only able to spend about fourteen days in the city each month before he mounted his horse, and was off again.

As the good work thus expanded in New South Wales, the need of additional labourers was keenly felt; and an earnest appeal was made to the Committee in England for the required assistance. But it was not till the Conference of 1817 that the Society was in circumstances to make arrangements for reinforcing the Mission. Towards the end of that year, however, the Rev. Walter Lawry embarked for the Southern World, and by the good providence of God, he landed in safety at Sydney on the 1st of May, 1818. When the new Missionary arrived, Mr. Leigh was out in the circuit, but on his return to the city on the following day, great was his joy on being favoured to welcome a fellow-labourer to the shores of New South Wales. A larger amount of ministerial labour was now given to the principal stations, whilst at the same time the Gospel was conveyed to several new places, which could not be reached when there was only one Missionary in the colony.

Two or three years afterwards, the Mission was still further strengthened by the appointment of the Rev. Messrs. Carvosso, Walker, Horton, and others; and as the population of the colony increased by the constant flow of emigration to its shores, the work was both consolidated and extended, to the great advantage of all classes of the community. The reflex influence of Methodism, in this as in other countries, was very observable, so that when Mr. Leigh visited England at a subsequent period, he could triumphantly exclaim, "When I commenced my Missionary work in Australia, there were only four clergymen of the Church of England, and very few communicants; now there are ninety-three thousand, one hundred and thirty-seven persons in connection with that Church! Then there was no Presbyterian minister in the colony; now the members of the Church of Scotland number eighteen thousand, one hundred and fifty-six! Then there were only fourteen accredited Wesleyans; now there are above ten thousand, and nearly as many children receiving instruction in the day and Sunday-schools! May we not say, in the language of admiration and gratitude, "What hath God wrought?"

From the very commencement of the work in the manner we have described, the entire course of the Wesleyan Mission to Australia has been one of steady progress and advancement. This was strikingly illustrated by the various addresses which were delivered in connection with the Jubilee services which were held at Sydney, in the month of November 1864, after the lapse of fifty years since the arrival of the first Missionary. These services commenced with an appropriate sermon by the Rev. Stephen Rabone, who took for his text Eccles. vii. 13. Early the following morning, a prayer-meeting was held, and at nine o'clock nearly five hundred persons sat down to breakfast together. Then followed a public meeting, at which Mr. T. W. Bowden, a descendant of one of the first Methodists in the colony, presided. The chairman apologised for the absence of Mr. Hosking, the son of the gentleman who took an active part in the commencement of the Mission, and then proceeded to relate how he remembered Mr. Leigh as an inmate at his father's house when he was a boy, and how he used to mount his horse, called "Old Traveller," and set off on his extensive circuit round the colony. He also gave an interesting account of the building first used as a Wesleyan place of worship at the corner of Essex and Gloucester-streets, now occupied by a shoemaker, and of the erection of the first new chapel in Sydney, in Prince-street, at the sole expense of Mr. James Scott, a sergeant in the 46th regiment, as already mentioned. He further related that, when this became too small for the congregation, the chapel in Macquarie-street, now occupied by the Unitarians, was built. Again there was a lack of room, when the still more commodious chapel in York-street, in which they were assembled, was erected. Other gentlemen and ministers also addressed the meeting in strains of gratitude to God for the prosperous state of the work, and a collection was made, when about £4,000 was given, or promised, towards the Jubilee Fund. This sum was afterwards increased to £12,000, for the purpose of founding a Wesleyan College, and for the relief of Church property.

With reference to this branch of Methodism in Australia, it is only necessary to add that, as the work expanded, a number of new circuits were organised in various parts of the colony of New South Wales, and that ultimately these were classified in four divisions, denominated the Sydney, the Bathurst, the Maitland, and the Goulburn Districts, which unitedly number *sixty-two ministers, five thousand Church members,* and *eleven thousand six hundred and seven scholars* in the Sabbath and day-schools.

QUEENSLAND.

On referring to the map, it will be seen that the north-eastern portion of Australia is now called Queensland. This extensive territory was formerly regarded as belonging to New South Wales; but a few years ago it was formed into a separate and independent colony, and as such its Missionary history claims a distinct and special record. A few brief observations on the course of events which led to this issue, will naturally conduct us to the main object we have in view.

Such was the spirit of agricultural and mercantile enterprise which animated the early settlers in New South Wales, that long before there was any lack of room in the old colony, individuals were seen pushing their way up the eastern coast of New Holland. On passing Point Danger, a large estuary was found sixty miles long and twenty broad, dotted with a number of beautiful little islands, and receiving the waters of five navigable rivers of considerable magnitude. This extensive sheet of water received the name of Morton Bay; and the land along the shores, and on the banks of the rivers, being found well adapted for agricultural purposes, it became the centre of a new settlement. The first trading establishment or town that was built was called Brisbane, being situated at the mouth of a river of that name, and is now the capital of the colony and the seat of government. Other towns and villages rapidly arose as the population increased, as Ipswich, Warwick, Maryborough, Rockhampton, &c.

Further exploration brought to light a number of beautiful harbours still further north, with extensive downs and alluvial plains in the interior, which pointed out the country as peculiarly adapted for colonisation. Arrangements were accordingly made with the Imperial Government to carry out this object, and a charter was granted in 1859, when Queensland became a separate colony. The principal agents in this important measure displayed the most laudable energy in pushing forward their favourite enterprise, and an emigration scheme was set on foot which brought a rapid influx of population from the mother-country,—too rapid, in fact: hence the collapse and serious embarrassment which have followed. But events such as these are not uncommon in a rising colony, and Queensland, which now comprises a territory four times as large as England, with a fine soil and a healthy climate, and a population of 107,427 persons will, no doubt, in due time surmount the financial difficulties with which she is at present contending, and be favoured to realise a grand and prosperous future.

Among the early emigrants to Morton Bay were a few pious Wesleyans, who did not allow the toils and anxieties incident to the commencement of colonial life, to quench the spark of Divine grace, which glowed in their hearts, but who met together for Christian counsel and worship as they had opportunity. These, and a few others, earnestly desired the ministrations and pastoral care of a Wesleyan Missionary. In consequence of the paucity of ministers, and other circumstances, some time elapsed before this laudable desire could be met. At first a Catechist was appointed to Morton Bay, to instruct the people and conduct public worship on the Lord's-day. Afterwards a supernumerary minister took up his residence among them, and gladly performed such service as his declining strength would permit. At length arrangements were made to occupy the place as a regular station. The first Missionary appointed to Queensland was the Rev. John Watsford, who commenced his labours in the Brisbane Circuit in 1850. A chapel had been erected in the town previous to his arrival, and such was the anxiety of the people to hear the Word of God, that its enlargement soon became necessary. The members of the Society increased in number during the first year to seventy-two, and they were said to "manifest their love to the Lord Jesus by the feeling of peace and love prevalent among them, by their upright deportment before the people of the world, by their zeal in seeking the conversion of sinners, and by their liberal contributions towards the support of the Gospel."

The subsequent history of the Mission was, in its main features, similar to that of the work in other new colonies. In every rising country there are peculiar temptations, trials and difficulties, which affect the Christian life of the individual member, as well as the onward march of the Church in its collective capacity. Everything connected with commercial and agricultural pursuits in such a place is liable to fluctuate, and the extremes of either prosperity or adversity are neither of them favourable to religious progress. It is pleasant to be able to state, however, that the cause of God in Queensland has continued steadily to advance from the beginning, and that it bids fair to surmount every difficulty, and to prosper more and more in time to come.

Mr. Watsford was succeeded by the Rev. Messrs. Millard, Piddington, Fidler, Curnow, Fletcher, Beazley, and others, and by their united and persevering efforts, the good work was extended to various parts of the province, several years before it became an independent colony, and it prospered still more afterwards. Several new circuits having been formed in localities remote from each other, to which ministers were appointed as openings presented themselves, they were organised into a regular Wesleyan district, in the year 1863, under the pastoral care of the Rev. Joseph H. Fletcher. In 1868 the Rev. Isaac Harding was appointed to the charge of the Queenstown district, and cheerfully travelled a distance of two thousand miles with his family from his former station in New Zealand, to enter upon his new sphere of labour. The writer had the pleasure of becoming acquainted with Mr. Harding at the Cape of Good Hope, where he was detained for some time when on his way to Australia in 1854, and from his known energy of character there is no doubt but the work will be still further extended and consolidated under his zealous and judicious superintendence. The immediate and pressing want of Methodism in this new and rising country is financial aid towards the support of the work in the present depressed state of the commercial interests of the colony. For this the chairman earnestly pleaded at the Conference held in Sydney, in January 1869, when it was unanimously resolved that a collection should be made in every chapel in the course of the year on behalf of the Home Mission Fund of Queensland. It is hoped that a liberal response will be made from those parts of the Connexion which are comparatively free from such painful embarrassment.

The work in this part of Australia is still in its infancy, and the impediments to its progress are great and numerous. It is matter of gratitude, however, that a good beginning has been made. We have now in connection with the Queensland district, *nine ministers, four hundred and twenty Church members*, and *one thousand, four hundred and sixty-one scholars* in the Sabbath and day-schools.

VICTORIA.

The colony of Victoria, formerly designated Australia Felix, is situated on the southern point of the great island continent, and immediately opposite to Tasmania, or Van Dieman's Land. It was originally included within the boundary of the colony of New South Wales, and only became a separate settlement in 1838. Previous to that period the country had been visited by a few individual adventurers, who, charmed with the splendid prospects which everywhere presented themselves to view, and attracted by the facilities which it afforded for agricultural pursuits, had taken possession of a few choice places as " squatters." When the first party of British colonists entered the splendid bay of Port Phillip, which is only two miles wide at the entrance, but afterwards spreads out to the breadth of from twenty to sixty miles, they were at once impressed with the numerous advantages of the locality. They went on shore at the head of the bay, at a place now known as Williamstown, but soon proceeded to a more elevated situation on the banks of the Yarra, where they fixed their headquarters, about two miles inland, where the splendid city of Melbourne now stands. In 1838, nothing was to be seen there but a cluster of rude huts, embowered in forest trees, presenting the appearance of an Indian village. Two wooden houses served the purpose of inns for the settlers who visited the place, and a small square frame building, with an old ship's bell suspended from a tree, was used as a place of worship by different denominations; whilst two or three so-called shops formed emporiums for the sale of every description of useful articles. How great is the change which has taken place in the short space of thirty years! Now the voyager on entering Port Phillip, has his attention arrested by the appearance of hundreds of vessels at anchor, from all parts of the world, engaged in an extensive and prosperous commerce: and on proceeding to Melbourne, he beholds a magnificent city, which bids fair to rival, if not to surpass, some of the splendid capitals of Europe.

When the first settlers arrived in this part of Australia, they found the country inhabited by scattered tribes of wandering natives, in every respect similar to those which had been met with in other places. When a party of these came down to the settlement on one occasion, there appeared among them a man in many respects different from the rest. Although nearly in a state of nudity, and assuming a savage aspect, he was evidently of lighter complexion, and had sharper features, than the rest of his sable companions. On full investigation, this strange-looking wild man of the woods proved to be an European, who had lived for many years among the Aborigines, and whose history is equal to any romance that was ever written. The leading particulars of this strange incident may be interesting to the reader, as they have an immediate bearing upon the Missionary enterprise, and the commencement of our work in that part of Australia.

The name of this man was William Buckley. He was a native of England, and formerly a soldier in the British Army. For some misdemeanour he was transported, with many others, to a penal settlement for seven years. The vessel in which the convicts were sent out touched at Port Phillip, it being intended, if circumstances were favourable, to form a convict establishment there. Those in command, however, considered the place unsuitable, and relinquished their design; they consequently proceeded in search of a more favourable place, and ultimately fixed upon Hobart Town, Van Dieman's Land. During the temporary disembarkation of the prisoners at Port Phillip, Buckley, with some others, absconded, and after a fruitless search for the missing convicts, the vessel sailed, and the fugitives were left in the country. From the information given by Buckley himself, it appears that he and his associates wandered together in the bush for a short time, and then parted; and from that period, he never saw or heard anything of his former companions. When

Buckley, who was a tall man, six feet six inches high, was first discovered by the natives, they manifested considerable surprise at the appearance of the gigantic pale-faced wanderer in the woods; but they treated him with kindness, and sympathising with him in his forlorn condition, provided him with food, such as they had. They moreover furnished him with skins for clothing, till he became accustomed to their savage mode of life. Having roamed about with these dark children of the forest for a considerable time, the Englishman abandoned all hope of getting away from the country; and at length allied himself to a tribe by marriage, according to native custom, and assimilated himself to their habits and mode of living. In this state he had continued for thirty-two years, and had completely forgotten his own native tongue, when he was discovered by the early European settlers. He gladly embraced the first opportunity of joining his countrymen; and, having abandoned his uncivilised mode of life, soon recovered a knowledge of the English language, and became useful both to the settlers and to the Missionaries in their intercourse with the Aborigines.

The Wesleyan Missionary Society having, from the commencement of their labours in Australia, cherished an earnest desire to attempt to Christianise the Aboriginal inhabitants when the way should open, regarded this as a favourable opportunity. The Committee in London, therefore, instructed the Rev. Joseph Orton, on his appointment to Tasmania, to collect and communicate to them all the information he could obtain as to the number and condition of the native tribes, and the most likely means of elevating them in the scale of being. With a view to fulfil this commission, Mr. Orton paid a visit to Port Phillip in the year 1836, and one of the first persons to whom he was introduced was the said William Buckley, who, together with other parties on whose testimony he could rely, communicated much valuable information. From these persons he learned that the number of natives within the distance of sixty miles on either hand of Port Phillip amounted to about one thousand; that they wandered about in small parties without any settled dwelling place, subsisting upon roots and such game, chiefly kangaroos and opossums, as they could procure in hunting; and that their moral condition was one of extreme degradation. Mr. Orton, moreover, held several meetings with a number of natives who were collected together for the purpose, their old compeer, Buckley, acting as interpreter. Such were the impressions made upon the mind of the Missionary by this tour of observation, and the favourable character of the report sent home upon the subject, that in the course of the following year two Missionaries, the Revs. Benjamin Hurst and Francis Tuckfield, were appointed to commence a mission among the Aborigines in the neighbourhood of Port Phillip.

As it was considered desirable to induce as many of the natives as possible to settle in one place, where they might be taught the arts of civilised life, and attend to religious instruction, Mr. Orton went to Sydney to lay the case before the Governor, and to obtain a grant of land for a native institution. The locality fixed upon for the station was on the river Barwann, about thirty miles from the township of Geelong. On the 12th of August, 1838, Mr. Tuckfield reported the safe arrival of himself and Mrs. Tuckfield at Melbourne, and they immediately entered on their new sphere of labour by holding meetings with the natives as they had opportunity. In the following year Mr. Tuckfield was joined by his colleague, Mr. Hurst, and, after some delay, they were put in possession of the land granted by Government, and removed to their wilderness home with a number of Aborigines.

The Missionaries had now to direct their attention to a variety of secular affairs, whilst at the same time they attended to the spiritual interest of the people. With the help of the natives they erected two wooden houses as residences for the Mission families, besides a number of necessary outbuildings. They also felled the trees, and brought under cultivation a considerable quantity of land for the support of themselves and the people. A flock of sheep and a herd of cattle were raised by degrees, and a measure of temporal prosperity was realised, in connection with the institution, which was truly gratifying. Nor were the efforts of the Missionaries to promote the spiritual welfare of the people destitute of results. A Mission-school was established and religious services regularly held with as many of the natives as could be induced to attach themselves to the station. Although the people were extremely ignorant and deeply degraded, having scarcely any idea of a Supreme Being, or of a future state of existence, they were not found wanting in capacity to receive instruction. Some of the children made considerable progress in reading, writing, and arithmetic, and the Missionaries were at times encouraged to hope that they would ultimately succeed in raising some of the tribes at least from the social and moral degradation in which they were involved.

On the whole, however, but little permanent impression was made on the native mind by the labours of the Missionaries. The difficulties with which they had to contend, from their imperfect knowledge of the language, the unconquerable propensity of the people to wander away from the institution, and the adverse influence of some wicked and unprincipled settlers in the neighbourhood, were insurmountable; and the Missionaries, who were undoubtedly men of God, and entirely devoted to their work, were doomed to see the people of their charge indifferent to their instructions, and frequently deserting the station, to resume their former savage mode of living in the bush. And this was not all. By means of the petty wars, which were so prevalent among the native tribes, and the diseases which were introduced among them by the depraved whites of the convict class, the people were gradually wasting away and becoming fewer every year.

Under these circumstances, the Missionaries were convinced that unless the institution could be removed further into the interior, beyond the influence of the settlers, and the number of labourers greatly increased, the evangelisation of the degraded Aborigines of Australia would be a hopeless task. Having laboured among them with but little fruit for several years, Mr. Tuckfield took an extensive journey of two hundred miles in search of a more suitable site for a Mission-station. After great privation and exposure he found, as he thought, an eligible place on the river Murray, and, with a measure of zeal and perseverance, worthy of more ample success, he was ready to prosecute his difficult enterprise on a new plan, when, in view of all the circumstances of the case, the Missionary Committee resolved, in 1848, after ten years of almost fruitless efforts, to relinquish the undertaking, and turn their attention to more promising fields of labour.

From the first arrival of the Missionaries at Port Phillip in 1838, they were deeply impressed with the necessity and importance of something being done to meet the spiritual wants of their fellow-countrymen who had already settled in the township of Melbourne to the number of about three thousand, and they embraced every opportunity of preaching to them, whilst engaged in preparing for their proper work among the natives. As some of the colonists had been connected with the Wesleyan Church, as members or hearers in their native land, and others were beginning to see the importance of the "one thing needful," they were not satisfied with this precarious and irregular supply of a Gospel ministry, but earnestly requested that they might be favoured with the stated services of a Missionary. This reasonable demand was at length met by the appointment, in 1841, of the Rev. Samuel Wilkinson to the Melbourne circuit. From this period the work of God rapidly advanced among the British settlers. A commodious chapel, to seat six hundred persons, was immediately built in the capital, at an expense of £3,000. To meet this heavy outlay the sum of £1,500 was raised by private subscription, and £1,000 and a suitable site for the building were generously granted by the local government. Two small chapels were also erected at William's Town and New Town, and the sum of £300 was subscribed towards the erection of a chapel at Geelong, a rising town about fifty miles from Melbourne. And what was still more pleasing, a rich spiritual blessing attended the preaching of the Word, and several enquirers were gathered into the fold of Christ, so that at the end of the first year, one hundred and fifty-two persons were reported to be united in Church fellowship in the Melbourne circuit, which, in fact, at that time embraced the whole colony of Victoria.

From year to year the work of God in Melbourne, and the other circuits which were successively formed in different parts of the colony, steadily advanced, and the accounts which were sent to the parent society from time to time were of a very pleasing character. From the very commencement of the Mission Melbourne was a self-supporting circuit, and in a short time it was able to render important financial aid to the dependent stations at a distance. But rapid as was the progress of the work in this part of Australia in the early years of its history, it was still more so from 1852, when the discovery of extensive gold-fields in Ballarat, Forest Creek, Bendigo, and other parts of the province brought such a large and rapid influx of population from almost every part of the world. It was a time of great excitement, and the numerous temptations to sin in various forms would no doubt have been still more appalling in their results if the Wesleyan Missionaries, and other Christian ministers, had not used their utmost exertions to stem the torrent of iniquity, and provide the means of grace for the vast multitudes of people which were soon congregated at "the diggings."

One of the most useful institutions which was called into existence by this influx of population to Melbourne, was the "Wesleyan Emigrant's Home," which was erected at an expense of £8,500, towards which the colonial government voted a grant of £1,000, from a deep conviction of the philanthropic character of the undertaking. This establishment was designed for the temporary accommodation of Wesleyans and others on their first arrival in the colony; and by means of the religious services which were held in connection with it, and the excellent management of Mr. and Mrs. Courtney, formerly members of the writer's congregation at the Cape of Good Hope, who were placed at its head, it proved a source of both temporal comfort and spiritual blessing to many a poor homeless emigrant. A large tent chapel was also pitched on the banks of the Yarra, on the outskirts of an extensive encampment called Canvastown, near Melbourne, and much spiritual good resulted from the services which were held there.

When the Wesleyan ministers nobly moved forward to the gold-diggings, and erected rough slab chapels in which to preach the Gospel, they sought the spiritual benefit of all classes of the community without distinction, and, at an early period of their labours, their attention was attracted to a large number of Chinese emigrants, who had found their way to the land of gold. But from the difficult and peculiar character of their language, little could have been done for these people had it not been for the instrumentality of one of their own number, who was providentially raised up for this particular work. This was a man named Leong-on-Tong, who, having been brought to a saving knowledge of the truth himself, laboured under the direction of the Missionaries at the diggings with unwearied diligence for the conversion of his fellow-countrymen. The Lord blessed him with much success, and he was made the honoured instrument of winning many souls to Christ. The Chinese converts thus gathered into the fold of the Redeemer were united in church-fellowship, and from time to time their number was increased.

On Sunday the 7th of June, 1868, an interesting service was held in connection with the Victoria Chinese Mission, when six more converts were presented for baptism. On this occasion Leong-on-Tong, their zealous teacher, made a noble speech. In the course of his address he said, "I have found some sheep which were going astray in the wilderness, and I wish you to rejoice with me and the angels in heaven. Their hearts were dark and hard; but God has shined into their hearts. They have sorrowed for their sins, and believed in Jesus; and now they are forgiven," &c. After the baptismal service, at which there was a large attendance of all classes, the Sacrament of the Lord's Supper was administered, when sixteen Christian Chinese joined their English brethren in commemorating the Saviour's dying love. In consequence of the increasing importance of this Mission to the large population of "Celestials" at the gold diggings, in 1867, the Rev. J. Caldwell, a European Missionary, was appointed to it; and it was hoped that still greater success would be realised in time to come. But a temporary check has been put upon the work by a painful dispensation of Divine providence. Mr. Caldwell proceeded to China to learn the language and prepare for his important enterprise; but, before he had been there long, he was unfortunately drowned while bathing in the river near Canton, on the 8th of September, 1868. This melancholy event has cast a gloom over the Chinese Mission in Victoria for the time being; but it is hoped that the Conference may yet set apart another Missionary for this important work.

In bringing to a close our brief and hasty sketch of the rise and progress of Methodism in Victoria, it is pleasant to be able to state that the good work is still advancing in a very satisfactory manner. The city of Melbourne has been divided into four circuits, in all of which beautiful and commodious places of worship have been erected; and a seminary of learning has recently been established, called "Wesley College," which promises to be a great blessing to the colony. The work has been gradually extended to Brighton, Berwick, Williamstown, Geelong, Portland, Ballarat, Hamilton, and many other places, where prosperous circuits have been formed, chapels built, and schools established. The colony has already been divided into three Methodist Districts, and the foundation of a great and glorious work has been laid, which it is believed will in time to come bring glory to God in the salvation of men on a larger scale than has yet been realised. We have now in connection with the Melbourne, Geelong, and Castlemain Districts in the colony of Victoria, *sixty-three ministers, ten thousand seven hundred and twenty-seven Church members*, and *twenty-five thousand scholars* in the Sabbath and day-schools.

But there is no sunshine without a shadow. In the midst of a cheering measure of spiritual prosperity, several events in connection with the history of Methodism in Victoria have recently occurred of a very afflictive character. On the 10th of January, 1866, the Rev. D. J. Draper and his excellent wife lost their lives by the foundering of the steam-ship *London*, in the Bay of Biscay, when on their passage to Melbourne; on the 8th of September, 1868, the Rev. J. Caldwell, of Victoria, was drowned near Canton; on the 14th of May, 1869, the Rev. William Hill

AUSTRALIA.

REV. J. D. AND MRS. DRAPER, OF AUSTRALIA,

Who lost their lives by the foundering of the Steamer "London," 10th January, 1866.

was murdered at Melbourne by a prisoner whilst visiting him in his cell in the prison: and these painful incidents were followed by intelligence of the somewhat sudden death of the Rev. Benjamin Field, from England, which occurred at Melbourne, where he had been labouring for some time with acceptance and success, on the 1st of September, 1869. These are so many calls to survivors to "work while it is day, for the night cometh when no man can work."

South Australia.

The colony of South Australia differs in many respects from those parts of Australia which have already passed under review. It comprises an extensive block of land, estimated at 300,000 square miles, being more than double the dimensions of Great Britain and Ireland. Much of this vast area has scarcely been yet explored, however, and many years must elapse before it can be fully occupied. The land in many parts of the country is said to be remarkably fertile, and easily brought under cultivation, being free from forest trees and fern roots, and ready for the plough. The country is far from mountainous in its aspect; but presents to the view a gently indulating surface, which redeems it from that flat monotony that would otherwise prevail. Large crops of wheat have been raised, from year to year; and, after supplying the home market, sufficient produce has remained to allow of the export of a considerable quantity to the neighbouring colonies. This portion of Australia is, moreover, possessed of considerable mineral wealth, extensive copper mines having for many years been worked to great advantage in the interior.

The capital of the colony is Adelaide, a considerable town with wide streets intersecting each other at right angles, and adorned with many excellent buildings. The town is situated about seven miles from the port, at the head of the Gulf St. Vincent; but it is reached with comparative ease by means of a recently-constructed railway. In the vicinity of the capital there are several villages rejoicing in the names of Kensington, Islington, Walkerville,

Hindmarsh, Bowden, Prospect, and Thebarton. Further up the country there are numerous rising townships; and farms are rapidly increasing in number with the influx of population.

It was by means of a remarkable dispensation of Divine Providence that the way was opened for the commencement of the first Mission-station in South Australia. Among the early emigrants to that rising colony there were a few earnest Wesleyan Methodists who united themselves in Christian fellowship, and met together at stated periods for Divine worship and mutual edification in the land of their adoption. To carry out their purposes more fully, and, if possible, to benefit their fellow colonists, they had built a small chapel, and were earnestly desiring the services of a regular Minister, when their wishes were met in a manner they little expected. This was by the shipwreck of a Wesleyan Missionary on their coast when on his passage from Tasmania to Swan River, in the year 1837. This incident is worthy of record as illustrative of the ever-watchful providence of God, and of the trials and dangers to which the Missionaries are often exposed in the prosecution of their important work.

The Rev. William Longbottom, with his wife and child, embarked at Hobart Town, for his appointed Station in Western Australia in a small vessel called the *Fanny*, about the middle of June. Soon after leaving the port, a fresh gale sprang up, which continued with increasing violence for several days. The storm had somewhat abated, but the sea was still running high, when about midnight on the 21st, the vessel struck on a coast unknown to the captain. The boat was immediately carried away by the violence of the surf, and it was with difficulty that they held on to the vessel, the sea breaking over them every minute, until the captain and seamen, with great exertion, succeeded in passing a rope from the ship to the shore, by means of which all lives were saved, though not without imminent peril to that of Mrs. Longbottom, who was under water for some time. After the shipwrecked party were landed, they suffered much for want of fire, till the second day, when some friendly natives, who ventured to approach them, supplied this want.

The passengers and seamen of the ill-fated *Fanny* had been for more than a fortnight in these forlorn circumstances, not knowing in which direction to proceed, when they were joined by the captain and crew of the *Elizabeth* another vessel that had been wrecked about a hundred miles to the eastward; but who had preserved their chart, and who informed the Missionary and his party that they were about fifty miles distant from Encounter Bay, a whaling station in South Australia. To this station the two captains and a few of the men at once proceeded; and after some delay a boat arrived for the remaining sufferers, or rather met them, for they had already set out, leaving behind them the property they had saved from the wreck, in despair of receiving the promised aid, having already been forty-five days in the bush. The boat carried them part of the way; they had then a fatiguing walk of twenty miles before they reached the whaling station, where they were received with great kindness by the residents. From thence they proceeded by sea to Adelaide, where the shipwrecked Missionary and his wife met with a most cordial reception from the members of the Methodist Society, sixty in number, and other colonists who gladly rendered all the assistance in their power to the whole of the sufferers.

No sooner had Mr. Longbottom in a measure recovered from the effects of his shipwreck, than he commenced preaching to the people at Adelaide, and the little chapel was crowded with attentive hearers of the Word of God. Being deeply impressed with the remarkable Providence by which a Missionary had been so unexpectedly brought to their shores, the people were unwilling to part with him, and united in an earnest request to the Committee in London for the continuance of his labours among them. This request was ultimately granted, and another Missionary was appointed to Swan River. On being authoritatively designated to the interesting sphere of labour on which he had been so strangely cast by the interposition of Him whom "winds and seas obey," Mr. Longbottom addressed himself with becoming zeal and diligence to the important duties of his office, and the blessing of the great Head of the Church attended his labours. The little sanctuary which he found on his arrival soon became too small for the increasing numbers who flocked to hear the Gospel, and it was ere long superseded by the erection of a more commodious place of worship in Gawler-street.

As the good work expanded, other chapels were subsequently built in Pier-street, Franklin-street, and Kermode-street, as well as at Bowden, Walkerville, Brigton, Thebarton, Kersbrook, and other villages in the neighbourhood of the capital, into which the Gospel was ultimately introduced. Nor were the labours of the Missionary, and the noble band of local preachers who were raised up to assist him, confined to the vicinity of Adelaide. A circuit was soon formed one hundred miles long and thirty broad, and comprising a large number of out-stations, where the Gospel was faithfully preached as opportunities presented themselves, and multitudes of perishing sinners were gathered into the fold of the Redeemer. On his removal to Tasmania, after an acceptable and useful term of service, Mr. Longbottom was succeeded by the Rev. Messrs. Eggleston, Weatherston, Draper, and others; and, notwithstanding occasional hindrances from the depression of trade, and other circumstances, the good work continued to advance in all its departments.

In the commencement of the Wesleyan Mission to South Australia, the Society had special reference to the evangelisation of the Aborigines, as well as the spiritual benefit of the European settlers, and native schools were established and continued for some time in the neighbourhood of the capital, under the patronage of the Government, but the same difficulties which had been experienced in other places, prevented the success of the enterprise. After persevering for some time with but little fruit, owing chiefly to the restless wandering habits of the natives, the undertaking was relinquished, and the Missionaries directed their attention more entirely to the spread of the Gospel among the colonists, who were rapidly increasing in number and pushing their way to distant parts of the country.

The subsequent history of the Mission was characterised by almost uninterrupted progress and success, the existing chapels, both in the city and in the rural districts, being enlarged, and new ones erected in various places to accommodate the rapidly increasing congregations. The number of ministers was also increased by arrivals from England, and by the raising up of faithful labourers in the colony to occupy the new stations and circuits, which were formed in various parts of the land. The result of this aggressive movement has far exceeded the most sanguine expectations of both Missionaries and people at an early period of its history. We have now, in connection with the South Australian District, *twenty-five ministers, five thousand and forty-five Church members*, and *nine thousand eight hundred and seven scholars* in the Sabbath and day-schools.

WESTERN AUSTRALIA.

The colony of Western Australia is situated at the head of King George's Sound, and the interior of the country is reached by ascending Swan River, on the banks of which, Perth, the capital, stands at a distance of about three hundred miles from the sea. The British settlement at this place was commenced in 1829, under circumstances of peculiar discouragement. The first party of emigrants were landed on the beach at the mouth of the river in mid-winter, in the neighbourhood of bare limestone rock, the country around being devoid of agricultural or pastoral capabilities, and inhabited only by wandering tribes of savage natives.

The process of debarkation was scarcely completed, when several of the ships were dashed to pieces on the shore, which was crowded with a heterogeneous mass of human beings,—families with infant children, ladies, officers, soldiers, sailors, and farmers; while horses, cows, sheep, goats, pigs, poultry, ploughs, piano-fortes, casks, furniture, bedding, and tools lay heaped together and drenched with rain. The confusion was complete ; the leaders of the enterprise were equally at a loss with the settlers to know how to proceed or what to advise. Several left the country in utter disgust by the first opportunity which presented itself; and we have heard some of them, who afterwards settled at the Cape of Good Hope, relate the story of their sufferings in the most pathetic manner. Others, however, ultimately pushed their way up the country, took possession of the lands assigned them, and, after encountering many difficulties, succeeded pretty well. Although the land in general, in this part of the Southern World, is not quite so fertile as in some other localities, the climate is acknowledged to be very salubrious, and the country is not subject to the droughts which prevail on the eastern coast. There are extensive forests of excellent timber in the interior, with intervals of excellent grazing ground for cattle, which, together with the mineral wealth which has recently been brought to light, promise for this small but rising colony a prosperous future.

We now call the attention of the reader to the means employed to promote the religious welfare of the British settlers, and the scattered tribes of Aborigines. Besides the appointment of a chaplain and schoolmaster to attend to the convict establishment which was soon formed, and the civil and military departments of Government, little or nothing had been done to supply the spiritual wants of the people, when, in 1838, the Wesleyan Missionary Society responded to an earnest request which was made for the appointment of a Missionary. The Rev. W. Longbottom was designated for the service, but suffering shipwreck, as already mentioned, he was authorised to settle at Adelaide, where he had been driven by stress of circumstances; and his place was supplied at Swan River, in the course of the following year, by the appointment of the Rev. John Smithies. On his arrival at Perth, Mr. Smithies was received with the liveliest demonstrations of gratitude and joy, by a few Methodist settlers who had already commenced to hold little meetings for their mutual edification. For the long period of sixteen years did this devoted Missionary continue to labour in the colony, during the first half of which it was his lot to minister to the same people without any colleague, amid difficulties and trials which might have discouraged a man of less firmness and energy of character. But although this zealous servant of God was left so long to toil alone, yet in another sense he was not alone, for the Master was with him, and if he was unable to do much in the way of extending the work, his labours were blessed to those whom he was able to reach, and the church was built up and edified by his instructive ministry.

As in the establishment of Missions in other places, so in the commencement of the work at Swan River, the Society had special reference to the welfare of the natives, who were found wandering about the country in small scattered tribes, the same as in other parts of the land. On the appointment of the first Missionary to Western Australia, he was instructed to pay particular attention to the Aborigines; and there can be no doubt but he discharged his duty faithfully in this respect, whilst at the same time he neglected no opportunity of preaching to his fellow-countrymen "the glorious Gospel of the blessed God." Failing in his efforts to impress or reclaim the adult natives from their wild and wandering habits, Mr. Smithies at length directed his chief attention to the children. Some of these were already in the service of the colonists, and several others, to the number of about forty, were placed by their parents, who occasionally visited the town, under the care of a Missionary and a teacher whom he hired to attend to them. These juveniles were found quite capable of receiving instruction, and being fed, clothed, and trained in the Mission school, for some time they made fair progress in learning.

In his report of this department of the work, for the year 1846, the Missionary says:—"The natives learn reading, writing, and arithmetic, and some have made considerable proficiency." Mention is also made of a public examination, at which His Excellency the Governor was present, and who was so pleased with the result that with his own hand he gave presents to six native youths, who had acquitted themselves remarkably well, in answering questions from the Catechism, as well as in other exercises, which included the singing of hymns both in English and in their own tongue. And, what was more encouraging still, some of these poor miserable outcasts were brought under the gracious and saving influence of the Gospel. On one occasion as many as eighteen native youths were received into the Christian Church by the initiatory sacrament of baptism, at a public service, which excited great interest; and with regard to most of these, there was good reason to believe that they had not only obtained an intelligent knowledge of Christianity, but that a genuine work of grace had commenced in their hearts.

The cheering measure of success which at first attended the efforts that were made to train and evangelise a few of the children of the natives of Western Australia renders it the more painful to relate the sequel of the story, and to acknowledge that, after all, the scheme resulted in bitter disappointment. After the native schools had been in operation for a few years, and some progress had been made in training the children, and after several hopeful conversions had taken place, and some happy deaths had been

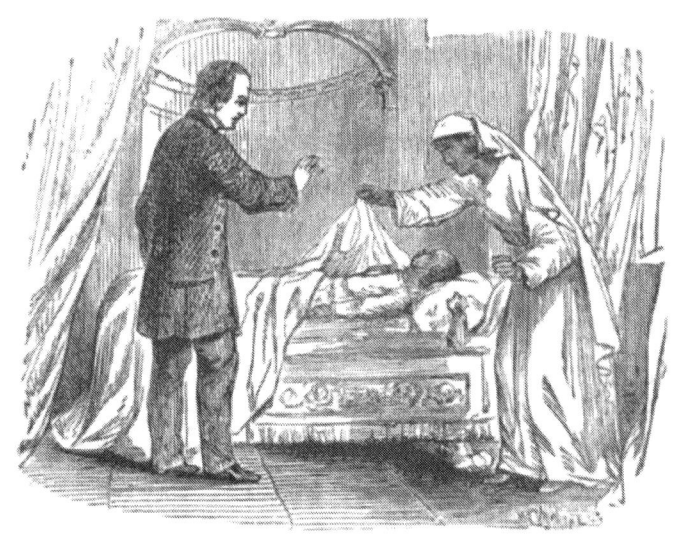

THE DYING AUSTRALIAN.

witnessed, it was found necessary to relinquish the undertaking. This was owing chiefly to the evil influence which the heathen parents exercised over their children. At first they seemed well pleased with the notice taken of their little ones by their European benefactors, and frequently came to see them in the school, and in their comfortable homes; but at length they decoyed them away into the bush with such frequency, that the efforts of the Missionary and teacher to promote their social and moral improvement were completely paralysed. In the meantime it became evident that the number of the Aborigines was rapidly decreasing here also, as in other parts of Australia, by means of the destructive influence of strong drink and the diseases which were introduced among them by immoral settlers and debased convicts.

Thus thwarted in their humane and philanthropic efforts to evangelise the degraded natives of Western Australia, the Missionary and his assistants had no alternative but to direct their attention henceforth to the European settlers, who, in consequence of the demoralising influence of the convict system, and other evils which might be mentioned, were in danger of becoming as thoroughly heathen in the land of their adoption, as the miserable natives whose hunting-grounds they were appropriating for their own use. In this important department of Christian labour there has not been the same amount of success realised here as in most of the other Australian colonies. Hitherto various circumstances have militated against the rapid progress of the work. Not only is the European population of the colony comparatively small, amounting to only six or seven thousand, but the convict system was longer continued and its baneful influence more powerfully felt than in most other places. The number of Missionaries employed in this part of the wide field has, moreover, always been very limited. For many years Mr. Smithies was left entirely alone, as already stated, and his services were necessarily confined chiefly to Perth, the capital of the colony. When he was afterward joined or succeeded by the Rev. Messrs. Lowe, Hardey, Simpson, Traylin, Lawrance, and others, the work was extended to York, Fremantle, Champion-bay, and other towns, villages, and hamlets, where chapels were built and societies formed, with much advantage to a scattered and neglected population. Still it may be said, "The harvest is great and the labourers are few." We have now in the Western Australia District *four ministers, one hundred and seventy-three Church members,* and *five hundred and forty-four scholars* in the Sabbath and day-schools.

TASMANIA.

Tasmania, or Van Diemen's Land, is a large island off the southern coast of Australia, from which it is separated by an arm of the sea called Bass' Straits, which is about two hundred miles wide. The land is generally high, diversified with moderate hills and broad valleys, which are well wooded and watered, and admirably adapted for agricultural and grazing purposes. In the year 1804 a British settlement was established on the south-east side of the island, at the mouth of the river Derwent, where Hobart Town, the capital of the colony, was built. The chief object of the Government was to provide suitable convict establishments to which criminals might be transported from the mother country. This system was carried on for many years, and gave a moral character to the colony which presented a strong claim for Missionary labour.

The introduction of Methodism into Tasmania was attended by circumstances which clearly show the superintending and overruling providence of God. The Rev. Benjamin Carvosso, having been appointed as a Missionary to New South Wales to assist the Rev. Samuel Leigh, was on his passage to that distant country, when in the month of April, 1820, the vessel in which he sailed put into the Derwent, to land part of her cargo and passengers at Hobart Town. On going on shore the Missionary found the people almost entirely destitute of the means of grace, and by far the greater part of them living in open violation of the laws of God, doing evil, "only evil, and that continually." Mr. Carvosso's spirit was greatly moved by what he saw around him; and, wishing to improve the opportunity by speaking a word in the name of his Divine Master, he took his stand on the steps of a small building then used as a court-house, with his devoted wife by his side to lead the singing, and in the open air preached the first Methodist sermon ever heard in Tasmania.

These services were repeated at intervals till the vessel sailed for Sydney, when the Missionary and his wife reluctantly took their leave of Hobart Town, cherishing the hope that some good had been done during their brief stay, and that Divine Providence would open the way for the establishment of a Mission-station there. The impression thus made upon the minds of the people was deepened by a similar visit from the Rev. Ralph Mansfield some time afterwards, and the need of something being done for Hobart Town seemed so urgent, that in the interim Mr. Carvosso wrote to the Missionary Committee in London, giving a description of the colony and of the spiritual destitution of the people, and urging the appointment of a Missionary to Tasmania as soon as practicable.

The Society readily responded to the call; but, before a suitable Missionary could be sent out, some time elapsed; and, during the interval, God in His providence was carrying on His work by other instrumentality. A few pious soldiers belonging to the forty-eighth regiment, who had been brought to a saving knowledge of the truth in New South Wales, arrived at Hobart Town. No sooner were these devoted servants of God settled in their barracks than they were painfully impressed with the wickedness that prevailed in the place; and, earnestly desiring to do good to others, as well as to make progress in religion themselves, they obtained the use of a room in the town, and began to hold meetings for prayer and exhortation. The meetings of the praying soldiers soon excited attention, and many of the townspeople found their way to the humble sanctuary, some of whom were convinced of sin, and brought to a saving knowledge of the Redeemer. At this Satan began to rage, and a spirit of persecution was evoked, which threatened to destroy the infant cause. A number of persons of the "baser sort" assembled around the cottage at the hour of prayer, and by loud and boisterous shouting, throwing stones at the door, and breaking the windows, attempted to daunt the humble worshippers and put a stop to the meetings. In this they were mistaken; for the more they opposed the more mightily grew the Word of God and prevailed. Tidings of these wicked proceedings soon reached the ears of the Lieutenant-Governor; the persecutors were silenced and peace restored; and, from that time to the present, no attempt at open opposition to the Gospel has been made in Hobart Town.

In 1821 the first Methodist class was formed in Tasmania, and before the end of the year the Rev. William Horton arrived from England to occupy the station as the first Missionary. The members of Society received him with open arms and grateful hearts, and he commenced his labours under the most favourable circumstances. No sooner was Hobart Town favoured with the stated services of a Wesleyan minister, than crowds of people flocked to hear the Word of God. The weather-board building used as a chapel soon became too small for the congregation. It was then enlarged, but the accommodation being still insufficient, it was resolved to attempt the erection of a commodious new chapel. A piece of land, in a suitable situation in Melville-street, was generously presented to the Society as a site for the building, by David Lord, Esq., and the foundation was laid in 1822. Numerous difficulties, however, arose, and long delays occurred, from various causes, which hindered the progress of the work, so that the edifice was not ready for dedication to the service of Jehovah till the 12th of February, 1826.

By this time the Rev. B. Carvosso, who first preached in the street of Hobart Town, from the steps of the Court House, had returned from New South Wales, to become the pastor of the people who had been gathered into the fold of Christ in the interim; and he had the high gratification of conducting the first public service which was held in the new and beautiful sanctuary. For five years subsequently did Mr. Carvosso minister within its walls to deeply attentive and increasing congregations, and the Church was built up and edified.

As openings presented themselves, the good work was extended to different parts of the island; and the Mission was reinforced by the appointment of the Rev. Messrs. Schofield, Hutchinson, Turner, Manton, Butters, and others. By the united efforts of these faithful servants of God, and other Missionaries by whom they were joined or succeeded, the work was gradually extended from Hobart Town to Campbell Town, Launceston, Lonford, Westbury,

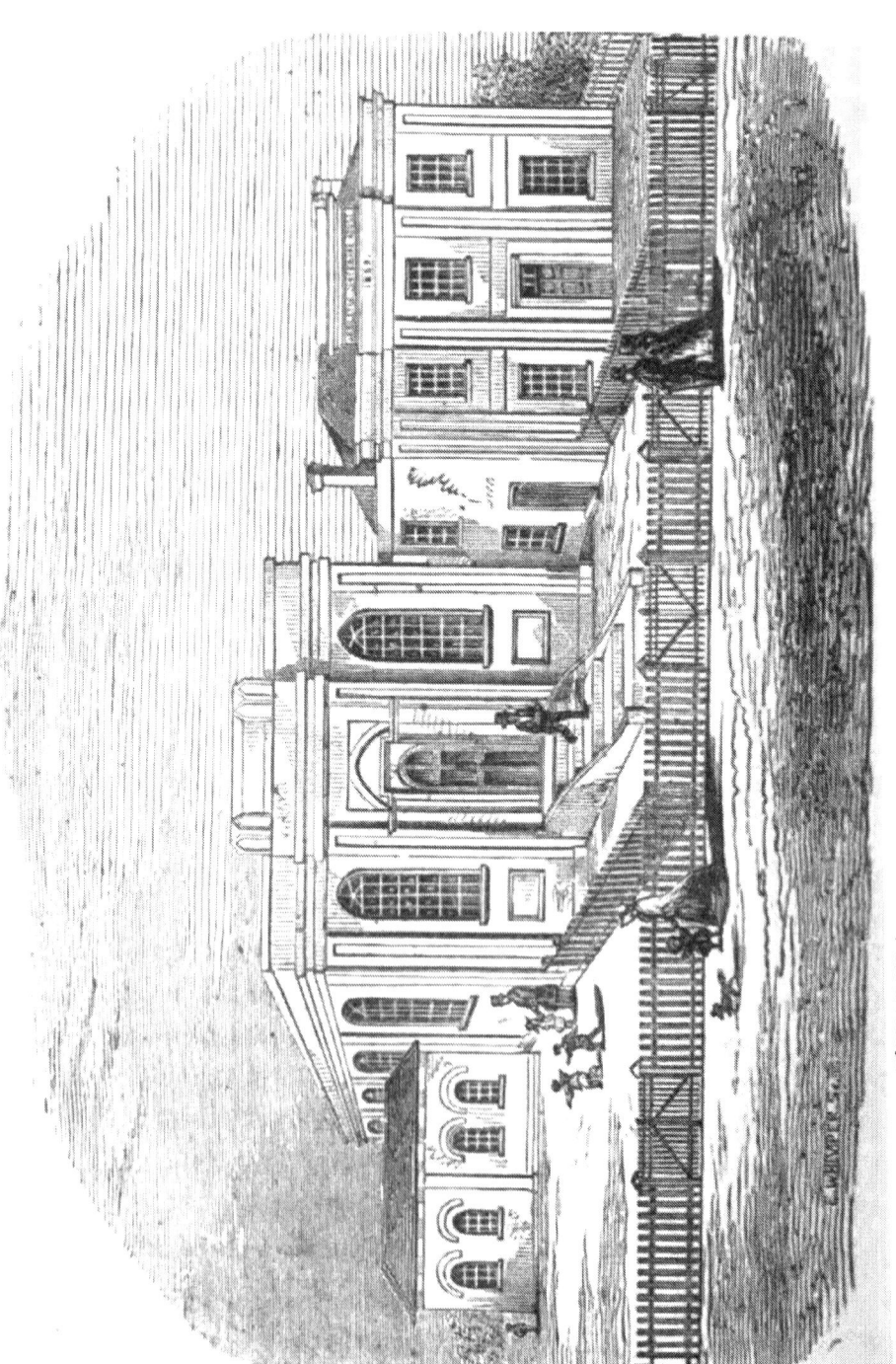

WESLEYAN CHAPEL AND MISSION PREMISES, LAUNCESTON, TASMANIA.

Deloraine, Mercy, Stanley, and Franklin, which ultimately became the centres of circuits, embracing a number of minor stations, where commodious chapels were erected, and where the people were regularly supplied with the faithful ministry of the Word of God, as preached by the Missionaries and the noble band of local preachers, who were raised up to assist them in the good work. Thus was every part of the island visited by the Missionaries or their assistants, and the community generally was permeated with the leaven of Christianity in the form of Methodism. Schools were, moreover, established in various places, and at Ross, a seminary of a superior character was erected, called Horton College, with a view to afford education of a higher class to those who require it, and to supersede the necessity of our people sending their sons to England.

This brief sketch of the origin and progress of Wesleyan Missions in Tasmania would be very incomplete without a more distinct reference to the efforts which were made for the benefit of the convicts sent thither, and the native inhabitants of the country. So long as the transportation of criminals to Van Diemen's Land continued this unhappy class of persons received the special attention of our Missionaries at their respective locations; and the Government were so sensible of the value of their services that they made considerable financial grants to aid the Society in carrying on the work. The principal convict stations were at Macquarie Harbour and Port Arthur, in connection with which the Rev. Messrs. Schofield, Butters, Manton, and others laboured for several years, and not without manifold tokens of the presence and blessing of God. Many of the poor convicts were led, by the faithful preaching of the Missionaries, to repent of their sins and to embrace the offers of that mercy in the land of their exile which they had despised and rejected in their own country. Macquarie Harbour was a penal settlement to which convicts of the most abandoned character were banished, when they were found incorrigible at the ordinary stations in New South Wales and other places. There the Missionaries were brought into contact with some of the vilest specimens of humanity which could be found on the face of the earth; and it is a pleasing fact that some of these even were brought under the subduing and renewing power of Divine grace. A few remarkable instances occurred of the conversion of convicts when under the sentence of death for crimes of the greatest atrocity, committed after their transportation. And so evident was the work of grace on the hearts of these miserable outcasts that they were enabled, in some instances, to praise the Lord for His pardoning mercy, and to express their unwavering confidence in the Redeemer, as they were accompanied to the fatal spot by the Missionary. So true is it that the Gospel of our Lord Jesus Christ is still "the power of God unto salvation to everyone that believeth." *

With regard to the Aborigines of the island, of whom comparatively few were found when the country was first discovered, we have but a very brief and gloomy account to give. We regret to state that they continued gradually to decrease in number till at length they became entirely extinct. The "last man" of the race was present at a public entertainment at the Government House in 1865, and it is believed that he has since then gone the way of all flesh. Several years ago the miserable remnants of the Aborigines of Tasmania were collected in a settlement provided for them by Government on the southern coast of the island. They were placed under the care of a medical gentleman, who paid every

---

* One of the first Missionaries to these miserable exiles, many of whom had been twice transported, was the late Rev. J. A. Manton, a personal friend of the writer. He reached the scene of his adventurous Mission in the month of May, 1882, and laboured for several years with remarkable success, although his life was frequently placed in jeopardy. The following honourable testimony to the importance and usefulness of this Mission was borne by Mr. James Backhouse, a member of the Society of Friends, who visited the settlement, and spent seventeen days among the convicts soon after the commencement of the work:—"We attended several of their religious opportunities to our comfort, and had liberty to labour in them; and had free access to the prisoners at all times. We have often seen the den of thieves become a house of prayer! for among those who have been turned from darkness to light, some were desperate hardened thieves. We heard one of the reformed convicts twice address his fellow-prisoners in exhortation to receive the doctrines of the Gospel, and to forsake their evil ways; and once he prayed for them in one of our religious assemblies, much to our comfort."

attention to their comfort, and, as far as they were capable and willing to receive it, religious instruction was given by the Missionaries; but the result was very discouraging, and they gradually wasted away in the presence of their pale-faced brethren, as it is apprehended the entire native population will do in every part of Australia.

The state of Methodism in Tasmania is reported to be thriving and prosperous. At the time of the general rush to the gold-fields of Victoria in 1852, a large number of colonists went thither from various parts of the island, and for two or three years afterwards the congregations were seriously diminished in consequence, and the progress of work was retarded. But many of the emigrants ultimately returned to their former homes, some disappointed, and others with increased means of supporting the cause of God, and the work has been gradually progressing ever since. We have now, in connection with the Tasmania District, *fifteen ministers, one thousand five hundred and seventy-three Church members*, and *three thousand and thirty scholars* in the Sabbath and day-schools.

By the blessing of God upon the preaching of the Missionaries and the rapid increase of population by means of emigration, the progress and expansion of the work in the Australian colonies was so remarkable, that the Committee in London was led seriously to consider by what means Methodism should be still further advanced and consolidated, and the respective stations be made self-supporting, that the funds of the Society might henceforth be available for the extension of the Missions in strictly heathen countries. In order to initiate the measures which were considered necessary for the accomplishment of this object, in 1845 the Rev. W. B. Boyce was appointed General Superintendent of the Missions in Australia and Van Diemen's Land. Mr. and Mrs. Boyce had rendered good service to the Society in Southern Africa for thirteen years previously, and their appointment to New South Wales was made a blessing to that country.

On arriving at his new sphere of labour, Mr. Boyce addressed himself to his arduous duties with a zeal and earnestness truly characteristic, and, having gained the esteem and confidence of his brethren, and of the people generally, with their aid and co-operation a financial system was inaugurated which prepared the way, a few years afterwards, for the organisation of an affiliated Conference. This grand measure was consummated in 1852, on the visit to the "Southern World" of the Rev. Robert Young, as a deputation from the British Conference. Mr. Young left England towards the close of the year, and having called at the Cape of Good Hope, where the writer had the pleasure of his company for a few days, in the month of March, 1853, he proceeded to Swan River, Adelaide, Melbourne, Sydney, Tasmania, New Zealand, the Friendly and Fiji Islands, and returned home in April, 1854, visiting India and Egypt on his way. In the year 1860 the Rev. Dr. Jobson was appointed to visit Australia, as a deputation from the British Conference, and performed his mission to the entire satisfaction of his brethren. Both of these eminent ministers published interesting narratives of their travels and observations, to which we have pleasure in referring for much valuable information on this important part of the Mission field.

The Australian Conference has taken under its management the Society's important Missions in the South Seas, and there are now, in connection with the respective circuits and districts included within its ample bounds, *two hundred and eighty-nine ministers, fifty thousand six hundred and seventy-four Church members,* and *ninety-eight thousand three hundred and forty-three scholars* in the Sabbath and day-schools.

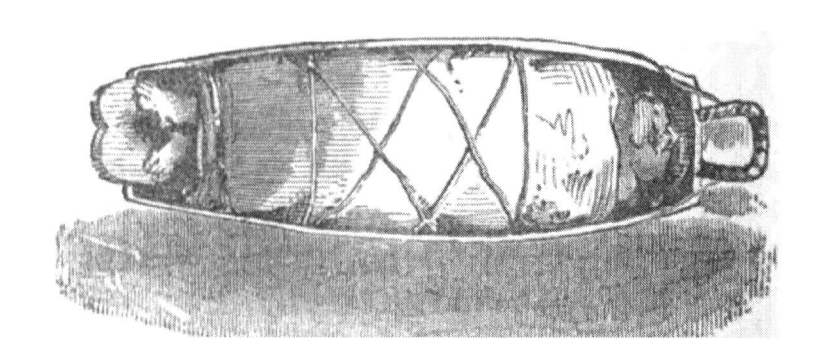

CHAPTER VII.

NEW ZEALAND.

DESCRIPTION OF THE COUNTRY—FIRST ATTEMPTS AT CIVILISATION—COMMENCEMENT OF WESLEYAN MISSION—THE WANGAROA STATION—SUSPENSION OF THE MISSION—RE-ESTABLISHMENT OF THE WORK—COLONISATION—ULTIMATE SUCCESS.

NEW ZEALAND is the name given to a group of islands in the Pacific Ocean, situated about fourteen hundred miles south-east of Sydney, in New South Wales. The principal of these are three in number, two larger and one smaller, distinguished as the Northern, the Middle, and the Southern Islands. The superficial area of the whole is said to be one-fifth larger than that of Great Britain. The climate is described as generally healthy,[1] and not very dissimilar to that of England, although it is, perhaps, on the whole, somewhat warmer and more humid. The interior of the respective islands exhibits great diversity of surface and scenery, the mountains, in some instances, rising to an altitude of nine thousand feet. From these elevated regions, numerous streams descend to the sea in various directions. The extensive forests which cover the mountain slopes, and the deep ravines which intersect the country, contain some excellent timber, and when the ground is cleared of these and of the fern roots which prevail in many places, it proves very fertile, and well adapted for almost all kinds of European produce, when well cultivated. The islands possess several good harbours, and, on the whole, the country is well adapted for agricultural and commercial enterprise.

New Zealand was first discovered by the Dutch navigator Tasman, in 1642, when he traced the eastern coast to a considerable distance, but being attacked by the natives as soon as his ship came to anchor, he was obliged to depart without going on shore. From this period the islands remained unknown to Europeans till 1770, when they were circumnavigated by our enterprising countryman, Captain Cook, who passed through the channel which separates the two principal ones, to which he gave his own name. New Zealand henceforth became a place of occasional resort for South Sea whalers, but no permanent European settlement was formed in the country till the commencement of philanthropic operations for the civilisation of the Aborigines in 1814. Subsequently numerous adventurers settled in the islands, and in 1840 they were organised into a regular British colony. The influx of European emigrants has since been very large, and New Zealand bids fair to become one of the most prosperous countries in the Southern World.

When first discovered, the Aboriginal inhabitants, called Maories, were remarkable for their warlike, savage, and cruel character, and it soon became well-known that they were addicted to the revolting habit of cannabalism, and that they generally feasted on the bodies of their enemies slain in battle. Some appalling instances of their savage manners, customs, and superstitions will come under our notice as we proceed. It will, therefore, be unnecessary to enlarge further on the general character of the country and the natives, and we may address ourselves at once to the duty of tracing the progress and the results of the efforts which have been made to promote their social and moral improvement.

First Attempts at Civilisation.

Any historical sketch of Christian labour for the benefit of New Zealand, by whatever denomination, without a distinct and honourable recognition of the services of the Rev. Samuel Marsden, the senior chaplain of the colony of New South Wales, who may be justly regarded as the father and founder of the enterprise, must be very imperfect. Soon after his arrival in Australia, Mr. Marsden was struck with the appearance and manners of individual natives of New Zealand, who were occasionally brought over to Sydney in vessels which visited the islands, and induced some of them, especially a young chief named Duaterra, to live with him for some time, and thus gained their confidence and esteem, as their friend and benefactor.

Having made the necessary preparations, on the 19th November, 1814, Mr. Marsden, in accordance with a long cherished desire to benefit the natives, embarked for New Zealand in a small sloop called the *Active*, with a company of European settlers, consisting of Messrs. Hall, King, and Kendall, and their families. These were not Missionaries, properly speaking, but laymen employed in connection with the Church Missionary Society, intended to teach the natives the arts of civilised life, and thus, according to the mistaken notions of the age, to prepare the way for the introduction of the Gospel. One was a schoolmaster, another a carpenter, and a third a shoemaker. They were also accompanied by the chief Duaterra, and two or three other natives, who were returning home from a long visit to Sydney, delighted with the prospect of their fellow-countrymen being taught some of the wonderful things that they had witnessed in the land of the white men.

Mr. Marsden and his party on board the *Active* had a favourable passage, and landed in safety at the Bay of Islands on the 22d of December, and on the following Sabbath, which was Christmas-day, Divine Service was celebrated for the first time in New Zealand. Duaterra had made a reading desk of an old canoe, and prepared seats for the Europeans with some planks which had been brought to the ground for the purpose, after the style of what he had witnessed in the colony. The whole population of the neighbourhood assembled on the occasion, the warriors being marched rank and file into the enclosure, whilst all who could be spared from the ship were landed to join in the service. The chiefs were dressed in regimentals, which had been presented to them by the Governor of New South Wales, with their swords by their sides, while the savages stuck their spears in the turf as they squatted in a circle on the ground. Mr. Marsden conducted the worship with great solemnity, Duaterra acting as interpreter in a very impressive manner. At the close of the service about three hundred natives surrounded the Minister and commenced their war dance, shouting and yelling in a most awful manner, in testimony of their joy on the auspicious occasion.

The impression produced by the religious services of the first Sabbath in New Zealand, appeared so favourable that it was deemed safe and necessary to proceed at once to procure timber and erect suitable buildings for the families of the settlers. On witnessing these proceedings, Duaterra became much excited, and exclaimed, with an air of triumph, "New Zealand will be a great country in two years! I will export grain to Port Jackson, in exchange for spades, axes, hoes, tea, and sugar." The grand object of his life, which he had studied for years during his residence in New South Wales, appeared to him on the eve of being realised. Under this impression he made arrangements for an extensive cultivation of the ground, and formed a plan for building a new town with regular streets, after the European mode, in a beautiful situation which commanded a view of the harbour and the adjacent country. Mr. Marsden accompanied the young chief to select a suitable site for the church, that everything might be satisfactorily arranged before his departure.

Thus pleasing was the prospect of success in these first philanthropic efforts for the benefit of New Zealand, when a dark cloud settled upon the scene and retarded the work for an indefinite period. This was the sickness and death of the young chief Duaterra, who had been under training by Mr. Marsden for several years with special reference to this enterprise. The chaplain's term of absence having expired, the *Active* was unmoored and sailed for Port Jackson; and Duaterra died four days after the departure of his friend from New Zealand.

The death of the friendly young chief was a severe blow to the infant settlement; and we regret to state that it did not meet with the success that was anticipated. The undertaking was arranged and entered upon with the purest motives by the philanthropic Mr. Marsden, in the interest of the Church Missionary Society; but the principle upon which it was based was erroneous. Past experience clearly proves that the real permanent elevation of a people cannot be effected by merely teaching them the arts of civilised life. It can only be expected as the result of establishing Christian schools in connection with the faithful preaching of the Gospel of Christ. In fact, a purely heathen people care little about arts and science till they are brought under the ameliorating influence of Christianity.

It was for want of clear views of the necessity and importance of the Gospel, as the best pioneer and companion of civilisation, that the secular Mission to New Zealand failed to accomplish much good, rather than to the death of the young chief, although that was no doubt felt to be a great calamity. The settlers undoubtedly did the best they could under the peculiar circumstances in which they were placed. The carpenter, with his edged tools, was regarded by the natives as a man of considerable importance; but the shoemaker and schoolmaster were lightly esteemed by the people. These wild men of the woods were delighted to see the trees fall by the application of the axe and saw; but nothing could convince them of the wisdom or necessity of confining their feet in cases made of leather; and the idea of sitting down all day to learn the letters of a book was, in their estimation, perfectly ridiculous, especially as their fathers had done very well without such punishment. The settlers being professing Christians, they held religious meetings for their own edification, and with the hope of benefiting the natives also; but not being allowed to preach, their services attracted but little notice; and year after year passed away without much impression being made on the minds of the people.

In 1818, when the experiment of civilisation had been tried between three and four years, Mr. Marsden prevailed upon Mr. Leigh of the Wesleyan Missionary Society, to take a trip to New

Zealand for the double purpose of recruiting his health and of inquiring into the state of the settlement. Soon after the arrival of the Rev. Walter Lawry to take part in the work of the Mission in New South Wales, Mr. Leigh, therefore, embarked for New Zealand, where he arrived in safety after a long and stormy passage. He was received by the settlers with much cordiality, and there is reason to believe that his wise counsels and prayers were made a blessing to them. Some little misunderstandings which had arisen between their families were happily removed by the Missionary's friendly influence, and much useful information was collected both with reference to the country and the people.

During the few weeks which Mr. Leigh spent in New Zealand on this occasion, several striking incidents occurred which painfully impressed his mind with a sickening sense of the cruelty and moral degradation of the natives, and of the great necessity of something more being done to effect their evangelisation. On the Sabbath after his arrival, he went out to a village near the settlement to converse with the people. As he entered it, he was surprised to see twelve ghastly tattooed heads of men, arranged in a row on the right-hand side of the path. He felt shocked at this appalling proof that he was indeed in the "region of the shadow of death." He sent for the Chief, and said to him, "I did not expect to witness so revolting a spectacle in your village. Why have you placed these heads here?" He replied, with an air of contempt, "Because I expected you to buy them!" "Buy them!" exclaimed the Missionary, "I buy spars, pigs, and flax, when I want them, but not the heads of men."

On coming to a hut, much superior in appearance to those around it, Mr. Leigh stooped down; and, on looking in, saw a little child lying naked between two large stones. He crept in on his hands and knees, the entrance being low, and wrapping the infant in his pocket-handkerchief, brought it out. Several persons having observed him, raised the cry, "The white man has gone into the Queen's hut!" The people were soon in motion; and the Queen herself arriving, demanded to know what business he had there. Holding up the child, he said, "I went in to save the life of this infant : why was it left alone naked on the floor of the hut?" The Queen replied, "I was planting potatoes, and could not attend to it. But I do not regret it; for your handkerchief, having touched my piccaninny, is forfeited, it is my property." Under the circumstances, he judged it prudent to let her have it.

He then went into the plantations and expostulated with such of the people as he found working on the Lord's-day. They declared that their gods were good for nothing, as they did not give them a Sabbath, or they might have been favoured with a day of rest like the white people. The Missionary visited six of the nearest villages in succession, assembled the people, and inquired whether they were willing to receive instruction. They generally replied in the affirmative, and assured him that if the white teachers would come regularly, they would stay at home themselves, and bring their children to be taught. He consequently formed them into a kind of circuit, and made a plan of visitation to which the lay Missionaries attached their names, and engaged to hold religious services in each village every Lord's-day.

Having finished his tour of observation, Mr. Leigh returned to New South Wales; and some time afterwards he embarked for England, fully resolved to recommend New Zealand to the Wesleyan Missionary Society as a promising field of labour.

Commencement of Wesleyan Mission.

When Mr. Leigh first laid before the Committee in London his proposal for the commencement of a Mission to the cannibals of New Zealand, there appeared to be little hope of success, as the Society was at that time labouring under a debt of £10,000. Whilst musing upon the subject, it occurred to the Missionary that, by a forcible appeal to the friends of Missions in different parts of England, he might, perhaps, obtain contributions of goods of various kinds, which, in New Zealand, would be more valuable than money itself. His proposal thus to provide the means to accomplish an object on which his large and loving heart was firmly fixed, having met with the sanction of the Committee and the Conference, Mr. Leigh held a number of meetings in the manufacturing districts for the purpose of setting before the Methodist people the necessities and requirements of the enterprise. His powerful and pathetic appeals were responded to in the most liberal manner, and in the course of a few months such a number of packages of merchandise were forwarded to London for the new Mission to New Zealand that it was with difficulty that storeroom could be found for them till the ship was ready to receive them on board. These packages consisted of ploughs, spades, saws, axes, grates, pots, kettles, fishhooks, and other descriptions of ironmongery from Sheffield and Birmingham, and prints, calicoes, and wearing apparel, with a variety of other useful articles, from Manchester, Liverpool, Bristol, and other places. The liberality of the friends of Missions was unbounded, so that the Society felt warranted in making arrangements for the commencement of the New Zealand Mission without further delay, especially as Mr. Leigh had already offered his personal services for the work.

In the meantime there arrived in London a distinguished New Zealand Chief named 'Hongi, together with Waikato, a chieftain of minor importance, his travelling companion. These two intelligent natives had come to England with Mr. Kendall, of the Church Missionary Society, and were regarded with much interest during their stay, especially by Mr. Leigh, who had known them in their own country. As the Church Missionary Society were about to place their settlement in New Zealand on a better footing, by appointing regular Christian Ministers to preach the Gospel to the people, it was no doubt thought that the appearance in England of these Maori Chiefs would give a new impetus to the work. The account which they themselves gave of the object of their coming to the white man's country was amusingly characteristic. "They had come," they said, "to see the king, the multitude of his people, what they were all doing, and the goodness of the land. They wished to remain in England one month, and then return home. They desired to take back with them one hundred men; miners to search for iron, blacksmiths, carpenters, and Missionaries, to teach them arts and religion in their own tongue. They were anxious to have twenty British soldiers, and three officers to keep the soldiers in order. They would protect them and grant them plenty of land. These are the words of 'Hongi and Waikato."

In some of these things they were gratified, but not in others. His Majesty King George IV. admitted them to an audience, showed them the armoury in the palace, and made them several costly presents. The chiefs lost no time in honouring Mr. Leigh with a visit. After a mutual interchange of salutations and enquiries, 'Hongi said, "As I have not been quite at home since I came to this land, I will stay with you while I remain in England." Mr. Leigh, knowing that in a few months the lifting up of the spear of 'Hongi would be equivalent to a declaration of life or death to himself and family, thought it prudent to accept of this proferred mark of respect, with as good a grace as possible. As the chief could not be induced to lie on a bed, the Missionary was obliged to place his mattrass on the floor, and sleep beside him.

Wishing to please and conciliate the two New Zealand chiefs as much as possible, as well as to encourage their laudable taste for the mechanical arts, the Wesleyan Missionary Society made them each a present of a chest of carpenters' tools. After they had examined, with evident satisfaction, the contents of the chests, they were told that the Committee would have pleasure in adding any other article that would be acceptable to them. "Then," said 'Hongi, "add, if you please, a dress for my wife." When this, with several other articles of female attire, was provided, he seemed pleased and satisfied. The Maories were delighted with the various sights which they witnessed in England; but it was soon found that the change of climate and the difference in the mode of living were exercising an unfavourable influence on the state of their health. They consequently accepted the offer of a passage in the Government ship *Spoke,* then about to sail, and returned to their own country by way of New South Wales.

The necessary preparations for the commencement of the Wesleyan Mission to New Zealand having been made, Mr. and Mrs. Leigh, together with Mr. and Mrs. Horton, and Mr. Walker, sailed from Gravesend in the ship *Brixton*, on the 28th of April, 1821. They were favoured with a pleasant passage, and on the 8th of August they reached Tasmania, where Mr. and Mrs. Horton remained to organise a Mission in that island, whilst the rest of the party proceeded to New South Wales. On reaching Sydney, Mr. Leigh was concerned to hear that a native war had broken out in New Zealand, and desolated that part of the country where he intended to commence Missionary operations. Perhaps this circumstance led him to spend a longer time in the colony than he would otherwise have done. The delay, however, was advantageous in many respects, as it afforded an opportunity of repeated consultations with his friend Mr. Marsden, who had spent several months in New Zealand during his absence, and was therefore well acquainted with the state of the country.

At length, notwithstanding the persuasions of his brethren to wait a little longer, Mr. Leigh preached his farewell sermon at Sydney, and on the last day of the year, he embarked with his heroic wife for their new sphere of labour. After an agreeable run, it was announced from the mast-head that New Zealand was in sight. "When I stepped upon deck," said Mr. Leigh, many years afterwards, "and looked toward the shore, and then at my dear wife, and reflected upon the probable consequences of our landing, I felt as if divested of all spiritual strength. We were running in upon a nation of ferocious bloodthirsty heathens, where there was no power to protect, and while the country was convulsed with war. Never shall I forget the agony of mind I endured, until reflection brought me to feel that I was surrounded by the Divine perfections, and that a hair could not fall from our heads without the concurrence of God." They sailed into the Bay of Islands on the 22d of February, 1822, where they met with a most cordial reception from their friends of the Church Mission, as also from several of the natives who had become acquainted with Mr. Leigh on the occasion of his former visit. These expressed their gratitude and joy at the arrival of the "white teacher," and hastened to salute him by rubbing noses, according to the native custom.

The Missionary and his wife were thankful thus to arrive at their appointed sphere of labour in safety, and to receive such a hearty welcome both from the natives and the agents of the Church Missionary Society. It is a pleasing fact that there was at that early period no feelings of jealousy or spirit of rivalry between them and their Wesleyan brethren. There had ever been the most cordial feeling of Christian kindness and friendship between the Rev. S. Marsden, the father of the Church Mission in New Zealand, and the Wesleyan Missionaries in the colony, and Mr. Leigh's former visit had been of essential service to the infant cause. The Church Missionary Committee in London had, moreover, duly acknowledged their obligation to their Wesleyan brother, and earnestly sought his counsel with regard to their future operations. It was probably in consequence of this that the Rev. J. Butler, a regularly ordained Minister, was appointed to New Zealand, that the work might henceforth be carried on, in conformity with the true evangelical principles which Mr. Leigh thought so essential to success. The field was wide enough for the operations of both Societies; and, as the Wesleyans had entered it with the perfect knowledge and sanction of their friends of the Church of England, it was their intention to commence their labours in another part of the country, among the more remote of the tribes on the banks of River Thames and at Mercury Bay, and to work at a sufficient distance from the existing station of the Church Mission at the Bay of Islands. Everything seems to have been wisely arranged; but it is painful to record that the plans of the Missionaries were upset, and the prospect of the future involved in the deepest gloom by a desolating war, which for several years swept over the land like a mighty torrent. And that which made it more appalling was the fact that the principal author and instigator of the sad calamity was the chief 'Hongi, who had received such marked attention and kindness on his visit to England a short time before.

The leading particulars of this melancholy occurrence were briefly as follows:—On the return of 'Hongi and Waikato from England, they called at Sydney, where they spent a short time under the hospitable roof of their old friend the Rev. S. Marsden. Here they met with Hanaki and another chief from New Zealand, who had taken their passage to London, that they also might "see the land of the white men." 'Hongi, in describing his visit to the country of " great muskets and big ships," dwelt with significant emphasis on the grandeur of King George, and the splendour of the military spectacles he had witnessed. He had marked the unwillingness of the King and his people, however, to supply him with muskets and gunpowder. Of the intelligence, industry, and religion of the English people he had taken but little notice. Mr. Marsden, perceiving that the bosom of 'Hongi was fired with ambition, and that the insight he had obtained of the wealth and power of Great Britain had only increased his desire for distinction and blood, endeavoured to persuade Hanaki and his companion to give up, for the present, their intended voyage to England and return to their own country with 'Hongi and Waikato; to this they agreed, when they heard of the unfavourable influence of the climate, and of the difficulty of procuring muskets and powder.

'Hongi gave to the other chiefs an intelligent and interesting account of his interviews with the Committees of the Church and Wesleyan Missionary Societies, and told them that Mr. Leigh might be expected in a few weeks to commence a Mission in New Zealand. After some discussion they agreed to recommend the establishment of the Mission in the neighbourhood of the River Thames and Mercury Bay, under the immediate protection of Hanaki and the other chief, his companion. While Hanaki was expressing his satisfaction with this arrangement, 'Hongi said abruptly, "Before that can be done, I have a small affair to settle with my friend Hanaki. During my absence I understand one of my people has been killed by the River Thames tribes, and I must have satisfaction." Then turning to Hanaki, he said, with a distorted countenance and a contemptuous sneer, "Go home with all speed, and put your *pa* in the best posture of defence, for as soon as I can get my people together I shall fight you." After this unpleasant occurrence the hostile chiefs, ate at the same table, slept under the same roof, united in the worship of God, and sailed to New Zealand in the same vessel, and it was hoped that friendly counsels would prevail; but it was not so.

During the voyage homeward every means were employed by Hanaki, consistent with his own dignity, to move 'Hongi from his hostile purpose and secure peace; but the haughty chieftain was implacable. On reaching the Bay of Islands, Hanaki and his friends hastened home to rouse the population of their respective districts to be ready to resist the threatened attack of the invader; while 'Hongi, at the head of three thousand warriors, lost no time in entering their territories. The opposing armies met like two whirlwinds moving in opposite directions, and the event of the conflict was for some time doubtful. At length 'Hongi, who had the best supply of muskets, and who displayed superior skill in strategy, prevailed, and the destruction and carnage which followed were awful beyond description. On perceiving his enemy fall mortally wounded, 'Hongi immediately sprung forward, and, with characteristic cruelty, scooped out his eyes with his English knife, and instantly swallowed them! and then, holding his hands to Hanaki's throat, into which he had plunged his knife, and from which the blood was flowing copiously, drank as much of the warm fluid as they could hold, with savage ferocity exulting in his victory. About one thousand of Hanaki's warriors fell in battle, three hundred of whom were roasted and eaten on the field by the troops of 'Hongi. When Mr. Leigh met with 'Hongi afterwards, and remonstrated with him on the atrocities perpetrated during his campaign against the tribes of the River Thames, the savage chief only smiled and remarked, "We must observe the customs of our country: the blood of Hanaki was sweet!"

We refrain from entering into further detail with reference to the scenes of cruelty and blood which characterised this fearful outbreak. To show the impression which a slight glance at them produced on the mind of a stranger, we may remark that, shortly after the first battle, a vessel, with the Rev. John Williams, of the London Society, on board, entered the Bay of Islands; and when writing home to his father, he says, " Large canoes are returning from the war in every direction. The day before yesterday several passed us; one or two of which had a man's head stuck on the front and stern, and several prisoners they had taken in the war were on board. One of our seamen went on shore, and saw ten heads of warriors, all preserved, brought from the field of battle: Mr. and Mrs. Leigh, of the Wesleyan Society, are here. When they have acquired the language, they will be a blessing to the people."

The circumstances of the Missionaries were rendered still more trying at this period by the irritation, jealousy, and reserve of 'Hongi, who was now the paramount chief over an extensive territory. Believing that the extreme difficulty which he experienced in obtaining muskets and powder was owing to the influence of the white teachers, he began to treat them with indifference and contempt. In this he was imitated by the natives generally, who refused to work for the Missionaries unless they were paid with muskets and powder. They, moreover, entered the Mission premises when they pleased, and took away what they liked; till Mr. Leigh was compelled to complain to the chief of the continued depredations of his people. After this there was a slight improvement in the conduct of the natives. But it was not long before 'Hongi again placed himself at the head of his army and went forth to battle, scouring the country in every direction. With scarcely any intermission these desolating wars continued for five years, till the very tribes whose evangelization the Wesleyan Missionary Society earnestly sought to promote, were either slain or scattered in various directions.

And yet, in connection with this dark and gloomy page in the history of the New Zealand Mission, we have a striking instance of that overruling Providence by which good is frequently brought out of evil. During his numerous conquests, 'Hongi gathered up the scattered fragments of many tribes, and sent them as slaves to the Bay of Islands. This was regarded at the time as a public calamity. It turned out, however, to be otherwise. The captives had been brought from various quarters to the only place in the country where Christian truth was shining amid surrounding darkness. They shared in the light; they attended the Mission schools and other means of grace; they learned to read and write; and some of them had firmly fixed in their minds the essential truths of the Gospel. After a time the rugged character of the chiefs and people in the Bay of Islands began to soften down under the continued influence of Christianity; these slaves were liberated, and permitted to return to their respective districts and friends. Some went to East Cape, others to Kawia on the west coast. A few advanced down the Wanganui River to its mouth. Several removed to Cook's Straits, where their tribes had located themselves; and it is a pleasing fact, that wherever they went, these returning captives spread abroad the leaven of Christian truth, and, by their simple account of what they had seen and heard at the station of the white teachers, created a desire for religious instruction in regions where the Missionaries had never been. The result of this was afterwards seen in the circumstance of messengers coming a distance of five hundred miles to the Bay of Islands to ask for teachers.

The Wangaroa Station.

The door being effectually closed, for the present, in the direction of the River Thames and Mercury Bay, by the proceedings of the ferocious 'Hongi; while the war was still raging in those regions, Mr. Leigh began to seek in other parts of the country for a suitable site for a Mission-station. He first paid a visit to a place called Ho-do-do, which had been recommended by 'Hongi, and where he had a sister residing who was anxious to have the white teachers near her. But this locality appearing, on inspection, ineligible for the purpose, the Missionary turned his attention to Wangaroa, which, after numerous adventures, ultimately became the headquarters of the Wesleyan Mission in New Zealand for several years. A brief reference to a few of these adventures may serve to illustrate some of the trials and difficulties of Mission life in heathen lands.

Being informed that several populous villages were situated near the harbour of Wangaroa, and that Europeans might visit them without much personal risk, Mr. Leigh hired a boat and five natives, and left home for the purpose of examining that part of the country. For some time they had a moderate breeze; but, as night approached, a storm came on which drove them out to sea. The native sailors yielded to despondency, lay down in the bottom of the canoe, and left the Missionary to manage the sail as best he could. After being tossed about till almost midnight, the moon arose, and land was distinctly seen in the distance. They bore down upon it and found themselves near the harbour of Wangaroa. They were compelled by stress of weather to enter and seek protection at the hands of the barbarous natives. Some time before a ship had called at this place to rescue the survivors of the massacre of the crew and passengers of the ship *Boyd*; but it is believed that Mr. Leigh was the first European who had landed and placed himself in the power of these cannibals since the occurrence of that sad event.

As the night was far advanced, and the people were asleep, Mr. Leigh's natives fired off their muskets to let them know that strangers had arrived, and that they were armed. The savages were aroused from their slumbers, and, seizing their arms, came out to defend themselves and take vengeance on the invaders. The Missionary sought an interview with the chief, who was present; he informed him of their stormy passage, and begged that a hut might be appropriated for himself and his boatmen for the night. This was readily granted, and they crept into it with hearts uplifted in gratitude and praise, and tried to compose themselves to sleep. They were kept awake most of the night, however, by the clamour of the natives outside the hut; and after breakfast and prayer next morning, the tumult of the people increased to such a degree that the Missionary became apprehensive that a hostile attack was about to be made upon him and his party. As personal resistance would have been perfectly useless, Mr. Leigh wisely sought to divert their attention by expressing his admiration of their beautiful country. He asked the chief, whose name was Tara, but whom the sailors called George, if he would step into the boat with him, as he was anxious to see a little more of their spacious harbour. He consented; and, after sailing a short distance, they passed the hulk of a ship deeply imbedded in the sand. It was the remains of the *Boyd*, which was captured and destroyed by the natives in 1809; and, pointing to the wreck with his finger, the chief gave the following ungarnished account of the tragic deed:—

"This is all that remains of the ship *Boyd;* the Captain no good. Myself and another met him at Port Jackson. He told us he was going to our country for spars, and he wished us to accompany him and assist him in getting good ones. He was very kind at first; but after we had been a few days at sea, he insisted on our working with the sailors. We refused to work, and told him that we were chiefs. He did not believe us, and ordered us to be flogged. I told him that on our arriving in New Zealand we should convince him that we were chiefs. We conducted the ship to Wangàroa; and on landing I told my father, who was principal chief, of the disgrace to which we had been subjected by Captain Thompson. He and the other chiefs resolved to have satisfaction; but, as there were seventy-four Europeans and five natives on board, armed with great guns and muskets, we could not at first see how it could be successfully demanded. At last it was suggested to request the Captain to go on shore and select his own timber. He manned three boats, which I piloted up the river Kaio, until out of sight of the ship. I then led the captain and his people into the woods, where I detained him until the tide turned, and left the boats dry upon the bank. While Captain Thompson was looking up at a lofty spar, and admiring its beauty, I cut him down with my tomahawk. The other natives who were with me struck the other Europeans at the same instant, so that all fell without being able to make the slightest resistance. They were well armed; but no one had time either to fire his musket or draw his sabre. We carried the bodies to the boats, and took them to the village, where they were roasted and eaten. We continued our course down the river, until we came within sight of the ship. At a given signal, which the natives on board well understood, they rose up and murdered the remaining portion of the crew and passengers, except five, who escaped into the rigging, and were not killed until the following morning; and two children, who, on seeing the blood flow on the deck, became quite frantic, and who, before they could be caught, touched a chief, were made sacred by the touch, and could not be killed. In plundering the ship, my father set fire to the gunpowder, which exploded and killed himself and many others. The ship was thus set on fire and burned down, as you see, to the water's edge." Having been repeatedly to Sydney, this chief could speak tolerable English, and entered into these details without the least emotion.

After sailing about the harbour for some time, the Missionary and the chief landed, and walked towards the village. Mr. Leigh desired his men, who refused to leave the boat, to keep near the shore, and to pull quickly in when he should give the signal. The villagers came down in considerable numbers; and, from their fierce, tumultuous, and ferocious appearance, the Missionary expected nothing less than personal violence; and, finding it impossible to reason with them, he began to move towards the beach. On observing this, the natives closed in upon him in a compact body, and almost surrounded him, flourishing their spears and clubs in a most threatening manner. The chief, who had hitherto been so friendly, looked on with apparent indifference, and declined to interfere. Believing the crisis to have arrived, Mr. Leigh cried out, "Stand back! I have fish-hooks;" and taking out of his pocket a handful of these coveted articles, he threw them over their heads. They were taken by surprise; and while they turned round and scrambled for the fish-hooks, he ran towards the beach, and succeeded in getting into the boat. With a thankful heart for this merciful deliverance, he stood out to sea, and reached the Bay of Islands in safety.

Having sought in various directions for a suitable site for a Mission-station without success, the thoughts of Mr. Leigh turned again to Wangaroa, as the place which appeared, on the whole, the most eligible, notwithstanding the coarse treatment which he received on the occasion of his first visit. Before deciding on a matter of such importance, he wished to examine more carefully the harbour, the river, and the adjacent country. A favourable opportunity for doing so occurred soon afterwards by the return of the ship *St. Michael* from the Friendly Islands, to which place she had just taken the first Wesleyan Missionary. Accordingly, Mr. Leigh embarked on his second visit to Wangaroa, on the morning of the 5th, 1823, accompanied by Mrs. Leigh and Messrs. Butler, Shepherd, and Hall of the Church Missionary Society, who manifested a laudable desire to assist their Wesleyan brother to the utmost of their power in his important enterprise. The distance being only about thirty miles from the Bay of Islands, they reached Wangaroa in the afternoon, and were much struck with the grand and romantic scenery at the entrance of the harbour. The water is deep close to the land, and, although the opening is narrow, when once entered, it is one of the finest harbours in the world. The interior is lined with lofty hills, richly wooded; and the site of the *pa*, or fortress of the natives, is an insulated rock, three hundred feet high, with almost perpendicular sides, and before the use of firearms must have been impregnable.

At an early hour of the morning of the 6th, the "St. Michael" was surrounded by native canoes filled with men, women, and children. Mr. Leigh and his friends, nevertheless, landed without fear, and proceeded up the river in a boat to the residence of the principal chief. When the Missionary stepped from the boat, on reaching the village, he was greeted by a number of natives, who cried out, "*Haere mai! haere mai!*" "Come hither! come hither!" This is the usual salutation, and when once uttered, the stranger has nothing to fear. On looking at Mr. Leigh very earnestly, several of them recognised him, and exclaimed, "This is the white man who gave us the fish-hooks." After a short interview, the chief returned with the Mission party to the ship in the harbour, and as they sailed down the river, he very humorously apologised for mixing the English with the Maori language in his conversation, observing, "Since I left the sea, my English has left me, and gone into the bush; but now that you are come into the country, it will soon return to me again." On Sunday, the 8th, Mr. Leigh conducted the first public religious service ever held in this part of New Zealand, preaching from the appropriate text, " Then Samuel took a stone, and set it between Mizpeh and Shen, and called the name of it Ebenezer, saying, Hitherto hath the Lord helped us."

Early on Monday morning Mr. Leigh and his friends manned a boat and proceeded up the river again, with a view to select a suitable site for a Mission-station. At length they came to a beautiful and fertile valley, in which dwelt the chief George, and Tepui, his brother, which they considered the most eligible place for a settlement, and to which they gave the name of Wesleydale. It was about seven miles from the mouth of the river, thirty-five miles north-west of the Bay of Islands, and twenty miles from Keri-Keri, the nearest station of the Church Missionary Society. Several native villages, containing a considerable population, were situated in this valley, and other small tribes were accessible at a short distance among the hills, so that this appeared to be a promising field of Missionary labour.

In order to provide a shelter for a few nights, on the evening of the 10th the Missionary and his friends proceeded to erect a booth with the branches of trees, a short distance from the side of the river. As the work proceeded, the natives were heard to remark that, in the event of a heavy fall of rain, it would be in danger of being swept away. Of this no notice was taken at the time. They had not long retired to rest, however, when "the rain descended, the winds blew, and the floods came," and swept their booth, together with several boxes, containing carpenters' tools and stores, which had been landed from the ship, into the river and down to the sea. The Mission party saved their lives by escaping at midnight to higher ground; but they suffered much during that dreary and inclement night. This misfortune suggested the necessity of shifting their position; and having obtained their canvas tent from the ship, they ascended to a more elevated situation and pitched it in the name of the Lord.

On the following day the foundation of a building was laid of sufficient dimensions to serve the purpose of a dwelling-house, store-room, and chapel. It was formed of posts planted in the ground, and the roof was thatched with grass. Calico was used instead of glass for the windows; and for want of boards, it remained without doors for several months. When this frail habitation was sufficiently advanced to be occupied by the Mission family, they removed from their canvas tent, and took possession of it with thankful hearts; and Captain Beveridge, who had no confidence in the natives, weighed anchor, and the *St. Michael* took her departure, calling at the Bay of Islands to land the members of the Church Mission, who now returned to their own station.

Mr. and Mrs. Leigh felt their loneliness when their friends had

NATIVE MISSION-HOUSE AND CHAPEL.

left them, but they addressed themselves to their important work with zeal and diligence, notwithstanding numerous difficulties arising from the wild and savage character of the people among whom their lot was cast. Even while engaged in cooking their food, which had to be done in the open air, they were liable to be plundered of their victuals. Never having seen boiling water before, the natives would sometimes plunge their hands into the pot as it simmered on the fire, with the intention of helping themselves to the meat; but, feeling the scalding heat, they would withdraw them suddenly, exclaiming, "The water has bitten our hands!" While the Missionary dressed their wounds with ointment, he tried to convince them that, in all their dealings with the white men, they would find "honesty the best policy." This seemed to have little effect, however; for, afterwards, they used sharp-pointed sticks, which, with great dexterity, they thrust into the pot, and frequently succeeded in emptying it of the pork, fish, or other contents, thus leaving the Mission family without a morsel of dinner. Still, with much that was trying and depressing, there were blended circumstances of encouragement. Religious services were held daily, morning, noon, and night, to which the natives were freely admitted, some of whom seemed disposed to attend to what they heard. Some progress was made, moreover, in teaching the children to read; and it was believed that everything would have gone on well, if it had not been for the war spirit that was abroad. But at the very time that Mr. Leigh was attempting to establish the first Wesleyan station at Wangaroa, 'Hongi and his warriors were laying waste the country at no great distance from the place.

For a length of time scarcely a day passed without alarming reports being brought to the station. These were sometimes true and sometimes false; but, in either case, they served to keep up a state of continual excitement. Nor were there wanting instances of actual attack and threatened violence. One case may serve as a specimen. On the 16th of July, the Mission family at Wesleydale were alarmed by the unexpected arrival of a war party from the Bay of Islands. They no sooner landed than the Wangaroa tribes flew to arms, and mustered their forces in front of the Mission premises. They commenced the war-dance, and became so excited, that in a few minutes they were prepared to advance to victory or death. Mr. Leigh went down and saluted the invaders, and spent two hours in earnest conversation with them. While thus engaged, the chief Tepui imprudently advanced and challenged them to the combat. At the request of the Missionary, the Bay of Islanders took no notice of this challenge. The chief George disapproved of the conduct of Tepui, and remonstrated with him. Hence ensued a scene of tumult and excitement which baffles description. The Missionary was thrown down, and with difficulty got into the house with his wife and Luke, his native servant. They barricaded the door, and, supposing they had but a few moments to live, knelt down and commended their souls to God in prayer. After repeated assaults, the attacking party were unable to force the door, and so, by the good providence of God, the Mission family were, for the present, preserved from harm. Towards evening the Bay of Islands' chief desired an interview with Tepui, when, after mutual explanations, they became friends, and ratified the agreement by the exchange of muskets. There was much noise and clamour around the station during the night; but the next day, after the Missionary had distributed a box of axes among the warriors as a peace offering, they quietly withdrew and returned home.

Notwithstanding frequent interruptions of this kind, at intervals between the alarms from wars and rumours of wars, the Missionary and his wife nobly persevered in the elementary work of the station. This consisted in studying the language, teaching the children to read and write, cultivating the ground, inculcating habits of industry and cleanliness; and, as far as they were able, explaining to the people the important truths of the Gospel. Many ludicrous and amusing scenes occurred in the course of these early attempts to instruct the natives in the arts of civilised life. Such was Mrs. Leigh's first effort to teach New Zealand girls to sew. When the white lady exhibited a small needle and handed it round among her pupils, that they might examine it for themselves, they were astonished. They expressed their surprise at the beauty of its polish and the sharpness of its point, which "bit them" as often as they touched it. Their wonder was increased when they saw a thread put through the eye of the needle. They were told that the artisan who made the needle had struck a hole in one end of it for the very purpose of receiving the thread. That so small a hole could be made in iron exceeded their belief, until, by taking hold of the thread at both ends, and moving the needle backwards and forwards, they had ocular demonstration of the fact. The needle being returned to Mrs. Leigh, she made a knot at one end of the thread, and began to sew a piece of calico. A needle was then threaded and given to each of the girls, with instruction to imitate the teacher. After a few abortive efforts, they were all in confusion. One complained that the thread would not stay in the cloth; another said she could not pull the needle through. The cause was soon ascertained; the one had not knotted the end of the thread, while the other had tied her thread to the end of the needle, instead of putting it through the eye. It was necessary to show them where the knot was to be made, and how to make it. Awkward as this first attempt may appear, and ignorant as these heathen children evidently were of the use of the British needle and scissors, it is a pleasing fact that in a few months, under the judicious teaching of the Missionary's wife, they could cut out and make articles of clothing for themselves and their relatives.

It would be an interesting exercise to dwell at length on many incidents, some pleasing and others painful, which continued to mark the early history of the Wangaroa station; but we must hasten onward to give a brief outline of the principal events which afterwards occurred. Towards the close of 1823, Mr. Leigh's failing health rendered it necessary for him to remove with his wife to New South Wales; but the Rev. Nathaniel and Mrs. Turner, and the Rev. William White, having previously arrived from England to strengthen the Mission, the work was carried on as usual. These devoted servants of the Lord were also assisted in their work by Messrs. Hobbs and Stack, two zealous young colonists from New South Wales, who commenced their career in connection with the Mission as artizans, but who were ultimately called to the higher work of the Christian ministry.

In the course of the following year, the station at Wangaroa was favoured with a visit from Messrs. Tyreman and Bennett, the honoured deputation of the London Missionary Society to their important Missions in the South Sea Islands, in the ship *Endeavour*. These Christian gentlemen were most favourably impressed with what they saw of their Wesleyan brethren and their work in New Zealand; and in a letter which they afterwards addressed to the the Wesleyan Missionary Committee in London, they gave an encouraging account of the progress and prospects of the station. Concerning the agents employed, they said : " Though the time we spent with your friends at Wangaroa was short, it was to ourselves truly pleasant and highly interesting, and animated us with a lively hope that God is about to do some great thing for the people among whom they dwell. We formed a high opinion of the good sense and missionary talents of the Rev. Mr. Turner and his coadjutor in office, the Rev. Mr. White, and also of Mrs. Turner. They appear to us well chosen for such an undertaking. We also think highly of their two young fellow-labourers, Messrs. Hobbs and Stack, who seem to be pious and diligent young men, of ingenious minds, and well adapted for usefulness in various ways. Most of your friends were doing well at the language, and appear to us to have made considerable progress. They appear to have established themselves in the good opinions of the natives, and have made some progress in removing their pagan superstitions, and in gaining their attention to the truths of the Gospel. We confidently anticipate their ultimate success."

We regret to add that on returning from Wesleydale to their ship in the harbour of Wangaroa, Messrs. Tyreman and Bennett were in danger of falling a prey to the cruel natives. In their absence the savages had surrounded the *Endeavour*, and crowded the deck in such numbers that they had become quite uncontrollable, demanding or taking possession of everything they saw. When the deputation came on board, the infuriated mob began to handle them very roughly, and would probably have proceeded to acts of violence, and taken possession of the ship, had not Mr. White and the chief George come down the river just in time to restore order and clear the decks before their departure to the Bay of Islands.

Suspension of the Mission.

We have now to advert to a crisis in the history of the Wesleyan Mission to New Zealand which is truly painful to contemplate, and which tried the faith and patience of the Missionaries to the utmost. When considerable progress had been made in preparatory work at the Wangaroa station, buildings erected, land brought under cultivation, two school-chapels built in native villages at a distance, and a hopeful impression made on the minds of some of the people, there arose a dark and gloomy cloud which entirely obscured the prospect of success in which the Missionaries had been wont to indulge, and involved the Mission family in perplexity and trouble. From day to day the darkness increased, till at length it culminated in a tempestuous outburst of hostile violence, which obliged the servants of the Lord to flee for safety, and the work was for a time suspended. A few particulars in reference to this painful event may be interesting to the reader.

In the year 1826 an English brig, called the *Mercury*, was taken and plundered by the natives of the Bay of Islands; and, although it was afterwards rescued from the savages, and conducted out to sea by two of the Missionaries, who restored it to its rightful owners, the circumstance created much excitement in the country, inasmuch as revenge, or a demand for "satisfaction," as they called it, was expected from the Europeans. The excitement in the neighbourhood of Wangaroa was increased by the sickness and death of the chief George, who was understood to have requested the people of his tribe to attack the Mission-station as soon as he was no more, in *utu*, or payment, for the death of his father in connection with the destruction of the *Boyd*. These sources of uneasiness made the wicked natives very overbearing in their conduct. They broke over the Mission fence, and committed numerous petty depredations on the property; and, on being admonished, they proceeded to acts of violence against Mr. Turner and his assistants, assaulting them with spears, and would, no doubt, have killed them, had they not been restrained by an invisible power in answer to prayer.

The Missionaries of the Church Society, hearing of their troubles manifested the liveliest sympathy with their Wesleyan brethren; and, with true Christian love, the Rev. Messrs. Williams and Kemp came over and urged that at least Mrs. Turner and the children should be removed to one of their settlements for a season. They were removed accordingly overland to Keri-Keri, where they received the kindest attention; but nothing could induce Mr. Turner and his fellow-labourers to leave the station, as they hoped the storm would blow over. For several days their circumstances were most critical. At length, on the death of the chief George, there came a party of natives to make an attack on the station, to demand satisfaction for the loss of the chief's father, and other real or imaginary injuries inflicted by Europeans several years before. After some consultation among themselves, however, they agreed to accept the blood of a bird as sufficient compensation. One of the party then jumped over into the Mission premises, bore off a duck, killed it, and so far all was over in respect to this matter. Mrs. Turner and the children now returned to Wangaroa, and it was hoped that all would be well; but it was not long before still worse troubles arose from another quarter.

The redoubtable chief 'Hongi, who had for several years been carrying on a devastating war in a distant part of the country, was suddenly prompted to invade the Valley of Wangaroa. On the 4th of January, 1827, whilst the Mission family was engaged in domestic worship, they received intelligence of the approach of the hostile chief and his warriors. The two tribes of natives inhabiting Wesleydale, among whom the Missionaries laboured, were thrown into a state of great excitement, and many of them, under the direction of the chief Tepui, seized their arms, and dropped down the river in their war canoes, to repel the anticipated attack. The Missionaries and their dependents were utterly defenceless, but endeavoured to put their trust in God. On the 9th, the assistant, Mr. Stack, was dispatched with a letter to the Church brethren at Keri-Keri, to request counsel and aid, but before he could return the crisis came. Early on the morning of the 10th, a party of natives were descried by the servant approaching the station. The Missionaries had hardly time to put on their clothes, when twenty savages, armed with muskets, spears, and hatchets, entered the Mission grounds, and were proceeding towards the house. It was demanded of them what they wanted. Oro, the chief, said, "We are come to make a fight. Your chief has fled; your people have left the place; you will be stripped of all your property before noon; therefore, instantly be gone!" At the same time he gave instructions to his warriors to commence the work of spoilation. They fired several guns at a signal, and others came to join them. The work of destruction and robbery having begun with merciless fury, Mr. Turner began to prepare for quitting the station. At six o'clock in the morning, when all hope of remaining in safety was gone, the sorrowful and affrighted household began to move off, saving scarcely anything from the wreck but the clothes they wore, and a change or two for the children. The company, apart from the native youths who clung to their teachers, consisted of Mr. and Mrs. Turner, their three children (the youngest of whom was an infant five weeks old), Luke Wade, the assistant and his wife, Mr. Hobbs, and Miss Davis, a young lady of the Church settlement who had come to spend a few weeks on a visit.

With the hope of reaching in safety the nearest Church Mission-station, which was twenty miles distant, they set off in that direction. As they went on, they were met by one of their own principal men, and also by a friendly chief from the Bay of Islands. To the latter, Mr. Turner made his appeal for help and protection, to which he immediately responded, and all the group moved on under his guidance. They had to cross the river repeatedly, and on turning a sharp bend in the channel, all at once they came upon a formidable party of fighting natives, armed with muskets and bayonets. The chief at their head caught a glance at the Missionaries, and loudly called upon his men to stop. He invited Mr. Turner and the rest of his party to sit down; and then came with several of his principal men to rub noses with the fugitives, in token of friendship and goodwill. On being made acquainted with the circumstances of the Mission party, the chiefs kindly protected them till the band of warriors had passed on, and thus they escaped another danger. The travellers now left the river and plunged into the woods, where they soon afterwards met with Mr. Stack returning from Keri-Keri, accompanied by Mr. Clarke and a few of the Mission youths. The boys were immediately despatched to the station for chairs on which to carry the exhausted females the rest of the journey. They were next met by another party of friends, consisting of Messrs. Williams, Davis, and Richey, and a dozen natives from Paihia, another Church Mission-station. From these excellent persons, and at Keri-Keri, where they soon arrived, the Wesleyan Mission party received every mark of sympathy and kindness that genuine Christian brotherly love could suggest. After refreshment and a temporary rest, Mr. Turner and his party removed, on the 17th of January, to the Paihia settlement, where they remained till the captain of the ship *Rosanna*, hearing of their disasters, kindly offered them a passage to Sydney; and thus they removed to the colony, and the work in New Zealand was for a while relinquished.

Adverting briefly to the deserted station at Wangaroa, we may just mention that the war party who made the first attack were proceeding with their work of destruction and plunder, when they were pounced upon and driven off by a band of warriors from Hokianga. What the first invaders had left these utterly demolished or carried away with them, burning the Mission-house and barn, with the crop of wheat, and killing the stock in the most wanton manner. They even dug up the body of Mr. Turner's infant, which had been recently buried, for the sake of the blanket in which it had been wrapped when interred, and left the station a complete ruin.

As to the terrible 'Hongi, whose warriors were the first to attack the peaceful station at Wesleydale, his days were numbered. Accompanied by his principal wife, Keri, who, though now blind, sustained him even in war by her presence and counsel, he went to his last conflict with a strong determination to conquer or die. Early in the day a fatal shot from the enemy struck 'Hongi, and he fell to the ground. He was carried from the field shattered and helpless, and although he lingered for some time, he never recovered. At length the end of New Zealand's greatest warrior drew near, and we regret to state that there appeared no signs of repentance in his last moments, although he had heard the Gospel faithfully preached both in England and in his own country. But "the ruling passion" was strong to the last. Just before he died, 'Hongi called for his gunpowder, muskets, and coat of mail, presented to him by George IV., which he bequeathed to his sons.

He then exhorted his followers to be valiant, telling them that this was all the *utu*, or "satisfaction," that he desired. After he had several times uttered the words, "*Kia toa, kia toa,*" "Be courageous, be courageous," he breathed his last. The usual barbaric honours of haranguing, crying, cutting, dancing, and firing of muskets were accorded on the occasion of his funeral; but, to the surprise of every one, the event passed off without the occurrence of those scenes of cruelty and blood which were wont to mark the death of great chiefs, for all seemed to feel that the greatest enemy to peace in New Zealand had been called away.

THE RE-ESTABLISHMENT OF THE WORK.

The chief Patuone, who kindly interposed on behalf of Mr. Turner and his family, and shielded them from native violence, as they fled from Wangaroa, seems never to have been easy at the removal of the Wesleyan Missionaries. The sad disaster evidently gave him the greatest concern, and towards the end of the year 1827, even before 'Hongi's death, he earnestly invited them to return. For this they held themselves in readiness, as they only regarded the suspension of the Mission as a temporary measure till the storm which drove them from their station had passed over. Hence it appears, that early in 1828 Mr. Stack and Mr. and Mrs. Hobbs, with their assistants, returned to New Zealand; Mr. and Mrs. Turner having embarked for the Friendly Islands, to which field of labour they had been appointed in the interim. The work of the Mission was resumed; not at Wangaroa, however, where the natives still appeared in a very unsettled state, but at a place called Mangungu, on the River Hokianga, on the western coast of the principal island. The place fixed upon by the Missionaries as the site of the new station was about forty miles distant from the scene of their former labours, and fifty miles overland from the Bay of Islands. The district contained a population of about four thousand natives, living in villages easily reached by boats, as they were situated near to the banks of a navigable river. Most of these people were subject to the friendly chief Patuone, whose protection and aid were promised to the Missionaries; the land was fertile, and everything seemed favourable for a permanent establishment.

The Missionaries addressed themselves with commendable zeal and diligence to the preparatory work of clearing and cultivating the ground which they had purchased for a station, and of erecting suitable buildings, whilst at the same time they neglected no opportunity of instructing the people in the things pertaining to their eternal welfare. In the secular part of their work they succeeded very well, and they were soon supplied with most of the necessaries, if not many of the comforts of life. But for a length of time the result of their spiritual labours was very discouraging. They had much to endure, not only from the carelessness and apathy of the people, but from their impertinence and rudeness, to say nothing of the shocking scenes of superstition, cruelty, and blood, which they were obliged almost constantly to witness. Sometimes, after an earnest and faithful discourse delivered by one of the Missionaries, the people would boisterously inquire, " What food do they eat in that world about which you have been speaking? How do they see? How do they hear? What is their employment? If a brave man die, how will he exercise his bravery? Are there no guns? no people to fight with?" &c.

It was not till the early part of 1831, when the Missionaries had toiled for nearly ten years, that their hearts were gladdened by the appearance of fruit. About that period, however, there was a general waking up among the natives to a sense of the reality and importance of eternal things. The children and young people attached to the station manifested increased earnestness to learn to read and write, and to become acquainted with the contents of the Bible and Catechism, whilst their parents and friends, in some instances, gladly became their pupils. The same spirit of inquiry was observed in the distant villages, which were visited at stated periods by the Missionaries; and they were surprised and gratified, on their return after a considerable interval, to find that their scholars had not only made considerable progress themselves, but that they had been busily engaged in teaching others. Both boys and girls were in the habit of walking through the woods a distance of many miles to school; and, when a broad river intersected their path, they would fearlessly plunge into the stream, and swim across with their books and scanty garments upon their heads, and hasten on to be in time for their much-loved lessons. Thus the progress made in elementary learning was remarkably rapid, and the demand for books, slates, pencils, and other school requisites, could not be met till additional supplies were sent from England. When the Missionaries became well acquainted with the native

NEW ZEALAND SCHOLARS CROSSING THE RIVER TO SCHOOL.

language, much of their time was occupied in writing out lesson-books for the use of their pupils, till, in after years, a printing press was sent out, when translations of portions of the Scriptures and other books in the Maori tongue were rapidly multiplied, and soon came into common use. Nor were the higher departments of Missionary labour less encouraging. The public services were well attended, and the natives listened to the Word preached as persons bent on receiving instruction. A gracious influence, moreover, frequently rested upon the congregation, and the Gospel became the power of God unto the salvation of multitudes of sincere enquirers.

The first genuine convert at the commencement of this movement was a youth named Hika, who, at his own request, had accompanied the Missionaries to New South Wales, when they were driven from Wangaroa, and who returned with them when they came to settle at Mangungu. This young disciple was brought to a saving knowledge of the truth in his last illness; and having been baptized into the Christian Church, and received the Sacrament of the Lord's Supper, he died happy in God, and was taken to heaven as the first-fruits of a glorious harvest, to be gathered from the once unpromising field of New Zealand. Others were afterwards gathered into the fold of the Redeemer, and a Christian Church was formed, which, as it extended and increased, became an unspeakable blessing to the land. A general desire having been manifested in various places for religious instruction, the Missionaries itinerated extensively; but, notwithstanding their utmost efforts, they were unable to meet the increasing demands made upon them, and they earnestly desired the society at home to send out more labourers.

In response to this request, in 1834, the Rev. John Whiteley * was sent out to New Zealand, and he was soon afterwards followed

---

* This devoted Missionary had laboured with exemplary zeal and diligence in New Zealand for the long period of thirty-six years, when he met his death in a manner truly painful to contemplate. On the 13th of April, 1869, he left his home, as usual, to preach at Pukearuhe, near the White Cliffs, and other places, on the following day, which was the Sabbath. It was a time of war, but Mr. Whiteley was unwilling to neglect his appointments. He had proceeded nearly to the end of his journey, when he encountered a party of hostile natives. They desired him to return, but he declined to do so, thinking, perhaps, that his presence might prevent the shedding of blood. Whereupon they shot first his horse and then himself, and immediately departed. On Monday morning the dead body of the Missionary was found lying near that of his horse, pierced with five bullets, but not otherwise mutilated. A whole family of Europeans was murdered in that neighbourhood on the same day, and when the intelligence of the massacre reached the nearest settlement, it was the cause of universal sorrow and mourning among the people.

by the Rev. James Wallis. These devoted servants of Christ, with their heroic wives, were subsequently joined or succeeded by the Rev. Messrs. Woon, Turton, Buller, and others, whose united labours were greatly owned and blessed of God to the conversion of sinners, and the building up of the Church of Christ. New stations were soon formed at Waipa, on the Waikato River, Wangungu, Taranaki, Waiuku, Kaipara, and other places; and, in the erection of chapels, schools, and other buildings, the converted natives came forward to assist the Missionaries with a readiness which called forth their highest commendations. In the following year, after the commencement of the great awakening, sixteen intelligent young men were reported as being employed as assistants to the Missionaries in teaching, exhorting, and preaching, and the blessed work advanced in the most delightful manner. Mr. Hobbs having removed to the Friendly Islands, to strengthen the Mission there, in 1836, Mr. Turner was re-appointed to New Zealand, and he rejoiced exceedingly on beholding the wonderful change which had taken place since the time when he was obliged to flee with his wife and family from Wangaroa.

But whilst the heart of the Missionary was gladdened by the prosperity of the work, he had many trials and afflictions to pass through, one of which was the total destruction of the Mission house at Wangungu, in which he resided, by fire. On the evening of Saturday, the 18th of August, 1838, Mr. Turner and his family retired to rest as usual; but before they did so, a large log of wood was placed on the fire to keep it burning, in case anything should be wanted during the night for Mrs. Turner, who was suffering from a long-continued illness. About two o'clock on Sunday morning the Missionary was awakened by a roaring noise, like that of fire. He instantly arose and went to the room which he had left some hours before, and found it full of smoke and flame. He attempted to enter, but could not for some time. At length he got through a window, and roused the settlement; but before water could be obtained, the fire had penetrated the roof of the house, which was of pine, covered with thatch, and all hope of saving the building was taken away. The Mission bell was rung, and the natives were soon on the spot, and laboured hard to secure whatever could be saved from the devouring element. The afflicted Mrs. Turner had to escape in her night-dress; and, in her endeavours to save the children, who were in an adjoining room, sustained a great shock, especially by falling down in the hurry, and being severely bruised. One of the children had also a narrow escape; but, through the kind providence of God, no lives were lost, nor were the flames permitted to desolate the adjoining buildings. Much valuable property in furniture, books, and other articles was destroyed, however, and the loss to the Mission was estimated at £600. Temporary accommodation was provided for Mr. Turner's family by the kindness of his colleagues, till the Mission-house could be re-built, and the zealous Missionary and his afflicted partner held on their way, being sustained by the mercy and goodness of God.

Colonisation.

The Missionaries had prosecuted their important work among the Aborigines of New Zealand for several years with a cheering measure of success, when an event occurred which was destined in the order of Divine Providence to produce a great change in the country and in the character of their labours—that was the commencement of a system of European colonisation. From a very early period white men had occasionally settled among the natives of the different islands; but before the Aborigines were brought under the civilising influence of Christianity none would venture on such a step, except persons of desperate character, such as escaped convicts or depraved seamen who absconded from the ships which visited those shores, and many of these were sacrificed by the savage cannibal inhabitants. In proportion as the Missions became influential and effective, however, the natives were willing to admit the settlement among them of trading adventurers, who by bartering British manufactured goods for articles of produce, such as timber, flax, and provisions, were disposed to carry on commerce in the country.

This led to the influx of a number of Europeans, who generally settled around the shores of the principal harbours; but especially in the neighbourhood of the Bay of Islands, where whalers and other vessels frequently anchored for refreshment. This part of the population was awfully corrupt; and, by the introduction of ardent spirits among the natives,—by their contempt of all moral restraint in the absence of all settled law,—their introduction of thoughtless native females to ungodly ship's crews, and their

WHALEFISHING.

fomenting of jealousies among native chiefs, they produced a misery little less than that of heathenism itself, and seriously impeded the labours of the Missionaries. These circumstances led first to the appointment of a British Consul to the country, and then to the adoption of a system of colonisation by what was called the " New Zealand Land Company." These arrangements were followed, in 1889, by an honourable treaty securing the cession of New Zealand to Her Majesty Queen Victoria, with a view to the settlement of a regular government; for the principal chiefs, being convinced of the inability of the Maori nation to govern the land efficiently, now sought the aid and protection of Great Britain.

For some time the Directors of the Wesleyan and Church Missionary Societies used their utmost efforts, by means of memorials and personal interviews with Government authorities, to prevent the plan for the colonisation of New Zealand being carried into effect, from an apprehension that it would be ruinous to the cause of Missions among the natives. At length, however, they were led to acquiesce in the measure, being convinced, perhaps, that the regular establishment of British law in any form would be better than the irregular and irresponsible settlement of the country by Europeans, which was rapidly progressing, despite the remonstrances of the Missionaries, and especially as advantage was frequently taken of the ignorance of the natives by wily settlers, who were attempting to buy up the land for a mere trifle.

To meet the emergency as best they could, the Wesleyan Missionary Society sent out a large reinforcement of labourers, consisting of the Revs. J. H. Bumby, Samuel Ironside, Charles Creed, and John Warren, together with the Rev. John Waterhouse as General Superintendent of the Missions in the South Seas, and the Rev. John Eggleston for Tasmania. This noble band of Missionaries, with their families, embarked at Gravesend, on board the ship *James*, on the 28th of September, 1838, and those who were destined for New Zealand arrived there on the 9th of March, 1839. Arrangements were now made for the extension and consolidation of the work, by the erection of additional chapels and the formation of new circuits, with a view to make provision for the rapidly-increasing European population in the respective towns and villages which were rising in every direction, whilst at the same time the spiritual wants of the natives were not neglected.

The Rev. J. H. Bumby, who had previously laboured successfully for several years in the home work, had only been in New Zealand about fifteen months when he was suddenly called to his reward in heaven by a most mysterious dispensation of Divine Providence. He was crossing an arm of the sea, known as the

Bay of Thames, on his homeward journey, after an absence of two or three weeks spent in visiting several distant stations. The weather was remarkably fine, as he sailed along in a large canoe, in company with eighteen natives. No danger was apprehended from any source, when one of the men stood up to set the sail, with a view to accelerate their progress, a gentle breeze having just sprung up. At the same moment several of the other natives rose from their seats, with eager haste to assist, and the canoe, being deeply laden, was upset, and the whole party submerged in the mighty deep. It was a moment of intense consternation; but as soon as the natives had recovered themselves a little,—for most of them were excellent swimmers,—they made a strenuous effort not only to save their own lives, but also that of their beloved Missionary. They soon succeeded in righting the canoe, and in getting Mr. Bumby, who was unable to swim, into it; but when partly baled out, and while hope was entertained of success, the frail vessel was upset again, by the rushing towards it of several of the men who were struggling in the water. Again they got the drowning Missionary lifted on the canoe, capsized as it was, and again he was washed off by the waves. As there was no other vessel in sight, all hope of deliverance was now taken away; and the devoted Missionary and twelve natives sank to rise no more, only six escaping to the shore to carry to their friends the news of the sad disaster. This melancholy event occurred on Friday, the 26th of June, 1840, and when the intelligence was conveyed to the Mission-station of Mangungu it produced a scene of lamentation, mourning, and woe, never to be forgotten by those who witnessed it.

ULTIMATE SUCCESS.

With the influx of European emigrants to the colony of New Zealand, and the excitement invariably connected with settling in a new country, numerous difficulties arose to impede the progress of the work of God, most of which were of a character different from those which had been previously experienced. The Missionaries had no longer to contend with the grosser forms of heathenism which so frequently appalled them when they first commenced their labours. Cannibalism and open idolatry had almost entirely ceased in every part of the country, and a large proportion of the natives had been brought under the influence of Christianity, and could read and write as well as the pale-faced strangers. But with the advent of the white men came the common use of ardent spirits, and the prevalence of intemperate habits among all classes, to say nothing of other revolting forms of sin. Then followed a manifestation of worldliness, avarice, ambition, and contention to which the natives had previously but few temptations.

Numerous and serious difficulties also arose between the Aborigines and the colonists with reference to the "land question." It was laid down as a fundamental principle by the Government arrangements for colonising New Zealand, that land must be fairly bought and honestly paid for; but it frequently happened that contending chiefs laid claim to the same tract of country, and it sometimes turned out that the wrong party had sold a block of land and received payment for it, whilst the real owner clamoured for his rights. After the Colonial Government had taken the matter into their own hands, the quarrels about land became so serious as to result in open war, and the sacrifice of many lives, both of natives and Europeans, to say nothing of the destruction of valuable property. Indeed, a state of warfare has been kept up between a small party of hostile natives and the colonists from year to year, with scarcely any intermission, to the present time, into the particulars of which it would be foreign to our purpose to enter.

All these things were unfavourable to the progress of religion; but perhaps the greatest trial which the Wesleyan Missionaries were called to experience at this period was the unexpected manifestation of a spirit of intolerance and exclusivism on the part of the Episcopalian Church of the colony. The utmost harmony existed between the agents of the two great societies, who had been so long and so successfully engaged in seeking to evangelise New Zealand, till the arrival of the Rev. Dr. Selwyn, in 1842, as the first bishop of the English Church. This distinguished dignitary being a person of great energy of character, and avowedly of "High Church" principles, he had not been long in the colony before he began to teach the doctrines of baptismal regeneration and apostolical succession, as they were held by the Puseyite party in England. This he might have done to his heart's content, if he had only confined his attention to his own people, and to that which immediately concerned him; but he so far forgot the claims of Christian charity, that he went out of his way to attack the unoffending Wesleyan Missionaries, by attempting to cast discredit upon their ministerial authority and character by denying the validity of their pastoral acts, because they had not been episcopally ordained. These, and kindred doctrines, as propagated by the bishop and his adherents among the semi-civilised natives, had the effect of inflating the minds of such as had been baptized by the Church Missionaries, and of causing them to look with feelings of contempt upon their Wesleyan brethren.

Clandestine efforts were, moreover, made to induce some of the people in the south to separate themselves, on these grounds, from connection with the Wesleyans, and such as were weak enough to be thus led away, were re-baptized, and admitted into what was called the *true* Church. These proceedings were for a long time a source of pain and grief to the Missionaries. At length the Rev. H. H. Turton, of the Taranaki station, deemed it his duty to address a spirited and yet most Christian remonstrance to Dr. Selwyn on the subject, in three able letters which were some time afterwards published in the local papers. There was no great amount of sympathy with this exclusivism, however, in the colony generally; and ultimately the Bishop acquired juster views of the Wesleyan cause, and these ill-judged and devisive proceedings were gradually abated, not, however, without weakening that blessed bond of attachment and respect which had formerly united the agents of both Societies.

When access to the native population had been rendered practicable and safe by the united labours of the Wesleyan and Church Missionaries for several years, a Roman Catholic bishop and a number of priests landed in New Zealand, and attempted to proselyte the simple-minded people to their corrupt system of religion. The pompous display and gaudy processions by which their religious ceremonies were accompanied, as a matter of course drew a few followers, but no lasting impression was made upon the minds of the native population generally. The Maoris, as a nation, had by this time become too well informed to be drawn away in any considerable numbers by the follies of Popery. The Mission press had happily been at work for several years before the arrival of the Romish priests, and a large proportion of the natives were able to read for themselves the numerous translations of elementary books and portions of the Scriptures in the Maori language, which were extensively circulated among them. The British and Foreign Bible Society having, morover, completed a large edition of the Maori New Testament in 1842, generously sent out to the Wesleyan Missionaries in New Zealand a supply of ten thousand copies, which were received with acclamations of joy at the respective stations, and helped, in no small degree, to counteract the pernicious errors of Popery, and to build up the people in the faith and knowledge of the Gospel.

Notwithstanding these and other impediments to the progress of the work, by the blessing of God upon the labours of His servants, the cause of truth and righteousness ultimately triumphed. When the Maoris were led to see the sin and folly of that system of idolatry and superstition in which they had been so long involved, and were fairly brought under the influence of Christianity, the desire which they manifested for religious instruction was very remarkable. The Mission schools were crowded, not only with children, but also with adults, all anxious to acquire a knowledge of letters. Their books became their companions wherever they went. Those who made the most progress in learning at school, taught the rest at home, in the field, and by the wayside; and when the Rev. Robert Young visited New Zealand as a deputation from the British Conference in 1853, he found that three-fourths of the adult population could read, and two-thirds could write their own language correctly—a proportion, perhaps, not surpassed in any part of the civilised world. And although the people did not show the same desire to imitate their teachers in their dress, habitations, furniture, and mechanical arts, yet they did, to some extent, adopt civilised habits, and were largely benefited, both temporally and spiritually, by the reception of the Gospel.

There were, among the civilised Maories, some remarkable instances of mental superiority, and of intelligent natives, who elevated themselves in the social scale, built handsome dwellings, furnished them respectably after the European style, and carried on business successfully as farmers, merchants, or Government officers. Nor was there wanting direct spiritual fruit of the most encouraging kind, as the result of the united labours of the Missionaries. At one period, on thirteen stations, the Wesleyan Missionaries reported three thousand two hundred and fifty-nine converted natives, united in Church fellowship; and four thousand children in the Mission schools. At social meetings, when opportunities were afforded to the native members to relate their religious experience, they frequently bore testimony to the regenerating and sanctifying power of Divine grace upon their souls, in a manner which excited feelings of the liveliest gratitude in the hearts of those who had been the means of their conversion to God.

In view of the cheering prospects which characterised the early history of the Missionary enterprise in New Zealand, it is with sorrowful feelings that we record the fact of the gradual decrease in numbers of the Maori race. Similar results have followed European emigration to other countries; and yet we see no reason why this need be the case, if proper precautions were used to guard the natives against the evils to which they are exposed when they come in contact with their pale-faced brethren. Unfortunately, thoughtless and unprincipled white men often introduce the use of ardent spirits and tobacco to the Aborigines of the countries where they settle, to say nothing about certain diseases almost as destructive of human life in their influence, to which the natives were previously strangers. Something may, however, in all fairness, be placed to the account of the people's own folly and imprudence in this matter: as early and unequal marriages, marriages with kindred, the remains of polygamy, improper treatment of infants, unwholesome food, and insufficient clothing, &c. When the natives become still better informed, and more fully Christianised, some of these hindrances to health and increase may, perhaps, be removed, and the permanency of the race be secured in a state of civilisation, if Europeans do their duty to their fellowmen. According to the latest accounts, the European population of New Zealand is estimated at two hundred and twenty-five thousand, whilst that of the Maoris scarcely exceeds forty thousand.

Since the colonisation of the country, the Missionary work in New Zealand has undergone an entire change in its character, as already intimated. From the removal of the people to different localities, the scattering of the tribes by war, as well as the decrease of the Aboriginal population already alluded to, the native department of the Mission is much more circumscribed than formerly, and fewer Church members are now reported. Yet we have some noble specimens of native Christians connected with our respective stations; and their spiritual interests and the education of their children are carefully attended to. Among the colonists, however, the work has greatly prospered, and many of the British emigrants, in that far-off country, can rejoice in the enjoyment of religious privileges equal to those with which they were favoured in their own highly-favoured land. Commodious and substantial chapels have been erected in the principal colonial towns and villages; common schools and seminaries of learning have been established, for the education of the rising generation of all classes; and, by the judicious arrangements of the Australian Conference, with which the work is now incorporated, we have reason to anticipate a prosperous future for Methodism in New Zealand. The Islands are divided into three separate Districts, which comprise about *thirty-two principal stations or circuits.* In connection with these, *forty-three ordained ministers* are usefully employed, with *two thousand five hundred and eighty-seven Church members* under their pastoral care, and *five thousand scholars* attending the Sabbath and day-schools.

CHAPTER VIII.

THE FRIENDLY ISLANDS.

THE COUNTRY AND INHABITANTS—A MISSION OF CIVILISATION—WESLEYAN MISSION COMMENCED—MISSIONARIES SENT FROM ENGLAND—PROGRESS OF THE WORK IN TONGA—MISSION TO HAABAI—MISSION TO VAVAU—GREAT REVIVAL—MISCELLANEOUS INCIDENTS—SAMOA.

THE Friendly Islands are situated in the South Pacific Ocean, the centre being in latitude 21° south, and longitude 18° west. The entire group is said to consist of nearly two hundred islands, from forty to fifty of which only are inhabited. The principal of these are Tonga or Tongatabu, Vavau, Nomuka, Eua, and the Haabais. They were first discovered by the great Dutch navigator, Tasman, in 1643, and in 1773 they were visited by our celebrated countryman, Captain Cook, who gave them their present name, from the real or supposed friendliness of the inhabitants, as compared with the savages of other groups with whom he came in contact. Like most of the other islands in the South Seas, they are of coral formation, and are supposed to have emerged from the ocean at a remote period, as the result of the industry of myriads of little insects which are constantly at work beneath the waves. Although the soil is but thinly spread over the coral rocks, it is, nevertheless, remarkably fertile, and produces the cocoa-nuts, bread-fruit, plantain, banana, sugar-cane, and yams, besides pumpkins, pine-apples, pepper, oranges, melons, and various other kinds of vegetables and fruits peculiar to the country. The climate, although warm, is said to be healthy, and the scenery is described as peculiarly grand and romantic, some of the hills being covered with forest trees, and others exhibiting evident signs of volcanic action.

It is believed that the Aborigines of the Friendly Islands, in common with the natives of other groups in the Pacific, originally came from the mainland of Asia. Their appearance, their language, and many of their customs, are regarded as justifying this view of their origin. At what period, and under what circumstances, these beautifully sunny islands were first inhabited, it is now impossible to say, as, when first discovered, the people had no written language or monumental records of any kind to chronicle their history. There are, however, in the appearance of crowded burying-places, in stories handed down from father to son, and in occasional traces of arts once known, but now lost, indications that many generations have succeeded each other since the Asiatic strangers first arrived on these shores. Tradition says that the population of the entire group was once immense, but it is now estimated at about thirty thousand.

With regard to their social and moral condition, it is quite clear that the inhabitants were awfully degraded, and fearfully sunk in depravity and sin, when they first came under the notice of Europeans. They were called *Friendly* Islanders, it is true, by those who paid a hasty and transient visit to their shores, and fabulous accounts of their innocence and happiness were freely circulated in Europe at an early period; but when Christian Missionaries came to live among them, and to witness their conduct from month to month and from year to year, their real state and character became more correctly and more fully known. It turned out that these *Friendly* Islanders were almost constantly at war among themselves, that they were cannibals, polygamists, and idolaters, and that they stood in need of the Gospel as much as any people whoever lived on the face of the earth. There were, nevertheless, traits of character and incidental peculiarities in these people, some of which will appear as we proceed, that seem to betoken a higher state of civilisation, at some remote period of time, from which they had degenerated—thus forcibly showing how man, when left to himself, may deteriorate in his condition; but, without the true knowledge of God, he can never raise himself in the scale of being.

A Mission of Civilisation.

It is to be feared that the impression made upon the minds of the Friendly Islanders by the first white men with whom they came in contact would not be very favourable. In connection with the visits of the ships of Tasman and Cook, some events occurred of a very exceptional character. And when escaped convicts or European seamen of depraved and dissolute habits occasionally landed on their shores, and took up their abode in the islands, the natives had still more objectionable specimens of people from a Christian country. These wicked men not only descended to the level of the savages in their dress and mode of life, without making any efforts to improve them, but they actually taught them deeds of daring and of sin which they had never known before. But we refrain from entering into a description of scenes of cruelty and of blood in which our countrymen were the chief actors, and proceed to notice events of a more pleasing character. At length the time came when the Friendly Islanders were to behold better specimens of white men; for a Mission was planned in England, by a truly philanthropic people, for the special purpose of seeking to promote their civilisation, concerning which a few particulars may prove interesting.

When the London Missionary Society was organised in the year 1795, it was arranged that their first enterprise should be a Mission to the South Seas, a part of the world which was then attracting considerable attention by reason of the wonderful discoveries of Captain Cook, which had just been made known to the public. After considerable delay, a ship called the *Duff* was purchased and fitted out for the voyage, and thirty persons were engaged as Missionaries. Only four of these, however, were ordained Ministers; the rest were mechanics or tradesmen, intended to teach the natives the arts of civilised life, as introductory to the Gospel, according to the erroneous notion generally entertained in those days. The *Duff*, with her noble band of Missionaries, sailed from London on the 10th of August, 1796, and after a favourable passage, she reached Tahiti towards the close of the year. Here the four ordained Ministers, and fourteen of the other brethren, were landed, and the ship proceeded to the Friendly Islands, for which group ten artizans were allotted, namely, Messrs. Shelley, Kelso, Wilkinson, Bowell, Harper, Buchanan, Cooper, Nobbs, Veeson, and Gaulton. They were put on shore at Tonga, on the 12th of April, 1797, and two days afterwards the *Duff* proceeded on her voyage to convey the remaining passengers to the Marquesas Islands, according to previous arrangement.

The persons engaged in this Mission of civilisation were generally young men of good sense and decided piety. Their trades and professions were various. There was a carpenter, a bricklayer, a cabinetmaker, a weaver, a tailor, a shoemaker, a hatter, and a cloth manufacturer; and it was intended that they should instruct the natives in every art with which they were acquainted. Nor was religious instruction to be neglected: but, so far as we are acquainted with their plan of proceeding, this was to be a secondary matter at the commencement, and to remain in the back-ground, from the mistaken notion that secular knowledge would prepare the way for communications of a purely spiritual character. The strangers were kindly received by the chiefs and people of Tonga, not so much, perhaps, from regard to the object of their Mission, as from the hope that they might become possessed of some of the goods they had brought with them; for the Missionaries were well supplied with various articles of merchandise, iron, edged tools, fish hooks, and other commodities which were highly prized by the natives.

A portion of land having been set apart for their use, the Missionaries soon began to turn it to good account. They stubbed up old bread-fruit trees, and prepared the ground for garden seeds; they planted peas, beans, and turnips; they made an enclosure for their pigs; they tried to make a forge for working iron, and moulds for bricks. These attempts to form a comfortable settlement interested the natives, who flocked around them in considerable numbers, and were at times exceedingly troublesome, asking numerous questions and examining their tools with evident surprise and delight. But, of all their possessions, none seemed to excite their wonder so much as a cuckoo-clock. Its motion and striking were caused, they fancied, by a spirit who lived in it. They gave it the name of "Akau lea," or "speaking wood." They dared not touch it, and they thought that if they stole anything, the bird-spirit would detect them. This superstitious fear was not without its use among a people who were addicted to theft, and who coveted almost everything they saw. Gifts of provisions were brought in large quantities to the Missionaries, who in return made many useful presents to the chiefs. The first Sabbath after they arrived, the Missionaries held a prayer-meeting in the morning, and in the afternoon Mr. Buchanan preached to his brethren. Thus everything at first seemed promising; but, after a short time, insurmountable difficulties presented themselves, and the result was the entire failure of the enterprise.

The first and greatest trial the Missionaries had to experience was from the unprincipled conduct of two dissolute Europeans, Ambler and Connelly, whom they found at Tonga on their arrival. These runaway sailors had been on the island about thirteen months, and having become tolerably familiar with the native language, they might have rendered good service to the Missionaries as interpreters, and in other ways; but instead of helping, they hindered them by their pernicious influence and example, and by various false and slanderous statements which they made to the chiefs as to the object of the strangers in coming to the country. The next trouble that overtook the Missionaries was the defection of one of their own number. George Veeson first absented himself from the prayer-meetings, then shunned the society of his brethren altogether, and soon afterwards they found him dressed like the heathen, and joining them in all their wicked practices. They mourned over their fallen brother, and did all in their power to recover him from the snare of the devil. But all their efforts were in vain. The fact was he had attached himself to a heathen woman, who lived with him as his wife, and he was ultimately excluded from the society of the faithful as an incorrigible transgressor.

Mr. Nobbs, whose health had failed, had left the island with the *Duff* when she called on her return voyage, so that only eight of the brethren now remained to attempt the civilisation of a barbarous race of people. These unwisely separated themselves into three bands, and probably fared the worse in consequence, when the country soon afterwards became involved in war between the native tribes. Ultimately the Mission premises were plundered and destroyed by the savages, three of the Missionaries were cruelly murdered, and the rest only escaped by getting on board a ship bound for Port Jackson, which called at Tonga just at the time they were exposed to the most imminent danger. Thus was the first Mission to the Friendly Isles relinquished after nearly three years of fruitless labour, exposure, and peril.

Wesleyan Mission Commenced.

Twenty-two years had elapsed since the surviving agents of the London Missionary Society had escaped from Tonga, when circumstances transpired which caused the thoughts of British Christians to turn once more to the Friendly Islands. After a long and gloomy night of toil, the Missions established in the Society and Marquesas groups had begun to bear fruit, and the hope was entertained that the Friendly Isles also might, perhaps, now be disposed to receive the Gospel, after what they had suffered by the desolating wars which had laid waste their country. On this occasion the honour was reserved for the Wesleyan Missionary Society to attempt to evangelise a people who had disappointed the anticipations of their benefactors. Before any arrangement could be made for sending a Missionary from England, the Rev. Walter Lawry, then stationed in New South Wales, was induced to undertake a voyage to the Friendly Islands as an experiment, preparatory to the establishment of a permanent Mission. Consequently he and his family sailed from Sydney in the ship *St. Michael*, in the month of June, 1822. He had with him two pious and active European colonists, George Lily, a carpenter, and Charles Tindal, a blacksmith. The Governor of New South Wales favoured the enterprise, and furnished the Missionary with cattle and sheep from the Government stock of the colony.

On the 16th of August the vessel anchored before Tonga. Among the hundreds of natives who, as usual, came off from the shore in their canoes, was an Englishman named William Singleton, who had lived sixteen years on the island, being one of the survivors of the ill-fated ship *Port au Prince*, whose crew had been massacred in 1806. He had become a thorough Tonga man in his manners and language, but his conduct was not so abandoned as had been that of Ambler and his companion, and he became very useful to the Missionary as an interpreter and in various other ways, ultimately joining the Church and dying in the faith and hope of the Gospel.

A few days after he landed, Mr. Lawry requested an interview with the principal chiefs, that he might state to them the object of his mission, for it was his determination to avow at once that he came not to trade or merely to teach them useful arts, but to preach the Gospel and to instruct them in the knowledge of the true and living God. His request was readily complied with, and he was conducted to a house of respectable appearance, the lofty roof of which was supported by pillars, and the floor covered with mats. Seven chiefs met him, and a vast crowd of people formed themselves in a circle outside. He spoke of the good will of the people of England in seeking to promote their welfare, of his own design in coming to their country, and asked many questions with a view to ascertain whether they were willing to receive instruction. The chiefs expressed themselves as being well pleased with what they had heard, promised to treat the Missionary and his companions kindly, and to send " thousands " of children to the Mission-school. They gave presents to Mr.

Lawry, and even stripped off their garments and handed them to him, which is one of the highest marks of Tongan courtesy. The principal chief of the island, named Palu, was very desirous that the Missionary should settle near him, and assured him of his protection and aid. For two or three months the kindness of the natives, and their readiness to receive instruction, raised Mr. Lawry's hope of success, and he wrote home for more Missionaries, a surgeon, a printer, teachers, books, and articles for barter. At the same time he held regular religious services with the people, both on Sabbaths and week-days, and instructed them in the best manner he could, Singleton acting as his interpreter.

Shortly after the departure of the *St. Michael*, however, in the month of November, things began to wear a different aspect. The characteristic fickleness and superstition of the people were again manifested. At the *Kava-ring* speeches were made against the new-comers, and it was suggested that they were spies, who intended to conquer the land. "See," said one, "these people are always praying to their God, as the other Missionaries who came here, and what was the consequence of their praying? Why, the war broke out and all the old chiefs were killed." Another told his dream, how in the night the spirit of an old chief had returned to the earth, seen the fence of the new Mission premises, and said in great wrath, "The white people will pray you all dead." These conferences influenced the conduct of the people in the most injurious manner. They became boisterous and insolent, and sometimes seized on articles of property belonging to the Mission, and carried them off without ceremony. Whilst these things were going on, Palu, the principal chief, was away, carrying on war with the people of Eua. On his return he expressed his displeasure at what had happened, and punished the offenders severely. The support of the Chief tended to allay the fears of the Missionary for the time being; but when in the most friendly mood, the natives were very rude, forcing their way into the Mission-house, and even into Mrs. Lawry's bed-room, as early as six o'clock in the morning, on the most trifling occasion. Earnest efforts were, nevertheless, made to instruct the people in a knowledge of Divine things; but, from his imperfect acquaintance with the language, and their total ignorance of such things, the Missionary found it extremely difficult to convey to their minds any distinct ideas of sacred truth.

Notwithstanding the disadvantages under which Mr. Lawry laboured, there were occasions when he had reason to hope that good impressions were made on the minds of some. For instance, one day, when he was telling Palu that the eye of Jehovah was upon him and upon all men in all places and at all times, the Chief seemed greatly astonished. The Missionary took advantage of the momentary impression to say, "When I can speak more of your language, I will tell you greater things than these;" and the promise was received with evident pleasure. On another occasion the Missionary walked into a village, where he met with several of the more intelligent natives with whom he entered into conversation. He spoke to them of the true God, and of his wonderful works in days of old; how he healed the sick, and raised the dead; and that he loved all men in every land, even the people of Tonga; and that he was come to the country on purpose to tell them of these things. The people seemed much interested in the truths thus simply spoken.

It is to be regretted that a Mission, in many respects so hopefully commenced, should have been relinquished even for a time; but so it was. After labouring about fourteen months in Tonga, visiting the powerful Chief Ata, building a Mission-house and blacksmith's shop, and cultivating and fencing in a large piece of ground, Mr. Lawry embarked with his family for New South Wales, the delicate state of Mrs. Lawry's health appearing to render this step necessary. The two artizans, Lilley and Tindall, remained in Tonga, and being pious men, they were willing to teach the people to the best of their ability; but after the Missionary was gone, the Chief Palu treated them very unkindly, and threatened to kill them. In the meantime three native teachers were sent to Vavau from Tahiti, by the agents of the London Missionary Society. Unhappily, the heathen influences by which they were surrounded proved too strong for the young converts,

THE FRIENDLY ISLANDS. 361

and they failed to win over the people to the adoption of Christianity, as their brethren had done in some other islands.

MISSIONARIES SENT FROM ENGLAND.

On receiving the report of Mr. Lawry, as to the condition and claims of the Friendly Islanders, the Wesleyan Missionary Committee in London were anxious to supply them with a Gospel minis-

DANGEROUS LANDING.

try, and permanently to carry on the work of evangelisation among them; but the work was delayed by various hindrances for upwards of two years. It was not till the month of June, 1826, that the Revs. John Thomas and John Hutchinson, and their wives, who had been appointed to this service, arrived at Tonga. The vessel which conveyed the Missionaries approached the island in the midst of a heavy storm, and it was found impossible to land at the old Mission-station. A few days of suspense and uncertainty passed by, and then good anchorage was found in an adjacent bay. Before this, however, the Missionaries had gone on shore in a boat, and obtained an interview with Charles Tindall, one of the mechanics left on the island by Mr. Lawry. From him they learned that it would not be safe to place themselves under the protection of Palu, as he had not kept faith with Mr. Lawry, but had ill-treated the young men who were left with him. They, therefore, sought for an interview with the great Chief Ata, living at Hihifo, who gave them a most friendly reception. He conducted the strangers into his house, and placed them upon a mat. Scores of natives gathered around and listened with marked attention, while Mr. Thomas explained their object in coming to their country. He told them it was not because Tonga was better than England, or that they wished to join in their wars, or to carry on trade, but because they desired to teach them the Law of God, and other good things. He then asked whether the Chief was willing for them to settle in the island, and whether he would permit them to conduct their own religious worship; whether they would send their children to school to be taught, give land for Mission premises, and protect the persons and property of the Missionaries. Much pleasure was expressed both by the Chief and his people with what they heard; full promises were made of protection and assistance, and a beautiful plot of ground, with a fine sea breeze sweeping over it, was at once allotted to their use.

But the fairest promises of the heathen are not to be depended upon. Within a week or two after their arrival, the Missionaries were convinced that their property was more coveted than their teaching. The Chief Ata, in particular, was very difficult to deal with. There was no knowing when he was pleased, or how to please him. On the 18th of July he was present at morning worship, and within a month of that time he withdrew his protection from the Missionaries altogether, allowing men, and even boys, to rob and insult them with impunity, and declared that he would burn down their houses. Every possible hindrance was thrown in the way of their benevolent design, and they had reason to fear for their personal safety. The Chief, moreover, called his people together, spoke contemptuously of the God of the Christians, and forbade them to go to His worship on pain of death. But, notwithstanding this threat, the religious services were continued, and many of the natives ventured to attend them. The wily Ata then set men to watch the gates of the sanctuary, and sometimes even watched them himself, on the Lord's-day, to prevent the people from going in, and some poor little children were actually chased away when they attempted to enter. The wife of the Chief having imbibed the spirit of her husband, took away from Mrs. Hutchinson a few young women whom she was teaching to sew and read. Difficulties were also thrown in the way of the Missionaries buying anything from the natives for the supply of their wants; and yet, all this time, the Chief called himself their friend, and went to the Mission-house to eat or beg almost every day.

Amid all these difficulties, the Missionaries continued earnestly to labour and fervently to pray for grace to enable them to bear up under their peculiar trials; and early in the following year, 1827, they were favoured to witness some improvement in the temper and spirit of both chiefs and people. They were also encouraged by seeing a number of people come from Nukualofa from Sabbath to Sabbath, to attend their services, the exhortations of two native converts from Tahiti having tended to arouse the people there to a concern for religion. About the same time Tubou, the Chief of Nukualofa, having become convinced of the folly of idolatry, gave up his gods, and built a chapel for Christian worship, the first instance of the kind which had occurred in the Friendly Islands. And although this was only an outward and nominal change, and did not, it was feared, proceed from a saving work of grace on the heart, it was, nevertheless, regarded as a hopeful sign of better days to come. Tubou was severely tried in his profession of Christianity. He resisted the threats of many of the other chiefs; but at length they overcame him by persuasion. They promised to make him paramount chief or king of all the islands in the group, if he would abandon the new religion. This temptation was too strong for him, and he promised to give up praying to Jehovah for the present. He, nevertheless, permitted the inferior chiefs and common people to do as they pleased, and the services were still largely attended.

As there now seemed to be a more general disposition on the part of the Friendly Islanders to receive instruction, an earnest request was forwarded to England for more Missionaries to be sent out. This call was promptly responded to, and in the early part of 1828 the hearts of the brethren were gladdened by the arrival at Tonga of the Revs. Nathaniel Turner and William Cross, with their excellent wives, who commenced their labours at Nukualofa, whilst Messrs. Thomas and Hutchinson continued at Hihifo. Schools were now established at both stations, which were soon attended by hundreds of children, who were taught chiefly from manuscript translations; but who made rapid progress in learning to read, as well as in committing to memory hymns, prayers, and lessons from Scripture. In the meantime the Sabbath congregations continued to improve, and they had frequently as many as two hundred natives joining with them in the public worship of God. Open opposition to the labours of the Missionaries in Tonga for a time almost entirely disappeared; and they were enabled to devote themselves fully to preaching, teaching, and translating, and acquiring a more perfect knowledge of the language. Although they were "in labours more abundant," they found it difficult to keep up with their work, especially as urgent calls for their services soon began to come in from other islands of the group.

For some time the Missionaries were so fully engaged that they were unable to extend their labours beyond the limits of Tonga. But the longer they were obliged to delay the work of extension for want of men, the louder and more frequent were the calls from every part of the group, for the confidence of the people was everywhere beginning to be shaken in their false gods. Finau, the Chief of Vavau, got an Englishman to write a letter for him to the Missionaries in Tonga, in which he says :—"I am so glad to hear that you are teaching my friend Tubou to know the Great God. I hope you will be so kind as to send to Port Jackson for some Missionaries to come to my island to teach me and my people. I am tired of my spirit-gods: they tell me so many lies, I am sick of them. I have had no sleep, being so uneasy for fear the Missionaries will be so long in getting here. My island will turn to the Great God, because I am the only chief on the Island; I have no one to control me; when I turn, they will turn. To be sure, I did try to take a ship, but I am sorry for it; there will be no more of that. Be so good as to go as quick about the Missionaries as time will allow."

The King of Haabai, who afterwards became the celebrated King George of the whole of the Friendly Islands, went even farther than this. He visited Tonga in person, begged earnestly for a Missionary, and did his best to persuade one of those already there to accompany him on his return. Although the brethren were unable at that time to comply with his request, they were pleased to hear, some time afterwards, that he had taken a solemn oath to cast away his lying spirits and turn to Jehovah; and that he had begun to observe the Christian Sabbath, by ceasing from work and from amusement. It afterwards transpired that when the King of Haabai could not procure a Missionary, he actually employed an English sailor to read prayers in a house which was used as a chapel on Sundays.

At Mua, the chief and his people spontaneously abandoned their idols, and built a neat Christian place of worship, in anticipation of a Missionary; and when a ship called there, and had no teacher on board, they were bitterly disappointed. These remarkable indications of the willingness of the people to receive the Gospel induced the Missionaries at Tonga to unite in a very earnest request to the Committee in London to send out a reinforcement of labourers. This request was readily responded to; but, from the great distance, and the difficulty of finding suitable men for the work, a length of time elapsed before they reached their destination. In the meantime the cause of God advanced on all the stations. Places of worship were erected, schools established, the Gospel faithfully preached; and multitudes of people were reclaimed from the worship of dumb idols, and gathered into the fold of the Redeemer.

PROGRESS OF THE WORK IN TONGA.

The evident change which was rapidly taking place in the views and feelings of the natives of Tonga, as manifested in their readiness to give up their idol-gods and embrace a nominal Christianity, was very gratifying to the Missionaries; but the great object of their Mission being to turn the people from darkness to light, and from the power of Satan unto God, they were anxious to witness more directly spiritual results. They knew that this outward change might result in part from the intelligence which was constantly coming to hand that other groups had relinquished their foolish and superstitious customs, and were learning to read; and partly from the direct influence of Divine truth upon their minds as the result of their instructions: but still they were not satisfied, from an apprehension that the people were resting in the mere external forms of the new religion. They met together for consultation and prayer, for the outpouring of the Holy Spirit; and after they had been about two years in the country, they were permitted to reap the first-fruits of their labour.

The first genuine convert to Christianity in the Friendly Islands was a youth named Lolohia, who resided at Hihifo, the station occupied by the Rev. John Thomas. From a child he was afflicted with a scrofulous disease, common in the Islands, and its ravages had made him an object of pity; but his countenance was fine, and his disposition mild and cheerful. Before Mr. Thomas came to Tonga, Lolohia had been staying with an elder brother at Vavau, where both their minds were much impressed by a few words about Jehovah, spoken by an English sailor who lived on that island. When they heard the same words advanced with still greater earnestness by the Missionary, their hearts yielded; they gave up their Tonga spirit-gods, and determined that the Lord should be their God. They were the first scholars in the Mission-school, and, being young men of rank and importance, from their mother having become the wife of the Chief Ata, their coming influenced others, and a considerable number of native youths were soon brought under instruction. Lolohia showed strong attachment to God's house and ministers, and when he was unable to walk to the school and chapel, on account of his affliction, he got the other boys to carry him there as best they could, which was sometimes in a kind of wheelbarrow constructed for the purpose.

In all the trials through which the Missionaries had to pass, in consequence of the strange conduct of Ata, the chief, and other adverse circumstances, poor Lolohia was their fast and sympathising friend, declaring that if they were obliged to leave the island, he would go with them wherever they went. As his views of Christ and His atoning work became clearer, his faith increased, and he was sweetly assured of his personal interest in the Saviour, and could rejoice in the hope of the glory of God. He was then at his own request baptized in the name of the Father, the Son, and the Holy Ghost; his mother and Ata offering no objection. For some time before his death, Lolohia was the head and guardian of a company of praying youths who lived near to him, and who often united in singing the praises of God and in supplicating at the Throne of Grace, in the room of the invalid. He bore his long affliction with perfect patience and resignation; and when the end drew near, and preparations were being made to remove him to a small house near the burying-ground, he said, "Yes; let us go." And when Mr. Thomas called to see him, he received him with a smile, and said, " My love to you; " " let us pray ;" and with the language of prayer on his lips, his redeemed spirit passed away to be " forever with the Lord," the first fruit of a glorious harvest from the Friendly Islands.

From this period the Missionaries were encouraged by evidences of a deeper spiritual work of grace among the people. Several of the young men who had been associated with Lolohia at Hihifo experienced a saving change of heart, and became active workers in the cause of Christ; and at Nukualofa, where Messrs. Turner and Cross continued to labour, several were brought into a state of acceptance with God through Christ. In the month of June, 1829, upwards of sixty natives were reported as meeting in class on this station, and the number of sincere inquirers after salvation was increasing every week. People came from distant parts of the island to hear preaching, and the congregations on the Sabbath-day became so crowded that it was necessary to enlarge the chapel. Among the early converts was the wife of the Chief and other distinguished persons whose example influenced many others to embrace the *lotu*, as they called the Christian religion. "All Nukualofa seemed moved. Learning to read, coming to class, being baptised, and going to heaven, were the principal subjects of conversation." About this time the King himself began to meet in class, and his voice was heard in the prayer-meetings. Christian marriages were now introduced, the Sabbath-day was kept holy, family worship was generally observed, and the whole deportment of the people showed that a genuine work of grace had taken place in the hearts of many.

Whilst this blessed work was going on at Nukualofa and in the neighbouring villages, the cause was less prosperous at Hihifo in consequence of the continued opposition of the Chief Ata. In fact, the opposition was so strong, and the hindrances to the progress of the work so numerous, that Mr. Thomas resolved to leave the place and go to the Haabai Islands, where the Chief was so anxious to have a Missionary, Mr. Hutchinson having previously embarked for New South Wales. Before this new enterprise was entered upon, it was thought desirable to wait for instructions from home; and, in the meantime, the prospect being so gloomy at Hihifo, Mr. Thomas joined his brethren at Nukualofa, which now became the principal station in Tonga.

The Missionaries having now more completely mastered the native language, preached the Gospel with the demonstrations of the Spirit, and with power; every week that passed witnessed new accessions to the Church, and multitudes believed and were baptized, as many as eighty-four being sometimes added to the number of professing Christians in one day. Monthly Missionary prayer-meetings were now commenced, at which accounts were given of what God was doing in other parts of the world; and at the first love-feast held in Tonga, one hundred and fifty members were present, and forty-six spoke, in a very simple and affecting manner, of their conversion from heathenism to Christianity.

But the most remarkable event of this early period was the baptism of the paramount Chief or King Tubou, which took place on the 18th of January, 1830. He stood up in the chapel before the pulpit, with his wife and children by his side, in the presence of a large congregation, as proof of his having abandoned his Toga gods, and embraced the true religion. He assured the Missionaries and his people, that he had cast away everything that he knew to be sinful, and that Jehovah was his God, and Jesus Christ his only Saviour, and that he made an offering of himself, his wife, and his children that day to the Lord, that He might dispose of him and his as He thought good. He exhorted his people to attend to the things of God, and to follow his example in being baptized in the name of the Lord Jesus. He then turned round, kneeled down, and the sacred ordinance was administered by Mr. Turner, amid the silent prayers and half-subdued emotion of a vast concourse of people. The King chose the name of Josiah; and having been himself thus dedicated to God, he presented his four children for baptism, so that the whole of the royal family were now received into the Church of Christ.

Mission to Haabai.

During the time that Mr. Thomas was detained at Nukualofa, a remarkable incident occurred which clearly shows the superintending providence of God in the affairs of the Missionary enterprise. Whilst waiting anxiously for communications from home, not daring to add to the financial burden of the Society by further outlay without the explicit permission of the Committee, a small box or packet was washed on shore and brought to Mr. Turner. It was found to contain a letter which set the minds of the Missionaries at rest, inasmuch as it authorised the commencement of a Mission in the Haabai group without further delay. The vessel that bore that letter, a schooner from Sydney, had foundered at sea, and all on board were lost. It is said that neither the vessel nor crew, nor any of the goods with which she had been freighted, were ever seen or heard of again. That letter alone, the messenger of mercy to a people waiting for the law of the Lord, guided by Him "whom winds and sea obey," escaped the general wreck, and was cast on shore at the right place, and at the right time, to relieve the minds of the Missionaries.

Mr. and Mrs. Thomas immediately embarked for their new sphere of labour, and arrived at Lifuka, one of the Haabai islands, after a stormy and dangerous passage, on the 30th of January, 1830.

A native teacher named Peter had previously been sent to this group, to instruct the people as best he could in the truths of the Gospel with which he himself had but recently become acquainted. Mr. Thomas was glad to find that the labours of this humble but earnest pioneer evangelist had not been in vain. Out of eighteen inhabited islands, all but three had embraced Christianity. Many houses, formerly sacred to idol gods, were either used as common dwellings, or set apart for the worship of Jehovah. The King took five of his principal idols and hung them up by the neck in one of these houses, in order that the people might see that they were "all dead." All classes of the community were anxious to learn to read and write, as well as to worship God in spirit and in truth; and the work was becoming too much for poor Peter when the first English Missionary opportunely arrived.

But notwithstanding this promising beginning, there was still a great work for the Missionary to do. The people were utterly ignorant and required instruction. All that they knew was that they were wrong, and that there was one among them who could set them right. On the day after his arrival, which was the holy Sabbath, Mr. Thomas preached to a congregation of about three hundred natives, in a large building which had been set apart for the public worship of God. From that day forward the congregations rapidly increased, and a gracious influence attended the preaching of the Word. In the course of the following week Mission-schools were opened, which were soon attended by upwards of two hundred male and female pupils, all anxious to learn to read the Word of God. Mr. and Mrs. Thomas, and their assistant Peter, were constantly engaged in teaching the crowds of people who flocked together to receive instruction.

To meet the ever-increasing demands on the time and attention of one Missionary would have been a truly herculean task, even if the usual aid of books and school requisites had been available, but in a country where letters were previously unknown, and where every book had to be written out with the pen of the teacher, the difficulty and labour were increased tenfold. Still the Missionary toiled on, preaching, teaching, and translating from day to day as the Lord gave him strength, and his labour was not in vain. Hundreds of children and young people soon learned to read and write their own language with fluency, native teachers were raised up to take a part in the good work, and the Mission prospered in all its interests.

There was, moreover, much cause for gratitude to God on account of direct spiritual results of the preached Gospel which were witnessed. Day by day not only young people, but also old and resolute heathens, were found yielding to the power of Divine truth, and many became Christians not in name only but in heart and in life. The decision and firmness of the Chief, King George, were of great use to the Missionary. In his communications to the society at home, Mr. Thomas spoke of him as "most hearty in the cause of Christ, and longing to see idolatry banished from all the islands." Before a year had passed away, one hundred and fifty converted natives had been united in Church fellowship, the Chief himself being one of the number; and a large chapel had been erected, at the opening of which between two and three thousand people were present, the King and his people, from the infant of days to the old and grey-headed, all bowing before Jehovah in humble adoration. Here, as in Tonga, the testimony of some of the new converts was very pleasing. One of the natives, the day after his baptism, said that his mind was very happy; that yesterday was a good Sabbath to him, and he was so happy when he lay down at night that he could not sleep. He added that he loved God very much, and hated the devil and all his works.

Considering the arduous nature of his work, it is not surprising that the health of Mr. Thomas should have failed after he had laboured in Haabai some time alone. On his partial recovery from a severe attack of illness in the spring of 1831, he was joined by the Rev. Peter Turner, who had recently arrived at Tonga from England, accompanied by the Rev. Messrs. Watkin and Woon. This was a valuable acquisition to the Station; and, through the united labours of these zealous and devoted servants of God, many were gathered into the fold of Christ, the church was built up, and the important work of education still further advanced among the people. With the aid of a noble band of native teachers, who were raised up in the Mission-schools, the good work was ultimately extended to most of the inhabited islands of the group, where chapels were built, congregations gathered, and promising societies organised. And, what is still more pleasing, the members of the native churches were generally remarkable for their consistent piety and godly conversation. The Sabbath was everywhere kept with the strictest sanctity, whilst prayer and praise ascended from almost every house, if not from every heart.

Mission to Vavau.

At an early period of the Wesleyan Mission to the Friendly Islands, Finau, the Chief or King of Vavau, had made application for a Missionary, professing to give up his idols, and praying to Jehovah as already stated. When he found he could not be supplied with a teacher, he turned again to his folly and superstition, and even became a persecutor of such of his people as embraced the *lotu*. Mr. Thomas had frequently conversed with Finau, and entertained the hope that he might, by and by, be favoured with an opportunity of carrying the glad tidings of salvation to the people of Vavau. As in many other instances, however, so in this, native converts were honoured to be the pioneer evangelists to their island neighbours. In April 1831, King George of Haabai visited Vavau with twenty four sail of canoes. He and his people went on worldly business; but their hearts were warm with their first love in the service of God, and they were bent on doing spiritual good to the utmost of their power. Peter, their own faithful Christian teacher, was with them. He carried a letter and a present to the chief from Messrs. Thomas and Turner, and their prayers followed the expedition. Finau opened his mind fully to his brother chief, and made many objections to the great change proposed.

The King of Haabai, finding difficulties in the way, wrote down the substance of Finau's remarks, and travelled back to Mr. Thomas at Lifuka for advice. On again reaching Vavau, he was able to promise a Missionary for that place in the course of a few months, if the chief renounced his idol worship, and turned to the true and living God. Many of Finau's doubts and scruples were now removed, and his royal guest pleaded so effectually with him that at last he exclaimed, "Well, I will; and I will spend the next Sabbath with you in worshipping your God." Two of his wives, as well as himself, many of his servants, another influential chief, and his sister Halaevu, and many more, joined the Christians from Haabai in prayer and songs of praise on the following Sunday.

The native Christians from Haabai remained some time at Vavau, with a view to confirm and establish the work so auspiciously commenced, and there was every token of sincerity in the Chief and his people. On the Monday morning after the memorable Sabbath, when they first publicly bowed themselves before the Lord, the Chief gave orders that seven of the principal idols should be brought out and placed in a row. He then addressed them in this manner:—"I have brought you here to prove you; and I tell you beforehand what I am about to do, that you may be without excuse." Then, commencing with the first, he said, "If you are a god, run away, or you shall be burned in the fire which I have prepared!" The god made no attempt to escape. He then spoke to the next in the same way, and so on till he came to the last. As none of them ran, the King gave orders that all the sacred houses should be set on fire. His commands were promptly obeyed, and eighteen temples with their gods were burned to ashes. The weather was damp, and it took three days to complete the work of destruction.

Many of the people joined in this work with all their hearts, yet hundreds were grievously troubled at what they considered the King's impious conduct, and sat trembling and silent to watch the result, looking for nothing less than some awful calamity. As no harm happened to the doers of the daring deed, they came to the conclusion that their gods must be liars, after all, and they, too, joined the praying people. Whilst they remained, the whole time of the visitors was taken up with teaching the new disciples. All ordinary work was laid aside, and the constant cry was, "We can do our work when you are gone; let us learn to serve God while you are here." And company after company, athirst for the water of life, resorted to the Christians to receive instruction. One of these said afterwards, " I was four nights and did not sleep. I was talking with the people, reading, praying, and singing all the time."

Two native teachers were immediately sent to Vavau, and at the following district meeting of the Missionaries, it was arranged that Mr. Cross should proceed to Vavau, and that Mr. Watkin should join Mr. P. Turner, at Haabai, while Mr. Thomas should return to Tonga. Mr. N. Turner had been compelled, by failing health, to leave the islands; and Mr. Thomas being now the senior Missionary, his presence at the principal station was desirable. According to this arrangement Mr. and Mrs. Cross embarked for their new sphere of labour; but on their passage they were overtaken by a mysterious dispensation of Divine providence. They suffered shipwreck, on which occasion the Missionary narrowly escaped with his life, whilst his beloved wife, and a number of those who sailed with him, perished in the waves. A few particulars concerning this mournful event may prove interesting to the reader.

Mr. and Mrs. Cross left Nukualofa for Vavau, on Saturday, the 7th of January, 1832, after having waited several days for a favourable wind. A large canoe had been lent to them by the Chief, Josiah Tubou; and they set sail early in the morning, after an affectionate parting with the natives, with whom they had lived and laboured for four years. Besides the Missionary, his wife, and about seventy natives, all Mr. Cross's books and other personal property were on board, and a large supply of Mission goods, for the purpose of barter, and for the erection of buildings for the new station. The voyage was long, and they proposed staying at Nomuka that evening, and spending the Sabbath there. For a few hours the wind continued fair and moderate, though there was a heavy swell on the sea. Afterwards, as the wind grew stronger, the swell increased, and, about noon, the yard broke, and then the mast. The large sail was instantly taken in, and a very small one set. Towards evening the storm increased, and all on board felt themselves to be in perilous circumstances. The sailors looked out anxiously for land, hoping that they were not far from Nomuka. No land appeared in sight, however, and the frail canoe was driven hither and thither till the break of day. About an hour after sunrise, the weary and alarmed travellers descried land. Not a man on board knew where they were. Some said they had got back to Tonga; others that they were nearing Fiji; but, reaching the land about noon, they found it was a small uninhabited island called Hunga Tonga.

The shore was steep and rocky, and the swell of the sea so great, that they found it impossible to land; and after consultation they resolved to try to return to Tonga. The mast, part of the yard, and all else that could be spared, were cast into the sea to lighten the canoe, and hopes were entertained that she would get back in safety. They now partook of some refreshment, which they much needed, as Mr. Cross had eaten nothing for thirty hours, and Mrs. Cross, who was in a delicate state of health, had tasted nothing but a little cocoa-nut milk. Towards sunset the little isle of Atata, near Tonga, appeared in sight. They hoped to reach it in a very short time, to spend the night there, and to get back the next morning to Nukualofa, only seven miles off. But, when within two or three miles of Atata, the wind changed from north to east, and blew a perfect gale. The men took in the sails with all speed; but almost before they could get to their paddles, the canoe struck upon a reef, and began to break up. To add to the horror of the moment, they were in darkness, the moon having just gone down. One of the natives exclaimed, "*Missa Kolosi, ke malohi ho tau lotu kihe O tua, he kuo tau mate.*" " Mr. Cross, be strong our minds towards God, for we are all dead." There was a short pause, in which they endeavoured to commit their bodies and their spirits into the hands of God, and then all were washed off the canoe into the sea, and the canoe was dashed to pieces.

Mr. Cross held his wife with his right arm, and they rose and sank repeatedly. With his left hand he caught a broken piece of the canoe that floated past, and resting on this, they took breath occasionally. Mrs. Cross uttered no word of complaint or fear; but, from time to time, she called on the Lord for help. A few more seconds and the buffetings of the waves conquered her feeble frame, and her spirit escaped to that place where all is joy, and calm, and peace. Mr. Cross's faithful arm still clasped the lifeless body of his beloved wife, till with the help of a native he got himself and his precious burden lifted on to some boards that were floating about. The shipwrecked Missionary, with a number of the natives, ultimately drifted on a small raft, which they managed to form, to an uninhabited island, called Tekeloke; but on landing they found that the body of Mrs. Cross had been washed away. It was recovered, however, a few days afterwards, and received Christian burial. Besides the Missionaries' wife, fourteen men, one woman and five children, were lost on this melancholy occasion, and no portion of goods were saved from the wreck. The survivors were rescued from the lonely island on which they had been driven by the arrival of a canoe from Tonga; and when the sad disaster became generally known, many hearts were filled with sorrow.

Notwithstanding this distressing bereavement, the zealous and devoted Missionary, Mr. Cross, had no sooner followed the remains of his dear wife to the grave than he embarked a second time for Vavau. He arrived in safety; and, although he felt his loneliness, he addressed himself to his important duties with characteristic earnestness, and his labours were made a great blessing to the people. In after years, the Revs. P. Turner, J. Thomas, T. West, G. Kevern, and other zealous and devoted Missionaries, were stationed at Vavau; and by the blessing of God upon their unwearied exertions, and those of the noble band of native teachers who were raised up, a wonderful change was effected in the entire group. Idol worship was totally abandoned, commodious chapels erected, native churches organised, schools established; and, what is best of all, there is reason to believe that thousands of sinners were brought to a saving knowledge of the truth by the faithful preaching of the Gospel. In the course of three months twelve hundred natives began to meet in a class, most of whom, it is believed, were sincere seekers of salvation. And at the opening of a new chapel, which would seat eight hundred persons, three thousand natives came together to take part in the services, which were necessarily held in the open air. From this time forward the work in Vavau and the neighbouring islands continued to prosper, and the same blessed change followed the introduction of Christianity that had been witnessed in other places.

The progress of the Mission at Vavau and in all the Friendly Islands was greatly aided by the arrival of a printing-press from England, in charge of the Rev. W. Woon, who was practically acquainted with its management, and who soon set it to work. Great were the surprise and joy of the natives of Tonga when they saw with what rapidity and neatness copies of school-books and other publications could be multiplied by the mysterious machine which had been brought from the white man's country. The printing office was besieged for several days by crowds of people, anxious to get a glance at the press in motion, and to receive the sheets as they were at first distributed among them to gratify their curiosity. In the course of nine months seventeen thousand copies of books of different kinds were printed; and the supply of paper brought from England was nearly exhausted. The progress of the people in education advanced with a rapidity proportioned to the increased facilities afforded for learning by the circulation of printed books.

The extension of the work throughout the islands had for a length of time demanded an additional supply of labourers; and towards the close of the year 1888, the Mission was reinforced by the arrival from England of the Rev. Messrs. Charles Tucker and David Cargill, with their excellent wives. The testimony of Mr. Tucker as to his first impressions of the work at Tonga is worthy of notice. Writing to the Committee in London he says, "We have abundant cause for devout thanksgiving and praise to the God of all grace for the good He is doing among this interesting people. The ordinances of His house are generally seasons of refreshing; and the people give evidence, by their regular and prayerful attendance on all the means of grace, that they love the habitation of God's house, and the place where His honour dwelleth. Their upright walk and conversation evince the change wrought in them. I never saw the Sabbath kept so holy as here; and I never heard half so much singing and praying in any part of the world before. To God alone be all the praise, for He alone the work hath wrought."

In marking the course of public events in connection with the introduction of the Gospel to the Friendly Islands, we can scarcely fail to notice the frequent interposition of the special providence of God. In 1833, Finau, the King of Vavau, died; and it was his dying request that King George, of Haabai, should be his successor in the Government. This request was agreeable to all parties concerned, and, accordingly, George became the supreme ruler over the united kingdoms of Haabai and Vavau. To those was afterwards added the dominion of Tonga, so that George ultimately became the king of the whole of the Friendly Islands—a circumstance which proved highly favourable to the development and establishment of Christianity, as he was a man of superior judgment and ability, and of unwavering religious principle. The most formidable difficulty with which King George and the Missionaries had to contend, after the people had generally declared for the *lotu*, was the determined opposition and hostility of a few minor chiefs and people who resolved, at all hazards, to adhere to their former superstition, and reject the Gospel. Most of these resided in a remote part of Tonga, and were encouraged in their hostile attitude to the teaching of the Missionaries, and the rightful authority of the King, by the heathen priests, and also by some wicked and abandoned Europeans who had settled among them. More than once these enemies of the truth were prompted to acts of violence and of blood; but the Christian forbearance of the King and his loyal subjects, and the pacific influence of the Missionaries, ultimately overcame every difficulty, and disarmed all opposition; so that, in a few years, the whole group of Friendly Islands became, at least nominally, Christian.

Great Revival.

We have now the pleasure of calling the attention of the reader to a remarkable religious movement which took place in the Friendly Islands at an early period of the Mission, which, in its character and results, has but few parallels in the history of the Christian Church. This great revival had its origin in the deep convictions, united prayers, and earnest efforts of the Missionaries and a few of their devoted people, who saw the danger of settling down into a mere profession of religion, when they had abandoned their idols, embraced the *lotu*, and who earnestly desired a richer baptism of the spirit. It commenced in the Island of Vavau, where Messrs. Turner and Cargill, and a little band of faithful leaders, had agreed together to enter into their closets every day at noon, to plead with God for this "one thing." Their prayers were soon and suddenly answered. A native local preacher was preaching at a village called Utui, on Tuesday, the 23rd of July, 1834, on Christ's compassion towards Jerusalem, when the word came with power to the hearts of the whole congregation. All confessed themselves to be sinners; and many were so deeply affected, that they cried aloud in the agony of their souls. They were unwilling to leave the place without a blessing, and actually remained together most of the night, seeking the pardoning mercy of God in Christ Jesus; and many, before morning, found peace in believing.

On the following Sabbath, at another village, similar results followed the ordinary services of the day. Five hundred persons, the whole of the inhabitants of the place, from the least to the greatest, joined in earnestly seeking salvation. Those who had been praying for the outpouring of the Spirit and the conversion of souls were amazed. They had asked largely; but God had given them more than they had asked or hoped to witness; and yet they were to "see greater things than these." The work spread from village to village, and from island to island, till the whole of the people seemed to be moved by one common impulse. In a single day, during this remarkable movement, there is reason to believe that more than one thousand persons were truly converted to God. The change was not now from dumb idols merely, but from sin to holiness, and from "the power of Satan unto God." Such was the general spirit of inquiry, and such the pressing claims of those whose hearts were set on obtaining a present salvation, that it was found necessary to give up the school for a week or two, and to hold six prayer-meetings every day. As soon as the Missionaries or the native teachers began to speak, the people were melted into tears, and multitudes fell upon their faces, "calling upon the name of the Lord," loud cries for mercy being frequently intermingled with the joyful acclamations of those who had found pardon. The whole island bowed before the power of God; and the society in Vavau soon increased to three thousand and sixty-six members, of which number as many as two thousand two hundred and sixty-two were the fruit of this extraordinary visitation from on high.

It is a delightful fact that King George and the Queen, who were then staying at Vavau, were among those who experienced a saving change of heart on this memorable occasion. They had long before renounced idolatry and embraced the worship of Jehovah, but they had not till now experienced a sense of the pardoning mercy of God through the atoning blood of Christ. When this blessed out-pouring of the spirit was given, the King and the Queen joined hundreds of their people in penitent confessions of sin, humbly kneeling with them to weep and pray for forgiveness. It was not, however, in the throng that they found the blessing which they earnestly sought. Having failed to realise the comfort they desired at the public prayer-meeting, they retired to their own house and continued together in fervent supplication till midnight, when they were enabled to believe to the salvation of their souls, and to rejoice in a sense of the Divine favour. Many prayers had been offered up by their people for the royal penitents, and now, when the happy crisis had come, and they had found peace with God, through our Lord Jesus Christ, the good news spread with amazing rapidity, and sincere songs of praise ascended to heaven from thousands of loyal and joyful hearts. King George himself immediately wrote to his Missionary, the Rev. J. Watkin, in Haabai, telling him "how great things Jesus had done for him."

Before the good news of what had taken place at Vavau reached Lifuka, the principal island of the Haabai group, the congregations there had been visited with tokens of good, and several persons had been made the happy partakers of the saving grace of God. On the 9th of August, the religious services were attended with a special manifestation of the Divine presence and blessing. In answer to the united prayers of the Missionaries and leaders, the spirit of conviction was given abundantly. The people were assembled in the large chapel, where four or five hundred men, women, and children "were pricked in their hearts," and began to cry, "men and brethren, what shall we do?" Some wept aloud, others smote upon their breasts like the publican, and breathed forth his humble plea, "God be merciful to me a sinner." The Missionaries went from one penitent to another, pointing their guilty and anxious spirits to "the Lamb of God that taketh away the sin of the world," praying with them and teaching them how to pray. About one hundred that night laid hold on Christ as their Saviour, and found "redemption through His blood, the forgiveness of their sins, according to the riches of His grace." Many who were still under conviction went home with sorrowful hearts; not to sleep, however, but to spend the night in wrestling with the angel of the covenant, like Jacob in earnest prayer and faith, and, like him, they prevailed, for the Lord blessed them there." The next morning, at dawn of light, the chapel and chapel-yard were crowded with people all in earnest about the salvation of their souls.

"As soon as the service began," says Mr. Tucker, "the cries of the people began. They were melted into tears on every hand, and many of them cried aloud by reason of the disquietude of their souls. O, what a solemn but joyful sight! One thousand or more bowed before the Lord, weeping at the feet of Jesus, and praying in an agony of soul. I never saw such distress, I never heard such cries for mercy, or such confession of sin before. These things were universal from the greatest chiefs in the land to the meanest of the people. The Lord heard the sighing of the prisoners, he bound up many a broken-hearted sinner in that meeting, and proclaimed liberty to many a captive. We were filled with wonder and gratitude, and lost in praise, on witnessing the Lord making bare his arm so gloriously in the sight of the heathen. We met again about nine o'clock, and had a similar scene; hundreds wept aloud, and many trembled from head to foot, as though they were about to be judged at the bar of God. We were engaged the whole day in this blessed work. I attended five services, and saw hundreds of precious souls made happy by a sense of a Saviour's love. There never was such a Sabbath in Haabai before; it was indeed one of the days of the Son of Man. Many will remember it with pleasure throughout eternity, as the day of their adoption into the heavenly family. During the following week, the concern of the people was so great that they laid aside their work. We had service twice every day but once, and the chapel was always full. It was a week of Sabbaths and of much prayer and praise. Not a day or a night passed but several were disburthened of their load of guilt and sin, by believing with their hearts unto righteousness."

Nor were there wanting satisfactory evidences of the genuineness of this remarkable work of grace. On the 24th of August, a society-meeting was held at Lifuka, when one thousand persons were present; and many gave a clear and satisfactory account of their conversion to God. At the same time the temper and spirit, the walk and conversion, of the new converts was most exemplary.

The Missionaries testify that the reality of the change which they had experienced was not so apparent in their rapturous joy as in the deep implantation in their minds of all Christian graces. They manifested in an eminent degree the "mind which was in Christ Jesus;" and what was said of Stephen, was especially true of the leaders and local preachers, "They were full of faith and of the Holy Ghost." This blessed work was not confined to the island of Lifuka; but speedily extended to the whole Haabai group. Mr. Tucker visited a small island at a short distance, where he found all the adult inhabitants, not one excepted, meeting in class; and after administering the ordinance of baptism to forty-nine persons, he regarded the whole population as members of the Christian Church. During the preceding fortnight, four hundred and fifty of these had been made happy in the pardoning love of God. At the little island of Foa, two-thirds of the inhabitants witnessed the same "good confession," and rejoiced in the same salvation. Other out-stations shared in the same general blessing; and it was estimated that more than two thousand conversions took place at the Haabai Islands alone in the course of two or three weeks.

At length the revival reached Tonga also. On the 6th of October a canoe arrived at Nukualofa from Lifuka, having on board a local preacher named Joel Maples. He gave the people an account of the wonderful work which had been going on in Vavau and Haabai, and earnestly exhorted them all to flee to Christ, the only refuge for poor sinners. At a prayer-meeting held the same day in the chapel, a gracious influence descended upon the congregation, and many became deeply affected by a painful conviction of their sin and danger. From that day the Christian natives assembled more frequently for prayer, and Mr. Thomas persuaded the chief to set apart a day for special supplication for a richer baptism of the spirit. At the time appointed the people assembled together in expectation of a blessing, and the spirit of prayer was poured out upon them in a very remarkable manner. All present engaged in earnest pleading with God, while many, unable to restrain the feelings, wept aloud. The people also held prayer-meetings in their own houses; and on some nights the village of Nukualofa was heard to ring for hours together with the voice of prayer and praise; several emerging out of darkness into the marvellous light of the Gospel. The number brought to a saving knowledge of the truth was not so great, however, in Tonga, as in some of the other islands; but they were sufficient to gladden the hearts of the Missionaries, and to inspire them with hope for better days to come.

Considering the comparative ignorance of the people, and the shortness of the time which had elapsed since they had abandoned the worship of dumb idols, it would not have been surprising if many of the new converts had afterwards fallen away. It is a pleasing fact, however, that this was not the case. There were but few backsliders, most of the people continuing steadfast to their religious profession, "growing in grace and in the knowledge of the Lord Jesus Christ." They, moreover, made rapid progress in learning to read and write, and in general civilisation, building better houses, and paying more attention to the cultivation of the ground, and to the comforts of domestic life. The females especially manifested a desire to adopt European modes of dress. Hitherto their garments had been made of native cloth called tapa, manufactured from the bark of a tree; but now there was a general demand for calico and prints. Mrs. Tucker taught her school-girls to plait straw and make bonnets; and great were the astonishment and joy of the people, one fine Sunday morning, when twelve of the female class-leaders appeared at chapel in new straw bonnets. More would have been done in this way, but the print and calico ran short, and so did the needles and thread; and this department of the work was somewhat retarded till supplies arrived from England.

From this period the history of the stations at Vavau and the Haabai Islands was that of regularly organised churches, the whole of the population professing Christianity; but in Tonga a war between truth and error had still to be waged, as a powerful party clung to the heathenish superstitions of their forefathers. It would be a pleasing task, if space permitted, to trace in detail the succeeding events which occurred in connection with the

Friendly Island Mission, from the period when idolatry was generally abolished to the present time; but they would be found very similar to those of other stations where Christianity has become dominant. All that appears necessary, therefore, is a brief notice of a few miscellaneous incidents of more than ordinary interest, and which are characteristic of the nature of the work in this important section of the Mission-field.

MISCELLANEOUS INCIDENTS.

The most remarkable events connected with the early history of the Friendly Island Mission were the conversion and subsequent career of King George and his noble Queen Charlotte. We have already mentioned how they were brought to an experimental knowledge of the truth as it is in Jesus, in the great revival, when on a visit to Vavau; and a glance at their steady, consistent, and upright course of conduct afterwards may serve to show the value of their influence and efforts to promote the interests of the cause of God. Soon after his conversion and return to Haabai, the King liberated all his slaves, and made known his views with regard to Christian liberty throughout his dominions. He had long taken a part in teaching such of his subjects as were less informed than himself; but now he gave himself up to close study, and was, before long, prepared to pass his examination as a local preacher. He entered upon his new duties with fervent zeal and intelligent views of his responsibility to God and His Church; and laboured with unwearied diligence to win souls to Christ. It was a pleasing sight to the Missionaries and their faithful people to see the royal preacher starting off in his canoe, on a Sabbath morning, to fulfil his appointment at a distant island; and still more pleasing to hear the song of praise wafted across the placid waters, ascending to heaven from the pious sailors and their zealous chief, as they glided along on their errand of mercy. At the same time Queen Charlotte was an earnest and devoted class-leader, and diligently employed her gifts for the benefit of her own sex. Thus was the promise of Jehovah to His Church, by the mouth of His Holy Prophet, literally fulfilled. "And kings shall be thy nursing fathers, and queens thy nursing mothers, and thou shalt know that I am the Lord."

Soon after his conversion, King George built a beautiful new chapel at Lifuka, the capital of Haabai, where he then resided. It was the largest and most elegant building that had ever been erected in the Friendly Islands, measuring one hundred and ten feet in length by forty-five feet in width. All the chiefs from the neighbouring islands met together to help forward the work, attended by about one thousand of their people. Most of the chiefs and head men were engaged in plaiting sinnet, a kind of ornamental cordage with which the timbers were bound together, whilst the common people were employed in the heavier kinds of labour. The large body of people thus drawn together to build the temple of the Lord, worked hard during the day, happy in each others' society; and at night, instead of employing themselves in sin and folly, they were constantly engaged in attending meetings for prayer and praise. The building was completed in the short space of two months. It was beautifully ornamented in the interior, and the communion rails were made out of the carved shafts of spears, with two large obsolete war-clubs at the bottom of the pulpit stairs, to remind the people of the happy change which had been brought about by the Gospel of peace and salvation.

The new chapel was formally opened for the public worship of God on the 9th of September, 1835, when not more than one-half of the congregated thousands could gain admittance within the precincts of the beautiful sanctuary. The King preached in the morning, and Mr. Tucker, the Missionary, in the afternoon. During the first prayer hundreds of the people were in tears, including the Missionary himself, who wept for joy at what his eyes saw, and his ears heard, of the goodness of God. Marked attention was paid while the royal preacher expounded Solomon's prayer at the dedication of the temple, and a gracious influence rested upon the congregation. At the close of this memorable service, Mr. Tucker baptized twenty adults; and he could now say that in the whole of the Haabai group there only remained *one* grown person unbaptized, and that was a poor man detained at home by sickness. Thus might it be said, almost without a figure, that " a nation was born in a day."

When the first attempt was made to introduce Popery into the islands, the King displayed great firmness and sagacity. On returning from the District Meeting in the month of October, 1837, Mr. Thomas was told that more Missionaries had arrived. His joy at the pleasing intelligence, however, was but temporary, for he soon found that the new Missionaries were a Roman Catholic Bishop and his companions, sent out by a Missionary institution in France. These gentlemen had already had an interview with the King, who was at that time residing at Vavau, and had asked permission to leave two or three of their party on the island. The King asked for what purpose they came, adding, " I and my people have all turned to God." His lordship told the King that his own religion was the old and true faith, and that the religion taught by the Methodist Missionaries was one that had lately sprung up. The King said, " We know but one God, and Jesus Christ our Lord, to whom we have all turned." He then advised the Bishop to wait till the return of the Missionaries from Lifuka. The Bishop, with five others, three of whom were priests, accordingly waited upon Mr. Thomas and his colleague, who observed that the matter must be settled between themselves and the King; that King George, and not the Missionaries, governed the islands. The Bishop stated, both to the Missionaries and the King, that he only wished to leave the priests at the Friendly Islands for two or three months to learn the language. The King saw through the artifice at once, and doubting whether they would learn much of the language in so short a time, asked in reply, " If they are to go away in two or three months, why cannot you as well take them away in the ship that brought them?" On being pressed to consent, the King said, " It is not my mind that they should stay." On the departure of the Romish Bishop and his companions, the Wesleyan Missionaries advised them to go where the people were still heathens, and not to trouble those islands which were already evangelised.

Soon after he had embraced Christianity, King George turned

his attention to the civil and social improvement of his people, as well as to their instruction in the principles of the new religion. He found that numerous and great evils arose from the subordinate chiefs and private persons taking the law into their own hands; and wishing that impartial justice should be dealt out to the poor as well as to the rich, to the servant as well as to the master, in 1839 he determined to give a written code of laws for the guidance of all classes. He appointed four of his chiefs as judges and magistrates, each of whom was to sit once a month, to hear and decide all cases of complaint that might be brought before them. When completed, the new code of laws was publicly read by the King to the assembled thousands of his people, and a copy given to each governing chief, with which all appeared well satisfied. From time to time these laws were modified and improved to meet the necessities of every case which might arise. The entire code is a remarkable document. The preamble commences thus:—" I, George, make known this my mind to the chiefs of the different islands, and to all my people. May you be very happy! It is of the God of heaven and earth that I have been appointed to speak to you. He is King of Kings and Lord of Lords. He doeth whatsoever He pleaseth. He lifteth up one and putteth down another. He is righteous in all His works. We are all the work of His hands and the sheep of His pasture; and His will toward us is that we should be happy. Therefore it is that I make known to you all, to the chiefs, and governers, and people, as well as to the different strangers and foreigners that live with me, the laws by which the land shall be governed." Then follow the laws on a great variety of subjects, divided into forty-eight sections.

The people generally submitted to the new laws with cheerful readiness. The only exception was in that part of Tonga which remained heathen, after the entire population of the other portions of the Friendly Islands had embraced Christianity. So inveterate were some of the chiefs and people of Hihifo and Bea against the new religion and the authority of the King, that first in 1837, and again in 1840, they declared war against the Christians. In this course of rebellion it is believed that the heathen were instigated by the emissaries of Rome, who had at length got a footing in Tonga. All possible means were adopted by King George and Josiah Tubou to conciliate the enemy and to preserve the peace; but their united efforts were in vain. At length, when the measure became inevitable, King George took the field at the head of a select band of his faithful subjects, with the hope of constraining the heathen to submit to the laws of the land. But the spirit in which this war was waged, so far as the Christian natives and their sovereign were concerned, is worthy of special notice, as it clearly shows the ameliorating influence of the Gospel. Previous to the final attack on the heathen fortress of Hihifo, in 1840, in haranguing his men, King George said: "Our late war with the heathen, three years ago, was by the mercy of God a victorious one. But though we got the victory, in some things we went astray. We fought not as Christians should fight. Our object was not to save, but to destroy. But you all now present hear me, that we do not so fight again. If, as may be expected, the enemy should come out of their fortress to-morrow morning, let every man endeavour to seize and save his man, but not one to shoot or strike, but in case of life or death."

Before daylight, the King and his army were in possession of the fortress, and the rebels were secured. Five hundred men thus came into the power of the Christians, all of whom King George pardoned, and not a single life was taken. This strange clemency on the part of the King was such a thing as had never been known in the Friendly Islands before, and made a deep impression on the minds of the heathen in favour of the *lotu*. With a dignity peculiarly his own, King George took his seat under the shade of a tree, and had the prisoners brought one by one before him, to receive their sentence; but when each trembling captive expected to be put to death, according to the former mode of Tongan warfare, he heard the voice of the sovereign say, "Live," and passed on. It was only the ringleaders in the rebellion that were banished to Haabai and Vavau, to prevent them from again stirring up the people.

There were still a few turbulent petty chiefs and their people higher up the country, at a place called Bea, who held out against the authority of the King, and who had cruelly murdered several small parties of native Christians who had occasion to visit the neighbourhood, and who refused to fight. It was not till the arrival of the Rev. John Waterhouse, General Superintendent of Wesleyan Missions in the South Seas, in 1841, that a permanent compact was made between the contending parties. Mr. Waterhouse had come from England some time before, in the Missionary

NATIVE CHRISTIANS REFUSING TO FIGHT.

ship *Triton*, with the Revs. Francis Wilson and George Kevern, to strengthen the Mission. On visiting Tonga, to inspect the state of the work on the occasion alluded to, the General Superintendent was requested by King George and the Chief Josiah Tubou, to use his influence to effect a reconciliation between them and their heathen enemies. This he did with pleasure, and proceeded at once to visit the Mua, or heathen fortress, with Mr. Tucker as his companion.

Fatu, the principal hostile chief, treated his visitors with the utmost politeness, listened attentively to the arguments used by Mr. Waterhouse, and expressed his readiness to act according to his wishes. But, being urged to go to Josiah and seek for pardon, he put his arm round the Missionary, and said: "You are my son. I want peace; but I am ashamed and afraid to go to Tubou. If he will visit me with you, I will humble myself." This was a grand point gained; and Messrs. Waterhouse and Tucker returned to King George and Josiah Tubou, and reported the result of their visit to the heathen fortress. Some doubts were entertained as to the sincerity of Fatu; but the Christian chiefs were at length induced to accompany the Missionaries to the Mua, where Fatu asked pardon, and was forgiven. The reconciliation was consummated by a large feast, consisting of several pigs, roasted whole, two large sharks, forty baskets of yams, and sundry other articles. After this, the work of evangelisation was carried on with renewed vigour in every part of the island, and several heathen chiefs and their people were brought under the power of Christian truth.

For several years the Missions in the Friendly Islands were dependent for their supplies on the precarious and uncertain visits of trading vessels from the Australian Colonies, or on the occasional charter of boats to convey goods to the respective stations. As the work extended, this method of supplying the Missionaries and their families with such articles as must necessarily be imported, was found to be both inconvenient and expensive, the brethren and their dependents being often left for weeks and months without some of the necessaries of life, after a high rate of freight had been paid, through the delay which occurred in sending supplies. It was, therefore, resolved, after mature deliberation, to provide a vessel on purpose for this service; and the brigantine *Triton* was purchased and fitted out under the direction of John Irving, Esq., of Bristol, for a four years' voyage among the islands. She sailed from England on the 14th of September, 1839, with a full cargo and twenty-six passengers, chiefly Missionaries and their families, who were appointed to different stations in Southern Africa, New Zealand, the Friendly Islands, and Fiji. The plan of employing a

Missionary ship to make periodical visits to the respective islands, to convey the General Superintendent when on his tours of inspection, and to remove the brethren and their families to their new appointments, as well as to convey the necessary stores to the different stations, answered admirably; and the *Triton* did good service for more than four years by the able management of Captain Buck, her skilful commander. The only fault that was found with this first Wesleyan Missionary ship was that she was rather too small to meet the requirements of the ever-expanding work of Methodism in the South Seas; and she was consequently sold and succeeded by a more commodious vessel, which was appropriately called the *John Wesley*.

The new Missionary vessel was a fine brig of two hundred and fifty tons burden. She was built by Messrs. White and Sons, of Cowes, and launched in the presence of a large concourse of spectators, on the 23rd of September, 1846. She sailed from Southampton on the 21st of November, under the command of Captain Buck, with the Revs. John Malvern and James Ford, and their wives and families on board, together with a full cargo, a considerable portion of which consisted of articles contributed by the friends of Missions for the respective stations. On reaching her destination, the *John Wesley* was found well adapted for her intended purpose, and for several years rendered good service to the Mission. Her periodical visits to the different stations were occasions of great joy to the Missionaries and their people, and proved a great comfort to the Mission families, as well as a saving to the Society's funds.

In 1851, it was found necessary for the *Wesley* to return to England for repairs, and to be furnished with tanks to receive the cocoa-nut oil which the natives were beginning to contribute in considerable quantities to the Mission Fund. She set sail a second time for the Southern World on the 25th of September, with the Rev. John Polglase and two trained teachers, Messrs. John Binner and William Collis, with their wives on board. The *John Wesley* continued her faithful services among the South Sea Islands till the 18th of November, when she was wrecked on the Tau

Reef, Haabai, not through any mismanagement in the navigation, but from the tumultuous waves of the sea caused by a violent shock of earthquake which occurred. There were on board at the time the Rev. Messrs. Davis, Lee, Baker, and Dyson, together with Mr. and Mrs. Moss, proceeding to the annual district meeting, which was to be held at Nukualofa; but through a kind and gracious Providence, no lives were lost, the vessel being lifted by a tremendous wave inside the reef, and left on the retiring of the sea in three feet of water. In consequence of this remarkable circumstance, most of the cargo was also saved; and although the Mission brig was a complete wreck, there was abundant cause for gratitude to God for His preserving goodness.

The South Sea Islands could not long be left without a Missionary ship, a second *John Wesley* was, therefore, immediately built and fitted out under the able superintendence of the late J. J. Lidgett, Esq. She weighed anchor at Gravesend, on the 18th of May, 1867, and proceeded on her long voyage, commended to the protection of the God of Missions by the fervent prayers of several ministers and friends who assembled on the occasion. The new Missionary ship arrived at Adelaide in safety on the 5th of September; and although the passage out was said to be not so auspicious as that of her predecessor, it is satisfactory to know that since she has reached her destination she has fully answered the purpose for which she was built, and promises to be a great blessing to the Mission.

In the year 1853 the Rev. Robert Young was deputed by the British Conference to visit Australia and the Mission-stations in the South Sea, and it may be interesting to glance at his impressions of the state of the work in the Friendly Islands. From the interesting narrative which Mr. Young published of his travels, it appears that he arrived at Tonga on the 21st of October, in the *John Wesley*. On approaching Nukualofa, the principal town, whilst standing on the deck of the vessel, he counted twenty verdant islands which studded the bosom of the placid waters, presenting a scene of loveliness which he greatly admired. But the beauty of the natural scenery was surpassed by the moral grandeur which he witnessed when he landed and saw for himself the wonderful change which the Gospel had produced upon a people who had but recently emerged from the darkness of paganism. Mr. Young was accompanied by Mr. N. Turner, who was no sooner recognised as their old friend and Minister by the crowds of natives who flocked to the beach to receive them, than they expressed their pleasure at his arrival in the most emphatic manner. On reaching the Mission-house—a structure of posts, reeds, and native cloth—the visitors met with a hearty reception from Mr. and Mrs. Adams, and Mr. and Mrs. Amos, and were plentifully regaled with bananas, cocoa-nut milk, and other dainties of tropical growth.

Having rested for awhile, they went to pay their respects to the King. They found him attired in native costume, occupying a mat on the floor; but when the deputation was introduced by Mr. Adams, his Majesty arose, shook hands cordially, and, having offered Mr. Young a chair in the most gentlemanly manner, resumed his squatting position. King George is described as a fine manly person, possessing powerful muscle, and exhibiting an intelligent, thoughtful, benevolent countenance. His smile was fascinating, and his whole bearing that of dignified meekness. The young prince, a most interesting boy of nine years of age, was introduced; but the Queen, being engaged, could not be seen. After examining the scattered town of Nukualofa, embowered in groves of cocoa-nut, banana, and bread-fruit trees, and meeting with many hearty congratulations from the natives, Mr. Young and his companions returned to the Mission-house to dinner. Ample provision had been made for the entertainment of the strangers in a humble way; but the establishment could furnish only one spoon for the use of the whole party. By way of apology, Mrs. Amos said, that in the morning they had several more, but the servants being so determined to rub them bright, as a compliment to their visitors, had broken them all but one, and that was much injured.

On the following day Mr. Young walked to the chapel, which stands on the only elevated ground in the town, and commands a fine view of the harbour. By order of the King some scores of men, women, and children, were engaged in cleaning and putting the sanctuary in order for the services of the morrow, that the deputation might see the station to the best advantage. The Sabbath which Mr. Young spent at Tonga was a day long to be remembered. At half-past five in the morning the chapel-bell was rung to call the people to the prayer-meeting, and in a few minutes about three hundred persons assembled together. The whole of the exercises were characterised by much fervour and animation; but none prayed with greater power and unction than the King and Queen, whose devout pleadings made a most favourable impression on the mind of the distinguished visitor. At eight o'clock the Sunday-school commenced; and the children, in addition to other exercises, were examined in the Conference Catechism with very satisfactory results. At nine o'clock, the chapel-bell was heard again, and in every part of the town the beating of the native drum also announced the hour for the commencement of the public worship of God.

The people repaired with joyful hearts to their beloved Mount Zion and the chapel, which was without pews or benches, but with its floor neatly matted to seat six or seven hundred persons was much crowded. After the reading of the liturgy in the native language by one of the Missionaries, Mr. Young preached, and Mr. Amos interpreted. At the close of the sermon several of the members, among whom were the King and Queen, engaged in fervent prayer for God's blessing upon the Word. At two o'clock in the afternoon, the school re-assembled, and thirteen classes were seen squatted on the floor, in so many circles around their respective teachers. The principal class was taught by the Queen, who takes a lively interest in the rising generation. At three o'clock the public worship again commenced, when the tribes of the Lord once more crowded His sanctuary. On this occasion Mr. Turner preached to the people in their own language, and many tears were shed when he feelingly referred to the wonderful change which had taken place in their condition since the time when he commenced his labours among them in the days of their heathen darkness. Such was the impression made upon the mind of Mr. Young by the services of the first Sabbath that he spent in the Friendly Islands, that he declared it to be " a day of light, and power, and glory, never to be forgotten in time or in eternity."

Most of the following week was occupied by the deputation in examining the Mission-schools, conferring with the Missionaries on the state of the work, and in visiting places of peculiar interest; and on the 28th, highly gratified with what he had seen at Tonga, he embarked on board the *John Wesley* for Vavau, where he arrived on the following morning, accompanied by King George, who embraced the opportunity of visiting Australia.

The Sabbath which Mr. Young spent in Vavau was equally memorable with the one in Tonga. In fact the exercises were in every respect similar. There was the same crowding of the sanctuary with attentive hearers of the Word preached, the same manifestation of deep feeling at the public services, and the same earnestness in the Sabbath-school. Some interesting meetings were held during the following two or three days, at which both King George and many of the other Christian natives spoke with pathos and power of what they had experienced of the mercy and goodness of God. The Mission-schools were also examined with very satisfactory results, a large number of children having learned to read and write with considerable fluency, and to answer the questions put to them in the most ready and intelligent manner. The state of the Mission reflected much credit upon the Rev. Messrs. Daniel and Miller, the resident Missionaries, and upon the staff of native teachers and preachers by whom they were assisted in their important work.

On the 3rd of November, Mr. Young and King George took their departure in the *John Wesley* for Fiji and Australia. On sailing down the placid waters of the Vavau harbour, and launching out into the Pacific Ocean, they passed in sight of thirty beautiful verdant islands. In closing this brief account of the visit of the deputation to the Friendly Islands, we may observe that Mr. Young was much pleased with what he saw of the results of the

Gospel in all their varied forms; but with nothing was he more delighted than with the conduct, spirit, and bearing of King George. In taking leave of his royal companion in travel, at the termination of their voyage, he says, "I had now spent several weeks in the company of the King, and during that period I had not observed an act contrary to the strictest Christian propriety, nor had

TRAINING SCHOOL AT NUKUALOFA.

I heard a foolish word from his lips. In all my intercourse with him, I was deeply impressed with his mental power and his genuine piety, and felt persuaded that had he possessed European advantages he would have been one of the greatest men of the age."

At all the Mission-stations in the Friendly Islands special attention is paid to the educational department of the work. For several years past, an excellent training school has been conducted at

Nukualofa, a view of which is here given. From this institution a number of efficient native teachers have gone forth to different parts of the district, to instruct the rising generation. We are happy to be able to state that this establishment has recently developed into a seminary of a higher class, and will henceforth be known as TUBOU COLLEGE, a name given to it in honour of King George Tubou, the distinguished ruler of the whole group of Friendly Islands. Additional buildings have been erected to accommodate eighty students, who are being trained as native teachers and ministers, with marked success by the able Missionary, the Rev. James E. Moulton. The first class of students consists of twelve, whose curriculum of study embraces algebra, history, arithmetic, astronomy, chemistry, Euclid, geography, mensuration, solids, trigonometry, Scripture history, and theology.

Some remarkable instances of native genius have, from time to time, been noticed. So recently as the 21st of January, 1869, two native Missionaries, David Kata and Barnabas Ahongalu, from Tonga, were introduced to the Wesleyan Conference assembled at Sydney, when, in answer to the welcome given to them by their European brethren, David responded as follows (the Secretary acting as interpreter):—"I thank the Lord for the welfare of this meeting, and the health of the ministers and chiefs who are assembled. I am thankful to witness the assembly that rules our Church in these seas, but more especially for this great love by which we two are recognised in the presence of this meeting. We had no expectation of being introduced; but thought our place would be outside: therefore we feel much the love of this meeting to two coloured men, and can say, with Peter, 'Now I know that God is no respecter of persons.' Besides, I thank this meeting for its love to the islands of the seas, which were without God in the world—the islands from which we come."

Among the fruits of genuine religion in the Friendly Islanders, their Christian benevolence is worthy of a passing notice. Of course some allowance must be made for a semi-civilised people, in countries where money, as a circulating medium for commerce, is almost unknown, and where receiving, and not giving, has long been the order of the day. Hence we find that but little was done towards the support of the Gospel at an early period of the Mission. But when the work became more fully established, and the doctrines of Christian obligation and responsibility were better understood, the Missionaries instructed the natives in the duty of supporting the cause of God with good effect. Missionary meetings were everywhere held, and noble speeches were made by chiefs, ministers, and people. It is now a pleasing sight to see men, women, and children bring their " offerings of love," as they call their contributions, marching in order, as they sing some beautiful native hymn. These offerings consist chiefly of articles of produce of various kinds, which are sold for the benefit of the Mission Fund. The amount thus contributed has increased from year to year, and the following extract from the report presented to the Annual Missionary meeting, held at Sydney on the 25th of January, 1869, will show what was done the previous year :—" The amount raised at the Missionary meetings in the Friendly Islands was upwards of £1,100; and we have just received by the *John Wesley*, contributions in oil to the amount of £1,200, making a total of £2,300 from this district for the past year." The Superintendent of the Vavau Circuit writes as follows : " The sum of £487 has been contributed at our Missionary meetings, which is an average of 4s. 7d. per member, and of nearly 1s. 11d. each for the entire population. Such a spirit of Christian liberality as this is worthy of being imitated in every land."*

---

* Remarkable as this may appear, whilst this sheet is passing through the press, intelligence comes to hand of still larger manifestations of Christian liberality on the part of the natives, the proceeds of which cover the entire expenses of the Mission for the past year. Thus the Friendly Island Mission has become self-supporting in an incredibly short space of time, and bids fair to take an active part in evangelising the "regions beyond." And what is better still, another gracious revival of religion has recently taken place in the Haabai group, in the course of which " eight hundred souls joined the Church, enrolled themselves as members of Christ's flock, and gave evidence of their desire to flee from the wrath to come." It is now confidently announced that there is *not one heathen remaining in any of the Friendly Islands.*

Samoa.

In the early part of the year 1835, the Missionaries in the Friendly Islands, having been repeatedly solicited to do so, decided to commence a Mission at Samoa, or the Navigator's Islands, and the Rev. Peter Turner was chosen for that purpose. He was to call at an island called Niua on his way, and remain there a few weeks to teach the people, who had hitherto been under the instruction of native teachers from Vavau. Mr. and Mrs. Turner, accompanied by a few Christian natives, embarked for their new sphere of labour in a small vessel built by a sailor at Fiji. They had a stormy passage, and for seven days and nights their frail bark was tossed about by contrary winds, much to the discomfort and even personal danger of the passengers. At length, by the good providence of God, they sighted Niua, and after great difficulty and considerable peril, owing to the stormy weather and heavy surf, they effected a landing, and were received with gratitude and joy by a people who were longing to be taught the way of God more perfectly. Mr. Tucker was induced, contrary to his intentions, to prolong his stay at this little island for several months, during which a blessed work was carried on. The King and Queen, with many others, were brought to a saving knowledge of the truth, two new chapels were erected, the schools reorganised, and everything put in train for future operations. The King himself, having become an acceptable local preacher, and other native teachers having been raised up, Mr. and Mrs. Turner took an affectionate leave of the people on this interesting station, and continued their voyage to the Navigator's Islands, according to their original intention.

The Missionary landed at Manono in the month of June, and met with a very hearty welcome; some of the people being acquainted with him and his work from the constant communication kept up between the natives of the Friendly Islands and the Navigator's group. Mr. Turner had studied the Samoan language at Tonga and at Niua, and was in part prepared to enter upon his labours. Such was the success which attended these early efforts to make known the glad tidings of salvation in these distant islands of the Pacific, that hundreds and thousands of the simple-minded natives embraced the *lotu.* Mr. Turner's encouraging accounts of the work of God among this people induced the Missionaries in the Friendly Islands to send the Rev. Matthew Wilson to assist him. About this time, the London Missionary Society commenced a Mission there, the Rev. Mr. Platt having landed in the month of August 1835, about two months after the arrival of Mr. Turner. Native teachers from Rorotonga, belonging to that Society, had, however, been labouring there for some time previously. This real or apparent clashing of interests and efforts was the cause of some unpleasant complication between the authorities and agents of the two great societies, the merits of which it is not our province to discuss. However desirable it may be, in general, distinctly to define the sphere of labour occupied by different religious bodies in foreign lands, circumstances may occur where a population is large to call for the efforts of more than one denomination of Christians, as at home. This appears to have been the case at Samoa in the estimation of those who have had the management of the work; and, notwithstanding some hindrances to the progress of the Gospel, both societies report their Missions to be in successful operation.

The Wesleyan Mission-stations in Samoa, in common with those of the other islands in the South Seas, have for several years past been carried on under the direction of the Australian Conference, who have formed the islands of the group into a separate district, extending the work to Upolu, Savan, and other places. In the respective Wesleyan Circuits of Samoa, *four European Missionaries, and twelve native teachers and catechists,* are employed, and about *eight hundred members* are reported as united in Church fellowship, with a proportionate number of scholars in the Mission-schools.

In conclusion, we may briefly state that in their general character and conduct, strict observance of the Sabbath, attention to the means of grace, and other Christian virtues, the converted natives of the Friendly Islands are truly exemplary and worthy of being imitated by professors of religion in other lands. They are, moreover, remarkable for their love for God's Word and private and family prayer. When the sun has gone down, and the labours of the day are finished, every household is assembled for evening worship; and in every town and village of the group, the hymn of praise may be heard ascending to heaven in connection with fervent prayer and the devotional reading of the sacred Scriptures. The regularity and seriousness with which these and other Christian duties are performed by this simple-hearted people has often arrested the attention of strangers, and excited their admiration and gratitude in view of the wonderful change which has passed upon these islands since they were brought under the influence of the Gospel. We have now in the Friendly Islands and Samoa districts *twenty-three Missionaries, one hundred and seventy-seven chapels, eight thousand two hundred and sixty-two Church members,* and *seven thousand two hundred and one scholars* in the Mission-schools. For these results of Missionary labour, all circumstances being considered, we may well "thank God and take courage."

HEATHEN CRUELTY.   CHRISTIAN HOPE.

CHAPTER IX.

THE FIJI ISLANDS.

THE ISLANDS DESCRIBED—CHARACTER OF THE PEOPLE—COMMENCEMENT OF MISSIONARY LABOURS—THE LAKEMBA CIRCUIT—THE REWA, VIWA, AND BAU CIRCUITS—SOMOSOMO—SUCCESS IN SUNDRY PLACES—MISCELLANEOUS INCIDENTS—ROTUMAH.

THE Fiji Islands are situated in the Pacific Ocean, about three hundred and sixty miles north-west of the Friendly group, with their centre in latitude 17° south, and longitude 178° east. They are said to be one hundred and forty in number, about eighty of which are inhabited. The rest are mere rocky islets, which are occasionally resorted to by the natives for the purpose of fishing, and taking *beche-de-mer*. The principal islands in the group are two of considerable magnitude—Viti-levu ("Great Fiji"), which is eighty-five miles long and fifty broad; and Vanua-levu ("Great Land"), which is ninety-five miles by thirty. The scenery in the larger islands, which are generally mountainous, is described as varied and interesting, and the soil, in many places, is rich and productive. The climate being warm and somewhat humid, tropical vegetation is rich and luxuriant, and presents to the view beautiful landscapes of ever-living green. The cocoa-nut, yam, taro, orange, banana, and other vegetables and fruits described as plentiful in the Friendly Islands, are also common in the Fijian group, and the land in some localities is well adapted for the cultivation of sugar, cotton, and coffee.

More than two hundred years ago some of these islands were discovered by the celebrated Dutch navigator Tasman; but after his voyage of exploration in the Pacific Ocean in 1643, they appear to have remained unnoticed till the temporary visits of our countrymen, Captains Cook, Bligh, and Wilson, towards the close of the last century. About the year 1806, Fiji began to be visited by traders for the purpose of procuring sandal-wood, to burn before Chinese idols, and *beche-de-mer*, to gratify the palates of Chinese epicures. It was from the men engaged in this traffic that the first items of reliable information were received in Europe concerning the islands and their inhabitants, which was so long desiderated in our national maps and gazeteers. Since this period, exploring expeditions have been sent out both from England and America, by which part of the Fiji group, in common with other islands of the Pacific, has been carefully surveyed, and accurately laid down on carefully-prepared charts, for the guidance of the mariner, rendering navigation much less dangerous than formerly.

Soon after the commencement of the present century, a number of European convicts escaped from New South Wales and settled among the natives at Bau and Rewa; but these desperadoes added nothing to the existing knowledge of the islands or the people. They were esteemed by the native chiefs principally on account of their knowledge of the use of firearms, and the aid which they rendered in carrying on the wars which then raged throughout the entire group. Being desperately wicked and abandoned in their moral character, these renegade convicts presented to the natives of Fiji a very unfavourable specimen of white men. Instead of trying to enlighten and benefit the heathen by their superior knowledge, they adopted all their superstitious practices, and most of them came to a premature end by their sin and folly. The last survivor of this party was an Irishman named Connor, who, in 1840, was despised and shunned by all classes of respectable people, both native and European, because of the savage and inhuman propensities in which he indulged, notwithstanding the progress of civilisation in the land.

CHARACTER OF THE PEOPLE.

In common with that of the natives of other groups of islands in the vast Pacific Ocean, the origin of the people of Fiji is involved in profound mystery. Both in complexion and in physical conformation they bear a greater resemblance to the Negroes of Africa than to the Malays of the Eastern Archipelago, from whom other tribes of Polynesia are supposed to have descended; but no one can tell at what period the islands were first inhabited, or whence the people came. After a considerable reduction by native wars and other causes, the population of the Fiji Islands is now supposed to amount to about one hundred and fifty thousand. In some features of their character these people resemble the Friendly Islanders and the Maories of New Zealand; but in others they present a marked difference. In personal appearance they are stout and robust, and care little about clothing, except on state occasions, when they paint their bodies, and pay special attention to the dressing of the hair, that they may be up to the fashion, as may be seen in the accompanying engraving. The Fijians are remarkably observant, shrewd, and sagacious; and they possess some mental qualities which, when brought under the civilising influences of the Gospel, raise them in our estimation as men and Christians. But when they first attracted the attention of Europeans, and before they became acquainted with the truths of Christianity, they were, perhaps, the most deeply degraded race of human beings that had ever been met with in any of the South Sea Islands. They were superstitious, cruel, and revengeful in the extreme, and addicted to war and bloodshed, in connection with which they often committed deeds of savage barbarity, a description of which would not be fit for the ears of civilised Christian people.

But the most appalling and disgusting feature in the character of the Fijians was their propensity to cannibalism. For a length of time Christian people in England seemed unwilling to believe

MODES OF HAIR DRESSING IN FIJI.

that human beings could be found anywhere so deeply degraded as literally to devour each other; but undeniable facts have been brought to light which prove that it is even so. Instances of a most shocking and revolting character have been known to occur in New Zealand and other islands, but Fiji has earned for itself the greatest notoriety for this abomination. At what period, and under what circumstances, cannibalism began to prevail in this part of the world it is impossible to say. Some have charitably supposed that the first instance might have occurred from stress of hunger when a party of natives were cast away at sea, or exposed to famine on shore. It is more likely, we think, to have had its origin in the cruelties of war, as it is a well-known fact that some heathen people, not habitually addicted to cannibalism, occasionally drink the blood of their enemies slain in battle, and feast upon their flesh, from feelings of revenge, and with the hope of thereby imbibing the courage and prowess of their fallen foes. But, however it may have originated, it is an appalling fact that cannibalism at length became fearfully prevalent in Fiji, and there are abundant proofs that the natives actually acquired a relish for human flesh. Indeed, it assumed, in a sense, the character of a religious institution; for at the building of a house, the launching of a new canoe, and on many other public occasions, it was customary to shed abundance of human blood to propitiate their demon gods and to render the enterprise successful. Then, also, the ovens were heated, the bodies of the victims cooked, and the assembled multitude feasted on the flesh of their fellow-men, proving the truth of the Scripture declaration that "the dark places of the earth are full of the habitations of cruelty."

An examination of the religious system of the natives of Fiji is attended with considerable difficulty. Their traditional mythology is exceedingly dark, vague, and perplexing. Each island has its own gods, each locality its own superstitions, and almost each individual his own modification of both. Yet amidst this confusion, there may be traced certain main tracks of belief which are common to the people generally. A confused idea of Deity, and a belief in the existence of an invisible superhuman power, controlling all earthly things, are entertained by all classes; but no direct homage appears to be offered to the Creator of all things. Superstitious reverence is paid to various objects, animate and inanimate, as rivers, mountains, stones, trees, serpents, lizards, and other reptiles, under the vague impression that the spirits of departed chiefs, which appear to be their principal gods, return to the earth and take up their abode in them. To the honour of these multifarious divinities, or *kalou*, to which various attributes and offices are ascribed, they build sacred houses or temples, called *bures*.

BURE, OR HEATHEN TEMPLE IN FIJI.

Nearly every town and village has one such, erected over the grave of a deceased chief, or in some other notable locality; not kept exclusively as a place of worship, but occasionally used as a council chamber, and for other purposes.

The people do not assemble, however, at these sacred shrines to offer sacrifices and prayers at stated periods, after the manner of the heathen in some countries, but at very irregular intervals, as on the death of a chief, the breaking out of war, or the occurrence of some other national calamity. Then they call upon their gods with savage shouts and furious yells; with tearing of the hair, and cutting the flesh; and not unfrequently with the offering of human sacrifices; for their *kalou*, or divinities, are supposed to delight in human blood. The temples are placed in charge of heathen priests, who are the objects of special awe and fear, and who subsist chiefly on the presents which they receive from their deluded votaries. There are, moreover, witches and wizards, who are supposed to have the power to detect crime and to cure diseases; and the manner in which they exercise their vocation, and deceive the people, is similar to that practised by the Kaffir witch-doctors in Southern Africa. The natives of Fiji regard the future or spiritual world as being in all respects like the present state of existence, where people will rally round their chiefs, and engage in their favourite pursuits of hunting, fishing, war, sensuality, and crime. Hence the feelings of indifference with which they regard human life. Suicide is fearfully common. For the most trifling cause, a native will cast himself headlong over a precipice, or from the top of a cocoa-nut tree; and young and sprightly widows will insist upon being strangled on the death of their husbands, to rejoin them in the spirit land.

As might be expected, the morals of the Fijians are on a par with their religion. The people are abandoned to almost every conceivable heathen vice. Cannibalism, war, polygamy, adultery, murder, suicide, deception, fraud, theft, and many other crimes which cannot be named, are described as prevalent among the natives. It is, moreover, worthy of notice that the most glaring sins are committed by the natives without any apparent sense of shame; and it was a length of time before the Missionaries could get the people to perceive the difference between the sin of theft and the disgrace connected with being detected in the commission of the crime. A somewhat ludicrous instance of this occurred shortly after the arrival of the first Missionaries, which we may relate as an illustration of the strange want of moral sensibility to which we have alluded.

At Bau a man one day jumped over the fence and went deliberately into the verandah of the Mission-house to steal a blanket. Being detected in the act, he immediately dropped his spoil and made his escape, not, however, before a passer-by recognised him, and gave his name. The Missionary at once complained to the Chief, who expressed his indignation, and declared he would kill the thief. It was now found necessary to plead for the life of the offender. The Chief yielded the point at last, saying, "Let us understand each other. You dislike being robbed, but you do not want the thief to be killed. Very well. I will only threaten to put him to death. Whatever I say or do, you must not be alarmed, as I shall only frighten him." The Chief then sent for the parents and uncle of the young man, and told them of the theft. "Not," said he, "that stealing is anything new among us; but it is new to do it so carelessly as to be found out. Your son has disgraced us, and he must die." The relatives at once consented to his death. As soon as the criminal was found, he was sent to the Chief, who thus addressed him: "You are a thief; a thief discovered in the very act of stealing. I am a thief; my father was a thief; my grandfather was a thief; but were we ever found out? Through your bad management you have discovered to the Missionary that we steal from him. You must die. Your father, and mother, and uncle have given their consent. However, as the Missionary has interceded for you, I am willing to offer you terms, by compliance with which you may save your life. You may either cut twenty fathoms of firewood for my wife, or furnish me with six pigs, or be strangled. Take your choice." After some deliberation the youth replied, "To cut twenty fathoms of firewood, sir, is very difficult, and would cause me great fatigue, I must, therefore, decline that. To furnish six pigs is not in my power, as I have not five friends who would each give me a pig to add to mine to save my life. To die is the easiest; so you will please strangle me." "Oh, very well," said the Chief, "then you shall be strangled." So the man was cleansed, oiled, and attired in the usual way; the friends were kissed, the knot was adjusted, and the cord was about to be pulled. At that moment the Chief again offered life to the culprit, but the offer was rejected with scorn. "Strangle me," said the infatuated youth. "I shall never give up stealing unless you strangle me. I wish to die." Oh! so you *wish* to die?" inquired the Chief.

"Yes, sir, I do," was the reply. "Then you shall NOT be strangled," exclaimed the now indignant Chief; "but you shall live, and you shall give up stealing as a punishment. Mind you are not caught again, or I will make you uncomfortable." And so ended the matter. The young man was not "caught" stealing again—for twelve months; when he was once more seized in the very act, on the same premises. Such is a specimen of the morals of the people of Fiji.

Commencement of Missionary Labours.

We now proceed to consider the means which have been employed to raise the natives of Fiji from the moral degradation in which they were involved. From an early period there had been occasional intercourse between the Friendly Islands, Tahiti, and Fiji; and when the *lotu* began to prevail in the places first named, the warlike Fijians must have been aware of the wonderful change that was taking place in several of the islands of the Pacific. Yet it does not appear that they manifested the same desire for Christian teachers as was sometimes evinced by other tribes. They were too deeply degraded to see the advantages of Christianity; and when some converted natives of other islands found their way to their shores, and declared what the Lord had done for them and their countrymen, they were slow of heart to believe the good news.

When the Wesleyan Mission was firmly established in the Friendly Islands, however, the Missionaries made arrangements to carry out a long cherished wish to try to do something for poor degraded Fiji; and at the District Meeting which was held at Lifuka, in December 1834, the Rev. Messrs. Cross and Cargill were set apart for the important enterprise. A vessel was expected from Australia to bring supplies, and to remove the Missionaries and their families to their respective spheres of labour about the end of March 1835; but it did not arrive till the beginning of October. Consequently the commencement of the Fiji Mission was delayed much longer than was at first expected. On Tuesday, the 8th of October, however, everything being ready, the Missionaries and their families embarked on board a small schooner, called the *Blackbird*, for the scene of their future labours in the Fiji Islands. Connected with the Mission party were several converted Friendly Islanders in the capacity of domestics and assistants, and also a few Fijians, who were returning to their own country. After many friendly adieus, and affecting partings, and earnest prayers for the blessing of God on the undertaking, the vessel weighed anchor, and stood out to sea towards the place of her destination.

On the evening of the Sabbath, after their departure from Vavau, the Missionaries got sight of Lakemba, the principal of the windward group of the Fiji Islands; but as the captain of the schooner had no correct chart of the coast or harbour, and had never seen the island before, he wisely shortened sail, and tacked about during the night. Early on Monday morning, the vessel was off the south-east part of Lakemba. As seen from the deck of the schooner, the island appeared to be surrounded by a continuous coral reef. The sea was comparatively calm; but the roar and foam of the billows, as they broke upon the reef, were terrific, and gave forth unmistakeable notes of warning; the space inside this barrier seemed capable of affording shelter for the vessel; but no passage to the harbour could be discovered. The Fijians who accompanied the Missionaries, pointed to a place where they said there was an opening in the reef, through which a canoe could pass. The captain, however, prudently resolved not to attempt to bring the vessel to anchor, until the size of the entrance, and the character of the harbour, could be ascertained, and if possible, the disposition of the natives known. In these circumstances Messrs. Cross and Cargill deemed it advisable to make an attempt to land in the schooner's boat, and to seek to obtain an interview with the King.

The boat was accordingly lowered, and intrusted to the care of the chief mate. Leaving their families on board, the Missionaries, with hearts uplifted to God in prayer, stepped into the boat, and steered for that part of the reef to which the natives had pointed, and where they assured them there was a passage into the harbour. Their account was found to be correct; but the entrance was so narrow that, although a small vessel might pass through, it could not tack about in it, and must, therefore, be entirely dependent upon a fair wind. As they approached the beach, they saw a number of natives running hither and thither, in apparent confusion; and when they drew near to the landing-place, about two hundred armed men took their station at no great distance from them, in a somewhat suspicious attitude. The appearance of this motley group of naked savages was by no means prepossessing, as with painted faces and hideous looks they grasped their muskets, spears, and clubs, and watched every movement of the strangers. As they stepped on shore, the Missionaries expressed their love to the natives in their own language, a little of which they had already learned; but they received no response to their friendly salutations, and felt somewhat perplexed to know how to proceed. They were at length relieved from their difficulty, on being informed that the King was waiting to see them, and to ascertain the object of their visit to his country.

The Missionaries, therefore, proceeded to the King's house, which stood in Tambōu, a large fortified place, and the principal town of the island, about a mile from the shore. The town was not large, but surrounded by a strong wall, with a reed fence on the top, and provided with numerous apertures, through which the defenders of the fortress might discharge their arrows and muskets, and keep off and annoy the enemy. The whole place was surrounded by a moat, eighty or a hundred yards wide, and was altogether a strong place of defence. The King's house was a large substantial building, at least a hundred feet long and nearly forty wide, without any partitions, and serving as kitchen, dining-room, and sleeping-room for the whole of the royal family. On being introduced to Tui Nayau, the King of Lakemba and neighbouring islands, in the presence of his chiefs and counsellors, the Missionaries made known the object of their visit, and were welcomed by the simultaneous clapping of the hands of all the natives present. The King asked many questions, and finally pledged himself to grant to the Missionaries a piece of ground to live on; to erect houses for them; to protect them and their families and property from molestation, and to listen to their instruction. In the meantime he offered them the use of one of his large houses within the fortress for their immediate use. This they respectfully declined, fearing the situation would be too confined, and expressed a preference for a large canoe-shed which stood on the beach, which was readily granted to them. With grateful hearts for the favourable reception they had met with, the Missionaries hastened on board the schooner to relieve the anxiety of their wives and families, by informing them of this encouraging prospect of success.

All on board were delighted with the good news, and on the afternoon of the same day the Mission families went on shore and took possession of the canoe-shed on the beach, the use of which had been granted for their accommodation by the King. The building was at least a hundred feet long, forty wide, and thirty high, and open at both ends. Such was the spacious but rude bedroom in which the Mission party spent their first night in Fiji, spreading their mattrasses on the deck of a large canoe, which still retained its place under the shed. Before they retired to rest, however, they were surrounded by hundreds of curious natives, all anxious to have a good look at the pale-faced strangers, and especially at the white ladies and children, having never been favoured with such a sight before. After a restless night, occasioned by the stings of myriads of mosquitos, which infested the shed in which they attempted to sleep, the Mission party arose early in the morning of the following day, and addressed themselves to the various duties which devolved upon them; the first and most important business was to select a suitable place for a Mission-station. They pitched upon what they considered an eligible site in a valley called Buthainambua, in the vicinity of the chief town of Lakemba. The King granted them the ground without any hesitation, and with apparent cheerfulness; and promised to erect upon it, with all possible despatch, a temporary house for each family.

In the meantime the captain of the *Blackbird* providentially succeeded in working his vessel through the narrow channel in the reef, and brought here safely to anchor in the harbour on the south side of the island. This was a necessary, but hazardous undertaking, owing to the dangerous character of the navigation, and the well-known determination of the natives to pounce upon both ship and cargo, and claim them as their own, in case any vessel should be so unfortunate as to touch the rocks on approaching their shores. Knowing the discomfort and privation to which the Mission families had been exposed in their vain attempt to sleep in the canoe-shed, the captain of the schooner kindly invited them all to come on board his vessel again, till their temporary houses were erected on the site selected for the Mission-station. In their peculiar circumstances this was a judicious arrangement. The Missionaries were well aware that the apparent cordial reception that had been given to them by the King and people of Lakemba was to be attributed, not to their desire for religious instruction, but to the hope which they entertained that they would derive temporal benefit from their coming, and that they would soon become possessed of the goods which they had brought for presents and for barter. They were, therefore, obliged to proceed with extreme caution, knowing that they had to deal with a designing, cruel, and treacherous people. There were instances fresh in the recollection of everybody illustrative of this, an entire ship's crew having been cut off, and the vessel seized, by the unstable and crafty natives not long before, which suggested the necessity of constant vigilance, prayer, and faith on the part of the brethren.

The Missionaries left their families on board, and frequently went on shore themselves to hasten forward the work, and after three days the two temporary houses promised by the King were finished. The whole of the Mission party now landed, and took possession of the frail dwellings provided for them. The materials of which the houses were made were the leaves of the cocoa-nut tree, plaited together, and laid one upon another on posts planted in the ground. They were only of small dimensions, and without any partitions; but by a little contrivance, a portion of each was screened off with native cloth for a sleeping apartment, whilst another corner was set apart as a store-room, and so the establishment was made tolerably comfortable. During the day, scores of natives, prompted by curiosity, surrounded the house to gaze at the strangers; and when they could not obtain a view of them through the doors or the windows, they occasionally lifted up the thatch of the roof, and thrust in their heads to see what was going on inside. It, moreover, required constant watchfulness on the part of every member of the Mission families to prevent pilfering, for the covetous natives took a fancy to everything they saw.

On the tenth day after her arrival, the *Blackbird*, having landed the last of the stores, weighed anchor and took her departure, leaving the Missionaries and their families strangers in a strange land of heathen darkness. Had their enterprise been of a worldly nature, they might have felt sad and sorrowful at the thought of being left entirely at the mercy of cruel savages, without any means of escape, whatever might happen; but they were engaged in a heavenly undertaking, and could put their trust in God, being happy in their work. There was, moreover, much to be done in connection with their new establishment, both of a temporal and spiritual nature, which constantly occupied their time and attention. The ground about the Mission premises had to be cleared of the reeds and bushes with which it was thickly covered. Roads had to be made, fences put up, and out-houses erected. From sunrise to sunset each day, all were engaged in useful employments; and everything that was done was regarded as preparatory or subservient to the great object of the Mission—the instruction of the people in the knowledge and worship of the true and living God, and of His Son Jesus Christ.

From the time of their first landing on the shores of Lakemba, the Missionaries neglected no opportunity which presented itself of speaking a word to the natives for their spiritual good; and as soon as they were somewhat settled in their temporary dwellings, they set about the work of religious instruction in a systematic manner, with becoming earnestness. Even the Missionaries' wives and their Christian domestics, who had come with them from the Friendly Islands, were unwearied in their efforts to impress on the dark benighted Fijians the superior advantages of the *lotu*.

On the first Sabbath that the Missionaries spent in Lakemba, public worship was celebrated with due solemnity, the King himself being present, and a congregation of natives numbering one hundred and fifty. The service was held in the open air, and the people listened with deep attention, whilst Mr. Cross expounded the first chapter of the Book of Genesis, and set forth the wonderful power of the Almighty, as displayed in the creation of all things.

The first Missionaries to Fiji had one great advantage over most of their pioneer brethren in other lands. They were able to commence their labours in the language in which they had been wont to minister, the way having been prepared by Divine Providence. For several years previously the natives of Tonga had resorted in considerable numbers to the Fiji Islands, for the purpose of commerce, and especially to procure canoes, mats, earthen pots, clubs, spears, and other articles for which the country was celebrated; and a few had become permanently settled in Lakemba, and other islands, where they had formed matrimonial alliances, and adopted the country as their home. This intercourse between the two countries had been the means of diffusing a knowledge of the Tongan dialect in Fiji to a considerable extent, and it was in this language that the Missionaries commenced to preach to the people. Indeed one half the congregation on the first Sabbath consisted of Tongans, and the other of Fijians, and all seemed to understand the word spoken, which was a great advantage to all parties.

Some of the Friendly Islanders who had thus settled in Fiji were nominal Christians, having heard the Gospel and abandoned their idols before they left their own country; but, like many nominal Christians in other lands, most of them were strangers to the nature of experimental religion, having degenerated in their moral character since they left their homes. By the blessing of God upon the labours of the Missionaries, however, a saving work of grace soon commenced in Lakemba, which resulted in the conversion of a large number of the resident Tongans, both nominally Christians and Pagans, as well as in that of a few native Fijians. On the 31st of October, nineteen days after the arrival of the Missionaries, a Tongan Chief, named Naufahu, and about fifty of his people, who had hitherto been avowed Pagans, joined the ranks of professing Christians by forsaking their idols and bowing before Jehovah for the first time. When this Chief, and other persons of influence, had embraced Christianity, hopes were entertained that Tui Nayau, the reigning king of the country, would do the same; but, notwithstanding his confessed convictions of the truth of the Gospel, he still procrastinated, assigning as a reason that, if he then renounced Paganism, he would incur the displeasure of his subordinate chiefs, and perhaps involve himself in war with neighbouring powers. In the meantime the Missionaries were diligent in their studies to acquire a competent knowledge of the Fijian language, that they might more effectually gain access to the masses of the people, whilst they carefully attended to the Mission-schools which they had established, and to the higher duties of preaching the Gospel.

The Lakemba Circuit.

Although Lakemba is not the largest island in the group, nor by any means the most important place in Fiji, it was, nevertheless, singularly fitted for the introduction of Christianity to the country, through the instrumentality of Missionaries from Tonga, from the circumstances already mentioned. It is, moreover, central to a number of others, with a considerable population, known as the Windward Islands, and which unitedly form a petty kingdom, with the seat of Government at Lakemba. These were, in the course of time, formed into an extensive and important Wesleyan Circuit, with numerous schools and out-stations under the care of native teachers, many of whom had been savingly converted to God at an early period of the Mission. The European Missionaries itinerate among the smaller islands and out-stations at stated periods, or as opportunities are available, to administer the ordinances of religion, and to direct and encourage the native teachers in their important work. It would be a very pleasant exercise to trace the origin and progress of these scattered stations in all their details, and to dwell on the various incidents, some serious and some ludicrous, which marked the commencement and course of the work; but we are obliged to limit our observations to the leading historical facts of the Mission.

The course of events at Lakemba, where the Missionaries commenced their labours in the manner already described, was for some time very checkered. They had no cause to complain of want of attention to their instructions, either on the part of the resident Tongans or the native Fijians, nor yet of the lack of fruit; but they had to encounter numerous petty trials and difficulties in the prosecution of their holy enterprise. In the first place, they found it difficult to procure food for themselves and their dependants. All the pigs on the island had been *tabu*, or prohibited, for more than twelve months, in consequence of the death of a chief, and none might be sold or eaten. The goods intended for barter at this station had been all landed at Tonga, and the Missionaries in Fiji were left almost destitute. Then came a destructive hurricane, which laid waste the whole country, blowing down most of the dwelling-houses, and doing much damage to the fruit-trees and provision grounds. Food now became scarcer than ever, whilst the Mission families were left for a time without a shelter, their frail houses having been levelled with the ground. These discomforts did not discourage them so much as the advantage which the heathen priests attempted to take of passing events, with a view to damage Christianity by representing the hurricane and other calamities as resulting from the anger of their gods at the presence of the Missionaries.

But the efforts which were thus made to work on the superstitious fears of the people were rendered futile by the increasing light which was being shed on their minds by the preaching of the Gospel. In answer to the wily insinuations of the priests that the storm had been sent by the tutelar god of Lakemba, because he was angry at the introduction of Christianity, the King, who was still a heathen, shrewdly remarked, "If the Missionaries be the objects of his resentment, why does he punish us who have not abandoned his service?" Receiving no satisfactory reply, and not being able to reconcile the conduct with the declaration of the supposed deity, his sable majesty took the liberty of saying that he must be "either a fool or a liar." Thus were the heathen priests set at nought by their own people, and the Missionaries continued to labour with considerable success. Other and more permanent dwellings having been provided for the Mission families, chiefly by the personal labours of the Missionaries themselves, a rude native chapel was constructed from the materials of the demolished houses, which did good service for three years, when it was succeeded by a more substantial and appropriate place of worship.

The year 1836 opened upon the Mission to Fiji with cheering prospects. The public services at Lakemba were well attended, the schools prospered, and there were some pleasing instances of conversion to God on the principal station. On the 20th of March thirty-two adults and twenty-three children were publicly baptized by Messrs. Cross and Cargill, whilst several other inquirers remained under instruction as candidates; and on Christmas Day they administered the Sacrament of the Lord's Supper to eighty devout communicants. Thus was a native Christian Church established in Lakemba, which continued to advance in numbers and in intelligence from year to year, whilst the Missionaries turned their attention to the neighbouring islands, in many of which the precious name of Jesus had never yet been heard, although the inhabitants of others had become imperfectly acquainted with the Gospel through the instrumentality of converted natives who had visited their shores.

The first place visited was an island called Oneata, where two native teachers from Tahiti had landed some time before, and had succeeded in imparting to several of the people a knowledge of the true and living God. These wished to be taken under the care of the Missionaries, and Mr. Cross embarked to pay them a visit on the morning of the 12th of February, 1836. He arrived at Oneata early in the afternoon, and waited on the Chief, by whom he was received in the kindest manner possible. He found a chapel already erected, which would contain about one hundred people, in which he preached in the evening to a crowded congregation, as many assembling round the outside as were able to get in. According to the earnest wish of the Chief and his people, this island was adopted as an out-station of the Lakemba circuit; and as the Tahitan teachers had failed to learn the Fijian language, or to teach any of the people to read, a more efficient agent was appointed, a Mission-school commenced, and the cause continued to prosper.

This is one of many instances which might be given of converted natives being honoured of God as the pioneers of the regular Missionary, and as the instruments of introducing the Gospel to dark benighted heathen tribes of their fellow-countrymen. Indeed, the Lord Himself appears to have prepared the way for the spread of His truth. In some cases the natives cast away their idols and began to worship Jehovah, without the intervention of teachers of any kind. A striking instance of this kind came under the notice of the Missionaries at an early period in connection with the remarkable manner in which Christianity was introduced into Ono, an island about one hundred and forty miles from Lakemba. A Chief of Oneata, named Takai, had visited Tonga and Tahiti before Missionaries arrived in Fiji, and had been much impressed with what he saw and heard there. On his return he had an interview with Wai, the Chief of Ono, whom he persuaded to abandon his false gods, and to begin to worship the God who had recently been made known in Tonga. According to the advice of his friend, Wai now commenced to be what he called "a Christian," by keeping part of the Sabbath-day holy, and by attending to his worldly affairs on the other part. A few of his people joined him in this partial profession of the new religion. They had learned that prayer was acceptable to the true God; but it appears they did not know that it was lawful to offer it on behalf of themselves; they therefore engaged one of the heathen priests to pray for them, with the strange idea that the sacredness of his character would ensure success. The priest, willing to oblige the Chief and his countrymen, or afraid to refuse, engaged to be their chaplain, and offered a prayer for them in some such language as this: "Lord, bless these Thy people; keep them from all evil.

They worship Thee. I turn my back on Thee for the present, and worship another god: but do Thou bless these Thy people."

Although the priest prayed for the people of Ono in the best manner he was able, yet they were not satisfied, and determined to send one of their number to the Friendly Islands, to request help from the Missionaries there. An English vessel bound for Tonga lying off Ono at the time, a passage for the messenger was speedily obtained in her. When the vessel reached her destination, the Rev. Messrs. Cross and Cargill had already proceeded to Lakemba, and the inquirer after teachers was directed to them. During the absence of the messenger the Ono people continued to worship God according to the light which they possessed, until some Tonga Christians, who were drifted to their island when voyaging to their own country, taught them the way of God more perfectly. Among those who were so unexpectedly, but so providentially, cast upon the shores of Ono at this important crisis, was a native teacher named Josiah, who remained for some time instructing the people. He was soon able to report to the Missionaries at Lakemba the conversion of forty Fijians to the faith of the Gospel, and that they had built a chapel which would contain one hundred persons, in which they regularly assembled for Divine worship. From this time Ono was taken under the care of the Missionaries, and visited at stated periods, or as opportunities presented themselves, in common with other islands. On his first visit to Ono, in 1840, the Rev. James Calvert baptized two hundred and thirty-three persons, and married sixty-six couples. Many gave clear evidence that they had been baptized with the Holy Ghost, and were living according to the Gospel. This has since become an important and prosperous station under the care of a native Missionary, who is assisted by several catechists, local preachers, and schoolmasters.

Some of the native teachers whose labours were thus blessed in the conversion of their fellow-countrymen, were very remarkable persons, both in their character and history. Many pages might be filled with interesting sketches relating to them, but the following may be taken as a specimen:—Joshua Mateinaniu, a native of

Lakemba, and related to a family of note, was a young man of such natural ability that, while in his heathen state, he was taken to the Friendly Islands by Fuki, a Tongan chief, to teach the people a Fijian dance called the *wesi*. In the order of Divine Providence, however, he was never permitted to accomplish his purpose. Before he had time to assemble the heathens together for the dance, he came under the power of the Gospel, and was brought to a saving knowledge of the truth. He often expressed his gratitude afterwards, that instead of being allowed to teach the Tongans the heathen dances and songs of Fiji, the Missionaries taught him to sing the songs of Zion. After his conversion he was employed as a local preacher, and accompanied Messrs. Cross and Cargill on their Mission to his native land, where he was made very useful in winning souls for Christ.

Through the instrumentality of this and other active and intelligent native teachers, both Tongan and Fijian, whom God in His providence raised up, combined with the zealous co-operation and able superintendence of the European Missionaries, the glad tidings of salvation were made known to seven of the towns and villages of Lakemba, and among the respective islands of the windward group. In addition to Oneata and Ono, already mentioned, a good work was commenced in Atoa, Ongea, Vulanga, Namuka, Mothe, Komo, and Kambra. Schools were everywhere established, and both old and young learned to read with a rapidity truly astonishing, all regarding this art as inseparably connected with the *lotu*. There are now connected with the Lakemba Circuit upwards of twenty islands, or out-stations, in charge of native Missionaries and teachers, in addition to those in the immediate vicinity of the capital of the kingdom, where a printing-office and a training institution were ultimately established, and where two English Missionaries reside to superintend and direct the work in all its departments.

The Rewa, Viwa, and Bau Circuits.

From the commencement of their labours the Missionaries did not regard Lakemba as the most important place in Fiji; but they justly looked upon it as the key to the central and larger islands of the group, and as the most appropriate locality for the first station, in consequence of the number of semi-civilised Tongans who had settled there, and to whom they could preach the Gospel in their own tongue. Hence as soon as they had got the station into tolerable working order, the two brethren arranged to separate, and attempt the extension of the work. The important task of endeavouring to break up new ground devolved upon Mr. Cross, as the senior Missionary; and on the 28th of December, 1837, he embarked with his family for Bau in the "Jess," a small vessel, belonging to Chevalier Dillon.

Bau is a small island two miles in circumference, and within a few hundred yards of the mainland of Viti-Levu, or Great Fiji, to which it is joined by a flat reef, which at low water is nearly dry, and at high water fordable. The island rises somewhat abruptly out of the sea, and is of a conical shape; and being nearly covered with the dwelling-houses and tall temples which composed the large town which bears the same name, it forms one of the most striking objects to be found in the varied scenery of Fiji, as may be inferred from the illustration. It is most inconveniently situated for everything except defence; but being a strong fortress and the most populous town in the group, it has for a long time been regarded as the capital of Fiji, and the centre of political power. Viwa is another small island, not more than two miles from Bau, and also near to the mainland, and a place of considerable importance. Rewa is a large town on an island in close proximity to the mainland to the South of Bau, at a distance of about twenty miles by water, and ten by land, and for population and influence ranks next to the metropolis. These three populous native towns have become the heads or centres of extensive Missionary circuits, and from their geographical position and historical associations they are so linked together that we may most conveniently regard them unitedly, in glancing at the history of their evangelization.

Mr. Cross embarked for the capital under the impression that if the paramount Chief or King of Fiji and his people could be in-

THE FIJI ISLANDS.

BAU, THE CAPITAL OF FIJI.

duced to abandon their idols, the minor chieftains of the land, with their respective clans, might, perhaps, follow their example, and so the whole group would ere long come under the power of Christianity. This view was no doubt correct, but the hope grounded upon it was too sanguine. After visiting Moala, the vessel anchored at Kiuva, a town about midway between Bau and Rewa; and the Missionary obtained an interview with Seru, the son of Tanoa, the King of Bau, the result of which convinced him that it would be imprudent to attempt the establishment of a Mission-station at the capital at that time. The country was only just recovering from the shock of a seven years' war, in which Tanoa had been deposed, and driven into exile; one of his sons had been killed, and the reins of government seized by a few daring and powerful chiefs. Seru had remained at Bau during the whole time, for which reason he received the name of Thakombau, that is, "Bau is bad;" and, although a mere youth, he so far outwitted the rebel chiefs as completely to effect their destruction, and prepare the way for his father's return to power. This remarkable young chief was carrying on his warlike work at the time that Mr. Cross arrived. In answer to the request of the Missionary for permission to take up his residence at Bau, Seru said, "It will be most agreeable to me, if you think well to do so; but I will not hide it from you that I am now engaged in war, and cannot attend to your instructions, or even assure your safety."

Under these circumstances Mr. Cross at once turned his attention to Rewa, the second place in Fiji in rank and influence. The Missionary landed at the place last named, on the 8th of January, 1838, and was received in the most friendly manner by the King, Tuindrcketche, who promised to protect him and his property, and to allow any of his people to embrace Christianity who wished to do so. Notwithstanding this favourable commencement of the work at Rewa, the cause was very weak and feeble for some time. On the first Sabbath after his arrival, Mr. Cross preached to a congregation of twelve persons, three of whom had come with him from Lakemba, whilst some of the others had been induced to renounce heathenism by a Tongan Chief who had visited Rewa some time before. As there were several Europeans residing in the town, the Missionary proposed holding Divine service in English for their benefit; but only two came: so indifferent were his countrymen to the great and glorious privilege of hearing the Gospel in their own tongue in a strange land; but perhaps this may be partly accounted for from the fact of their being, to a great extent, under French influence, for the Chevalier sent his boat to Rewa to trade, notwithstanding it was the Sabbath.

But discouraging as were the circumstances of Mr. Cross and his family at the commencement of the Rewa Mission, they were rendered more so by a severe attack of illness by which the lonely Missionary was now visited, and by which he was prevented from ministering to the people during the six following Sabbaths. This attack of fever was, no doubt, induced by the unwholesome and uncomfortable dwelling which had been provided for the Mission family. It was a house containing but one room, built on low, damp ground, and almost surrounded by stagnant water, from which the effluvia emitted in rainy weather was almost unbearable. When Mrs. Cross was nearly exhausted with watching and attention to her afflicted husband, she was cheered and assisted by the arrival of a white man, an American, named David Whippy, from Ovalau, an island about fifty miles from Rewa. This kind-hearted man rendered considerable help to Mrs. Cross during the night watches, and the invalid was, through mercy, soon raised from a bed of sickness. He continued in such a state of weakness, however, that it was thought that his removal to a colder climate would be necessary to save his life.

Happily, about this time arrangements were made for the reinforcement of the Mission. The circulation of a powerful and pathetic appeal to the Christian people of England on behalf of poor cannibal Fiji, written by the Rev. James Watkin, produced such an effect that the Society felt warranted in sending out the Revs. John Hunt, T. J. Jaggar, and James Calvert, with their wives, in April 1838, and towards the close of the year they landed safely at Lakemba, with a printing-press and materials for printing and binding books, &c. Fiji was now made a separate District, of which the Rev. David Cargill, M.A., was appointed chairman. At the first district meeting, which was held shortly after the arrival of the Mission party from England, it was resolved not to attempt the commencement of any new station till the brethren from home had acquired some knowledge of the language; but to strengthen the existing Missions. The most pressing business was to relieve Mr. Cross, who, on account of the shattered state of his health and constitution, had received permission to remove with his family to Australia. Mr. Hunt was, therefore, appointed to Rewa to take the place of the invalid Missionary; but when he got there, he found Mr. Cross much better, who, feeling unwilling to leave his young brother alone, a stranger to the language and to the people, nobly volunteered to forego the privilege of visiting the Colony, that he might labour on a little longer in a cause which was so dear to his heart. The King having provided a more convenient and suitable house for the Mission families, they lived and laboured together with comparative comfort, and with a cheering measure of success.

Schools were now formed for the instruction of the rising generation, and preaching was commenced at several towns and villages in the neighbourhood of Rewa. The Missionaries also visited Viwa once a fortnight, frequently calling at Bau to converse with the King and his Chiefs, with the hope of preparing the way for the introduction of the Gospel to the heathen metropolis. It was not without repeated instances of opposition and persecution on the part of the pagan priests and people, sometimes encouraged by those in power, that these zealous labours were at first prosecuted; but the Lord greatly blessed the efforts of His servants, and in a short time one hundred and forty natives avowed themselves the worshippers of Jehovah. As the work advanced, and as the Missionaries gained a more perfect knowledge of the language, the country, and the people, it became more and more apparent, from its central position with reference to the population generally, that Rewa must necessarily become one of the most important stations in Fiji. In view of this fact, it appeared necessary to make some new arrangements for the more efficient prosecution of the Mission; and for this purpose a special district meeting was convened at Rewa, the Rev. Messrs. Cargill and Calvert having come from Lakemba for the purpose of conferring with their brethren.

At this meeting, which was held in the month of May 1839, it was resolved to remove the printing-press from Lakemba to Rewa, and to attempt, by the commencement of new stations, an aggressive movement on the mass of heathenism which pervaded the land, especially as the new Missionaries were making satisfactory progress in the language, and other brethren were expected shortly from the Friendly Islands. In July the Rev. Messrs. Lyth and Spinney arrived from Tonga; and from their acknowledged ability, zeal, and experience the most sanguine expectations were entertained with reference to their appointment to Fiji. These were fully realised with regard to Mr. Lyth, who served the Mission well for many years, especially in connection with the efficient training of young men as native teachers, and in the medical treatment of the afflicted; but poor Mr. Spinney's health entirely failed, and he was obliged to remove to Sydney, where he died, happy in God, on the 10th of February, 1840.

After the reinforcement of the Mission the boundaries of the Rewa Circuit were extended by the addition of a number of outstations, to which native teachers were appointed; and subsequently, after a desolating war had laid waste the country for several years, both Viwa and Bau were occupied by resident Missionaries, and became the centres of important circuits. Thus was Christian truth, from the pulpit, the schools, and the press, brought to bear, with powerful effect, upon a dense mass of heathen people, thousands of whom were induced to relinquish their barbarous habits, and to turn from the worship of dumb idols to serve the true and living God. Many and fierce were the conflicts which the Missionaries had to encounter from the prevalence of cannibalism, war, and superstition; and appalling were the scenes of cruelty and of crime which they were compelled to witness; but the Gospel of Christ was aggressive in its onward march, and proved to be "the power of God" to the salvation of many precious souls. Perhaps there never was such a struggle between light and darkness, truth and error, Christ and Belial, as that which took place in the course of the Fiji Mission, before Bau, the stronghold of heathenism, yielded to the *lotu*. But the Missionaries, having obtained a firm footing at Rewa and Viwa, persevered, and pushed forward their noble enterprise with a moral heroism deserving the highest commendation; and they had their reward in the complete victory with which their efforts were crowned at last.

Various circumstances combined to keep the Missionaries out of the capital for several years after they had succeeded in introducing the Gospel to other places in Fiji. This was the place where there was the largest number of heathen temples, and where the priests exercised the greatest power over both King and people. The country was, moreover, almost constantly embroiled in war, first with Rewa, and then with Somosomo, and afterwards with other places. It was to Bau that the bodies of the victims were brought by scores and hundreds, when the savage warriors had vanquished their enemies, or succeeded in surprising a party of unoffending natives, when they wanted to make a cannibal feast for the entertainment of their visitors. There human blood was made to flow most copiously in honour of the demon-gods of Fiji, and there the ovens were kept constantly ready for the disgusting festivals and midnight orgies of a people led captive by the devil at his will. But perhaps the greatest hindrance to the reception of the Gospel at Bau was the inconsistent vacillating conduct of the ruling powers. The old King Tanoa continued in his heathen state to the last, notwithstanding the many warnings which he received; and at his death in 1852 five women were strangled to accompany him into the spirit world, in the face of the most faithful remonstrances of the Missionaries. Thakombu, his son and successor, was convinced of the truth of Christianity long before he yielded to its influence; and it was only after he had suffered numerous reverses and afflictions that he at length bowed his knee to Jehovah. But when he did turn to God, Thakombau began at once to use his powerful influence in favour of the truth; and great was the triumph of Christianity in Bau, and in other parts of Fiji, when he yielded to the power of the Gospel.

Somosomo.

One of the places fixed upon for a new station when the Missionaries in Fiji found themselves in circumstances to extend the sphere of their operations was Somosomo, a large and important town situated in Taviune, an island off the south-east point of Vanau Levu, or Great Land. Tuithakau, the King, accompanied by his two sons, and some hundreds of his people, had visited Lakemba soon after the arrival of the first Missionaries, and, being favourably impressed with all that they saw at the Mission station, especially with the knives, hatchets, iron pots, and other useful articles which the white strangers had brought with them, he earnestly pleaded for Christian teachers. The wily monarch urged his plea by a reference to the fact of his superior power and influence, as compared with the King of Lakemba, alleging that, if he embraced the *lotu*, all Fiji would do the same. At that time it was not in the power of the Missionaries to commence a station at Somosomo; but, at length, the number of Missionaries being increased, they made arrangements to do so. They knew that this was pre-eminently, next to Bau, the stronghold of heathenism, a den of iniquity, a very hell upon earth; but with a firm reliance on the God of Missions, and the promised protection and patronage of the King, they hoped to overcome every difficulty. This promised protection and patronage proved, however, as in some other cases, false and deceitful, the King's motives being entirely selfish and ambitious; and the attempt which was made to introduce Christianity into Somosomo presents to our view one of the darkest chapters in the history of the Fiji Mission. It is now our painful duty to tell the mournful story, at least so much of it as is fit for civilised ears, for some of the abominations of the savage cannibal natives had better sink into oblivion.

It was in the month of July 1839, that Mr. Hunt removed from

Rewa, and accompanied by Mr. Lyth, went to Somosomo. When they landed they met with no welcome greeting, as in some other places; but every one seemed to regard them with perfect indifference. An old house belonging to the King was given up for the use of the two families, it is true, but beyond this little notice was taken of them. This cold reception was trying enough to the Missionaries and their devoted wives; but severer troubles awaited them. They saw around them, in every direction, abundant proof that they had come to a land of superstition, cruelty, and blood. When they had got all their goods landed, and before the vessel in which they came had taken her departure, tidings reached Somosomo that Ra Mbithi, the King's son, had been lost at sea, with all who sailed with him; and that several women were set apart to be strangled. The Missionaries, therefore, began their work by pleading for the lives of these wretched victims. All that they could do was to get the execution delayed till further search had been made for the missing canoe. This proving fruitless, sixteen women were forthwith strangled in honour of the young chief and his companions, and the bodies were buried within a few yards of the house occupied by the Mission families.

When the Missionaries had toiled on for about six months, in the face of every kind of opposition and insult to which they could possibly be exposed, Mr. Hunt makes this touching record in his Journal, under the date of February 7th, 1840:—"Last Monday afternoon, as soon as our class meeting was over, a report came that some dead men were being brought here from Lauthala. The report was so new, and so indefinite, that at first we did not know what to make of it. Almost before we had time to think, the men were laid on the ground before our house, and the chiefs, and priests, and people met to divide them to be eaten. They brought eleven to our settlement, and it is not certain how many have been killed, but some say two or three hundred, others not more than thirty. Their crime appears to be that of killing one man; and when the man that did it came to beg pardon, the chief required this massacre to be made as a recompense. The principal chief was killed and given to the great Ndengei of Somosomo. I saw him after he was cut up and laid upon the fire to be cooked for the cannibal God of Somosomo. Oh! shame to human nature!" But we forbear. This is only a specimen of what the Missionaries and their families had to endure at this trying period; and it is believed that the full amount of their sufferings will never be known in this world.

Whilst these appalling scenes were being enacted, Divine service was held by the Missionaries every Sabbath and at other times, and occasionally a considerable number of people would collect together to hear the Word of God; but these were chiefly strangers from a distance, as the King strictly prohibited any of the inhabitants of the place becoming Christians, or attending the services. Fierce persecution and open violence were moreover brought to bear on the Missionaries, and the few who ventured to attend upon their instructions. One day the King's son, club in hand, came in fury to kill Mr. Lyth, who had refused to purchase part of a melon from the King's favourite wife. Mr. Lyth escaped to his bedroom, and Mr. Hunt held the angry chief in conversation till his rage had cooled down. Every day the position of the Missionaries and their families became more trying and more dangerous, and they were perplexed to know what was best to be done.

Early in 1840 Commodore Wilkes, with two ships of the United States Exploring Expedition, visited Somosomo, and expressed great sympathy with the sufferers, placing at their disposal one of the vessels, if they chose to remove with their effects, and go to any other part of Fiji. The great kindness of the United States officers was highly valued by the Missionaries, but their work was begun, and they were resolved not to leave it till they had made further trial. Soon afterwards the Rev. John Waterhouse, the General Superintendent of the South Sea Missions, visited the station, where he found Mrs. Hunt very poorly, while her husband was away at Rewa, whither he had gone to afford brotherly sympathy to Mr. Cargill, whose excellent wife had just died. In the meantime there were occasional instances of spiritual good resulting from the labours of the Missionaries, which excited a gleam of hope for the future, but in general the darkness and gloom in the prospect seemed to preponderate.

The health of the Mission families continuing to suffer from the confined and unsuitable dwelling which they occupied in the centre of the town, they succeeded at length in erecting two tolerable houses in a more open and airy situation by the sea-shore, and they were beginning to entertain hopes of the ultimate success of the Mission, when several untoward circumstances occurred to blight their prospects. They first heard of the lamented death of the Rev. John Waterhouse in Australia; and then of the serious

GRAVE OF THE REV. W. CROSS.

illness of Mr. Cross, at Viwa. Hoping to save the life of such a beloved and valuable labourer, the Missionaries promptly made arrangements for the removal of Mr. Cross to Somosomo, where he might have the advantage of Mr. Lyth's medical skill, which had been very successful in other cases. This arrangement was carried out, and Mr. Hunt went to take charge of the Viwa station, on the departure of his suffering brother. But the fatigue of removal, and the want of efficient servants, added to the exhaustion caused by the disease, proved too much for Mr. Cross, and in spite of Mr. Lyth's diligent attention, he died on the 15th October,

1842. A native house was built over the grave of the devoted Missionary, and beneath the same roof in this land of strangers were interred the remains of two or three little children, who were removed to a better country, while their bereaved and afflicted parents were striving to plant the standard of the Cross in dark benighted Somosomo.

We need not further dwell on the long and gloomy night of hope deferred which brooded over the Missionaries and their work in cruel·blood-thirsty Somosomo, but hasten to relate the mournful sequel. After labouring under the most trying and discouraging circumstances, and suffering to an extent, only known to God, for eight years, with no improvement in their prospects, the Missionaries began to entertain serious thoughts of relinquishing the Somosomo station, that they might spend their strength in more promising parts of Fiji. At the district meeting of 1847, it was, accordingly, resolved to abandon this comparatively barren field, and to enter some of the openings which were presenting themselves in other places. When the removal was once decided upon, it required the greatest care in carrying it into effect. The Missionaries, therefore, began to prepare in the most silent and quiet manner, so as not to arouse the anger and cupidity of the natives. They packed up all their goods, unscrewed the windows and doors of their houses, and got everything ready for embarkation. According to previous arrangement the *Triton* anchored off Somosomo on the 28th September; and, with the aid of two of their brethren, who came from Lakemba for the purpose, every thing was got on board as well as could be expected. Of course pilfering took place to a considerable extent; but when they had secured all they could possibly remove, the Missionaries were glad to weigh anchor and leave a place which had given them so little satisfaction.

A few years afterwards the notorious persecutor, Tuikilakila, King of Somosomo, died a violent death, and his dominions were plunged into a civil war. Some of the most active opposers of the Mission were killed, and others had to flee for their lives. "Verily there is a God that judgeth in the earth." Somosomo, after many vicissitudes, is again to have a Missionary. May the people now know and improve the day of their gracious visitation!

Success in Sundry Places.

About twenty miles from Viwa, to the northward, there is a very important island called Ovalau. Its central position, with a good harbour and anchorage, has made it the chief place of resort for such ships as visit the group. The principal entrance, through the reef which almost surrounds the island, is on the east side, opposite Levuka, the capital, or chief town. This is the place where most of the foreigners who have, from time to time, settled in Fiji have fixed their residence. These white men from America, England, Ireland, Scotland, and other countries, have generally connected themselves with native women, and have families of coloured children. They employ themselves in building boats, making chests, planting provisions, and trading with the natives. Several of the principal men of the settlement own small vessels, in which they cruise about and make short trading voyages to the different islands of the group.

At an early period of their labours in Fiji, the Missionaries saw and felt that in time to come these American and European settlers and their descendants would necessarily exercise a powerful influence upon the country for good or evil, and they were anxious to promote their spiritual welfare to the utmost of their power. Before any arrangement could be made by the brethren for the benefit of their fellow-countrymen, so peculiarly circumstanced, and as early as the month of May 1839, Messrs. Cargill and Calvert were unexpectedly cast upon the shores of Ovalau. They were proceeding in a small vessel on a visit to Ono and Rewa, when they were driven out of their course by contrary winds, and anchored off the town of Levuka. During the fortnight that they were detained there, the Missionaries were cordially received by the white residents and natives in the neighbourhood of the settlements, to whom they preached repeatedly, especially on the Sabbath; and an earnest desire was expressed by all parties for their continued services; but when the wind became favourable, they were obliged to weigh anchor, and proceed on their voyage.

A Mission-station being deemed indispensable for the settlement, in 1840, a piece of ground was purchased of the King of Levuka, and generously presented to the Wesleyan Missionary Society, by Mr. W. R. Waldren, Purser of the United States Exploring Expedition; and in the following year Mr. Cross took two native teachers to instruct the children of the settlers, and to hold religious services for the benefit of their fellow-countrymen. It was the intention of the Missionary to visit the station occasionally till more ample arrangements could be made to supply the spiritual necessities of the people; but his failing health prevented him from carrying out his purpose to the extent he desired.

On the arrival of Mr. Hunt at Viwa, in 1842, he felt it his duty to pay special attention to the whites and their families at Levuka; and on his frequent visits he preached to them in English, and found them quite willing to receive instruction, and to alter their mode of life, which had hitherto been fearfully depraved. The settlers now began to observe the Sabbath, to wear better clothes, and to procure shoes for their feet, that they might not descend below the level of the degraded natives, which they were in danger of doing. Several of them became lawfully married, and such was the general reformation, that they bid fair to become an industrious, thriving, community. And, what is better still, a few gave their hearts to God, who were formed into a class, and taken under the pastoral care of the Missionary, whilst some of their sons were taken to Viwa for special instruction and training, with the hope that they might be made useful in time to come.

For some time after this favourable commencement, the good work was retarded by the prevalence of war and other difficulties, into the particulars of which we cannot now enter. But when the country became more settled, the Missionaries resumed their visits, and ultimately Ovalau became an important station, with a resident European Missionary and an English schoolmaster. When Mr. Calvert visited Levuka, in 1849, he had good congregations, and was pleased to find that the wives and children of the settlers especially had made considerable progress in learning to read. When a chapel had been erected, and the station was fully occupied, more ample provision was made for the religious instruction, both of the white settlers and their families, and the native population of the island.

Among others, a mountaineer chief of high rank, living at a town in the interior called Lovoni, became nominally Christian, and desired Paul Vea, a Tongan teacher, who was residing at a village on the coast, to become his instructor. In urging Paul to go, the chief promised to feed him well; and, as an inducement, waving his hand round towards the towns belonging to Lovoni, promised him plenty of snakes, saying, "All these parts are subject to us, and the people will bring you and me plenty of snakes to eat with our vegetables." Paul intimated that the promise was not likely to entice him from the coast, as he did not desire such diet. "Ah!" said the chief, "they are excellent food; superior to pork, or fish, or fowls." Notwithstanding the difficulties arising from the strange mode of living of these wild mountaineers, as illustrated by this incident, and other peculiarities of the country, the *lotu* prevailed in various parts of Ovalau, places of worship were erected and schools established in several towns and villages, and numbers were gathered into the fold of the Redeemer. The good work has recently been extended to Thakaundrovi, and other neighbouring islands, which, unitedly, will form an important and extensive circuit.

To the south of Viti-Levu, at a distance of about one hundred miles, there is an important island called Kandavu, which, together with a small group of islets in its immediate vicinity, forms an interesting Missionary circuit. Soon after the Rewa station had been commenced, this place attracted the notice of the brethren, and two native teachers were sent over as the pioneers of Christianity. These humble messengers of the churches were received with much cordiality, from an impression which had gone forth that the *lotu* was designed universally to prevail, and the people showed a remarkable readiness to attend to their instruction. On one occasion a deputation was sent from a town a long way off to the capital, where the teachers lived, begging that instruction might be given to their people also. One of the teachers accompanied the messengers on their return, and met the priests of the town, who acknowledged their conviction of the falseness of their own religion, and desired to be more fully informed about the *lotu*. They were so pleased with what they heard, that they requested the teachers to visit them frequently; but this being impossible, in consequence of the distance and their numerous engagements, the people of that place determined to remove and settle near to the capital, that they might enjoy the benefit of religious instruction. At this town, the chief and people, with the permission of the King of Rewa, to whom it was subject, became Christians; and there was a cheering prospect of still greater success, when it was sadly blighted by the breaking out of a cruel and bloody war. This resulted in the withdrawal of the teachers, and the station was for a time relinquished.

For several years the country continued in a very unsettled state. Kandavu being so intimately connected with Rewa, it necessarily shared in the commotion resulting from the long-continued war between that place and Bau. It was not till the arrival of King George, of the Friendly Islands, at Fiji, in 1853, that a better understanding was established among the people, and a measure of peace was restored to the country. The royal visitor went to Kandavu with his fleet of canoes, and both there and at every other island where he called, he used his powerful influence for the promotion of peace and the spread of Christianity. So soon as the way was once more open, native teachers were again sent to Kandavu. The Missionaries also visited the islands themselves, and were much pleased with the favourable prospects which they beheld in every direction for the spread of the Gospel. When writing to a friend in England, Mr. Moore says, "I have been all round Kandavu on foot, and I am surprised at the work of God. You would be astonished to hear many pray who have only just begun to serve the Lord." Ultimately the station was occupied by a European Missionary, with a staff of eight efficient native assistants, to labour in the respective towns and villages of the group. A theological institution was, moreover, established there for the purpose of training native agents for the whole district, and a cheering measure of success was realised in every department of the work.

We must now turn our attention to the larger islands of Fiji. With respect to VITI LEVU, we may regard the Rewa, Viwa, and Bau stations as immediately connected with it, and as bearing directly on its vast population, all three being in close proximity to it. A considerable number of places, regarded as continental towns and villages, were, moreover, included in the three circuits which we have mentioned, and were occupied by native teachers at an early period, and visited by the Missionaries as occasion required. At the same time there are thousands of people in the interior, and on the distant shores of the mainland, who have not yet been brought under the influence of Christianity. These will, it is hoped, be visited and instructed as opportunities are afforded, and as the means at the disposal of the Missionaries and their agents will permit.

The other large and populous island, called VANUA LEVU, attracted the attention of the Missionaries at an early period; but their arduous duties on the stations which they already occupied for some time prevented them from doing anything effectual for the spiritual benefit of the inhabitants. At length, about the year 1843, the heathen Chief of Bua, the principal town of the "sandal-wood district," on the western point of the island, procured a native teacher from Viwa, to instruct a friend of his who had renounced idolatry in favour of the *lotu*. This teacher, and others who were afterwards sent to his aid, laboured under the direct sanction of the Bua Chief, and were favoured with such encouraging success that, although the district had been unsettled by war, the converts amounted, in 1845, to three hundred. Presently this fair prospect was darkened by a sudden change in the views and conduct of the Chief, who, on the conversion of one of his relatives, became a violent persecutor of the Christians. Thus the good work was retarded for some time. In 1847 the Chief of Bua died, and three of his wives were strangled in connection with his funeral. The refusal of the native Christians to take part in these appalling superstitious rites subjected them to the still heavier displeasure of the sons of the deceased, who were now in power, and they were annoyed in various ways till the appointment of a regular Missionary to take charge of the station.

When the Somosomo station was given up, as already stated, this was one of the new spheres of labour entered upon, as more likely to repay the labours of the Missionaries. In anticipation of the new arrangement, Mr. Hunt had caused a house to be built in a village called Tiliva, where most of the native Christians lived; and on the 3rd of November, 1847, the Rev. Thomas Williams arrived from Somosomo to occupy the station. In a letter which he soon afterwards addressed to the Missionary Secretaries in London, Mr. Williams gives the following account of the locality of the station, and the commencement of his labours:—" With the locality of this new station I am much pleased. It is embosomed in tropical luxuriance, and on the edge of a good river, and two miles from the sea. The village of which my house forms a part is Christian; that on the opposite bank of the river is heathen. My congregation on Sunday last numbered about one hundred and twenty souls, most of whom were seriously attentive. The physical appearance of this people is far below that of the Fijians among whom I have laboured previously; but there appears a willingness to be taught, and to make my way as pleasant as they can. The mind which produces these dispositions is of more worth than a noble exterior. Several small places at a distance of from three to ten miles are open to me, at three of which we have a few Church members."

For some time the aspect of the work was pleasant and encouraging. The Christian village of Tiliva, where the Missionary resided, was separated from the heathen town of Bua by a river; and, being inhabited chiefly by *lotu* people, who had congregated there from various parts of the country at the close of a desolating war, it was a place of refuge, where the ordinances of religion were highly prized. The regular attendance of the converted natives on the means of grace, after all the sufferings which they had passed through, was a source of great comfort to the Missionary. Soon after his arrival he was favoured with a visit from the Rev. Walter Lawry, the successor of Mr. Waterhouse as General Superintendent of the Missions, when the people had their school-feast, sang hymns, repeated various portions of Scripture, and presented offerings of sandal-wood, mats, and oil, as marks of respect to their distinguished visitor, and of their love for the cause in which he was engaged.

At an early period of the Mission a few remarkable cases of conversions occurred, and two or three of the native converts died happy in the pardoning love of God, and gave pleasing testimony in their latest moments of their blessed hope of heaven. When the new station was in a measure established, the Missionary felt at liberty to visit several places at a distance, where a few native Christians were settled, and where there seemed to be openings for the introduction of the Gospel among a people who were still, to a large extent, heathen. In the course of the first journey, he came to a village called Nai Vakasinga, the chief of which gave him and his people a cordial welcome. After a frugal supper they were conducted to the heathen temple, or god-house, to lodge, where they found several old cannibals in possession. Among these strange occupants the Missionary, weary with travel, stretched himself upon the floor, and tried to compose himself to sleep. "On the following morning," he writes, "we conducted a short service among our heathen bed-fellows, and then set off to our canoe."

Notwithstanding numerous hindrances, arising from occasional wars and rumours of war, and the hostility of heathen priests, and others, the cause of God continued to advance in this new and interesting sphere of labour. When the Bua Circuit had been formed about three years, and Mr. Williams had been joined by the Rev. William Moore, in 1852, the Missionaries were able to report the opening of six new preaching-places and the erection of three substantial chapels. The principal of these, which adorned the headquarters of the Mission, was acknowledged to be the best place of worship in the entire group. Mr. Williams, who appears

CHAPEL AND MISSION PREMISES AT BUA, FIJI

to have been a skilful mechanic as well as a faithful preacher of the Gospel, also erected for himself a commodious dwelling-house, and arranged everything about the station in a manner likely to impress the natives with a favourable view of the manifold blessings of Christianity, as may be seen from the accompanying engraving. And, what is better still, about three hundred native converts had been received into the church by baptism, many of whom gave satisfactory evidence of a change of heart.

About this time the newly arrived Missionary built a temporary house on the other side of the river, and took up his residence near the heathen town of Bua, that he might bring his labours to bear more directly upon the pagan chief and his people. This was a bold step on the part of Mr. Moore, especially as Mr. Williams was obliged soon afterwards to remove to Australia, on account of failing health, and this large circuit was again left to the care of one minister. The arrangement, however, resulted in a wider diffusion of Christian truth; and, in subsequent years, by the blessing of God upon the zealous labours of Messrs. Malvern, Wilson, and others, who were appointed to this station in succession after the removal of Mr. Moore, the work has now spread over an extensive district on the mainland, and to the Yasawa Islands, where out-stations have been formed; and it is carried on, with a prospect of still greater success, by two European Missionaries and four native Ministers whom God has raised up to take part in this noble enterprise.

Another important station was afterwards formed on the southern coast of Vanua Levu at a place called Nandi, and it has been maintained, amid similar scenes of opposition, from the horrible cruelties of heathen superstition and war to those which were witnessed at Bua. The pioneer evangelist in this instance was a devoted native teacher named Joel Bulu; and whilst the cause was in its infancy, the place was occasionally visited by the Rev. John Hunt and others from Viwa, under whose direction a Mission house was erected in a village where most of the native Christians had taken up their residence. In 1847 the station had become so important that it was found necessary to make more adequate provision to meet the increasing demands which were made for religious instruction by a people just emerging from the darkness of heathenism; and the Rev. John Watsford, who had been labouring at Viwa, and the Rev. James Ford, who had just arrived from England, were sent to occupy it.

The newly arrived Missionaries found their people occupying a very unfavourable position in a low, swampy place, by the side of a creek, hemmed in by dense forests of mangroves, and infested with swarms of mosquitoes. To the inconveniences and discomforts incident to such a locality, the Mission families were obliged, for a time, to submit, as native houses had been erected for them there, and there the *lotu* people were settled. The brethren had scarcely commenced their labours, however, when the country was visited by one of those desolating hurricanes to which many of the South Sea Islands are so liable. Their dwellings were almost entirely demolished, the village was inundated, and they had to make their escape with their wives and children, as best they could, wading through deep water to a more elevated position. There they waited till the fury of the tempest had abated, and the waters began to subside, when they returned to the station and witnessed an appalling scene of destruction. Furniture, books, and wearing apparel were either entirely destroyed or seriously damaged; and, what was worse still, Mr. Watsford's little daughter caught such a severe cold from the exposure, that she sickened and died about two weeks afterwards, and was buried in a land of strangers.

The Mission-village was now removed to a more elevated and healthy locality, and the Missionaries rebuilt their frail dwellings, and proceeded with their work as usual. But their troubles were not yet ended. The health of Mr. and Mrs. Ford so completely failed, that they were obliged to return to England when they had been only about a year in Fiji; and Mr. Watsford being removed to Lakemba, the new station at Nandi was occupied, in 1848, by the Rev. David Hazlewood, and a few zealous native teachers. By the blessing of God upon their united labours the work prospered, schools being established, and preaching commenced at out-stations in various directions, especially at a place called Solevu, where a number of white settlers had taken up their residence, and also at Nandundu, a village about fifty miles further up the coast. Mr. Hazlewood had not been long on the Nandi station, when he was plunged into deep distress by domestic affliction and bereavement. On the 7th of February, 1849, he lost a sweet little girl, who was cut down after a short but severe illness, and before the end of the month, he was called to follow to the grave, in a strange land, the remains of his beloved wife, who died suddenly three days after giving birth to an infant. The lonely and afflicted Missionary was visited by his friend and brother, Mr. Williams, from Bua; and all the Mission families in Fiji sincerely sympathised with him, and his three motherless children, in the great loss which they had sustained.

On the removal of Mr. Hazlewood to Australia, he was succeeded at Nandi by the Rev. Messrs. Moore, Polglase, Malvern, Waterhouse, Fordham, and others, who prosecuted the work amid various trials and difficulties resulting from personal and domestic affliction, the prevalence of war and cannibalism, and the hostility to the Gospel naturally arising from heathenish superstition in a pagan land. But notwithstanding every obstacle, Christianity continued to advance; schools being established and chapels built in various directions, whilst a goodly number of sinners were brought to a saving knowledge of the truth; and it is hoped that the *lotu* will ultimately prevail throughout the length and breadth of Venua Levu, as well as in every other part of Fiji.

Miscellaneous Incidents.

It is a pleasing sight to see dark benighted heathens, by hundreds and thousands, casting away their idols, and bowing down in humble worship before the Great Jehovah; and it is still more delightful to behold indubitable evidences of a genuine saving work of grace upon the heart. In the history of the Fiji Mission there were some remarkable instances of the outpouring of the Holy Spirit in answer to prayer. If the revivals of religion were not so

extensive as those which occurred in the Friendly Islands, they were not less marked in their character as the real work of God. In the month of October 1845, at Viwa especially, a gracious influence descended upon the people, when assembled together for the purpose of seeking a fresh baptism of the Spirit. Concerning one of these meetings, Mr. Hunt wrote soon afterwards as follows:—
" Nothing was heard but weeping and praying. Many cried aloud for mercy, and not in vain. The merciful God heard their cries, and blessed them with pardon and peace. This was the commencement of a series of meetings which were held every day, and sometimes many times a day, not only in the chapel, but in almost every house in the town. A penitent meeting was held by almost every family night and morning; in some instances nearly the whole family were crying for mercy, with one heart and with one voice. Business, sleep, and food were almost entirely laid aside. We were at length almost obliged to force some of the new converts to take something for the sustenance of the body. I think about seventy persons were converted during the first five days of the revival. Some of the cases were the most remarkable I have ever seen, heard of, or read of; yet only such as one might expect the conversion of such dreadful murderers and cannibals would be. The work has spread throughout the circuit. I think every place, more or less, has been blessed. 'The people that sat in darkness have seen a great light.'" Many remarkable conversions also occurred, from time to time, when there was no particular excitement, as those of King Thakombau, the Chief Varini, and others, who became eminently useful in promoting the spread of the Gospel. The religious experience of the native converts, as given in the class-meetings and love-feasts, and on other occasions, is described as generally satisfactory, and sometimes affecting beyond measure.

A brief tribute of respect to the memory of the Rev. John Hunt, the eminent Missionary to Fiji, may with propriety be placed on record here. His short but useful life is a study for young men, fraught with important and admonitory lessons. He was born at Balderton, near Newark, on the the 13th of June, 1812, and in early life he gave his heart to God. Soon after his conversion, he was called to preach the Gospel to his fellow-countrymen. When he had acted as a local preacher for some time, he offered himself, and was accepted, as a candidate for the Missionary work, and placed as a student in the Theological Institution at Hoxton, where he remained nearly three years, a pattern of attention, diligence, and Christian consistency, to the admiration of all with whom he had to do. Mr. Hunt was appointed as a Missionary to Fiji in 1838, and he arrived at the scene of his future labours at the commencement of the following year. For nearly ten years he was "in labours more abundant," crowding the services of a long life into a comparatively short period. He speedily acquired a knowledge of the Fijian language, and was incessantly engaged in preaching, translating the Scriptures, composing theological and other works, training native teachers, and laying himself out in every possible way for the advancement of the cause of Christ in the islands of Fiji, to which he was devotedly attached. Mr. Hunt was a man of singular intellectual energy; of a piety which breathed the purest love to God and charity to man; of a patience which accumulated trials and difficulties failed to move; and of a "calmly fervent zeal" which in sickness and in health, in strength and in weakness, was always in pursuit of its one great object—the salvation of souls. Worn out with incessant toil, he was at length seized with a severe illness from which he never recovered. His death admirably corresponded with his life. "You see a bright prospect before you," said Mr. Lyth. He replied, "I see nothing but Jesus." On another occasion, Mr. Calvert read for him the seventieth chapter of St. John's Gospel, and engaged in prayer. Towards the close Mr. Hunt began to weep. At length he cried out, "Lord, bless Fiji! Lord, save Fiji! Thou knowest my soul has loved Fiji." Again he said, with great vehemence, "O, let me pray once more for Fiji! Lord, for Christ's sake, bless Fiji! save Fiji! save Thy servants! save Thy people! save the heathen in Fiji!" The dying Missionary then became more composed, and after taking an affectionate leave of his family and brethren, and repeatedly expressing his unwavering confidence in the atonement of the Redeemer, he slept in Jesus, on the the 4th of November, 1848, at the early age of thirty-seven.

Although the names of but few Missionaries have been brought so prominently before the public as that of John Hunt, from his being cut down in the midst of his usefulness, and other circumstances, there have been many excellent humble labourers in the Mission-field who have been equally devoted to their work, of whom little has been heard at a distance; but they will have their reward in heaven. Yea, and a goodly number of zealous, holy, self-denying Christian women, too, have been engaged in the enterprise to whom the cause of Missions is indebted to an extent that many are not aware of. In illustration of this, one instance of female heroism may be given as a specimen of numerous cases which have come under our notice, but which were never brought to light before the world.

Mrs. Calvert and Mrs. Lyth were left alone with their children at Viwa whilst their husbands were gone to the District Meeting, when a report was brought one day that fourteen women were to be killed and cooked on the morrow. What could be done? The Missionaries had often interceded, with more or less success, for human life. Would it be of any use for their delicate wives to exert their influence to save the lives of their dark heathen sisters? They resolved to try. A canoe was immediately procured, and the two ladies, with a few natives, jumped into it. As they proceeded, poling over the fat, a distance of two miles, they drew near to the blood-stained capital of Fiji, and heard, with trembling hearts, the wild din of the savage cannibals grow louder and louder with the dismal sound of the death-drum, and horrid shrieks at intervals told that the dreadful work of murder was begun. Nothing daunted, the noble-minded Englishwomen urged on the boatmen to increase their speed. At length they reached the beach, and, on jumping on shore, they met a *lotu* chief, who dared to join them, saying, "Make haste! some are dead; but some are alive!" Guarded by an unseen power, the Missionaries' wives passed through the savage throng unhurt.

They pressed forward to the house of the old King Tanoa, the entrance to which was strictly forbidden to women. With a whale's tooth as a present in each hand, they urged their plea that the remaining lives might be spared at the footstool of his sable majesty. The old man was startled at the audacity of the fair intruders. His hearing was dull, and the ladies raised their voices higher and yet higher in pleading for mercy. When the King fully understood the nature of their request, he said: "Those who are dead, are dead; but those who are still alive shall live." At that word a messenger was immediately sent to stop the work of murder, and he soon returned to say that five of the women were still alive, the rest of the fourteen having been killed. Having faithfully executed their mission of mercy, the Missionaries' wives returned to their homes with mingled feelings of gratitude and sorrow, and with renewed resolutions never to neglect an opportunity of doing good.

The watchful care of Divine Providence over the Missionaries and their families whilst exposed to numerous dangers in foreign lands, has, for many years, been very remarkable; but, in a few instances, a melancholy loss of precious lives in the service of the Lord has been permitted by infinite wisdom. A most afflicting case of this kind occurred in Fiji a few years ago, when the Rev. Thomas Baker and his companions were murdered in the interior of Viti Levu, a brief account of which may interest the reader.

The station occupied by Mr. Baker was Davuilevu, in the Rewa Circuit, about twelve miles from the mouth of the river; but, several native teachers having been appointed to interior stations among tribes who had recently abandoned their idols and embraced the *lotu*, it was thought desirable to pay them a visit of inspection. With this object in view, Mr. Baker left home, accompanied by a few native youths, on Saturday, July 13th, and ascended the river in his boat to a place called Natoaika, where he preached on the Sabbath. The following week was spent in visiting various out-stations and scattered tribes higher up the country, with which he had been more or less acquainted before. When he reached Dawarau, Mr. Baker seems to have resolved upon attempting to cross the country to the northern coast, an object which he had long secretly cherished, as he wished to penetrate to the interior regions, with the hope of inducing other tribes to embrace the *lotu*. From this place he wrote a letter to his wife, stating his intention, and the probability of his returning home by sea. On proceeding forward, Mr. Baker and his party, which now consisted of a native Missionary, two teachers, and six young men from the training institution, came in contact with a tribe of savage heathens at a place called Navosa, the chief of which plotted their destruction. They were allowed the use of a hut to lodge in on Saturday night; and, having cooked their supper and united in their evening devotions, they retired to rest. But the noise and confusion which was kept up outside made sleep impossible, and from what they heard they had reason to believe that mischief was intended. This circumstance hastened their departure from the town next morning; but they had not proceeded more than a hundred yards, when they were attacked by a band of armed men, with the chief at their head, and were all murdered in cold blood, with the exception of two of their young men, who escaped as by miracle, and fled with all possible speed to communicate the mournful intelligence of the sad disaster.

Reference having already been made to the visit of the Rev. Robert Young to several stations of the Wesleyan Missionary Society in the South Seas, we are glad to be able to give a brief notice of his impressions of the work in the Fiji Islands. When on their passage, in the *John Wesley*, from the Friendly Islands to Australia, Mr. Young, King George, and Mr. N. Turner reached Lakemba on Sunday morning, the 6th of November, 1853, and immediately went on shore, where they were received by a group of half-naked savages. On ascertaining who the strangers were, the countenances of the men on the beach brightened, however, and they escorted them to the chapel, where the people, to the number of about four hundred, were assembled at the morning service. The Rev. John Polglase was the officiating minister and, although he had only been in Fiji a short time, he preached in the native language with considerable fluency. At the close of the service Mr. Young and his companions proceeded to the Mission-house, where they were introduced to Mr. and Mrs. Lyth, and also to Mr. and Mrs. Binner, who had been obliged, in consequence of war, to leave their station at Ovalau. In the afternoon a fellowship meeting was held, at which many of the native converts spoke with much clearness of their personal religious experience, and of the blessed change which the Gospel had produced in the country. Two or three of the following days were spent by Mr. Young in examining Mr. Lyth's theological class and the Mission-schools under the able superintendence of Mr. Collis, a trained teacher from England; and the result was very satisfactory. On Wednesday, King George preached, much to the edification of the people; and, in connection with the service, the Rev. J. Polglase was united in marriage to Miss Mary Fletcher, the daughter of the Rev. Joseph Fletcher, of Taunton.

On Saturday, the 12th, Mr. Young embarked with his companions, and some of the Missionaries, for Viwa. The Sabbath was spent on the sea, and the Mission-party held Divine Service. On the following day they entered the harbour of Viwa, where they received a hearty welcome from the Rev. Messrs. Calvert and Waterhouse. The next few days were spent by Mr. Young in business with the Missionaries, religious services with the natives, examining the schools, and in a visit to Bau, where he had an interview with the far-famed King Thakombau, and witnessed many scenes of peculiar interest. He also visited, with solemn feelings, the grave of the devoted John Hunt; and, on embarking for Sydney, on Friday, the 18th, he expressed his admiration of the zeal, courage, and perseverance of the Missionaries, as well as his gratitude to God for what he had witnessed of the triumphs of Christianity on the respective stations of the Fiji District.

Many valuable testimonies to the usefulness and importance of our Missions in Fiji, from parties entirely unconnected with the Society, have appeared at different times; but the most recent is from the pen of the Rev. J. B. Smythe, a pious clergyman of the Church of England, who was chaplain on board H.M.S. *Brisk*, when she visited Fiji in the month of November 1867, to inquire into the circumstances connected with the murder of the Rev. T. Baker and his companions. Writing to the Rev. Stephen Rabone, General Secretary of the Australian Missionary Society, Mr. Smythe says :—" I cannot refrain from recording my high appreciation of the great and good work which the Missionaries are accomplishing in Fiji; and which must be apparent to every unprejudiced and Christian man visiting these Islands. It is, indeed, a rare pleasure to attend the native services; to see a large and flourishing congregation imbued with the spirit of devotion and godly reverence; to hear heartfelt praise to God; to observe their fervour in prayer, and their love for their Bibles. Never was I so much impressed with the power of Divine truth as when I stood in the midst of a native congregation at Bau, of over seven hundred; the King seated in a dignified manner in an armchair, with his large Bible before him; the Queen, the finest specimen, as regards flesh and bones, 'of the human face divine' that I ever saw, in a conspicuous place among the women; and heard the Gospel preached by a native minister, and the accents of their praise ascending on high, like the voice of many waters. The church is a large native building, capable of holding one thousand persons, and displays great ingenuity in its style of architecture. It is situated within a few yards of the ruins of an old heathen temple, where human sacrifices were wont to be offered to the gods previous to their being cooked and eaten. The ovens which were used for this revolting purpose of cooking the victims are still to be seen, filled with earth, and quite close to the church.

"I was well repaid for my visit to the Richmond Native Institution, on the island of Kandavu. The clean and airy schoolroom, the tidy little houses of the students, and the beautiful order in which the grounds are kept, delight the eye of the visitor. When we entered the institution, a well-defined air of satisfaction gleamed in the faces of forty-five fine-looking young men; and, as we proceeded to ascertain their mental attainments, slates and paper were quickly placed before them, and the examination passed off in a manner alike creditable to themselves and their energetic teacher. This institution is clearly the hope of Fiji, for native teachers must be largely employed; therefore a constant number of not less than a hundred should be kept under instruction."

The introduction of the Gospel to the Fiji Islands is effecting an entire revolution in the condition, views, and habits of the natives, who are rapidly becoming at least nominal Christians.* From the

FRIGHT OF NATIVES ON FIRST SEEING A HORSE.

* In the year 1869, the Rev. Messrs. Rabone and Watkins visited the whole of the Wesleyan Missions in the South Seas, as a deputation from the Australian Conference, and their report of the state of the work and the advancement of the natives in religious knowledge and general civilisation is most encouraging. Of Fiji they say: "Almost all things exceeded our expectations. The islands, their size, beauty, and fertility. The people, if not in their personal appearance, certainly in their behaviour. They are the politest Polynesians we saw—the Frenchmen of the South Sea Islands. Gentle in their movements and low in the tones of their voices, you would think that they could not be violent; but they can be so on occasions, as has been shown through the whole of their known history. It would be a good thing if the British Government would assume the protectorate of these islands, in compliance with a request made by the native chiefs." We learn from other sources that European emigrants are flocking to Fiji by hundreds, and that the cultivation of cotton and other articles of export is being carried on very extensively. For much additional interesting information the reader is referred to an excellent work recently published by the Rev. James Calvert, entitled, *Fiji and the Fijians.*

instructions of the Missionaries, and the increasing number of European and American settlers who are flocking to their shores, they are obtaining a knowledge of arts, science, civilised ideas, and useful animals of which they were previously ignorant. When the Rev. Mr. Hazlewood imported a pair of horses in 1851, the natives on the Nandi station were quite alarmed, and fled in terror from the presence of the strange-looking creatures, having never seen such animals before, but now farming stock is becoming common. The principal thing now to be feared is the influence of that irregular emigration and colonisation which is rapidly taking place in Fiji. It is questionable whether the rule of King Thakombau, with all the aid he can command, will be equal to the emergency. One thing is quite clear, the Missions, which have been the principal means of producing the wonderful change which has been experienced, must be vigorously prosecuted and liberally sustained, that the great work of evangelisation so auspiciously begun may issue in its intended results.

ROTUMAH.

Rotumah is a solitary island of the Pacific, situated at a distance of about three hundred miles to the north of Fiji, in latitude 12° 30' south, and longitude 177° 10' east. It is fifteen miles long, and varies in breadth from two to seven miles. The island is evidently of volcanic formation, and its surface is covered with scoria, or ashes, among which lies a scanty but productive soil, well adapted to the growth of cocoa-nuts, bananas, yams, and the usual variety of vegetables and fruits found within the tropics. The inhabitants, who are estimated at about four thousand in number, are of smaller stature than the Fijians, and are different in many of their customs as well as in their language. When they first attracted the notice of Europeans, these people were deeply debased, although, perhaps, not so cruel, bloodthirsty, and warlike as their nearest neighbours. They encumbered themselves with very little clothing, but tattooed their persons with curious devices, and besmeared their skins with a thick coat of turmeric and cocoanut oil, which they used so plentifully that not only their scanty wrapper of native cloth, but their mats and houses, and even the trees on the roadside, were bedaubed with the rich yellow compound, rubbed off from time to time from the bodies of the people.

For a long time the Missionaries in the Friendly and Fiji Islands were anxious to do something for the degraded inhabitants of Rotumah; but their hands were so full, and the distance was so great, that they were unable to commence a Mission-station among them, although it was known that they were quite willing to receive instruction. At length, in the year 1841, three Tongan native teachers were taken by Mr. Waterhouse to instruct the people, and a good work was commenced which has continued to advance from that time to the present. The native teachers from Tonga soon obtained some knowledge of the Rotumah language, and laboured successfully; but after a while it was found that Fijians could more readily learn, and more perfectly pronounce, this peculiar dialect, from its affinity, in some respects, with their own. From this and other circumstances, arrangements were ultimately made for connecting the Rotumah station with the Fiji District, from whence it was supplied with native teachers, till several were raised up on the spot to take a part in the good work.

But however excellent native teachers may be, they require the constant supervision of European Missionaries; and, from the isolated position of this station, it could seldom be visited. This lack of ministerial oversight soon began to be more painfully felt from the circumstance of the Romish Missionaries having gained a footing in the island. At length the case became so urgent that it was arranged that an English Wesleyan Missionary should occupy the station, with a suitable staff of native assistants. From this time the work of evangelisation rapidly advanced. Additional places of worship were erected, schools established, and portions of Scripture were translated; which, to a considerable extent, counteracted the baneful influence of Popery, and raised the people to a position which they had never occupied before. Idolatry has waned in Rotumah, and more than half the native population has been brought under the benign influence of Christianity. The Rev. W. Fletcher, B.A., has been on this lovely island five years, and has laboured most diligently, and with great success, in every department of the work. He has effected a translation of the entire New Testament, which he has carefully revised and prepared for the press; and the British and Foreign Bible Society has generously sent out paper and binding materials to Sydney, where Mr. Fletcher will pass the work through the press, and prepare the boon for circulation among the people.

The last account published by the authority of the Australian Conference, under whose direction the whole of the Wesleyan Missions in the South Seas have been placed, are of a very encouraging character. There are now employed in the Fiji Islands and Rotumah *thirteen European and forty-four native Missionaries*, with upwards of *twenty-five thousand Church members and probationers* under their pastoral care, whilst over *fifty-one thousand scholars* are receiving instruction in the Mission-schools. Of subordinate agents mention is made in the Report of 1 English schoolmaster, 839 catechists, 494 local preachers, 2,260 class-leaders; with 105,947 attendants on public worship in 472 chapels and 891 other preaching places.

Special attention is also given to the training of native agents to enable them to take an efficient and larger share in the great work of evangelising their fellow-countrymen. Besides the training institutions at the head-quarters of each circuit, for several years past an able Missionary has been entirely devoted to this important branch of the work at the Theological Institution at Kandavu, where between forty and fifty of the choicest young men, selected from all parts of Fiji, are receiving instruction of a higher class; and those who have gone forth from this institution have proved its value.

Considering the deeply degraded state of the people, when the Missionaries first arrived at Fiji, thirty-four years ago, and the numerous difficulties with which they have had to contend in the prosecution of their arduous enterprise, the results of their labours are truly astonishing; and they should excite in our hearts feelings of sincere gratitude to Almighty God for what has been already achieved by the power of His Gospel, whilst they encourage us to renewed efforts for the accomplishment of what still remains to be done before the whole of the people can be said to be won for Christ.

CHAPTER X.

INDIA.

THE COUNTRY AND THE PEOPLE—COMMENCEMENT OF WESLEYAN MISSION—CEYLON—MADRAS—BANGALORE—CALCUTTA—LUCKNOW.

WE have now to call the attention of the reader to the origin and progress of the Missionary enterprise in a country and among a people different in many respects from those which have hitherto passed under review. In the East we meet with heathen temples and systems of idolatry and superstitions which bear upon their front evident marks of hoary antiquity, and which are not so easily overthrown. We will not anticipate, however, but proceed at once, according to the plan adopted in other cases, to take a glance at the country and its inhabitants, as preparatory to a brief account of the means employed for their evangelisation.

India, or Hindustan, as it was formerly called, is a large and important portion of the British Empire, situated in Asia, having Persia and Arabia on the west, and China and Burmah on the east, with the Himalaya Mountains on the north, and the Indian Ocean on the south. In a country of such vast extent, comprising an area of one million three hundred thousand square miles, we are not surprised to find almost every variety of climate and scenery; but from its position, chiefly within the tropics, the heat in many places is oppressive during the greatest part of the year, and it is only in a few mountainous districts that a cool and bracing air is generally to be found. Hence the climate of India has proved trying to the European constitution, and only a few Englishmen, who go out early in life, become so acclimatised as to endure a residence there for many years without a change. The general aspect of the country presents to the view towering mountains, dense jungles, and extensive verdant plains, which are almost inundated at certain seasons, and which are thereby rendered very productive, especially in paddy, or rice—an article on which the natives chiefly subsist. In addition to the provisions grown for home consumption, various articles of produce are cultivated in India for exportation; among which may be mentioned hemp, cotton, tobacco, sugar, coffee, rice, spices and drugs of various kinds, and numerous other commodities, to the use of which we have been so long accustomed in England, that we now regard them as included among the common necessaries of life.

The island of Ceylon, which is two hundred and seventy-one miles in length, and one hundred and thirty-seven in breadth, and is separated from the mainland by Palk's Straits, differs in some respects from Continental India. The central portions of the island form a vast mountain plain, enclosed on all sides by rugged heights, with a broad belt of low land stretching round its exterior border, reaching thence to the sea. The celebrated mountain called Adam's Peak, is a conspicuous object from almost every point of view, as it rises to the height of 7,420 feet above the level of the sea, and it is associated, in the minds of the natives, with many curious traditions. Ceylon abounds with extensive forests and vast tracts of fertile land, on which most of the articles already mentioned are cultivated, especially coffee, spices, and some other important items of export.

In turning our attention to the inhabitants of India, we are somewhat perplexed as to the best course to pursue. It is no easy task to give an intelligible and succinct account of a population amounting to one hundred and seventy millions, comprising nations and tribes of such diversity of character, language, and religion, as are found in our vast Indian Empire. It may be sufficient for our present purpose to state that the entire population of Continental

HEATHEN TEMPLES AT BENARES.

India and Ceylon are chiefly Hindus and Mohammedans, with a few Parsees or fire-worshippers. But if we were going into a minute analysis, which is not necessary, we should have to subdivide these two grand classes of religionists, and describe each portion separately. The Mohammedans originally came from Arabia, and at an early period received the Spanish name of Moors, which has ever since been applied to them. Being shrewd, designing, fanatical and powerful, they became the dominant race, both in Ceylon and on the Continent, previous to the advent of the Europeans, and they ruled the poor timid Aborigines with a rod of iron. Their religious system needs no description here, as it is the same in every part of the world where it prevails. It is only necessary to say that, wherever the Moors succeeded in establishing their authority, they required all, by the powerful arguments of fire and sword, to submit to the dogmas of the false prophet.

The Hindus, or original natives of India, whether professedly Buddhist or Brahmins, are Pagans, and consequently idolaters. They build splendid temples to the honour of their numerous gods, in which are set up idols of gold, silver, brass, wood, and stone, frequently of the most hideous and repulsive form. To these idol shrines are brought offerings of food, fruit, and flowers; and although the gods cannot appropriate the offerings, the priests in attendance, who live in ease and indolence, can: and thus the simple people are deceived. Nothing can be more affecting than to see Hindu parents with their children coming to the temple to present their sacrifices to dumb idols, and thus training up the rising generation to worship gods made by the hands of men. But it is on the occasion of their great festivals, when the people congregate to the number of tens of thousands, that the sin and folly of these miserable idolaters are most apparent. Then may be heard the wild and frantic shouts of the multitude as they drag along the car of Juggernaut, crushing beneath its ponderous wheels the wretched victims devoted to destruction, to propitiate their blood-thirsty deities. Then may be seen devotees with iron hooks thrust through their flesh, swinging in the air amid the deafening plaudits of the maddened throng, who regard the act as highly meritorious. And so deluded are these poor heathens, that mothers may often be seen casting their sickly children into the sacred waters of the Ganges, to be devoured by the crocodiles, not so much perhaps with a view to be relieved from attending to them,

THE YOUNG IDOLATER.

as to appease the anger of their cruel gods, to whose displeasure they attribute all the afflictions which come upon them.

Such a state of things is sufficient to awaken in the breast of every true Christian the tenderest emotions of sympathy and sorrow. But, although more than three hundred years have elapsed since the Hindus first came in contact with the pale-faced strangers from the West, comparatively little has yet been done to bring them to a saving knowledge of the truth. When the Portuguese arrived in Ceylon in the beginning of the sixteenth century, and established their rule over a considerable part of the island, they zealously propagated Roman Catholicism; but this did little good, as, in its pompous ceremonies, picture-worship, and moral influence, it was not much better than the Paganism which they found pervading the land. This first race of settlers in Ceylon was superseded by the Dutch in 1556, when a certain kind of Reformation was introduced among the natives. As an inducement to embrace Lutheranism, in preference to Roman Catholicism or Paganism, offices under Government were offered only to such as were baptized into the national faith. This well-meant, but mistaken policy, brought hosts of nominal Christians within the pale of the Church, and to attend the commodious places of worship which were everywhere erected; but it did little for the cause of true religion, as it is well known that many of these professed converts never relinquished their idolatrous rites and ceremonies, but were, in fact, the most accomplished hypocrites.

When, at a later period, nearly the whole of Continental India and Ceylon were brought under British rule, a brighter day dawned upon the country than it had ever seen before. With all its faults, our Government of India has been merciful, mild, and benign, compared with that of its Mohammedan rulers, who previously swayed the sceptre; and it has been more likely to benefit the people than the partial and temporary rule of other European powers which it has in a great measure superseded. At the same time it must be confessed that for many years the British East India Company discouraged every effort that was made to evangelise the Hindus, and even prohibited Christian Missionaries from settling in the country so long as it was in their power to do so. In the midst of numerous difficulties and discouragements, however, the Church, Scottish, London, Baptist, American, Wesleyan, and other Missionary Societies, have done something towards spreading the light of the Gospel among the dark, benighted, teeming millions of India. We now proceed to trace the origin and progress of one important branch of this glorious work.

Commencement of Wesleyan Mission.

The Wesleyan Mission to India, the history of which is so distinctly marked by the providence and grace of God, originated with the venerable Dr. Coke, who has been appropriately styled the "Father of Methodist Missions." The zealous Doctor had already crossed the Atlantic eighteen times; planted Missions, and laboured indefatigably to establish the Word of God in America and in the West Indies; and worked hard for Ireland, to say nothing of his literary toils and travels in England. And now, in the evening of life, at the age of sixty-six, when most men would have thought of taking a little rest, he conceived the noble idea of inaugurating a Methodist Mission to India. In view of his advanced age, and the risk to health and life which his residence in the torrid zone would involve, many of his friends tried to dissuade him from his purpose; but so firmly was he convinced of a Divine call, and so fully was his heart set upon the project, that in writing to one of them, he gave expression to the following noble sentiments:—"I am now dead to Europe, and alive to India. God Himself has said to me, 'Go to Ceylon.' I am so fully convinced of the will of God, that methinks I had rather be set naked on the coast of Ceylon, without clothes, and without a friend, than not go there."

At the Wesleyan Conference of 1813, which assembled in Liverpool in the month of August, Dr. Coke brought forward his proposal for a Mission to India. The certain costliness of the undertaking, and the many difficulties attending it, appeared so formidable that the ministers spent a whole day in discussing the question. The matter being still undecided when the session closed, the Doctor repaired to his lodgings with a heavy heart. The Rev. B. Clough, who accompanied him, afterwards testified that he shed a profusion of tears as they walked along the street, on reference being made to the opposition of some of his brethren to his cherished project. The next morning, when the Conference assembled, the Doctor was absent, and on calling at his lodging, Mr. Clough was admitted to his chamber, and he perceived at once that his venerable friend had passed a night without repose. In fact the man of God intimated to his visitor that he had spent much of it on the floor in prayer for India.

When the Conference met again, the debate on the Indian Mission was resumed; and Dr. Coke, being now in his place, at the proper time arose, and told his brethren all that was in his heart, in an address so clear, and with an appeal so convincing, that every difficulty seemed to disappear. He detailed the Providential circumstances which had led him to desire the establishment of the Mission; the favourable disposition which some men in power had manifested towards it; the grand duty of preaching the Gospel of the Grace of God to the perishing millions of the East; and then, making the offer of himself, and mentioning the proffered services of the Ministers who had consented to " brave with him the dangers of the enterprise," he added boldly and generously, that " if the Connexion could not furnish the means, he would gladly defray the expenses necessary to the outfit and commencement of the work himself, to the extent of six thousand pounds." Awed into acquiescence by so splendid an example of devotion and generosity, his brethren in the Conference at once gave their consent, and Dr. Coke and six young Ministers—namely, the Revs. William Ault, James Lynch, George Erskine, William M. Harvard, Thomas Squance, and Benjamin Clough—were at once appointed to proceed on a Mission to the East Indies.

From the moment that the Conference gave its sanction to the enterprise, Dr. Coke and his companions were busily employed in preparing for their embarkation. Some attention had to be paid to the languages spoken in the East, while at the same time suitable outfits of books and wearing apparel had to be provided. On the zealous little Doctor himself devolved a large amount of care and responsibility connected with stores, passages, and other matters. As it was found impracticable for the whole Mission-party to sail in the same ship, passages were engaged for Dr. Coke, Mr. Clough, and Mr. and Mrs. Harvard, on board the *Cabalva;* and for Messrs. Lynch, Erskine, and Squance, and Mr. and Mrs. Ault, in the *Lady Melville*. It being war time, it was arranged for these vessels to sail in convoy; and every necessary preparation being completed, Dr. Coke and his companions proceeded to Portsmouth in the month of December to join their respective ships. There they had to wait some time, but they were not idle. Some very interesting religious services were held during the period of their detention. Dr. Coke preached his last sermon in England in St. Peter's Chapel, Portsea, from his favourite text, "Ethiopia shall soon stretch out her hands unto God." And when the Mission-party were all together afterwards, he exclaimed with delight, "Here we all are before God, six Missionaries and two dear sisters, now embarked in the most glorious work in the world. Glory be ascribed to His blessed name, that He has given you to be my companions and assistants in carrying the Gospel to the poor Asiatics; and that He has not suffered parents, nor brothers, nor sisters, nor dearest friends, to stop any of you from going with me to India."

A signal having at length been given that the fleet was about to weigh anchor, Dr. Coke and his party met at Mr. Keets', where they spent a short time in singing and prayer. Having thus commended each other to God, they proceeded to embark on board their respective ships on the 29th December. On the following morning, the last day in the year 1813, the beautiful panorama of the Isle of Wight, and the grand sights which Portsmouth, with its towers and spires, its ramparts and battle-ships, presented in time of war, had vanished from their sight, and the fleet was on its way down the English Channel. When tolerably settled on board, and somewhat recovered from sea-sickness, the Missionaries commenced a systematic course of study, to prepare themselves more fully for their great work; and they also held religious services at stated periods, for their own benefit and that of their fellow-passengers.

On the 10th of February, 1814, an event occurred which cast a

PORTSMOUTH.

gloom over the Mission-party. It was known that Mrs. Ault was ill, and that she had been unable to sit up ever since she came on board; but on the morning of that day the Union Jack was seen flying half-mast high on board the *Lady Melville*, and it was soon announced by signal that the dear sufferer had passed away to her eternal rest. The whole fleet joined in the token of mourning, and the same evening her remains were committed to the mighty deep, with a solemn religious service, in hope of a glorious resurrection to eternal life. But this was only a prelude to a still heavier trial which awaited the Mission-party. Whilst several of the brethren had been sick and confined to their cabins, Dr. Coke was generally pretty well, active, and cheerful, although some of the passengers thought that he had, for a few days past, looked more pale than usual. After their usual devotional exercises, he retired to his cabin one night slightly indisposed, accompanied by Mr. Clough, who was wont to see that his venerable friend had everything that was necessary. Before lying down, the Doctor requested to have some medicine brought from the chest, which he intended to take that night. This was done, and various little arrangements made for his comfort. Mr. Clough then requested permission to watch at his side all night; but Dr. Coke thanked him, and said this was not necessary, as he hoped he should be better in the morning. This was the last time that his gentle voice was heard on earth. At half-past five o'clock next morning, the 3rd of May, the faithful attendant, as usual, stood at the Doctor's cabin door, and knocked. He listened in vain for the accustomed acknowledgment. At length, moving the latch, he noiselessly entered the room, and petrified with surprise and awe, beheld the form of the venerable man of God stretched lifeless on the floor.

After recovering in a measure from the shock which this melancholy spectacle had given him, the man hastened to communicate the discovery to Captain Birch, who, startled and perturbed by the intelligence, sent in the first place for Mr. Clough, and made him acquainted with what had come to pass. Endeavouring to master his own agitation, Mr. Clough proceeded to break the news to his colleague and the other brethren on board the *Lady Melville*, which was still in company. It would be in vain to attempt to describe the feelings of intense sorrow and anguish which this mysterious dispensation of Divine Providence produced on the minds of those most immediately concerned. It is distressing to dwell on such a painful subject. It may be sufficient to say, that Captain Birch, having expressed a decided opinion that it would not be prudent to attempt to preserve the remains of the dear departed servant of the Lord till the ship reached her destined port, arrangements were at once made for the funeral at sea; and in the evening, amid the sighs and tears of the Missionaries, the passengers, and the sailors, and with the usual solemn religious service, the body of Dr. Coke was committed to the mighty deep in latitude 2° 29′ south, and longitude 59° 29′ east, "in sure and certain hope of a glorious resurrection to eternal life," in that day when the last trumpet shall sound and "the sea shall give up the dead that are therein."

Believing that this afflictive dispensation of Divine Providence, however dark and mysterious, was intended for some wise and good purpose, the Missionaries endeavoured meekly to bow in humble submission to the will of God, and resolved, in the name and strength of their Divine Master, to do their best to fulfil their important Mission to India. On the 21st of May both ships arrived at Bombay; and as soon as they had cast anchor, Messrs. Harvard and Clough went on board the *Lady Melville* to consult with the other brethren as to the steps it would be necessary to take in their peculiar position. It was now discovered that Dr. Coke had left no letters or papers authorising anyone to draw money or transact any business on his account or that of the Missionary Society, in whose service they were engaged. The Missionaries felt themselves to be in a dilemma; but, implicitly relying on the good providence of God, they brought their case before their Heavenly Father in fervent prayer, and He prepared their way before them. Captain Birch, whose kindness and sympathy for the young evangelists had been uniform and constant from the beginning, and especially in the time of their trial, generously offered to represent the case to Thomas Money, Esq., a respectable merchant in Bombay, to whom Dr. Coke had a letter of introduction. Such was the effect of this representation that when Mr. Harvard, at the request of his brethren, went on shore and presented the said letter to the Indian merchant, he declared his readiness to advance any amount of cash the Missionaries might

BOMBAY.

require, on behalf of the Committee in London, and to render them any service in his power.

After spending about a month in Bombay, the Missionaries embarked for Ceylon, the place of their destination, on the 20th of June, with the exception of Mr. and Mrs. Harvard, who remained some time longer on account of family circumstances. On reaching

Point de Galle, after a pleasant passage of nine days, the brethren met with a most cordial reception from Lord and Lady Molesworth, His Excellency General Brownrigg the Governor, and other friends whom they had never seen before, but who took a lively interest in their welfare in consequence of letters which they had received from Mr. Money and others; so that they were unexpectedly welcomed to the country by persons of station and influence who were in a position to render them essential service.

CEYLON.

But thankful as the Missionaries were for the friendship and hospitality of such distinguished personages as Governor Brownrigg and Lord and Lady Molesworth, and others,—for the Government House being placed at their disposal as a temporary residence, and for the use of the church at Galle on the first Sabbath after their arrival in Ceylon,—they would not have been satisfied without suitable openings for the commencement of their proper Missionary work among the natives. It was not long, however, before their highest wishes were gratified. The Government authorities named several places in the island where ministers of the Gospel were much required, as well as schools for the training of native children. It was also intimated that in aid of the educational department of the work financial grants would willingly be made from Government funds.

After mature deliberation, it was decided to commence stations, in the first place, at Colombo, Galle, and Matura, in the south, among a native population speaking the Singhalese language and at Jaffna and Batticaloa, in the north, where the Tamil language was in common use. Then came the important question of how the preachers should be stationed. This might have been a comparatively easy matter under ordinary circumstances; but this band of zealous young Missionaries had lost their father and their head, and were left without Bishop, President, Chairman, or Superintendent. They seem, however, to have been inspired by a sincere desire to do the work of the Lord anywhere and every-

BRIDGE OF BOATS AT COLOMBO.

where, as He might seem fit to appoint. They foresaw that those Missionaries who might occupy stations where they must necessarily learn the Singhalese language would never be able to interchange with brethren who had acquired a knowledge of Tamil. This consideration seemed to enhance the importance of the question, and made them more earnest in prayer for Divine direction. At length they agreed to fix the appointments by ballot, when it was arranged for Mr. Clough to be stationed at Galle, Mr. Erskine at Matura, Mr. Ault at Batticaloa, and Messrs. Lynch and Squance at Jaffna, whilst Mr. Harvard was to occupy Colombo on his arrival from Bombay. All appeared perfectly satisfied with the arrangement. Not a murmuring word was heard, and it is believed that not a thought or feeling was experienced contrary to perfect acquiescence.

In taking a brief survey of the respective Mission-stations which were established in Ceylon, the first place which demands our attention is Colombo, inasmuch as it is the maritime capital of the island, and the head of the Wesleyan South, or Singhalese, District. The town is situated on the west coast, and is built more in the European style than most other garrison towns in India. It is remarkable for a very strong fort, upwards of a mile in circumference, which stands on the extremity of the peninsula, the sides of which are washed by the waves of the Indian Ocean. A striking and picturesque object which arrests the attention of the visitor is a curiously-constructed bridge of boats, over which he has to pass on entering the town.

The population of the cantonment has been estimated at fifty thousand, and comprises persons of different casts and shades of character, speaking the Singhalese and Portuguese languages. The Rev. W. M. Harvard, the first Missionary who was appointed to this interesting sphere of labour, arrived at Colombo in the month of March 1815, and entered upon his work in the true Missionary spirit. He found a valuable assistant in Mr. A. Armour, a zealous and devoted Christian gentleman who had formerly belonged to the British Army, but who had now retired from military service, and was engaged as Government schoolteacher. Mr. Armour had been a member of the Wesleyan Methodist Society in early life; and, having retained his first love, and laboured to be useful according to his ability in the land of his adoption, he hailed with feelings of gratitude and joy the arrival of a Wesleyan Missionary, and offered him his cordial co-operation.

Mr. Harvard, being a man of considerable mental ability, sound good sense, and gentlemanly manners, was admirably adapted for his position, and he soon won the confidence and goodwill of all classes of the community. His first concern was to make himself more fully acquainted with the languages in which he would have to minister; but, in the meantime, he frequently preached and held other religious services in English, both for the benefit of soldiers and civilians. It was not long, however, before he was able to proclaim the glad tidings of salvation both to Singhalese and Portuguese congregations in their own tongues; and the Word preached came with convincing power to the hearts of some of his hearers. Before the end of the year he formed a class of fifteen members; and thus the foundation of a native church was laid in Colombo, which has continued to prosper from that day to this. In his evangelical labours Mr. Harvard was efficiently aided, not only by his countryman, Mr. Armour, already mentioned, but also by several intelligent native young men who were raised up on the station as the fruit of Missionary labour.

Christian schools were also organised for the training of the rising generation; and, in the course of the following year, a neat and commodious chapel was erected, towards the cost of which the inhabitants of all classes contributed liberally. A printing press was also imported and set up, for the purpose of multiplying copies of portions of the Scriptures and school-books, which were soon translated into the native language, and which were urgently needed as the schools began to make an impression on the population. The superintendence of the printing-office and the educational department of the work at Colombo involved so much labour and responsibility that Mr. Harvard found it necessary to apply for help, and Mr. Clough was instructed to join him. A

Singhalese grammar and dictionary were now compiled and put to press, and the good work expanded and prospered in all its departments—literary, educational, and evangelical. The Colombo station has been served by many able and devoted Missionaries since the holy men who have been mentioned passed away to their heavenly rest, and a goodly number of native ministers have, from time to time, been raised up to take a part in the good work. The city has recently been divided into two circuits, the South (Colpetty) and the North (the Pettah). These, with their headquarters, out-stations, and schools are now worked on an extensive scale, and will, no doubt, in the future, as in the past, be productive of much spiritual good to the people.

At Galle the Dutch church was placed at the service of Mr. Clough, for the time being, and he commenced his labours among a dense but mixed population with characteristic zeal and diligence. Till he acquired the languages of the people among whom his lot was cast, he preached in English to the military and other European residents, who, in many instances, received the Word with gratitude and joy. At the same time attention was paid to the rising generation, and Christian schools were established at this as at other stations, the Missionary communicating with the people, in the commencement, through the medium of an interpreter. But Mr. Clough's superior mental ability and indomitable perseverance soon enabled him to conquer the difficulties of the principal languages of the people, and he began to make known the truths of the Gospel both in Dutch and Singhalese. The blessing of God attended these early efforts, and in a short time a class was formed of twenty hopeful converts. This number was afterwards largely increased, and ultimately commodious chapels were built and schools established, not only in the town of Galle, but also in a number of neighbouring villages, which were formed into an extensive circuit. When Mr. Clough removed to Colombo to assist Mr. Harvard, the station of Galle was worthily occupied by the Rev. John M'Kenny, from the Cape of Good Hope. Under the judicious superintendence of this devoted Missionary, and that of other zealous servants of God who were appointed to labour there from time to time, the station has advanced in importance and usefulness, and been made a great blessing to the people of all classes.

Proceeding southward we come to Matura, where Mr. Erskine commenced his evangelical labours under very favourable circumstances. His reception by the people and mode of proceeding were very similar to those of his brethren on other stations. His time was fully occupied in studying the native languages, establishing Mission-schools, and in preaching the Gospel, as he had opportunity, to both soldiers and civilians in English, and to the natives, first through the medium of an interpreter, and afterwards in the vernacular tongue. On his removal to another station in the north, Mr. Erskine was succeeded in Matura by the Rev. John Callaway, who was sent out from England to strengthen the Mission. Other zealous Missionaries laboured from time to time in this interesting part of the wide field, and, by the blessing of God upon their persevering efforts, a considerable number of hopeful converts were gathered into the fold of Christ, some of whom were called to preach the Gospel to their fellow-countrymen, whilst others were honourably employed as interpreters and teachers in the Mission-schools. Special mention is made of one young man, named Andris, who, although of parents professing Christianity, and baptized in infancy, was for many years a priest of Budha, but was savingly converted to God, and employed as a teacher at a village altogether heathen about half-way between Matura and Galle.

On the stations already mentioned, and in connection with others which were afterwards formed in the south of Ceylon, the principal language used by the Missionaries in preaching to the natives was the Singhalese; but, in order to benefit another important section of the population called "Burghers," descendants of a former race of colonists, a knowledge of Dutch and Portuguese was necessary. As the work expanded, additional Missionaries were sent out from England, and new ground was occupied in various directions. Important stations were ultimately established at Negombo, Kandy, Caltura, Pantura, Seedua, Morotto, Wellewatta, and other places, the history of which, if given in detail, would resemble those of other circuits already described. As the result of the united efforts of the noble band of Missionaries, both European and native, who successively laboured in this part

KANDY.

of the island, a sound Christian education was given to a considerable portion of the rising generation, many heathens were converted to the faith and hope of the Gospel, whilst more correct views of the nature of true religion were made to prevail among professing Christians of every grade of society.*

We must now turn to the North, and take a view of the Tamil department of the work in Ceylon. The most important station, and the head of the District, is Jaffna, to which Messrs. Lynch and Squance were appointed when the work was apportioned on the arrival of the first Missionaries. Jaffna is situated on the northern point of the island, and is regarded as the capital of an extensive district called Jaffnapatam. The population is large, but it does not materially differ in its general features from that of other parts of the country; only here the prevailing language among the natives is Tamil, whilst that of the south is chiefly Singhalese. When the Missionaries first arrived they were struck with the ignorance, superstition, and degradation of all classes of people, whether professedly Christians, Mohammedans, or Pagans. Many of the descendants of the Dutch and Portuguese, who still made use of the respective languages of those nations, seemed to be as deeply degraded as the Aborigines themselves; and there appeared to be a loud call for Missionary labour. Numerous difficulties had to be encountered at Jaffna, such as had not been experienced in the south; but, by diligence and perseverance, they were ultimately overcome. Commodious premises were

---

* In the months of July and August 1869, special services were held in several of the circuits of the South Ceylon District, which resulted in a very remarkable revival of religion. At Kandy "thirty-five persons professed to have received a sense of God's pardoning love: of these ten were Singhalese. At a band-meeting held on the Sunday following about forty persons stood up and spoke of what God had done for their souls." In another circuit, at one of the services, "fourteen souls tasted of the joys of salvation." After another meeting it was found that "seven others, including a Buddhist, had experienced a saving change." At another place "every house was opened for prayer-meetings, and seventy-five persons were made to rejoice in knowing that God for Christ's sake had pardoned their sins." From another station it is reported, "Ten persons have found Jesus, and one or two Buddhists have joined the Society." At Pantura there were "sixty-six persons who found peace in one week." At Galle there were "seventeen penitents, of whom twelve obtained the blessing. A love-feast on the Monday following concluded the services, at which fourteen spoke, giving a clear testimony as to their acceptance with God." "The special services at Matura were also successful."

MISSION-SCHOOL AND CHAPEL AT JAFFNA.

secured for the use of the Mission, and an elegant and substantial chapel and school-house were erected, a view of which we are able to present to the reader, and the foundation of a great and good work was laid which has continued to prosper to the present time. When the arduous task of learning the languages had been accomplished, and two or three native assistants had been raised up, the work rapidly extended to other places in the north, chapels being built and schools established, not only in the villages adjacent to Jaffna, but in places at a considerable distance, which were ultimately occupied as separate stations.

On the eastern coast of Ceylon, at the head of a deep bay, stands the important town and fortress of Batticaloa. To this station the Rev. William Ault was appointed on the arrival of the first party of Missionaries. It will be remembered that Mr. Ault had lost his beloved wife by death on her passage to India, and the bereaved young Missionary proceeded to his lonely station with a heavy heart. Being a man of genuine piety and entire devotedness to God, and of a meek and humble spirit, he endeavoured to reconcile his mind to the afflictive dispensation of Divine Providence with which he had been visited, and entered upon his work at Batticaloa with a full determination to spend and be spent in the cause of his Divine Master. At this, as at some other places, there was a church without a clergyman, and the building was politely placed at the disposal of the Missionary by the Government authorities, till permanent Mission buildings could be erected. A very favourable impression was made upon the minds of the people by the zealous manner in which Mr. Ault commenced his ministerial labours; but whilst engaged in studying the native languages, and in preaching by an interpreter, and otherwise exerting himself in the work of the Mission, he was seized with an illness which baffled the skill of the physician and terminated fatally. Having been prostrated by fever repeatedly, the final attack came at last, and the faithful servant of the Lord was called to rest from his labours on the 1st of April, 1815,—the first of a considerable number of Wesleyan Missionaries who have fallen a sacrifice to the climate of India. It is a true saying that

"God buries His workmen, but still carries on His work." The vacant station of Batticaloa was soon occupied by another Missionary; and such was the success which attended the labours of the Rev. Messrs. Jackson, Osborne, Erskine, and others who were appointed to labour there in succession, that it was ultimately divided into two Circuits, and the work was extended to various parts of the surrounding country.

When the Ceylon Mission had been efficiently reinforced by the arrival of several brethren from England, a Missionary was stationed at Point Pedro, which was made the head of a separate circuit, after having been supplied for a length of time from Jaffna. Another place which was occupied by the Society with great advantage to all classes of the community, at an early period, was Trincomalee, on the eastern coast, where chapels were erected, schools established, and native converts gathered into the fold of Christ, the same as on other stations. Indeed, the plans adopted for carrying on the work of God in Ceylon, and the results which everywhere followed the faithful preaching of the Gospel, were so similar, that a more detailed account of each station would be superfluous. In connection with the progress of the Mission several interesting incidents occurred on which it would have been pleasant to dwell, but we must confine ourselves to a few observations on the native agents that were raised up to take a part in the great and glorious work.

The most prominent of these was a young man named John Philips Sanmugam, whose parents, being professing Christians, had presented him for baptism in his infancy, and afterwards sent him to a school taught by Christian David, a convert of the celebrated German Missionary Schwartz. When the boy was fifteen years of age, and began to think of doing something for himself in the world, Mr. Squance arrived at Jaffna, and began to preach with a power and unction previously unknown in that place. Sanmugam was much interested in the proceedings of the Wesleyan Missionary, who officiated in the Dutch church in the fort, and was seriously impressed with the truths which he heard preached. Some time afterwards the native youth became personally acquainted with

Mr. Squance, who was made the honoured instrument, in the hands of God, of leading him to Christ. In return for the kind attentions he received at the Mission-house, young Philips, as he was now generally called, manifested a cheerful readiness to assist the Missionary to the utmost of his power in the good work in which he was engaged. He daily read the Scriptures in Tamil with Mr. Squance, and thus aided him in the acquisition of that difficult language, whilst at the same time his own mind was enriched with the precious treasures of Divine truth, as expounded by his benefactor. John Philips was then employed as a Mission-school teacher and catechist, and ultimately as a Native Minister, having carefully prepared himself by diligent study for the highest department of the work of God. For some time subsequently to his having devoted himself fully to the work of the Mission, the young evangelist was associated with Dr. Hoole, at Negapatam, on the Continent, and gave great satisfaction by the zeal and earnestness with which he served his Divine Master.

Soon after he returned to Ceylon, in 1829, Mr. Philips was sent by the Rev. Joseph Roberts on a Mission to the western shore of the island, to preach to a large concourse of people who assembled there at the season of pearl-fishing. Here he was "in labours more abundant;" and by his fidelity in proclaiming the glad tidings of salvation, distributing tracts, visiting the sick, especially during the prevalence of cholera, he was instrumental in the salvation of many precious souls. Thus during a long and useful life did Mr. Philips labour for the spiritual welfare of his fellow-countrymen, till worn out with incessant toil, he finished his course, and fell asleep in Jesus, on the 22d of April, 1864, in the sixty-fifth year of his age—a fine specimen of a large number of native Ministers and teachers who have been raised up as the fruit of our Missions in Ceylon and Continental India.

If we were to pursue this interesting theme of a native ministry further, we should have to speak of Richard Watson, W. A. Salmon, Paul Rodrigs, and a host of others, some of whom have been called to their reward in heaven, whilst others are still spared to labour in the Lord's vineyard. It may suffice to say, however, that the Wesleyan Mission to Ceylon has been a grand success; and, if faithfully prosecuted, it will no doubt be a still greater blessing in time to come. The unwearied labours formerly of such men as Robert Newstead, Joseph Roberts, Daniel Gogerly, Robert Spence Hardy, and more recently of John Walton, John Scott, John Kilner, and many others, in addition to the Missionary

NATIVE MISSIONARY.

pioneers already mentioned, have had a rich reward. But a still more blessed recompense awaits the faithful servants of the Lord in the world to come. There are now in connection with the North and South Districts into which the island of Ceylon is divided, *thirty-one Missionaries, one thousand five hundred and ninety-four Church members, and three thousand seven hundred and sixty-five scholars* in the Mission-schools.

MADRAS.

Madras is the capital of the British possessions on the east side of the peninsula of Hindustan. The city stands on the margin of the Bay of Bengal, and is of vast extent, stretching along the shore a distance of nine miles, and between three and four miles inland. The great centre of population in this large area is known as Black Town, which is separated from Fort St. George by a broad and open esplanade. In common with all the European settlements on this coast, Madras has no port for shipping, and every vessel which arrives must cast anchor in the roads at a considerable distance from the shore, which is washed by a heavy surf that sometimes makes landing difficult, if not dangerous. As viewed from the sea this part of the city presents a somewhat imposing appearance. A line of substantial and handsome buildings, often three stories high, and each protected from the sun with a broad verandah, is seen extending for a mile along the beach, and includes merchant's offices, law courts, the custom-house, and the terminus of the Madras Railway. Behind this line of buildings are narrow streets occupied by the humbler classes of English and East Indians, with crowded shops or bazaars, markets, temples, mosques, and churches of various denominations of Christians. Within the municipal limits of Madras there are also several large surburban villages, each numbering its native population by tens of thousands. The broad intervals between these villages are occupied by the spacious residences of English merchants and other civilians, surrounded by park-like gardens. The population of Madras is estimated at half a million, and although the first Protestant church erected in Hindustan was built there, and more Missionary effort has been put forth in this city than in any other place in India, it is believed that more than three-fourths of the people are still heathen, and loudly call for the sympathy and aid of British Christians.

It was in the year 1817 that the first Wesleyan Missionary commenced his labours in this part of India. A few pious Methodists from England residing there, had been in the habit of meeting together for the purpose of prayer and Christian fellowship, and to read Mr. Wesley's sermons for their mutual edification. They heard with delight of the arrival of Wesleyan Missionaries in Ceylon, and earnestly requested that one of the party might be spared to labour among them. This reasonable wish was readily met by the British Conference, and Mr. Harvard was appointed to Madras. But the claims upon this devoted Missionary at Colombo, in connection with the Mission-press and the work of translation, was such as to prevent his removal to the Continent without serious injury to the cause. It was therefore ultimately arranged that Mr. Lynch should go to commence the Mission at Madras. The arrival of this zealous servant of God marked the commencement of a new era in the populous heathen city which we have described. His statements of Christian experience, and especially his distinct enunciations of the doctrine of the direct witness of the Spirit, were such as had never been heard there before. All classes wondered at his boldness and success. His talent for reproving sin was extraordinary, and wherever he went, he was hailed as a faithful Minister of Christ. During the time that Mr. Lynch laboured in Madras, he was instrumental in the erection of a beautiful new chapel for English services in the centre of the East India population of Black Town, which he left entirely free from debt. He also witnessed the gathering into the fold of Christ of a goodly number of hopeful converts as the seals to his earnest ministry.

The work thus auspiciously commenced in Madras has been zealously maintained ever since, and the faithful preaching of the Gospel, in connection with the educational department of the Mission, has been made a great blessing to the people. Among the devoted Ministers who have laboured here, but who have long since passed away to their reward in heaven, the names of Jonathan Crowther, Joseph Roberts, and Thomas Cryer, are deservedly held in grateful remembrance by a few of the surviving old members. Other zealous Ministers have entered into their labours, who are still spared to the Church of Christ. The chapel, which was considerably enlarged in 1861, will seat about five hundred persons, and it is generally filled on Sunday evenings. The English Missionary on the Madras station is entirely supported by the members of the church and congregation to whom he ministers, and they also contribute liberally towards the support of the Mission cause generally.

But, whilst thus careful to provide for the spiritual welfare of Europeans and their descendants in India, the Wesleyan Missionary Society is not unmindful of their chief work among the Hindus. They have, moreover, expected that the English work in Madras would be auxiliary to that which is carried on directly for the benefit of the natives. Nor have they in this been disappointed. Black Town has given both men and money, and the native Church will not soon be able to repay the debt of gratitude she owes to her elder sister for her friendly aid in various ways. For many years it was customary to hold Tamil services in the vestibule of the English chapel, for the benefit of a small native society and congregation. But in 1859, by the exertion of the Missionaries, aided by a committee of the English congregation, a commodious Tamil chapel was built close to the English sanctuary; and this is now the centre of the Madras North (Tamil) Circuit, where an important native work has for several years been carried on.

The Madras South (Tamil) Circuit has its centre at Royapettah, a populous district three miles distant from Black Town, where the Wesleyan Mission concentrates its principal labours. The Mission premises are of ample dimensions, and occupy a "compound," or lot of land, some acres in extent. The most conspicuous building is the native chapel, which stands in a convenient position near to the conjunction of several roads. Neat, substantial, and well-built, this sanctuary is no bad specimen of Indian architecture. It will seat about five hundred persons. Venetian folding-doors on three sides take the place of windows; which, standing open during Divine service, invite passers-by to enter and hear the Word of Life. Many have thus been brought under the saving influence of the Gospel, and been led to unite themselves with the people of God.

If we were to enter this chapel on a Sabbath morning we should behold a beautiful sight. The males and females sit apart, after the manner of olden times in England, as arranged by Mr. Wesley. The foremost seats on the women's side are occupied by the neatly clad girls of the boarding-school, and the corresponding seats on the other side, in part, by the young converts from the boy's school. Behind these are arranged the elder members of the church and congregation. The worshippers are generally of the poorer classes of the community; for in India, as in other places, "not many mighty, not many noble are called." If we remain during the service, we shall hear loud and earnest singing, if it be not very melodious. The language is Tamil, and the hymn, which is one of Wesley's, was translated by that excellent Missionary, Elijah Hoole, in his youthful days. The preacher is a native Minister; his face is as dark as those of his hearers, now upturned towards him in wrapt attention, but it glows with affection and zeal in his Master's service. If it is the day for public adult baptisms, we are struck with the promptitude and earnestness with which the native converts answer the questions proposed, and assign their reasons for renouncing heathenism and embracing Christianity, whether we can understand their language or not; and when we remember the persecution to which the native Christians are frequently exposed, and that by thus espousing the cause of Christ, these poor converted Hindus may be severing themselves from home and kindred, and everything dear to a feeling heart, we cannot fail to be convinced that the work must be of God which can produce such wonderful results.

Immediately behind the native chapel which we have described, is the noble range of buildings occupied by the Anglo-Vernacular Schools. These buildings were erected, and the institution brought into excellent working order, several years ago, through the instrumentality of the Rev. Messrs. Jenkins, Hobday, and Burgess, who have occupied the station in succession. The gentleman last named has been the longest connected with the institution, and to his unwearied exertions and able superinten-

INDIA.

PERSECUTION OF NATIVE CHRISTIANS.

dence is to be mainly attributed the efficient state to which the establishment has been brought.

If we accompany Mr. Burgess and look into the boys' school first, we shall witness a strange sight. On entering the large hall, we see standing in orderly groups nearly three hundred youths, perhaps a dozen wear English dress, a few the coloured loose silk drawers of the Mahommedans, but the great majority the white tunic of the Hindu; all, except the English lads, leave their slippers at the entrance of the building, but wear their turbans. Going to his desk in the centre of the hall, the Missionary kneels, and asks the Divine blessing on the labours of the day. The first lesson is from the Holy Scriptures, taught in every class by a Christian teacher; and many pleasing instances have occurred in which heathen youths have been convinced and converted by means of the truths brought home to their hearts and consciences in the course of these exercises. English literature is probably the next subject of study, when the works of Goldsmith, Macaulay, or De Quincey, are familiarly used as text-books. Then follow lessons in the histories of England and of India, in geography, astronomy, or chemistry.

The conducting of such an institution is a heavy tax upon the time and strength of a Missionary, and some may doubt whether he is right in devoting himself so much to secular teaching. But it must be remembered that it is the desire for such teaching that attracts the pupils, and makes them willing to listen to higher truth. It is a fact, moreover, that each lesson the Missionary gives in Western literature or science, not only tends to undermine the faith of the Hindu in his ancestral religion, and prepare him to receive the truth as it is in Jesus, but it increases the influence his instructor has over him. The institution is chiefly supported by the fees of the pupils, which in the year 1867 amounted to £254 4s. 6d. The Wesleyan Missionary Society has eight of these Anglo-Vernacular Schools in the Madras District; but the one we have described is the largest and the most important.

When female education was first proposed in India, it seemed a strange paradox to the Hindu mind, and it was met with the most strenuous opposition. Native prejudice has, however, been to a considerable extent overcome, and a number of schools for the training of Hindu girls have been established in connection with our various stations in British India, especially since the organisation of the Ladies' Committee for the promotion of female education in connection with the Wesleyan Missionary Society. None of these institutions are more important or more prosperous than the girls' school at Royapettah, Madras. Near to the buildings already described, but further back, and almost concealed from view by the straight branches of silk cotton trees and the thick foliage of the mangoes, is the girls' boarding school. The building at present occupied was opened on the 21st of November, 1867, and it has been pronounced the neatest and most commodious erection of the kind in Madras. It occupies nearly the same site as the former establishment, in which, for twenty years, about forty poor native girls had been fed, clothed, and taught, whilst others attended as day scholars. The cast prejudices of the Hindus make it impossible to secure, as pupils in such an establishment, the daughters of the higher classes, so that the school has been recruited chiefly from the families of servants in English employment. A few of the girls have Protestant Christian parents, several are of Roman Catholic origin, but the majority have been rescued from heathen homes. In the school all are treated with equal consideration and kindness. They are taught to read and write Tamil with fluency; they become familiar with the elementary rules of arithmetic, so as to be able to keep bazaar accounts; they gain some knowledge of geography; and those who have been longest in the school can read an easy English book, and converse in that language on familiar subjects. All are instructed in the Conference Catechisms, and made familiar with the leading events of Scripture history, whilst singing is a favourite exercise. The elder girls are drafted in rotation for duty in the kitchen, and thus become acquainted with practical household work, as well as with the use of the needle, in which they greatly excel. But what is more pleasing still, every year a few of the pupils are brought under religious influences and received into the Church by baptism, and at least twelve or fifteen of these Christian girls are members of the Society. On more than one occasion the school has been blessed with special visitations of the Holy Spirit, and the girls have met together for prayer in their hours of recreation, when many have found peace with God through faith in Christ Jesus. Thus conducted on genuine Christian principles, our Mission-schools become nurseries of the church, and important auxiliaries to the efforts which are put forth by the Missionaries for the advancement of the Redeemer's kingdom.

After the accounts we have given of a few Mission-stations and schools, as specimens of a large number of others which might have been described with equal fulness, our references to the remaining circuits in the Madras District must necessarily be brief. At an early period after the commencement of the work in Continental India, stations were formed and schools established at St. Thomas's Mount, Negapatam, Manaragoody, and Trichinopoly, and more recently at Melnattam, Warriore, Trivalore, and Caroor. At all these places the Gospel is faithfully preached, both in English and Tamil, and a goodly number of natives have been converted, from time to time, and gathered into the fold of the Redeemer, whilst the sphere of the Society's labours is continually widening by the occupation of new ground, and the formation of out-stations. The trials and difficulties which the Missionaries have to experience in carrying on the work on the respective stations are so similar, as well as the modes of operation in seeking to enlighten the minds of the dark benighted people, that it is unnecessary to dwell at greater length on the progress of the work from year to year. The greatest drawback to the prosperity of the Mission has been the frequent removal of the Missionaries in consequence of the failure of health. This has been in a measure compensated by the raising up of a number of native Ministers to preach the Gospel to their fellow-countrymen in their own vernacular tongue; and it is hoped that in time to come still more will be qualified and called of God to engage in this noble enterprise.

Among the numerous instances of providential interposition by which the early history of our Mission in India was marked, none is more worthy of notice than the burning of the *Tanjore*. This noble ship sailed from Gravesend, on the 19th of May, 1820, with the Rev. James and Mrs. Mowat, and the Rev. Elijah Hoole on board, besides Sir Richard Otley, Mr. and Mrs. Browning, of the Church Missionary Society, and two Singhalese converts, who had been educated in England under the care of Dr. Clarke, and other passengers. Nothing very particular occurred during the former part of the passage, which occupied more than three months; but on approaching the shores of India, a sad disaster occurred. On Sunday morning, the 3rd of September, the ship made the Island of Ceylon to the eastward of Point de Galle. Not being able to reach the port, the wind and current being adverse, she steered for Batticaloa. On Tuesday, the 5th, she came to anchor off the river, and landed Sir Richard Otley and suite, Mr. and Mrs. Browning, and the other Ceylon passengers. On the following day, about noon, having finished her business with the port, the *Tanjore* weighed anchor, and stood away for Madras, with a light breeze and fine weather, but at sunset the sky assumed a threatening aspect.

Then came a fearful thunderstorm, and about eight o'clock the ship was struck with lightning, and immediately set on fire. The consternation occasioned by an event so sudden and appalling may be more readily imagined than described. The captain used every possible effort to quench the flames, which first appeared in the main hold, but finding the fire and smoke increasing in all directions, and seeing no prospect of subduing the devouring element, he ordered the boats to be got ready. All on board now made haste to leave the burning ship, and the scene of confusion and dismay was indescribable; the darkness of the night, relieved only by vivid flashes of lightning, which had already proved fatal to two of the seamen, adding to the terror which prevailed. At length all the survivors, forty-eight in number, got into the boats, and made their escape, nothing being saved except a compass, the ship's papers, and a box of dollars. In this trying hour the

Missionaries were enabled to look up in faith and prayer to their heavenly Father, and to commend themselves and their companions to His care and protection. For some time the burning ship was driven after the boats by the tempest, and appeared to pursue them like a thing of life. At length they got out of its track, and with peculiar feelings, during that long and gloomy night, they watched the burning mass till all was quenched in darkness.

Early on the following morning they caught sight of land, which gladdened their hearts, and about ten o'clock they fell in with a native boat, which took them all on board. They now found that they were about fifteen miles from Trincomalee, for which port they immediately steered, being anxious to get on shore as soon as possible. The current being against them, it was not till the next morning that they were able to reach the port. The Mission-party landed in pitiful plight; poor Mrs. Mowat was without bonnet or anything of her own to cover her, and Mr. Hoole was without a hat; but they were truly thankful for life, and rejoiced to be permitted to set their feet on the shores of India, after such a remarkable interposition of Divine Providence on their behalf. They were kindly received by the Rev. Messrs. Carver and Stead, the resident Missionaries at Trincomalee, who soon supplied them with a few necessary articles of clothing, and, after resting a few days, they proceeded to Madras, where they safely arrived on the 17th of September. It is pleasing to be able to add, that the two devoted Missionaries, thus mercifully preserved in the hour of peril, were spared to render important service to the Church of Christ for many years, both at home and abroad, and that they both still survive after the lapse of nearly half a century since the occurrence of this affecting incident, Dr. Hoole being the esteemed and worthy senior Secretary of the Wesleyan Missionary Society, and Mr. Mowat a venerable and happy retired Minister on the list of honourable Supernumeraries.

Although the Wesleyan Missionary Society has been labouring in this part of Continental India for more than fifty years, the work is still, to a considerable extent, of a preparatory character. Religious knowledge is being extensively diffused by means of

Mission-schools and the faithful preaching of the Gospel; and it is hoped that the ancient systems of idolatry and superstition, by which the people have been so long deluded, are being sapped at their foundation. In the meantime, the value and importance of the Mission must not be estimated by its statistical results, but by the influence it is exerting upon a heathen people, "sitting in darkness and in the shadow of death." In connection with the respective stations comprised in the Madras district, we have now *seventeen Missionaries, two hundred and eight Church members, and two thousand one hundred and six scholars* in the Mission-schools.

BANGALORE.

The province of Mysore embraces a large tract of country in the interior of the peninsula of Hindostan, situated between the east and west ridges of the Ghauts, and forming a high table-land nearly three thousand feet above the level of the sea. This district is in some places subject to drought, and altogether less fertile and productive than many other parts of Southern India; but by artificial means, such as dams and tanks, the water is collected from numerous rivers and mountain torrents in large quantities for the purpose of irrigation, and considerable crops of cotton, sugar, rice, and other articles are raised. From its elevated position, the Mysore is favoured with a climate comparatively temperate and healthy; and if the extensive jungle, amid which the elephant and other wild beasts still roam at their pleasure, were more fully cleared, and the country more generally opened up to cultivation, fever and cholera would, perhaps, entirely disappear.

The localities which are inhabited sustain a dense population of a somewhat mixed character, both the Tamil and Canarese languages being extensively spoken. The province is under the nominal government of a native Rajah, but it is in reality subject to British rule, in common with the surrounding territory of the Madras presidency. Although not, properly speaking, the capital of the province, Bangalore is the most populous and important city in the country. Here the British Government keep up a large military establishment, and here also have been located the headquarters of the Wesleyan Missionary Society in the Mysore district for many years, during which all possible means have been employed to shed the light of Divine truth on the surrounding darkness.

As early as 1820, an earnest request from Bangalore had reached the Missionary Committee in London, that Missionaries might be sent to that important centre of population in Southern India; and encouraged by the character of the beginning which had been made in Ceylon and Madras, the Rev. Messrs. Mowat and Hoole were selected and set apart for this service. On their voyage to India, these devoted servants of the Lord were shipwrecked, and "suffered the loss of all things" by the burning of the *Tanjore*, as already stated. This circumstance, together with the demand for Missionary labour in Madras and Negapatam, where some of the brethren were laid aside by illness, prevented the two Missionaries from proceeding up the country to their appointed sphere of labour so soon as they intended. It was not till the month of May, in the following year, that Mr. Hoole arrived in Bangalore, which is about two hundred miles from Madras, and where he was joined a few weeks afterwards by Mr. Mowat. They met with a very kind reception, and appeared to have received a favourable impression of the place as a promising field of Missionary labour. In their communications to the parent Society, they describe the Fort of Bangalore as square, regularly built, fortified by a ditch and wall, and by a quantity of jungle or thick underwood, permitted to grow on every side, with a view to hinder the swift approach of banditti, who were accustomed to come upon the people unawares for the purpose of spoil and plunder. The scenery of the surrounding country was similar to that which prevails in other parts of India, and the habits of the people were simple in the extreme; but all were involved in midnight heathen darkness.

The population of the Pittah, or suburb, was estimated at thirty thousand, consisting chiefly of Canarese, who sustained themselves by their manufactures and cultivation, and of a number of people

SCENE IN INDIA.

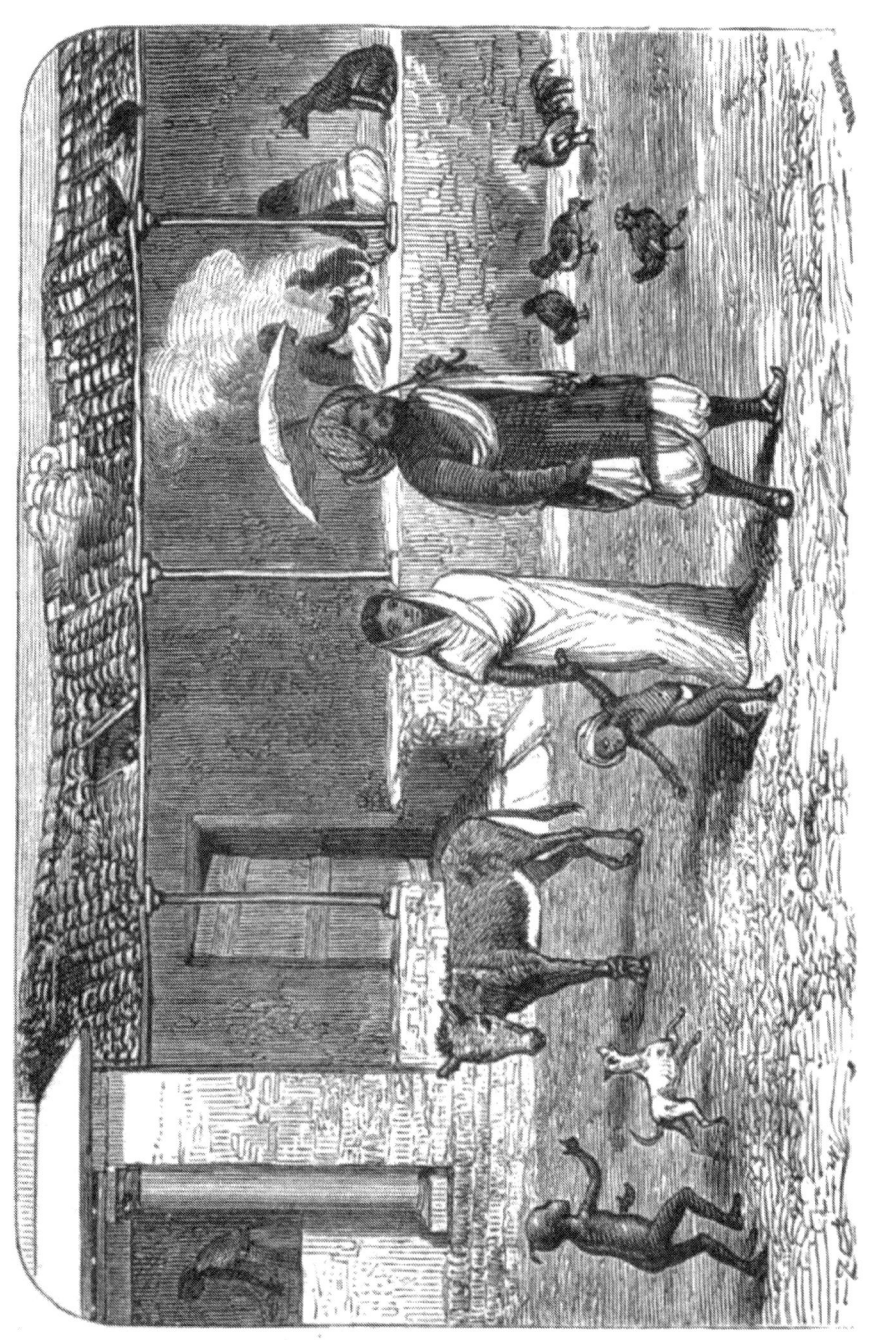

from various places, who use the Tamil language. The cantonment, built for the accommodation of the troops, is described as being about a mile distant from the Pettah. The bungalows occupied by the British officers and other Europeans, presented the appearance of a neat English village, whilst the bazaars and huts built by the followers of the army formed a town as large and populous as the Pettah itself. With a few exceptions this part of the population spoke Tamil, and understood no other language, so that to them especially the Missionaries hoped to be made useful at once, having acquired some knowledge of that dialect during the time that they were assisting their brethren on the coast.

On their arrival at Bangalore, the Missionaries found that Hinduism and Mahommedanism were the predominent religious systems there, the same as in other parts of the Mysore and Southern India generally; and the natives were addicted to the usual idolatrous and superstitious rites and ceremonies. Mr. Hoole, having made considerable progress in the acquisition of Tamil, commenced immediately after his arrival to hold open-air services, at which he generally preached first, and then held familiar conversations with the people on the important truths of the Gospel. On the arrival of Mr. Mowat, arrangements were made for conducting public services in a native house which was obtained for the purpose. The first of these was held on the 20th of July, 1821, and, difficult as it was to get Hindus to enter a place set apart for Christian worship, twenty-seven natives were present, and on the following Friday the congregation numbered thirty-three. The Missionaries were, moreover, encouraged by the spirit of enquiry and attention manifested by the people who came to be instructed in Bangalore, as well as by the result of their visits to other promising places in the province of Mysore during the time that they occupied the station. We regret to state, however, that before steps could be taken to erect suitable buildings and fully organise the Mission, both Missionaries were called away to supply vacancies which had occurred at Madras and Negapatam through the failure of the health of some of the brethren.

During the following two or three years, Bangalore was left without a resident Missionary, being only visited occasionally as opportunities presented themselves. But in 1826 the station was occupied once more by the appointment of the Rev. John F. England, who commenced his labours under circumstances as favourable as could be expected, all things considered. He directed his attention in the first place to the European troops in the cantonment, a considerable number of whom attended the English services, which he held chiefly for their benefit. Several of the soldiers were brought under the saving influence of Divine truth, gave their hearts to God, and were united in Church fellowship in a class formed expressly for them. At the same time, the Missionary did not neglect the heathen population around him, but as soon as he was conversant with the Tamil language, he began to preach the Gospel to the people in their own tongue. Native classes were also formed for the religious instruction of enquirers, who were led to renounce their heathenish practices and embrace the truth as it is in Jesus. A considerable number of these ultimately gave satisfactory evidence of genuine conversion to God, and the foundation of a native Christian Church was laid, which has continued to grow and expand from year to year, even to the present time.

Mr. England was enabled to report before long that he regularly conducted four services weekly, in three places of worship—two in Tamil and two in English. He also reported the baptism of a number of converted natives, particularly of a whole heathen family, and the subsequent exemplary conduct of the adults, who all appeared deeply concerned for their personal salvation. Schools were also established for the instruction of the rising generation of both sexes, and the Bangalore station was placed on a permanent and substantial footing. On the removal of Mr. England from this interesting sphere of labour, he was succeeded by the Rev. Messrs. Cryer, Hardy, Male, Arthur, and other devoted Missionaries, and by the blessing of God upon their zealous labours, the good work continued to prosper in all its departments.

For several years the religious services in Bangalore were conducted in English and Tamil only, in consequence of the agents employed being unacquainted with any other language; but in 1836, the Rev. Thomas Hodson, who understood Canarese, having been appointed to the station, he began at once to preach in that tongue. Thus a new department of Missionary labour was entered upon, which was ever afterwards followed up and attended with a pleasing measure of success. The designation of Mr. Hodson to Bangalore and the Mysore appears to have been peculiarly fitting and providential; for he has spent more than a quarter of a century in connection with our Mission in that country, and he still labours there with an earnestness and zeal worthy of the highest commendation. As the result of his unwearied efforts, combined with those of his excellent colleagues, from time to time, the Bangalore station has risen to a high state of efficiency. The Mission-house, chapels, schoolrooms, and other buildings, which have been erected at different periods, and at little or no expense to the Society's funds, are on a convenient and ample scale; and the new sanctuary which stands at the end of the esplanade is said to be the largest and the best Methodist Chapel in Asia. The printing establishment, which has sent forth tens of thousands of copies of portions of the Scriptures and other good books, is second to none in India, whilst the schools for the training of children, and the education of more advanced pupils, will bear a comparison with those of Royapettah, Madras, already described, or with any similar establishments in any part of the world. And, best of all, the Gospel of Christ, as faithfully preached by the Missionaries in English, Tamil, and Canarese, not only in the beautiful places of worship which have been erected, but in the bazaars and streets of the city, and in twenty-five surrounding villages, has been made the power of God unto salvation to many precious souls.

Almost simultaneously with the first efforts which were made, by the Wesleyan Missionary Society for the evangelization of Bangalore and its neighbourhood, attention was directed to Seringapatam, that last grand stronghold of Mahommedan despotism in Southern India. At that time the fortifications of the city had been dismantled, and the gigantic ruins which were seen on every hand presented to the view striking evidences of the power and grandeur of the celebrated TIPPOO SAIB, who fell in his last struggle for supremacy, when the city was captured by the British in 1799. The place had still a population of about fifty thousand, among whom were a few God-fearing people, chiefly Europeans and their descendants, who had built a small place of worship and met together for reading and prayer every Sabbath;

ORIENTAL TRAVELLING.

but, having no minister, they felt their destitute condition, and made an earnest request for a Wesleyan Missionary to labour among them. In response to this appeal, the Rev. Titus Close paid them a visit in the month of May 1821, when he was welcomed with feelings of gratitude, known only to those who have been long deprived of a Gospel ministry. On the Saturday evening after his arrival, Mr. Close delivered the first sermon that was ever preached in the little church that had been erected in Seringapatam, and on the Sabbath, and during the following week, he was constantly engaged in dispensing the Word of Life, administering the sacrament of the Lord's Supper, marrying, baptizing, and visiting the people. On entering the little sanctuary, at an early hour on Sunday morning, the Missionary had an opportunity of witnessing the mode of worship adopted by a few Christian natives, when left without a regular pastor. About twenty were assembled together, and the person conducting the service was a modest and respectable country-born female, who read the Scriptures and the Prayers in Malabar with great propriety, she being the only individual in the place capable of doing so; and after the second lesson, the Missionary stepped forward and married a couple, according to previous arrangement.

As a Missionary could not be spared at that time to reside at Seringapatam, arrangements were made for the place to be visited once a quarter from Bangalore. This duty devolved most frequently upon Mr. Hoole during his connection with that station; and his earnest ministry and diligent pastoral attention made a deep impression upon the minds of the people, and were remembered with gratitude many years afterwards. At length, when the Mission in Southern India had been re-inforced by the arrival of additional labourers from England, a Missionary was set apart for Seringapatam and the City of Mysore conjointly. Chapels were now erected and schools established at both places; and although the Mission cannot as yet boast of great apparent results, the foundation of a good work has been laid, which, with the Divine blessing, will be productive of much good in time to come. The City of Mysore is the capital of the province, and the place where the reigning Rajah has his regal palace and splendid equipage of tame elephants and household troops. This distinguished personage, although a rigid Hindu, is favourable to the Wesleyan Mission, and patronises the educational department of the work especially in various ways. The Mission-schools have already made a deep impression in favour of Christianity, and a few converted natives have been united in Church fellowship.

As the work expanded, Mission-stations were ultimately formed at Coonghul, Goobbee, Toomkoor, Shemoga, and other places;

but the dark benighted state of the people, the means employed for their enlightenment, and the trials and difficulties of Missionary life are everywhere so similar that it is unnecessary to enter into a minute description of every place where chapels have been built and schools established. It may be sufficient to say, that in connection with our Mission to Bangalore, and other important centres of population in the Mysore country, a considerable amount of success has been realised, and a power is at work which, it is hoped, will help to sap the foundation of idolatry in British India, and hasten the coming of the Redeemer's kingdom. We have at present in the Mysore District *fifteen Missionaries, two hundred and seventy-three Church members, and two thousand eight hundred and seventy-four scholars* in the Mission-schools.

Calcutta, &c.

A considerable number of Wesleyans from England having from time to time settled in Calcutta, the capital of Bengal, they were very anxious to have a Minister of their own denomination to labour among them; but, for several years, the Society at home, for want of means, were unable to respond to their earnest request. At length, in 1829, the Conference appointed the Revs. Peter Percival and Thomas Hodson to commence a Mission-station there, with the hope of doing something towards evangelization of the heathen population, as well as of supplying the spiritual necessities of their fellow-countrymen. These excellent brethren entered upon their work in the early part of the following year with becoming zeal and earnestness. They not only collected an English congregation, and carefully dispensed the Word of life to Europeans and their descendants, according to the original arrangement; but they studied the Bangalee language, built a native chapel, established schools, and exerted themselves in every possible way for the benefit of the dense Pagan population, by whom they were surrounded. These zealous labours were not without fruit; but after they had been prosecuted for three or four years, the results were not considered such as to warrant the continuance of the heavy expenditure which the maintenance of the Mission involved. Just at that time also, in consequence of the sickness and removal of some of the Missionaries, the work in the Ceylon, Madras, and the Mysore Districts, was suffering for want of men. Under the circumstances, the Missionary Committee in London resolved to withdraw their agents from Calcutta, that they might strengthen the other Indian stations, and thus the Mission to Bengal was suspended, Mr. Percival removing to Ceylon, and Mr. Hodson to Bangalore.

After the lapse of about thirty years, the way seemed to open for the re-establishment of the Wesleyan Mission at Calcutta. Arrangements having been made for the appointment of Ministers to labour for the benefit of Methodist soldiers in British regiments stationed at Barrackpore, Kurrachee, and other important garrisons in Northern India, the brethren designated to this work were necessarily brought into contact with the capital of Bengal, and such were the impressions which they received of the spiritual necessities of the vast population of that great city, that they felt it their duty to urge the Committee to give it another trial. This led to the appointment, in 1862, of the Revs. James H. Broadbent and Henry G. Highfield to Calcutta. They arrived there on the 17th of September, and entered upon their work with sanguine hopes of success. These hopes were not disappointed. The use of a commodious building, known as the "Freemasons' Hall," having been secured, the Missionaries at once commenced preaching to large and attentive congregations. At the commencement of their labours their ministrations were necessarily confined to the English language, but, with a view to reach the dense native population, and to render themselves generally useful, they soon made an arrangement for one of them to devote his principal time and attention to the study of the Bengalee, that he might preach to the Hindus in their own language the glorious Gospel of the blessed God. This desirable object has now been attained without neglecting the military at Fort William, or the English-speaking population resident in the city, and the results have already been of a very encouraging character. A commodious and beautiful

WESLEYAN CHAPEL AND MISSION PREMISES, CALCUTTA.

new Chapel and Mission premises have been erected in a convenient situation, a view of which we are able to give, and the Mission, with its Schools and Bible-classes, has been placed on a firm and substantial footing, so that we may hope in time to come its influence will extend to various other places in the populous presidency of Bengal. At the Conference of 1869, the Mission-stations in this part of India were formed into a regular district, to which the Rev. John Richards, an experienced and able Missionary, was appointed as Chairman and General Superintendent.

To the places already mentioned as military stations occupied by Wesleyan Ministers in Northern India, the City of Lucknow, so famous in the Indian Mutiny, has recently been added. Here a neat little chapel has been built, and an English-speaking congregation collected by the Missionaries of the Methodist Episcopal Church of America. The pressing claims of their native work in Bareilly preventing them from giving that attention to this charge which it required, they offered to transfer it to us, if an English Wesleyan Missionary could be appointed to the garrison at Lucknow. This generous offer was accepted by the Committee, and in 1864 the Rev. Daniel Pearson proceeded to Lucknow, where he met with a kind reception both from soldiers and civilians, and entered upon his work with cheering hopes of success. Of course the congregations are very fluctuating at all the military stations, as the regiments often move from place to place. But, surely, it is a grand and noble work in which British Methodists are engaged when they aid in supplying a Gospel ministry for the benefit of the sons of our people in a far distant land, as well as for the evangelization of the heathen. In connection with the Calcutta District and the military stations in the north of India, we have *three Missionaries, one hundred and ten Church members, and one hundred and thirty-nine scholars* in the Mission-schools.

The reader may remember that the first party of Wesleyan Missionaries sent out to India landed at Bombay, and that the Rev. W. M. Harvard was detained there for some time after his brethren had embarked for Ceylon. This interval was improved by the Missionary in preaching to the people as he had opportunity, and such was the impression made by his faithful ministry, that an earnest request was sent to the parent Society, that they also might be favoured with the services of a Wesleyan Missionary. This led to the appointment to Bombay of the Rev. John Horner, who arrived there, with Mrs. Horner, in the month of September, 1817. In the following year he was joined by the Rev. Joseph Fletcher, and for some time their prospect of success was promising. From various causes, however, among which may be noted the failure of the health of the Missionaries, the experiment ultimately resulted in disappointment, and in 1821 the Mission was relinquished, the brethren being withdrawn to supply vacancies in other places.

The island of Mauritius can scarcely be said to belong to India; but, whilst adverting to stations hopefully commenced and afterwards relinquished, we may here remark that at this place also an experiment was tried by the Wesleyan Missionary Society for the evangelization of the negroes and others, which likewise proved a failure. At the earnest request of several of the inhabitants two Missionaries, the Revs. Henry D. Lowe and John Sarjant, were appointed to the Mauritius in 1830; but after labouring there for a year or two with but little fruit, owing chiefly to the opposition manifested by the planters to the religious instruction of the slaves, the station was given up. In the meantime, Mr. Sarjant, a zealous and promising young Missionary, had fallen a sacrifice to the climate, and was buried in a land of strangers. His grave may be seen in the beautiful cemetery of Port Louis, close to that of Harriet Newell, a Missionary's wife who was interred there about eighteen years previously. The resting place of Mr. Sarjant is marked by a plain stone, erected by the subscriptions of a few pious soldiers who had been benefited by his ministry. Mr. Lowe ultimately returned to England, and was engaged for several years in the home work.

In 1865, the Rev. William S. Caldecott was appointed to the Mauritius, to minister to the Wesleyan troops in the garrison, and it was hoped by some that this would lead to the establishment of a regular Mission-station there for the benefit of all classes. This hope was not realised, however. In consequence of a fatal epidemic fever, which ravaged the Island in 1858, the regiments were dispersed, and Mr. Caldecott's own health having failed, he was removed to the more important military and naval station of Malta, in the Mediterranean.

In bringing to a close our brief review of the origin and progress of Wesleyan Missions in India, we may remind the reader of the numerous and powerful obstacles which have tended to impede the advancement of the work in this important section of the wide field. In addition to the complicated and elaborate system of Hinduism, with its fascinating superstitious rites and ceremonies, and its idol worship in which the masses of the people have been trained for ages, there is the soul-withering influence of cast; and the barrier which cast raises against religious enquiry and Christian fellowship can only be fully appreciated by those who have had to do with it, and seen the poor Hindu convert to the faith of the Gospel cursed, disowned, abandoned, and left to perish by his idolatrous and cruel kindred. We say nothing now about the exclusiveness, pride, and obstinacy of that portion of the population who are professed Mahommedans. We only glance at the peculiar hindrances which stand in the way of the progress of Missionary work in India, for the purpose of showing that we must not measure its value and importance by mere statistical and visible results, but rather entertain the hope that the faithful preaching of the Gospel in the vernacular languages of the people, the translation and circulation of the Holy Scriptures, and the education of the rising generation, as it is conducted in the Mission-schools, will gradually sap the foundation of idolatry, and hasten its entire downfall.

In the meantime, it is satisfactory to know that the labours of the Missionaries are not without tangible and visible results. By the blessing of God upon the numerous agencies which are employed to evangelize the people, tens of thousands have been won over from the worship of dumb idols to serve the true and living God; and it is hoped that in time to come a still more plentiful harvest will be gathered into the garner of the Lord. In the respective

INDIA.

CONVERTED NATIVES DESTROYING THEIR IDOLS.

circuits and districts of Ceylon and Continental India, the Wesleyan Missionary Society employs about *seventeen Missionaries*, a large proportion of whom are native Ministers. These have *two thousand one hundred Church members* under their pastoral care, and there are upwards of *eight thousand scholars* receiving instruction in the respective Mission-schools. In view of the peculiar nature of the work, and of the numerous difficulties at which we have briefly glanced, surely this is a measure of success which may well encourage the friends of Missions to renewed and more vigorous efforts in the prosecution of the holy enterprise.

CHAPTER XI.

CHINA.

THE EMPIRE AND ITS INHABITANTS—FIRST EFFORTS TO EVANGELIZE THE CHINESE—COMMENCEMENT OF WESLEYAN MISSION—THE CANTON DISTRICT—THE WUCHANG DISTRICT.

CHINA is an extensive country of Eastern Asia, lying between the parallels of 20° and 41°, and extending from the meridian of 97° eastward to the Pacific Ocean. Its superficial area is estimated at one million three hundred thousand square miles, or more than one-third the size of Europe. All the natural features of China are on a gigantic scale, and correspond with the vast extent of the country. Chains of mountains, which appear almost interminable, intersect its surface, and in the north-west rise into snow-covered peaks, and its rivers are superior in length to any others in the Eastern Hemisphere. Nor are the works of human industry by which China is distinguished less imposing, as the remains of the Great Wall, which separates it from Tartary, and extends across hill and valley for one thousand two hundred and fifty miles, and its Grand Canal, the longest in the world, abundantly testify. The Empire is divided into eighteen provinces, which exhibit considerable difference of aspect, soil, and climate. Besides the vegetables and fruits peculiar to the country, it produces most of those that are grown in Europe. The Chinese are great agriculturists, but the article for which they are the most celebrated is the tea plant, the leaves of which are now so well known in Europe. It is said that they not only cultivate every available piece of land within their reach, but also the bottoms of their waters, and that the beds of their lakes, ponds, and rivulets, produce crops unknown to us.

The population of China is estimated on good grounds at the enormous number of four hundred millions, equal to one-third of the entire human race! Many of the provinces are extraordinarily populous, containing upwards of six hundred persons to the square mile. Thousands of the people constantly live upon the water, in boats or vessels of various kinds, without ever spending a day on the dry land. The Chinese belong to the Mongol, or olive-coloured, variety of mankind. They have large foreheads, small eyes, short noses, large ears, long beards, and black hair, and those are thought to be the most handsome who are the most corpulent. The women affect a great deal of modesty, and are remarkable for their small feet. So anxious are they to excel in this respect, that little children, especially the girls, have their feet encased and confined in small boots, to prevent their growing too large. Of course they feel very uncomfortable, and they are often in great pain whilst passing through this trying ordeal; but their parents and little brothers try to amuse them with playthings to prevent their crying and to reconcile them to their fate. Many other foolish and ridiculous things might be related of the child-life of the Chinese; but when they grow up to years of maturity they are a most industrious people. They are famous for their manufactures in porcelain, cotton, paper, and various other articles. They are great smokers, however, and many of them are fond of opium, and shorten their days by indulging in its use.

Much more might be said in reference to this wonderful country and the strange people by which it is inhabited; but, in a Missionary point of view, the language, literature, religion, and morals of the Chinese are most important, and demand a few passing observations. The Chinese language is very peculiar, and was once thought almost inaccessible to Europeans, but a more intimate acquaintance with it has proved that it is not so. The characters are somewhat of the form of hieroglyphics, and are read not from left to right as the English, nor from right to left as the Hebrew, but from top to bottom, being arranged in perpendicular columns. Learning is much cultivated by the Chinese, and their schools and colleges are, in their way, of a very respectable

CHILD-LIFE IN CHINA.

character. They have among them numerous books on a variety of subjects, which are indicative of a higher state of civilisation, having existed at some previous period of their history than that which they now enjoy.

The religion of the Chinese is sheer Paganism, of the Buddhist type. They have no Sabbath, nor even such a division of time as a week. The principal pagodas or temples are dedicated to a god whom they call Fo; but they are not much frequented, for the people generally have their own household gods, and private heathen altars in their respective dwellings, where they perform their idolatrous and superstitious rites and ceremonies. Confucius, who flourished about two thousand years ago, is regarded as their great philosopher and reformer; but, however his works and his character may be eulogised, no very favourable impression appears to have been made upon the morals of the population of China by his teaching. With all their high pretensions to a superior civilisation, the moral character of the people is as debased as that of the Hindus, or any other pagan nation with which we are acquainted. In addition to the various forms of idolatry and superstition which are openly professed by the Chinese, there are prevalent among them polygamy, infanticide, debauchery, gambling, and other revolting forms of vice, to say nothing of the malignity, deceit, and fraud by which they are characterised. From this brief statement it will be clearly seen that the teeming millions of the population of China stand in need of the Gospel; and we shall now proceed to consider what has been done by the enlightened nations of Europe to raise the people from their morally degraded condition.

First Efforts to Evangelise the Chinese.

For many years China was inaccessible and almost unknown to foreigners. The people flattered themselves with the idea of superior civilisation, and with a fabulous antiquity, which raised them, in their own estimation, to such a point, that they looked with contempt on all the world besides, and regarded all other nations as races of "barbarians." They are, moreover, extremely ignorant with respect to the character and condition of other nations. A Chinese author says, "I felicitate myself that I was born in China. What, if I had been born beyond the seas, where the people are clothed with leaves of trees, eat wood, lie in holes of the earth, where the cold freezes, or the heat scorches? I should not have been different from a beast. But now, happily, I have been born in China; I have a house to live in; drink, and food, and elegant furniture; I have clothing, and caps, and every blessing. Truly the highest felicity is mine!" Thus ignorant and puffed up with pride, the Chinese for a length of time declined to have any dealings with strangers, and would not allow any foreigner to enter or to reside in their country.

How long this spirit of exclusiveness would have continued it is difficult to say, had not the famous Chinese plant, with which we are now so familiar, become known in Europe, and originated a branch of commerce which, in a measure, broke down the barrier which had so long enclosed the "Celestial Empire" against the intrusion of the so-called "barbarians." It was with great caution, and under many restrictions, that the Chinese ultimately admitted foreigners to their shores, and at first only one or two ports were accessible to foreign vessels, according to the treaties which were entered into, from time to time, with the Western Powers. As early as the year 1807, when the way began to open, the first effort was made by the Protestant Christians of Europe for the evangelisation of China. This honour was reserved for the London Missionary Society, who, at that period, sent out the Rev. Robert Morrison, D.D., for the special purpose of securing, if possible, a faithful translation of the Scriptures into the difficult Chinese language. After many years of arduous and plodding perseverance, this grand object was accomplished, and the name of Dr. Morrison will be handed down to posterity as the apostle of China and the founder of the first Protestant Mission to this extensive and populous country.

Dr. Morrison had studied the Chinese language for a brief period before he left home, under a learned native named Sam Fok, then residing in London. Going to China by way of New York, the Missionary received from Mr. Maddison, the Secretary of State, an introduction to the American Consul, which proved of great service to him. On arriving in Canton, he conformed to the prevailing usages of the country, in diet, dress, and manners. He handled chopsticks instead of knife and fork, curled up his hair in orthodox pigtail form, and allowed his finger-nails to grow. But, after pursuing this method for some time, he was led to see the folly of such a degrading conformity to the habits of a heathen people, and henceforth assumed a dignified and distinctive character and aspect. At first Dr. Morrison found it extremely difficult to obtain tutors to aid him in the acquisition of the language; and for several years he was, to a considerable extent, excluded from social intercourse with the people. It was not long, however, before he was able to report to the Directors of the Society that "the Chinese *Grammar* was ready for the press, the *Dictionary* was filling up, and the manuscript of the *New Testament* was, in part, fit to be printed."

In the year 1813 Dr. Morrison was joined by the Rev. William Milne, D.D., who was also honoured to render efficient service in the Chinese Mission; and in the following year they baptized their first native convert, a man named Tsai-Ako, who continued faithful to the day of his death, in 1818. The work of evangelisation was very slow in its progress for a length of time; but, as it gradually expanded, the honoured Missionaries whom we have named were followed by the Rev. Messrs. Medhurst, Legge, Hobson, and others, and stations were established in Canton, Hong Kong, Shanghai, Macao, and other places. Much of the time of the brethren was, at first, necessarily, occupied in studying the language; but at length they were enabled to commence preaching the Gospel to the people in their own tongue; and, among the few converts who were gathered into the fold of Christ through their instrumentality, some were raised to the honourable position of native evangelists.

When the country became open and accessible to foreigners by the more liberal treaties and other arrangements which resulted from the Chinese war, a number of other Christian agencies, both from America and Europe, were brought to bear upon the dense mass of heathenism which pervades the Celestial Empire. Ultimately that section of the Christian Church, the history of whose Missions we have traced in other lands, was able to take its share in the important work of endeavouring to evangelise this vast and populous country, and not without encouragement to persevere in their labours.

Commencement of Wesleyan Mission.

The Wesleyan Mission to China was organised at a comparatively recent period. This was owing, not to the lack of disposition on the part of the Society, but to the want of means. When, in 1845, China was thrown open to foreigners to an extent it had never been before, by the publication of an important document notifying that every form of Christianity might be freely professed, and by an alteration in the law, permitting Missionaries to make extensive journeys beyond the limits of the "five free ports" to which they had been previously confined, a strong desire was felt by many that our Society should enter the country and take its proper share of Missionary work in the "Flowery Land." But at that time the entire resources of the Committee were more than absorbed by the claims of the work in the South Seas, the West Indies, Africa, India, and other places. Consequently it was impossible to send out Wesleyan Missionaries to China at that time; and it was not till actually pressed into the work by the special providence of God that it was ultimately entered upon.

The conversion of China to the faith of the Gospel was a burden laid upon the heart of a pious young man in Yorkshire, named George Piercy, and he could scarcely rest day or night, from a deep conviction that he ought to give himself entirely to this great work. This conviction was deepened by a communication from a few pious soldiers stationed at Hong Kong, and ultimately Mr. Piercy, impelled by the constraining love of Christ, went out to China at his own expense, and without any pledge of support from any Missionary Society. He arrived at Hong Kong on the 20th of January, 1851, expecting to find a pious sergeant, with whom he had formerly been acquainted, at the head of a small band of praying soldiers. He stepped on shore in a strange land with peculiar feelings, and, walking towards the barracks, he inquired of the first soldier he met where he should find Sergeant Ross, and he received the startling reply that he was dead! He then inquired for Corporal D——, another member of the little Methodist class,

VICTORIA, HONG KONG.

and his grief and disappointment were somewhat relieved on finding that the man to whom he was speaking was the person himself, who at once gave him a cordial welcome to China.

Having listened to the affecting story of the sickness and death of his friend, Sergeant Ross, and of other members of the little class, for Corporal D—— was the only survivor, Mr. Piercy proceeded to make arrangements to labour for the benefit of his fellow-countrymen in the garrison, till he could acquire the Chinese language, and prepare to enter upon his Mission to the natives. On calling upon Dr. Legge, of the London Missionary Society, Mr. Piercy was received as a brother in Christ, and cordially offered a home in the Doctor's house till he could make suitable arrangements for his own accommodation in connection with his work. After residing about three weeks under the hospitable roof of his friend, the young Missionary hired rooms in Hong Kong, one of which, capable of containing about sixty persons, he turned into a preaching-place for the English soldiers. At the same time he commenced visiting the sick in the hospital; and, under the direction of Dr. Herchberg, applied himself to the study of medicine as well as to the acquisition of the language of the people among whom his lot was cast, that he might be more fully prepared for future usefulness. The Lord greatly blessed the labours of Mr. Piercy among the soldiers and their wives, and about twenty of them were soon formed into a Society, of whose sincerity he had good hope. Those among whom he laboured showed a disposition to contribute to his support, and, although his own funds were expended much sooner than he anticipated, what they raised, coupled with small sums sent by his friends in England, enabled him to devote all his time to Mission work, without engaging in any secular employment, as when he went out he expected he might be obliged to do.

At this stage of his evangelical labours, Mr. Piercy, who had long been a consistent member of the Methodist Church, offered his services to the Wesleyan Missionary Society; and, after such an examination as he could be subjected to at that distance, involving a written statement of his Christian experience and doctrinal views, he was accepted as a candidate for our ministry. This course was adopted by the Missionary Committee and Conference, under a deep conviction that the Society was now called upon to do something for China, and that Divine Providence was calling them into the field by thus raising up and thrusting into the harvest suitable labourers to carry on the work. In the meantime Mr. Piercy was studying the Chinese language diligently, and labouring to do good to the utmost of his power. On hearing that his offer of service was accepted by the Wesleyan Missionary Society, he began to arrange his plans for future action. These plans involved his removal to Canton, where he believed there was a more ample and appropriate sphere of labour. He had, from the beginning, regarded his stay at Hong Kong as merely temporary, till he should be in a measure initiated into his proper Missionary-work.

The Canton District.

On proceeding to Canton, Mr. Piercy met with a cordial reception from Dr. and Mrs. Hobson of the London Missionary Society, who did everything in their power to promote his comfort and success. Having hired apartments, as before, and being supplied with the services of a native assistant, named Leang Afa, by the kindness of Dr. Hobson, Mr. Piercy continued his studies at the language, and soon began to hold religious services for the benefit of the natives. But his position and prospects will best appear from his own statement. Writing to the Committee in London soon after his arrival at Canton, he says: "As to the field before me, I need not say it is large. I am a temporary resident in a house not far from the factories, close to the river, and to a ferry over which nine thousand persons frequently pass in a day. It is a little way into the western suburbs, over which, from a lofty verandah, I have an extensive view. I can look two miles to the west, and two-and-a-half to the north; and in this small space are crowded the abodes and persons of four hundred thousand human beings. Through every street of this given space I can pass

CHINA.

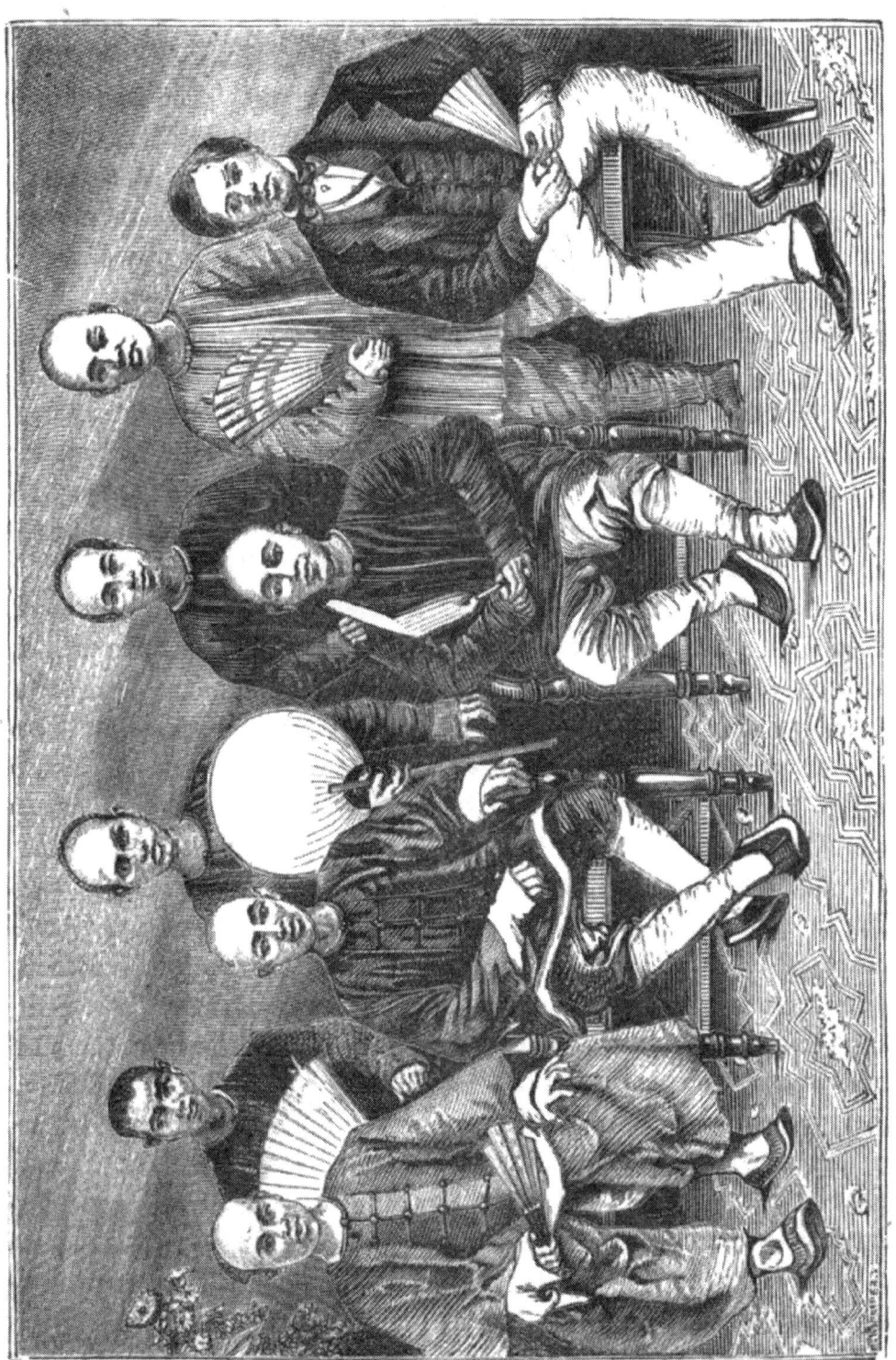

THE REV. GEORGE PIERCY AND HIS CLASS OF CHINESE CATECHISTS.

unmolested, and in many places I can enter shops and leave a tract, or speak a few minutes with the people. I think I perceive a difference in the treatment of foreigners of late. The free intercourse of the Missionary families with the people has had a very beneficial effect. As to the people themselves, there is a moral and mental apathy respecting the truth which is a great discouragement to the Missionary. Yet still numbers are willing, and some desirous, to receive Christian books and tracts. They come into the preaching-room, and, in many instances, pay close attention to the speaker. The idolatry and temple rites have no hold on their hearts, but as seasons of show and mirth, of amusement and relaxation from business. In this field are found rich and poor, learned and unlearned in vast numbers. If a Chinese is of equal value with any other human being, what a number of islands and large tracts of territory elsewhere will even this city outweigh."

It was clearly understood by the Society at home, when they adopted Mr. Piercy as their recognised agent, that measures would have to be taken to strengthen his hands and place the work on a permanent basis; and it is gratifying to observe that the means required for that purpose were soon forthcoming. Many noble friends and liberal supporters of the China Mission were raised up in various parts of the country, just at the time when they were required. Among the foremost of these was the late Thomas Farmer, Esq., the respected treasurer of the Society, who contributed £1,000 at the commencement of the work and £100 a year afterwards. Thus encouraged to prosecute the important enterprise with zeal and perseverance, the Committee selected and sent out the Revs. William R. Beach and Josiah Cox to aid Mr. Piercy, and they arrived in Canton on the 20th of January, 1853.

The newly arrived Missionaries were of course constantly employed for a length of time in learning the language, and preparing for future labours; whilst Mr. Piercy, who had in a great measure conquered these difficulties, was busily engaged in preaching, teaching, translating, and other active Missionary-work. A boys' school was now commenced under auspicious circumstances, into which the Conference Catechisms, which had been translated into

Chinese by Mr. Piercy, were at once introduced with good effect. At intervals, to relieve the tedium of their studies, the junior Missionaries engaged earnestly in the work of distributing tracts and copies of the Scriptures, the British and Foreign Bible Society having generously undertaken to provide one million copies of the New Testament for gratuitous distribution in China. As the work began to expand, an earnest appeal was made to the Society at home for more labourers, that they might be preparing to enter the openings which appeared to present themselves in various directions.

Encouraged by the liberality of their friends, and by the increase of special contributions to the fund for the support of the China Mission, the Conference of 1854 appointed the Revs. Samuel Hutton, Samuel S. Smith, and John Preston to this interesting part of the Mission field. They were solemnly ordained in City Road Chapel, and embarked for their distant sphere of labour early in the following year. After a pleasant passage of eighty-nine days from Gravesend, they reached Hong Kong, whence they proceeded to Canton, and, having with considerable difficulty procured a place of residence, they applied themselves to the study of the language with becoming zeal and diligence. The preparatory and active work of the Mission was going on hopefully when the commencement of hostilities between Great Britain and the Empire of China seriously interrupted the work, and obliged the Missionaries to leave Canton and take refuge in Macao, in the month of November, 1856.

But during the period of their comparative exile, the brethren were not idle; they continued the study of the language with unabated application, and held meetings for religious instruction and worship with the people as they had opportunity. It was during their sojourn at Macao, that three of their earliest converts, who had accompanied them, were admitted to the Church by baptism, after long training and a full conviction of their sincerity and soundness in the faith of the Gospel. In the midst of their troubles, the Missionaries set apart two days for special prayer and intercession for China, and to ask God so to interpose by His providence, that passing events, however painful and threatening for the time being, might be overruled for the advancement of His cause and kingdom in the land. Soon after this they thus expressed themselves in writing to the Committee in London:— " Important changes must follow the present employment of arms. Our diplomatic relations will, no doubt, be improved. Commerce will receive advantage. Our position as Missionaries cannot be worse than it was. It would, perhaps, be fair to claim a decided improvement in it, from the change that will probably occur; but we feel very jealous of depending on the protection and support even of own blessed country in efforts for the conversion of men. The work is of God. It belongs to Christ and Christians. It is 'not by might, nor by power, but by My Spirit, saith the Lord.' Let not war divert us from looking to Christ. Let Christ be magnified, and the excellency of His power will rest on us. We should pray that the few and feeble messengers of the churches may be filled with the Holy Ghost. God will then delight to employ us in entering the open doors which may be set before the Church."

For nearly two years the Missionaries were obliged to continue in exile, during which period they held four meetings weekly for the benefit of the Chinese, by whom they were surrounded at Macao, and they had the pleasure of adding two more to the number of their converts from among those who became impressed by their instructions. At the same time they were constantly employed in study and in distributing tracts and copies of the Scriptures, Mr. Piercy and Mr. Cox making excursions to the Straits and Shanghai occasionally. At length, towards the close of 1858, the success of the Allied Powers having secured the objects for which the war was undertaken, the restoration of peace was followed by the re-occupation of Canton as a station of the Society. Four of the five Missionaries happily succeeded in securing suitable residences, Mr. Smith having remained some time longer at Macao, by desire of the brethren. Two places of worship were also provided, one adjoining Mr. Hutton's residence, and the other in the old city, which afforded a preaching-place, a schoolroom, and a residence for an unmarried Missionary.

The following year was marked by circumstances of an interesting character. One of the brethren having thought proper to retire from the Wesleyan Connexion, and join another community, the Rev. John S. Parks was sent out to strengthen the Mission. Four day-schools were established in different parts of Canton, one of which was for girls; and some of the elder scholars displayed a very encouraging measure of progress in the knowledge of the plan of salvation. The number of native converts was, moreover, slowly but constantly increasing, and mention is made of one who sickened and died happy in the pardoning love of God. With reference to the character of the rest, the District Minutes contained this pleasing testimony:—"We have great joy in recording that the general conduct of our Chinese members has been in accordance with the Gospel, and we believe they are steadily advancing in the knowledge and love of our Lord Jesus Christ, whilst three of them have cheered us by their marked zeal for the salvation of their countrymen." Nor did the Missionaries neglect the British soldiers stationed at Canton, but laboured for their benefit as they had opportunity, and were richly rewarded by seeing a considerable number of them brought to a saving knowledge of the truth.

The next event which claims our attention in connection with our China Mission was a remarkable providence, by which the means were provided for placing it on a more substantial and permanent basis than it had ever been before. From the commencement of the work considerable difficulty had been experienced in obtaining suitable premises for the residences of the Missionaries and for schoolrooms and places of worship, which had in every instance to be hired, as the Society was not in a position to erect buildings of their own. But in 1860, by the munificent legacy of Thomas Pooll, Esq., of Road, of £10,000, especially for the India and China Missions, the Committee were enabled to make arrangements for the erection of commodious Chapels, Schools, and Mission premises, in different parts of Canton. As the new places of worship were opened, from time to time, a fresh impulse was given to the work, which continued to advance slowly but gradually in all its departments. The prospect of the future was for the moment bright and cheering; but Missionary experience is often very checkered and fluctuating. The new Mission premises were scarcely completed when, in the month of July 1862, Canton was visited by a terrific storm, by which the property of the Society, as well as that of many other parties, was placed in great jeopardy. Indeed, some of the buildings were wholly destroyed, and the effects of the brethren scattered to the winds. In a few months, however, the damage done by the hurricane was repaired, and the work went on as usual.

About the same time, one of the brethren was exposed to "perils among robbers." Mr. Preston, in company with an American Missionary and consular Chaplain, took a journey into the interior of the province, for the purpose of distributing New Testaments and tracts and preaching to the people. The journey occupied fourteen days, and extended over a distance of two hundred and forty miles. At most of the places they were kindly received by the people, but on passing through a ravine they were captured by banditti, stripped of nearly all their clothing, and robbed of their horses and other property. Having led them away three or four miles among the mountains, repeatedly threatening their lives, the robbers took them into a remote valley, and re-searched their persons, to ascertain that nothing valuable remained in their possession, and then returning to each of the Missionaries a coat, marched off, leaving them to find their way as best they could. On arriving at the town from which they had started in the morning, the Missionaries were kindly provided with food and lodging, and with equal kindness and generosity were helped onward by officials and others to their homes in Canton.

The China Mission having now become well established, the work advanced from year to year, if not rapidly, yet with marked improvement and uniformity. Some of the brethren having been obliged to return to England, temporarily or permanently, on account of the failure of their health, the staff of labourers were strengthened by the appointment of the Revs. Joseph Gibson, John H. Rogers, Silvester Whitehead, and Thomas G. Selby.

The City of Canton was ultimately divided into two circuits, east and west, and a promising station was commenced at Fatshan, and several new converts were baptized and added to the native Church from time to time. The Schools also increased both in number and efficiency; and to give the girls a better chance of improvement, a trained female teacher from Westminster College was sent out to the assistance of Mrs. Piercy, under the auspices of the "Wesleyan Ladies' Committee for the Promotion of Female Education in the East." This arrangement, however, did not result in the permanent advantage which was expected, in consequence of the failure of the young lady's health, which necessitated her return home to die under circumstances peculiarly affecting. A brief account of this touching incident may appropriately conclude this section of our work.

The first female teacher sent out to China in connection with the Wesleyan Mission to that Empire, was Miss Mary Gunson, of Ayside, near Windermere, whose brief career is worthy of a passing notice. In early life Mary gave her heart to God, and being deeply impressed with the conviction that she ought to do something to promote the cause of that Saviour who had done so much for her, she resolved to devote herself entirely to the important work of teaching. She therefore sought and obtained admittance into the Wesleyan Training Institution at Westminster, in January 1860, to prepare for the undertaking. Her college life was marked by diligence in study, entire devotedness to her work, and an exhibition of humble piety and Christian consistency which endeared her to all with whom she had to do. At the end of her second year of training, Miss Gunson obtained a place in the third class in the Government Examination, and also a prize for skill in drawing. Instead of taking charge of a school in England, as her friends anticipated, she was unexpectedly requested to go out to China to teach the young "Celestials."

Miss Gunson arrived at Canton on the 8th of August, 1862, and addressed herself to her work with an earnestness and zeal which gave promise of marked success. She soon became endeared to Mr. and Mrs. Piercy, with whom she resided, as well as to the other members of the Mission. She had only been a few months in China, however, and begun to battle with the difficulties of the colloquial language, and to make herself useful in the girls' school, when her health failed. There appeared in her fair and amiable visage evident marks of pulmonary consumption. The hectic flush and frequent cough told their sad tale; and her medical attendant recommended her immediate departure for England as the only likely means of saving her life. With feelings of great reluctance, but with humble resignation to the will of God, the poor invalid embarked for her native land on the 29th of April, 1863, accompanied by Mrs. Piercy, who was proceeding on a visit to England. The strength of the afflicted sufferer continued to decline during the voyage; but she was mercifully spared to reach her home in safety, and to embrace once more her beloved parents, and brothers and sisters, who had felt very anxious on her account. Contrary to all expectation, Miss Gunson lingered for several months; but at length, on the 19th of May, 1864, the Master called her, and she entered into the joy of her Lord in the twenty-third year of her age.

The Wuchang District.

At an early period of their labours in Canton and the neighbourhood, the Missionaries were convinced of the necessity and importance of establishing a strong Mission in the north of China, if they would make any sensible impression upon the vast heathen Empire. Hankow, a most important centre of commerce, was, accordingly, unanimously recommended to the Committee by the brethren as a suitable place for the headquarters of such a Mission. Densely crowded with people, the city affords facilities for preaching the Gospel to myriads who never before heard the glad tidings of salvation. It also affords easy access to the city of Wuchang, an important provincial capital, and other populous towns, and is favoured with a communication twice a week with Shanghai, by means of the splendid navigable river Yangtsye. Writing from Hankow on the occasion of his first visit, Mr. Cox says: "The whole heathen world cannot produce a field whose population is so great, accessible, and intelligent, nor one where the marked providence of God so loudly demands our co-operation." For the commencement of the Mission, the District Meeting asked for the appointment of three Missionaries in addition to Mr. Cox, who was already there; but Mr. Cox, in the midst of the openings which surrounded him, strongly recommended the appointment of six Missionaries, one of whom should have a knowledge of medicine, and a trained teacher. He would not only occupy Hankow by the appointment of two Missionaries, but would also place two and a schoolmaster at Wuchang, and two at Kiukiang.

Mr. Piercy, when writing to the Committee in support of the proposals for the extension of the Mission made by Mr. Cox, thus expresses his conviction that the hand of Providence was pointing to their adoption:—"I feel grateful to Almighty God for the manifest guidance vouchsafed to my beloved brother in his journeyings to the north, and I regard his determination to stay there, pending your action, as a wise one. I trust the Conference of 1862 will be able, ten years after the establishment of our first Mission at Canton, to undertake the commencement of a second, with at least three or four men in the very heart of this great Empire. What obstacles has Divine Providence removed during these ten years! Now all the country is open before us. Men are wanted who will give themselves to the work of evangelising this country in its length and breadth, who are willing to leave the old posts, and penetrate into new localities, and, with self-denying love to perishing souls, encounter the difficulties of opening up new fields of labour."

These warm-hearted and earnest appeals met with a noble response. The Committee authorised the purchase of ground and the erection of suitable Mission premises at Hankow; and the Rev. William Scarborough proceeded to join Mr. Cox there, whilst the Revs. David Hill and Frederick P. Napier were appointed to occupy the new station of Wuchang. At these important centres of population, the usual labours of studying the language, organising Mission-schools, preaching to the people, and distributing tracts and copies of the Holy Scriptures, were carried on with a pleasing prospect of success; Kiukiang being also visited occasionally with a view to its being occupied as soon as circumstances would permit.

In connection with the headquarters of the Mission at Hankow,

NATIVE TEACHER CIRCULATING THE SCRIPTURES.

a new element was, moreover, brought into operation, as an important auxiliary to evangelistic work,—namely, the dispensing of medicine to the afflicted. The Chinese have a high opinion of the skill and benevolence of Europeans; and they will make application for their medicine, when nothing else would induce them to come in contact with the Western strangers. The

American and London Societies had long availed themselves of this means of usefulness with good effect, and our Missionaries had done what they could according to their knowledge and circumstances; but in 1863 the Committee in London secured the services of Dr. J. Porter Smith, a pious and skilful Methodist physician, to proceed to China and organise a regular medical Mission at Hankow. Dr. Smith reached the scene of his future labours early in the year 1864, and commenced the study of the language and the practice of his profession in the true Missionary spirit.

The plan adopted was to dispense medicine gratuitously to the poor, and to give spiritual counsel and instruction to the invalids, as far as practicable. A commodious hospital was accordingly fitted up in connection with the Mission-premises at Hankow; and the days appointed for the application of patients were Mondays, Wednesdays, and Fridays. When the poor sufferers were assembled, one of the Missionaries, already acquainted with the language, delivered an address before Dr. Smith commenced the examination of each case respectively; and whilst he was afterwards busily engaged in the dispensary, conversations were continued with the waiting patients in the adjoining chapel. The people distinctly understood, that in connection with the healing of the body, the Missionaries sought the salvation of the soul; and yet they came together in large numbers, and not only received with gratitude the medicine prescribed, but often listened with devout attention to the instruction given.

The report of the results of the Medical Mission for the first year stated that a total of eighteen thousand seven hundred and sixty-four patients was actually registered, with the addition of others admitted irregularly. The persons applying for medical aid were of every rank and degree, from the haughty grandee to the poor beggar in the streets, and from every province in the Empire. Much suffering was relieved, many diseases cured, some lives preserved; and the moral effect produced was, in many instances, very gratifying, considering the strong prejudices and other obstacles which had to be encountered in the prosecution of the work. Some who had received benefit from the medicine of the Missionaries, began to regard them as their friends and benefactors, attended to their religious counsel, were brought under the renewing influence of Divine grace, and there is reason to hope that they will be their "joy, and the crown of their rejoicing, in the day of the Lord Jesus."

The Wesleyan Mission to China is in active and vigorous operation, and in all its departments—evangelical, educational, and medical—it has already been a means of both temporal and spiritual good to many; and with God's blessing on the zealous and persevering labours of His servants, still greater success may be expected in time to cóme. From the peculiar character of the work, it will require much faith, and patience, and perseverance, on the part of the Missionaries who are engaged in it, and continued sympathy, prayer, and liberality on the part of the friends of Missions at home. In connection with the respective stations in the two districts into which the work is divided in China, there are now *eleven Missionaries, seven Catechists, eighty-five Church members*, and *three hundred and twelve Scholars* are receiving instruction in the Mission-schools. For these results, comparatively small as they may appear, we would render sincere thanksgiving to Almighty God, and devoutly pray that the leaven of Gospel truth, which has been deposited in the dense mass of heathenism which exists in that dark benighted pagan land, may work effectually till the whole Empire shall be permeated with the light and life of our Divine Christianity.

CHAPTER XII.

THE RETROSPECT.

THE SPECIAL PROVIDENCE OF GOD—THE SUCCESS WHICH HAS BEEN REALISED—THE WORK WHICH REMAINS TO BE DONE—APPEAL TO THE FRIENDS OF MISSIONS.

HAVING conducted the reader over the varied scenes of labour occupied by the Wesleyan Missionary Society in different parts of the world, we may now, with profit to ourselves and advantage to the cause in which we feel deeply interested, pause for a moment to take a retrospective view of the past and a glance at the probable future of the great and glorious work in which we are engaged. Whilst briefly tracing the rise, progress, and present state of the respective Missions which have passed under review, numerous thoughts and enquiries have suggested themselves, in which we did not indulge at the time, after the manner of some historians, lest we should break the thread of the narrative, divert the attention of the reader, or occupy time and space to an extent which would have been incompatible with the plan of our work. Hence the propriety of indulging in a few reflections in our concluding pages, that we may fully comprehend the magnitude and importance of this branch of the grand Missionary enterprise, and feel the full weight of the responsibility which rests upon us, as individual professing Christians, henceforth to prosecute the work with renewed and increased vigour in certain hope of its glorious consummation. In the history of the past, in the aspect of the present, and in the prospect of the future, we see much to stimulate and encourage us in our work of faith and labour of love. We also behold ample cause for deep humiliation before God, for searching self-examination, and for a fresh consecration of ourselves with all we have and are, to the service of Him from whom we have received every temporal and spiritual blessing which we are favoured to enjoy. On some of these encouragements and stimulating motives we shall dwell, for a few moments, with the hope that, under God's blessing, our observations may lead to practical results. We may first remark on

The Special Providence of God.

Nothing can be more pleasing and encouraging to the mind of the Christian believer, in view of the work which he is called to do in connection with the spread of the Gospel throughout the world, than clear and enlightened conceptions of the doctrine of Divine Providence. If man were left to himself in his humble efforts to evangelise the world, it would, indeed, be a hopeless task. But it is not so. Supernatural aid and the special blessing of God, are promised to every attempt which is made by His servants to promulgate a knowledge of the Redeemer. When Christ gave to His disciples that great command, "Go ye into all the world and preach the Gospel to every creature," He also said, "Lo, I am with you alway even to the end of the world." And this promise implies, not only the gracious influence of the Spirit upon the hearts of preachers and hearers, for their comfort and salvation, but also the over-ruling and superintending Providence of God, opening doors of usefulness, defending His servants in times of danger, over-ruling passing events for the advancement of His cause and kingdom among men, and making all things work together for good to them that love Him.

The History of Wesleyan Missions presents to our view a succession of such interpositions of Divine Providence during the past century as is scarcely to be found in the records of the Church within the same space of time, at any previous period. On some occasions the elements of nature were controlled by the almighty power of God, and pressed into the service of Him whom " winds and seas obey," to bring the messengers of His mercy to lands where the people were waiting for His law, and thirsting for the water of life. This was especially the case when Dr. Coke and his companions were driven by a storm to the West Indies when on their passage to America, and when Mr. Longbottom was shipwrecked on the coast of South Australia, not to mention numerous instances in which the Gospel was introduced to the islands of the Pacific Ocean by adverse winds, so called, and storms and tempests by which frail barks freighted with native evangelists were wafted to places which they had no intention of visiting at the time. Nor are the instances less remarkable in which the Hand of God is clearly seen in the preservation of His servants from danger and from death in the hour of imminent peril. When Missionaries have been exposed to the fury of wild beasts and savage men; to the raging tempest, the earthquake, or the hurricane by sea and by land; and to the " pestilence that walketh in darkness, and the arrow that wasteth at noon-day," in unhealthy climes, they have been shielded by an unseen power, and rescued from peril in the most marvellous manner.

To the same interposition of Divine Providence must be ascribed the numerous openings which have presented themselves at different times for the introduction of the Gospel into heathen lands, and the raising up of suitable agents for the work just at the time when they were specially required. In some instances we have seen populous countries, as India, China, and Japan, which had remained for ages effectually closed against foreigners by the extreme jealousy of the ruling powers, all at once thrown open to commercial intercourse, and to the efforts of the Christian Missionary for the evangelisation of the teeming millions of their idolatrous inhabitants. In other cases where the light of Protestant Christianity had long been excluded from vast populations by restrictive laws and regulations, originating in Popish intolerance, as in Italy, Spain, and other places, the barrier has been broken down, religious liberty proclaimed, and the country thrown open in the most surprising manner. Nor have the facilities for the introduction of the Gospel been less remarkable which have occurred in countries such as New Zealand, Fiji, and the Friendly Islands, which a few years ago seemed closed against the messengers of God's mercy by the deep degradation, and the cruel, murderous, and cannibal propensities of the inhabitants. In these places, which were " full of the habitations of cruelty," we have seen the unruly passions of men controlled by an invisible power, and the heralds of peace going forth to unfurl the blood-stained banner of the Cross without fear and without molestation. And when occasions of imminent danger have occurred from threatened personal violence, the protecting power of the Almighty has often been displayed in the most signal manner. We have known an enraged savage brandish his spear and point it at the Missionary's breast; but when the man of God lifted his hand to heaven and assured the assassin that if he dared to strike Jehovah would see and punish him; and that white men, on hearing of his death, would come and demand satisfaction, the implement of destruction has fallen to the ground, and the intended murderer has turned away trembling with fear.

It is true, instances have occurred in which precious lives have been sacrificed in the Missionary enterprise, not only by the wasting influence of pestilential climates, but by the devouring elements and the murderous hands of savage men. The friends of Wesleyan Missions will never forget the names of the Rev. Messrs. Threlfall, Thomas, Bumby, Draper, Baker, Whiteley, and Hill; and of the zealous native teachers who honourably fell at the post of duty. The afflictive dispensations of Divine Providence by which useful labourers have been suddenly removed, when their services were so much required, were no doubt permitted for some wise and good purpose, and it must be admitted that the number of such casualties has been but small indeed, compared with the thousands of agents employed for many years in the Mission-field, and the peculiar dangers to which they have been exposed. The wonderful preservation of Christian Missionaries can only be attributed to the special providential care of that God whose they are, and whom they serve, and without whose permission a sparrow cannot fall to the ground, nor a hair on the head of one of His people be injured.

The infidel and the sceptic may laugh or sneer at these references to the superintending providence of God in connection with the work of Christian Missions; but the true believer has a full conviction of the truth of the doctrine, and it is a source of great comfort and encouragement both to the Missionaries themselves and the friends by whom they are sustained in their hallowed labours. It is this view of the Divine government, in connection with the promises which God has given in His holy Word, which more than anything else stimulates the friends of Missions to fervent persevering prayer for His blessing upon the labourers and their work. And often has the writer been sustained and comforted, when exposed to difficulties and danger in foreign lands, by the assurance which he has felt in his heart, that he was the subject of the ever-watchful care of his Heavenly Father, and that he and his brethren were remembered by Christian friends at home at the throne of the heavenly grace. " The Lord reigneth, let the earth rejoice, let the multitude of the isles be glad thereof."

The Success which has been Realised.

The duty of the Christian to persevere in his humble endeavours to propagate the Gospel of our Lord Jesus Christ is not dependant upon the success which may attend the first efforts made for that object. If no fruit for a long time appeared as the result of Missionary labour, the obligation to obey the commands of the great Head of the Church would remain the same. But when success is realised, and that soon after the work has been commenced, it is matter of encouragement and of sincere gratitude to God, inasmuch as it clearly indicates the truth of the Gospel, and the Divine approval of the means employed for its dissemination. When the husbandman has scattered abroad with a liberal hand precious seed upon good ground carefully prepared for its reception, if he does not see the blade spring up at the appointed time, he naturally feels disappointed, and begins to surmise whether the seed sown was the genuine article which it professed to be. So would the Christian Missionary be exposed to grave temptations and serious misgivings if permitted to toil year after year without seeing any indications of the fruit of his labour. But when showers of blessing descend upon the heritage of the Lord, causing the good seed of the Kingdom to germinate and spring up, " first the blade, then the ear, then the full corn in the ear," and in due time the fields to appear white unto the harvest, they who sow and they who reap are favoured to rejoice together.

As the soil on different lands varies, so the circumstances of different countries and populations are diversified, some being more and some less fruitful; but if we go forth in the name and strength of the Lord, trusting in Him for success, we shall not labour in vain or spend our strength for nought. We may meet with discouragements as we "go forth, bearing precious seed," but, if faithful, we shall, doubtless, "return again with joy, bringing our sheaves with us." Jehovah Himself has said: "As the rain cometh down and the snow from heaven, and returneth not thither, but watereth the earth, and maketh it bring forth and bud, that it may give seed to the sower, and bread to the eater; so shall My word be that goeth forth out of My mouth: it shall not return unto Me void, but it shall accomplish that which I please, and it shall prosper in the thing whereto I sent it."

The Wesleyan Missionary Society has been highly favoured in this respect. In the most unpromising soil the agents of this institution have seldom been permitted to labour long without the appearance of tangible fruit; and that fruit has often been of a character and on a scale far beyond the most sanguine expectations of the parties concerned. It is matter of gratitude to the friends of Missions to see the work of Christian civilisation advance among dark benighted heathen tribes,—peaceful villages formed, places of worship erected, schools established, and the arts of civilised life promoted in all their diversified forms. But that which is still more welcome and delightful to all who love the Saviour in sincerity and in truth, is the appearance of real spiritual fruit as the result of Missionary labour. Wherever the Gospel of our Lord Jesus Christ has been faithfully preached, it has proved to be "the power of God unto salvation to everyone that believeth." Sinners have been awakened from their slumber, brought in humble penitence and prayer to the foot of the cross, and by faith in the precious atonement have found pardon and peace, and been savingly converted to God. Many of these converts from heathen darkness and superstition have themselves been called to preach the Gospel to their fellow-countrymen, and in Africa, India, and the South Sea Islands, the work is, to a great extent, carried on by native agency. Prosperous Christian churches have, moreover, been organised in various parts of the Mission-field, and there are, at the present time, *One hundred and sixty thousand, two hundred and ninety five members* united in Church fellowship, on the various stations occupied by the Wesleyan Missionary Society, whilst nearly *two hundred thousand scholars* are receiving instruction in the Mission-schools.

THE WORK WHICH REMAINS TO BE DONE.

But whilst we rejoice over these indications of the Divine approval and blessing, and render sincere thanks to Almighty God for the success which has attended the Missionary enterprise, we must not lose sight of the fact that much, very much, yet remains to be done before the world can be said to be won for Christ. Largely as the leaven of Gospel truth has diffused its influence of late years in various parts of Europe, there still remains a mighty mass of infidelity and popish superstition to be removed, that the Word of the Lord may have " free course, run, and be glorified." On the Continent of America, and in the Islands of the West Indies, many sinners yet remain to be converted, whilst the churches already gathered need much pastoral care and attention. But when we turn our eyes to Africa, and call to mind the appalling fact that thousands and millions of her deeply degraded inhabitants are still involved in midnight heathen darkness, we might well despair of ultimate triumph, if it were not for the evidences of the power of the Gospel, which we behold on the numerous Mission-stations which have already been formed in various parts of the country.

The same remarks will apply to Australasia. Notwithstanding the wonderful achievements of Christianity in many of the islands of the South Sea, there are still whole nations and tribes of people who have never yet heard the name of Jesus, or seen that Book which alone reveals the mercy of God to poor sinners, whilst the tens of thousands of converted natives in Fiji and the Friendly Islands must for many years require constant instruction and vigilant oversight. Nor are the claims of India and China, with their teeming millions of population, less urgent, or less deserving, of the sympathy and the care of British Christians. Sufficient of success has been realized to prove the excellency and efficiency of the armour with which the "Captain of our salvation" has furnished his faithful followers; but the great battle with idolatry, pagan darkness, and Mahommedan superstition, has yet to be fought. A few of the outposts of Heathendom may have been taken, but the citadel of the strong man remains to be captured. In view of these appalling facts, we may well ask with the Apostle, "Who is sufficient for these things?" And we have the same blessed response which cheered his heart, "Our sufficiency is of God!"

Appeal to the Friends of Missions.

In conclusion, and in full view of the special providence of God, the success which has already attended the Missionary enterprise, and the work which yet remains to be done, we may ask who is willing to "come up to the help of the Lord against the mighty?" In the presence of enemies so numerous and powerful, and with responsibilities so weighty and momentous, every professing Christian should inquire, What can I do to help forward the work of God, and the spread of the everlasting Gospel throughout the world? All may not be equally able to take a part in the glorious enterprise; but all may do something. To some God has given suitable physical and mental endowments to fit them for personal service to plead the cause of the perishing heathen, or actually to go forth to labour in the Mission-field. Whilst such are prudently careful not to "run before they are sent," they should be equally on their guard against disobeying the heavenly call and allowing themselves to be deterred from engaging in the blessed work by apprehensions of the real or imaginary difficulties and dangers connected with it. If any pious, intelligent, and devoted youth, whilst reading these pages, has felt in his heart those mysterious stirrings and Divine aspirations which, in connection with concurrent providential indications, constitute the call of God to the Missionary work, let him not resist the promptings of the Holy Spirit, or disobey the commands of the Almighty, but heartily respond in the language of the prophet, "Here am I, send me." Nor should Christian parents withhold their full consent, or throw difficulties in the way of their children whose hearts God Himself has disposed to engage in personal service in the cause of Missions. Rather let them imitate the example of the noble-hearted parent who said, "If I had a dozen sons or daughters, I should be glad to see them all engaged in making known the glad tidings of salvation to the perishing heathen."

To others God has given a considerable portion of the good things of this world; and where much is given, much is required. Of whatever nature the talents may be which are committed to our care, we are only entrusted with them as "Stewards of the Lord." Nor should we forget that the time is approaching when the Master will say, "Give an account of thy stewardship, for thou mayest be no longer steward." Wealth is never better employed than when consecrated to the service of the Redeemer; and the highest department of that service is making known His dying love to those who had never before heard of His great salvation. Let those who have it in their power, support the cause of Missions at home and abroad with princely liberality, remembering the words of Him who said, "Freely ye have received, freely give," for the "Lord loveth a cheerful giver." But if our means be very limited, we are not on that account excused from the faithful discharge of our duty, or debarred from the privilege and honour of being identified with this department of the work of God. We are, in that case, to contribute as the Lord hath prospered us; and He, whose eye was on the treasury, and who marked with His approval and blessing the widow's mite, so cheerfully consecrated to His service, will accept our offerings if presented in appropriate measure, and with a single eye to His glory.

But those who have nothing to give but their prayers, may render important service to Christ and His cause in connection with the Missionary enterprise. He who taught His disciples to say, " Thy kingdom come, Thy will be done on earth as it is done in heaven," will appreciate every petition presented at the throne of grace for God's blessing on the Missionaries, their families, and their work. Let this sacred duty not be neglected, for without the influence of the Holy Spirit to render effectual the faithful preaching of the Gospel, and the watchful care of Divine Providence over those who go forth to dwell in heathen lands, we cannot expect the cause to succeed. But with the blessing of heaven in answer to fervent persevering prayer, every obstacle shall be overcome, for "the fervent prayer of a righteous man availeth much."

Whatever talents have been entrusted to us by the providence and grace of God, whether they be gifts of physical strength, mental power, worldly wealth, moral influence, or power with God in prayer, let them all be devoted to the honour and glory of Him whose we are and whom we profess to serve. Having consecrated ourselves and all that we have and are to the service of the Redeemer, let us live and labour for God and heaven, remembering that we are not our own, we are bought with a price, and that it is our duty, as it is our privilege, to " Glorify God in our bodies, and in our spirits, which are His." If we come up to the help of the Lord against the mighty, and engage in the great Missionary enterprise in this spirit of self-sacrifice and entire consecration to God, we shall not live or labour in vain;

the enemies of the Cross will be vanquished; hindrances will be removed out of the way of the onward march of truth; and every knee shall bow to Jesus, and ultimately every tongue confess Him to the honour and glory of God the Father; and He, whose right it is to reign, as King of Kings, and Lord of Lords, shall sway His sceptre over a subjugated world.

The signs of the times warrant our anticipation of the speedy fulfilment of ancient prophecy and the second advent of Christ to reign and rule more fully in His Church and in the hearts of all His faithful people. How wonderful the changes which have taken place during the past half century, all tending to prepare the way of the Lord! Slavery has been abolished throughout the British Empire, and by " terrible things in righteousness," America has been constrained to relinquish her favourite domestic institution; whilst the different nations of Europe are giving up their claim to the right of property in their fellow men. Africa has been explored and made known to Christian philanthropists to an extent never before realized; and the diseases peculiar to the unhealthy western coast are now better understood, and consequently less fatal than formerly. India, China, and Japan are thrown open to the commerce and Christian enterprise of the Western World. France, Spain, and Italy are no longer closed against the Bible and Protestant truth. The dreadful war which has desolated some of the fairest portions of the European continent may be overruled in the providence of God, as in former similar cases for the wider extension of religious liberty and the freer promulgation of the everlasting Gospel. The temporal power of Papal Rome is a thing of the past, and popery itself seems to totter to its foundation. The way is now open to the Wesleyan Missionary Society, as well as to other kindred evangelical institutions, to plant the standard of the cross in the eternal city, and St. Peter's itself may soon resound with the free proclamation of that Gospel for which the fisherman-apostle lived, laboured, suffered, and died. Christian England can communicate with all parts of the world, by means of steam and the electric telegraph, on a scale which was never known before.

Thus all things are ready for the Church of Christ to march forward like a grand conquering army to take possession of the world; or, to use another figure of a milder type, the way is prepared for the noble band of labourers in the Lord's vineyard to go forth and reap a glorious harvest, to the honour of His blessed name. The field is the world. The harvest is great and the labourers are few. Pray ye therefore the Lord of the harvest to send forth more labourers into the field; so shall the whitening harvest be gathered into the garner of the Lord, and the word of prophecy receive its accomplishment: "There shall be a handful of corn in the earth upon the top of the mountains; the fruit thereof shall shake like Lebanon: and they of the city shall flourish like grass of the earth. His name shall endure for ever: His name shall be continued as long as the son; and men shall be blessed in Him: all nations shall call Him blessed."

"O, multiply the sower's seed!
And fruit we every hour shall bear,
Throughout the world Thy Gospel spread,
Thy everlasting truth declare."

TABULAR VIEW OF THE RESULTS OF WESLEYAN MISSIONS AT HOME AND ABROAD, 1870.

Districts in	Principal Stations.	Ministers or Missionaries.	Church Members.	Attendants or Adherents.	Contributions to Mission Fund.
1. EUROPE	1,000	2,800	400,000	1,500,000	£150,000
2. AMERICA {United States .	12,000	15,000	2,500,000	7,000,000	80,000
{British Dominions	902	955	92,000	250,000	10,000
3. WEST INDIES	73	93	40,434	105,610	2,500
4. WESTERN AFRICA . . .	20	81	8,900	30,319	400
5. SOUTHERN AFRICA . . .	58	75	11,808	60,975	2,000
6. AUSTRALIA	143	185	22,308	150,880	5,000
7. NEW ZEALAND . . .	80	38	2,351	15,652	1,000
8. FRIENDLY ISLANDS . .	5	19	8,613	23,484	2,500
9. FIJI ISLANDS	9	58	7,836	190,098	500
10. INDIA	82	104	3,039	15,629	600
11. CHINA	18	28	1,519	8,463	250
Total throughout the world	14,340	19,386	3,098,808	9,346,110	£254,750

N.B.—In this Table the statistics of all the branches of Methodism are given so far as they could be gathered from the most reliable sources.

TABULAR VIEW OF THE PROGRESS OF THE WESLEYAN MISSIONARY SOCIETY.

Dates.	Principal Stations.	Ministers or Missionaries.	Church Members.	Scholars in Mission Schools.	Attendants or Adherents.	Contributions to Mission Fund. £ s. d.
1780	9	16	2,221	200	5,624	1,844 6 3
1790	16	22	8,620	542	9,461	2,365 4 2
1800	31	37	5,752	2,163	14,652	5,460 7 4
1810	48	56	10,564	4,621	32,460	15,260 8 8
1820	123	164	27,451	18,463	142,164	38,977 9 4
1830	185	218	41,206	28,463	246,740	50,204 17 9
1840	295	371	78,504	55,078	413,123	92,697 18 8
1850	324	427	105,394	78,548	532,649	111,685 13 11
1860	509	763	132,726	121,760	743,221	140,005 7 5
1870	788	987	160,295	181,840	867,189	145,750 17 10

N.B.—The statistics in this table for some of the earlier dates, before the publication of Annual Missionary Reports, must be regarded as approximations to the exact figures as near as practicable.

INDEX.

	PAGE
Aborigines	264, 283, 295, 298
Adams, Rev. Thomas	394
Addison, Rev. Edward	199
Adelaide, S. Australia	292
AFRICA, WESTERN	155
AFRICA, SOUTHERN	206
African ingenuity	152
Ahongalu, Barnabas	398
Albany	237, 238, 243
Alder, Rev. Dr.	80
Alderney	29
Algoa Bay	235, 240
Alice	259
Allen, Rev. William	198, 199
Allison, Rev. John	255
Amampondas	254
Amazulu	254
Ambler and Connelly	356
AMERICA	51
Ames, Rev. William	132
Amos, Rev. R.	174, 394, 395
Anguilla	119
Annear, Rev. R. S.	174, 198
Anshaw	252
Antigua District	110
Antigua, Island of	114
Appeal to Friends of Missions	540
Appleyard, Rev. J. W.	242
Archbell, Rev. J.	217, 251, 254
Army and Navy Work	12, 49, 506
Arthur, Rev. W.	499
Asbury, Rev. Francis	62, 63
Ashante	203
Ata, Chief	360
Ault, Rev. William	446, 481
AUSTRALIA	262
Author's Personal Mission	183, 224
Backhouse, Mr. James	306
Badger, Rev. H.	174, 175, 193
Bahamas	141
Bailie, Rev. J. A.	217, 219, 223
Baker, Rev. John	168
Baker, Rev. Thomas	451
Baltimore	61
Bangalore	495
Baralongs	251
Barbadoes	127
Barber, Rev. W.	234
Barnley, Rev. G.	84
Barra Point	194
Barratt, Rev. J. C.	40
Barrington	93
Barrowclough, Rev. W.	176
Barry, Rev. R.	91
Bartholomew, Rev. J.	47

	PAGE
Basutus	252
Bathurst, Gambia	178, 179
Bathurst, S. Africa	138
Batticaloa	481
Bau, Fiji	425, 430
Baxter, Mr. John	112
Bay of Islands	311, 319
Beach, Rev. W. R.	522
Beal, Rev. William	23
Bechuana District	251
Belfast College	68
Belize, Honduras	140
Bell, Rev. William	180
Bellamy, Rev. G.	132
Benares, Temples at	461
Bensonville	252
Berbice	133
Berkley	242
Bermudas	104
Berrie, Rev. J. W.	177
Berry, Rev. J. R.	174
Bethel	219
Bible Society	349
Bickersteth, Rev. E.	201
Binner, Rev. J.	399, 452
Birch, Captain	470
Birch Town	83
Bishop, Rev. A.	96, 124
Black, Rev. W.	90, 98, 102
Blackbird, Schooner	412
Black Town	485
Blanchard, Rev. T. W.	177
Blencowe, Rev. G.	255
Bloemfontien	253
Boardman, Rev. R.	60
Bombay	471, 506
Bowden and Hoskings	266, 278
Boyce, Rev. W. B.	240, 247, 261, 307
Boyd, Ship	325
Brackenbury, R. C., Esq.	28
Brazier, Rev. Mr.	136

	PAGE
Bridgart, Rev. J.	176, 193
Brisbane	280
British Columbia	86
British Guiana	131
British Rule in India	464
British Settlers	235
Broadbent, Rev. S.	251
Broadbent, Rev. J. H.	504
Brooking, Rev. R.	197, 198
Brown, Rev. John	144
Brown, Rev. Samuel	168
Browning, Rev. Mr.	87
Buchanan, Mr.	356
Buck, Captain	399
Buckley, William	283
Bulpit, Rev. James	99
Bumby, Rev. J. H.	345
Buntingville	247
Bure, Fiji, Temple	408
Burg-street Chapel	228
Burger's Dorp	252
Burgess, Rev. A.	488
Burning Mission Premises	343
Butterworth	245
Cabalva, Ship	467
Cadiz	44
Calcutta	503
Caldicott, Rev. W. S.	507
Caldwell, Rev. J.	289
Calvert, Rev. J.	422, 427
Calvert and Lyth, Mesdames	449
Cameron, Rev. J.	240, 255
Cameron, Rev. J. R.	255
Canada	69
Canarese, Preaching in	500
Cannibalism	432, 447
Canton District	520
Canvas Town	288
Cape Briton	96
Cape of Good Hope	208

Cape of Good Hope District	211
Cape Town	227
Cargill, Rev. D.	378, 411, 428
Carribs	123
Carver, Rev. R.	494
Carvosso, Rev. B.	277, 301, 303
Case, Rev. William	33
Castlereigh	272
Castletown	23
Cathcart, Sir George	219
Catts, Rev. James	144
Centenary Celebration	61
Ceylon	450, 472
Champness, Rev. T.	176, 201
Chapel Openings	221, 386
Chapman, Rev. B.	189
Chapman, Rev. G.	198
Channel Islands	27
Charlotte Town	100
Chatham	32
CHINA	289, 511
Chinese	514
Christian Benevolence	399, 541
Civilisation	310, 354
Claremont	230
Clarke, Rev. Dr.	22, 29, 42
Clarke, Rev. Isaac	173
Clarkebury	245
Class-meetings, Origin of	9
Clement, Rev. V. E.	194
Clough, Rev. B.	469, 476
Coke, Dr.	15, 28, 64, 465
Colenso, Dr.	256
Colesberg	252
Collis, Rev. J.	399
Colombo	472
Colonisation	343
Columbus	57
Commemoration Chapel	226
Concordiaville	226
Convicts, Mission to	305
Cook, Rev. E.	226, 233
Cook, Rev. Dr.	25, 47
Cook, Captain	263
Coolie Mission	134, 137, 257
Cooper, Rev. R.	143
Cork, Mr. Wesley at	17
Coughlan, Rev. L.	28, 101
Courtus and May	171
Cox, Rev. J.	522
Cox, Rev. M. B.	205
Crabb, Rev. James	27
Cradock	241
Crane, Rev. R. H.	94
Cranswick, Rev. M.	96
Creed, Rev. C.	345
Crocodile Worship	160
Croggan, Rev. W. O.	47
Cromwell, Rev. J. O.	47
Crosby, Rev. B.	173
Cross, Rev. W.	364, 374, 411, 426
Crowther, Rev. J.	486
Cryer, Rev. T.	486
Cuthbert, Rev. J.	201
Damaraland	226
David, Katta	898
Davies, Rev. W.	167
Davis, Rev. W. J.	240, 255
Daw, Rev. Robert	194
Dawson, Rev. S.	170, 182
Demerara	130
Devil Worship	161
Diaz, Bartholomew	207
Diep River	230
Dominica	115
Duglas	22
Dove, Rev. T.	174, 175, 186
Draper, Rev. J. D.	290
Drew, Mr. S.	66
Duaterra, Chief	311
Dublin, Mr. Wesley visits	15

Dunham, Rev. D.	77
Dunn, Rev. S.	21
Dunwell, Rev. J.	198
Durban	255
East London	241
Edendale	256
Edmondson, Rev. J.	33
Edney, Rev. J.	176
Edwards, Rev. E.	216, 227, 251
Edwards, Rev. J.	240
Edwards, Rev. T.	174
Eggleston, Rev. J.	345
Egypt	49
Elephant Fountain	226
Elsey's River	230
Emancipation of Slaves	148
Emigrants' Home	288
Emigration	53
Embury, Philip	54, 58, 75
England, Rev. J. E.	499
English, Rev. W.	192
Erskine, Rev. Mr.	464, 477, 482
Essequibo	133
EUROPE	3
Evans, Rev. Dr.	84, 87
Farmerfield	238
Fauersmith	253
Female Education	491
Fentin, John	28
Field, Rev. B.	291
Field Preaching	7
Fijians	405
FIJI ISLANDS	403, 454
Fiji, King and Queen of	452
Findlay, Rev. Mr.	199
Fingoes	240
Fish, Rev. William	187
Fleet, Rev. Henry	174
Fletcher Memorial Chapel	87
Fletcher, Rev. J.	452, 457, 507
Fletcher, Rev. J. H.	281
Foolas	165
Ford, Rev. J.	339
Fort Beaufort	239
Fox, Rev. W.	186, 199
France	30
Frazer, Rev. E.	47
Freeman, Rev. T. B.	197, 199
French Prisoners' Mission	31
FRIENDLY ISLANDS	356
Friendship and Buxton	133
Galle	476
Gama	207
Gambia, River	178
Gardener, Rev. E. A.	200, 201
Garrettson, Rev. F.	63, 93
Garry, Rev. W. P.	175
Gaskin, Rev. J.	255
George Town	131
German Village	242
Germany	38
Gibraltar	41
Gibson, Rev. W.	46
Gilbert and Fletcher	176
Gilbert, Nathaniel, Esq.	111
Girls Learning to Sew	331
Godman, Rev. M.	192, 217
Gold and Silver Washing	120
Gold Coast	194
Gold Fields	288
Graham's Town District	235
Graham's Town	237
Greaves, Rev. T. T.	198
Greece	47
Green, Rev. R.	46
Grenada	124
Griffith, Rev. W.	42
Grimmer, Rev. M.	201, 202
Guernsey	29

Guinea	194
Gunson, Miss	527
Gurney, Rev. A. J.	193, 200
Haabai	365, 369
Haddy, Rev. R.	222, 226, 230, 257
Halifax, N. S.	94
Hall, Rev. J.	177
Hammett, Rev. W.	113, 117, 136
Hankow	508, 529
Hardey, Rev. S.	234, 300
Harding, Rev. J.	281
Hardy, Rev. R. S.	499
Harrop, Rev. J.	199
Harrop, Rev. P.	196
Hart, Rev. F.	200
Harvard, Rev. W.	467, 474
Hawkins, Rev. R.	180
Hawkshaw, Rev. J.	122
Hawtrey, Rev. John	84
Hayti	144
Hazelwood, Rev. Mr.	455
Heald Town	239
Heck, Mrs. Barbara	54, 75
Heck, Mr. Paul	54, 75
Hesk, Rev. T.	197
Highfield, Rev. H. G.	504
Hihifo	362
Hill, Rev. D.	529
Hill, Rev. W.	290
Hillard, Rev. C.	199
Hindus	464
Hirst, Rev. Henry	193
Hobert Town	301
Hobbs and Stack	238, 332
Hobson, Dr.	520
Hocart, Rev. J.	37
Hodgson, Rev. T. L.	228
Hodson, Rev. T.	500, 503
Hokianga River	338
Holden, Rev. W.	255
Home Missions	11
Honduras	140
Hongi, Chief	316, 337
Hoole, Rev. Dr.	493, 496, 502
Hoole's Fountain	223, 224
Hope Street Chapel	229
Hopper, Rev. C.	12
Hornabrook, Rev. R.	133
Horner, Rev. John	507
Horton, Rev. W.	277, 303
Horton College	303
Hottentots	209, 236
Huddlestone, Rev. John	169
Hudson's Bay Territory	84
Huff, Mr. Paul	77
Human Sacrifices	162
Hurlburt, Rev. Mr.	85
Hurst, Rev. B.	285
Hunt, Rev. John	487, 432
Hutchinson, Rev. J.	432, 487
Hutton, Rev. S.	525
Idolater, The Young	453
Idolatry	462
Impey, Rev. W.	245
Inanda	256
Indaleni	256
INDIA	459
India, Mission to	465
Indians, American	82
Ireland	15
Ironside, Rev. Mr.	345
Isle of Wight	25
Italy	45
Jackson, Rev. J.	217
Jackson, Rev. J., Jun.	255
Jacobs, Rev. Peter	83
Jaffna	479
Jamaica	135
James, Rev. W.	186

	PAGE
Jager, Joannes	222
Jagger, Rev. Mr.	427
Jehu, Rev. David	174
Jenkins, Rev. E.	488
Jersey	28
Jessop, Rev. William	94
Jobson, Rev. Dr.	308
Johnson, Rev. T.	140
Jones, Rev. Peter	83
Jones, Rev. T. W. S.	46
Jonker, Africaner	226
Kaffraria, British	241
Kaffirs,	209, 236, 248
Kalk Bay	230
Kamastone	247
Kandy	479
Kandavu	453
Kava-Ring	359
Kay, Rev. S.	240, 243
Keeling, Rev. John	47
Keightley, Rev. John	172
Kemp, Rev. W.	334
Keri-Keri	335
Kerpezdron, Rev. Mr.	82
Kevern, Rev. G.	376, 390
Khamiesberg	217
Kingston, Jamaica	137
King, John	47
King William's Town	241
King, George	385
Kingstown, St. Vincent's	123
Korannas	252
Kumasi	203
Kwangubeni	256
Lady Melville, Ship	470
Lady Gray	232
Lady Smith	256
Lakemba	412
Lakemba Circuit	218

	PAGE
Lane, Rev. G.	120, 169
Launceston	204
Laws of Tonga	588
Lawry, Rev. W.	276, 314, 357
Lean, Rev. R.	189, 193
Lees, Mr. John	272
Leigh, Rev. S.	267, 313, 317, 330
Lerwick	21
Losse, Rev. William	75
Lesseyton	247
Le Sueur, Mr. P.	27, 102
Lewis, Rev. John	103
Lidgett, J. J., Esq.	393
Lily Fountain	217
Lifuka	370, 385
Links, Jacob	222
Lolohia	336
London Miss. Society	210, 221, 354
Longbottom, Rev. W.	293, 297
Lord, David, Esq.	203
Lowe, Rev. H. D.	507
Lucknow	506
Lusanne	37
Lynch, Rev. W.	467, 479, 486
Lynn, Mr.	192
Lyons, Mr.	72
Lyth, Rev. Dr.	89
Lyth, Rev. R. B.	429, 437
Macarthy's Island	184
Macpherson, Rev. D.	47
Macquarie Harbour	305
McAllum, Dr.	21
McArthur, W., Esq., M.P.	69
McBrair, Rev. R. M.	188
McCarty, Mr. James	72
McCornock, Rev. W.	115
McDugall, Rev. George	85
McGeary, Rev. John	102
McKenny, Rev. John	211, 477
McMuller, Rev. James	41

	PAGE
Madras	485
Maer, Rev. Edward	172
Mahaica	132
Malays	210
Malta	47
Malvern, Rev. John	299
Man, Isle of	22
Mandanaree	179
Mangungu	338
Mann, Rev. John	92
Man-of-War Class Meeting	310
Mansfield, Rev. R.	302
Manton, Rev. J. A.	206
Maories	216, 310, 349
Maria, Mail Boat	121
Maritzburg	255
Marsden, Rev. S.,	275, 311, 319
Marsden, Rev. J.	105
Martin, Rev. J.	198
Mason, Rev. Mr.	87
Maxfield, Rev. T.	8
Maynard, J. M., Esq.	230
Meadows, Rev. W.	193
Medical Mission	531
Melbourne	287
Methodist Episcopal Church	66
Methodism, Origin of	5
Mercury, Ship	334
Milan	46
Milne, Rev. Dr.	516
Milward, Rev. W. H.	200
Mohammedans	462
Money, T., Esq.	471
Montigue	232
Montserrat	116
Moore, Rev. W.	77
Moravians	6, 210
Morgan, Rev. John	179
Morrill, Rev. J. M.	40
Morris, Mr. James	219, 224
Morris, Rev. J.	219, 224

	PAGE
Mortier, Rev. John	132
Morley	245
Morton Bay	279
Mosquito Shore	140
Moss, Rev. W. S. F.	188, 192
Mount Coke	242, 243
Mount Arthur	247
Moulton, Rev. J. E.	398
Mowbray	229
Mowatt, Rev. J.	493
Morrison, Rev. Dr.	515
Mua	365
Müller, Mr. C. G.	88
Munroe and Peck	171
Muzenberg	230
Mycock, Rev. J.	198
Mysore	502
Namaqualand	219, 204
Namaquas	214
Napier, Rev. P. F.	529
Natal District	254
Neal, Major George	71
Negro Character	150, 153
Negroes	114
New Brunswick	65, 96
Newell, Mrs. Harriet	507
Newfoundland	101
Newlanders	252
Newlands	230
Newmanville	237
Newport, Isle of Wight	25
New Providence	142
New South Wales	266
Newstead, Rev. R.	85
Newtondale	241
New York	56
NEW ZEALAND	309
Nicholson, John	19
Nisbett, Bath	228
Nobbs, Mr.	355

Nova Scotia	89
Nukualofa	363, 368, 384, 397
Oneata	420
Ono	422
Oporto	45
Otley, Sir Richard	493
Osborn	247
Osborne, Rev. Mr.	482
Oriental Travelling	501
Orton, Rev.	284
Palestine	47
Palm Wine	164
Palmer, Rev. Mr.	240
Palmerston	240
Paramatta	275
Parkinson, Rev. J.	191
Parks, Rev. J. S.	525
Paris	35
Parsonson, Rev. G.	189, 192, 217
Patterson, Rev. J.	173
Pearce, Rev. B.	127
Pearce, Rev. H.	255
Peard, Rev. J. E. and Mrs.	191
Pearson, Rev. D.	506
Peelton	23
Peet, Rev. H.	193
Peddie	241
Percival, Rev. P.	404
Perks, Rev. G. T. (M.A.)	46
Persecution	123, 125, 127, 138, 145
Philadelphia	61, 62
Philips, Rev. S.	482
Picott, Rev. T. R.	202
Piercy, Rev. G.	517
Piggott, Rev. J. B.	46
Piggott and Hart	170
Pilcher, Rev. J.	255
Pilmoor, Rev. Joseph	60
Pilter, Rev. J.	141
Plaatberg	252
Plaat, Rev. Mr.	401
Point Pedro	182
Polglase, Rev. J.	399, 451
Pooll, T. Esq.	526
Popery	387
Pope, Rev. W. B. (M.A.)	46
Port-au-Prince	146
Port Elizabeth	240
Port Jackson	263
Port Philip	262
Portsmouth	467
Portugal	45
Potter, Captain	195
Powell, Mr.	132
Preston, Rev. John	523
Priestley, Rev. John	223
Prince Edward's Island	99
Printing Establishments	377, 500
Providence of God	534
Purslow, Rev. Mr.	175
Queen Charlotte	385
Queensland	278
Queen's Town District	242, 247
Quettevill, Rev. De Jean	29, 34
Quick, Rev. W. A.	174
Quilter, Rev. H. J.	194
Quinte, Bay of	72, 76
Rabone, Rev. S.	453
Raby, Rev. John	21
Raikes, Mr. Robert	81
Raithby	232
Ramsay	23
Rankin, Rev. T.	62
Raston, Rev. Mr.	174
Rawlins, Mr.	246
Rayner, Rev. J.	67
Reay, Rev. L. D.	176

INDEX.

	PAGE
RETROSPECT, THE	533
Revival in Ceylon	479
Revival in Tonga	379
Rewa	423, 426
Rhenish Missionary Society	226
Rhodes, Rev. J.	202
Richards, Rev. J.	223, 506
Richmond, Rev. Legh	27
Richmond, Rev. H. H.	201
Ridgill, Rev. R.	233
Ridsdale, Rev. B.	223
Rigg, Rev. John	42
Rigg, Rev. Dr.	42
Rigging Loft	56
Ritchie, Rev. W.	172
Robertson	232
Robinson, Mr.	246
Robinson, Rev. G.	201
Roblin, Mr. John	76
Robson, Rev. Mr.	87
Rogers, J. H.	526
Rondebosch	229
Rotumah	455
Rowlands, Rev. Mr	198
Royapettah Schools	491
Rule, Rev. Dr.	42
Rundle, Rev. Mr.	84
Salem	237
Samoa	400
Sanders, Rev. W.	173
Sandfleet	232
San Salvadore	142
Sargant, Rev. S. S.	523
Scarborough, Rev. W.	529
Schmelen, Rev. Mr.	213, 217, 243
Scholars Swimming to School	340
Scilly Isles	24
Scotland	12, 13, 14
Scott, Rev. Dr. G.	40
Scott, Sergeant James	271, 278

	PAGE
Selby, Rev. T. G.	526
Selwyn, Dr.	347
Seringapatam	502
Seymour	239
Shadford, Rev. G.	62
Sharp, Rev. Mr.	201
Sharracks, Rev. J.	145
Shaw, Rev. B.	200, 213
Shaw, Rev. W.	228, 235, 237
Shawbury	247
Shelburne	92
Shenston, Rev. W. E.	108
Shepstone, Rev. W.,	245, 248
Shrewsbury, Rev. W. J.	132, 245
Shipman, Rev. S. A.	197
Shipwreck	129, 293, 347
Sierra Leone	164
Simon's Town	230
Slaves, Institution of	237
Slaves Liberated	385
Slavery, African	161
Smith, Rev. S. S.	523
Smith, Dr. Porter	531
Smithies, Rev. J.	297
Smyth, Rev. J. B.	452
Somerset, West	282
Somosomo	431
South Australia	292
Southern, Rev. A.	194
Spain	43
Spencer, Rev. Mr.	202
Spenceley, Rev. C.	255
Spinny, Rev. Mr.	429
Squance, Rev. T. H.	467, 479
Stark	29
St. Christopher's	117
St. Eustatius'	118
St. Helen's	28
St. John's, N.B.	97
St. Martin's	118
St. Mary's, Gambia	179

St. Mary's, Scilly	28
St. Vincent's District	121
Stegman, J. A., Esq.	230
Stephenson, Rev. John	105
Stephenson, Rev. J. R.	40
Stillenbosch	231
Stockholm	40
Stott, Rev. S. H.	257
Strand	232
Strawbridge, Robert	58
Strong, Rev. John	79
Swallow, Rev. W.	188
Swan River	296
Sweden	40
Switzerland	36
Swellendam	234
Success realized	359
Sunday, John	83
Suttcliffe, Rev. Joseph	24
Sydney-street Chapel	128
Sydney, City of	268
Sykes, Rev. C. B.	201
Symons, Rev. S.	189
Tabou College	398
Talboys, Rev. T.	132
Tamil	479, 484
Tanjore, burning of	493
Tanoa, Chief	430
Tasmania	301
Taylor, Rev. A.	201
Taylor, Jeremiah	81
Toase, Rev. W.	31
Tobago	128
Teal, Rev. Mr.	176
Terrington Grove	232
Terry, Rev. G. (B.A.)	40
Thaba Uncha	251
Thakombau, King	452
Thackwray, Rev. Mr.	197
Thomas, Rev. J.	199, 223, 361
Thomas, Rev. J. S.	246
Thompson, Captain	324
Threlfall, Rev. W.	222, 240
Thurles	19
Tindall, Rev. John	145
Tindall, Charles	326
Tindall, Rev. Joseph	223, 226
Tindall, Rev. H.	224, 226, 232
Tonga	357, 366
Tortola	119
Tregaskes, Rev. B.	177
Trinidad	124
Triton, Mission Ship	309
Tucker, Rev. C.	378, 382, 390
Tuckfield, Rev. F.	205
Tuffy, Mr.	71
Turner, Rev. N.	332, 364, 394, 451
Turner, Rev. P.	372, 400
Turton, Rev. J.	342, 348
Turton, Rev. W.	143
Tyas, Rev. V.	194
Tyreman and Bennett	332
Uitenhage	241
United States	241
Umhali	256
Vancouver's Island	86
Van Dieman's Land	301
Vasey, Rev. Mr.	64
Vavau	364, 372
Veeson, George	356
Verulam	256
Victoria	88, 238
Victoria and Golden Grove	133
Virgin Islands	49
Viwa	424
Waite and Fletcher, Messrs.	177
Walbridge, Elizabeth	27
Walker, Rev. Mr.	277, 317

	PAGE		PAGE
Wall, Rev. Thomas	191	Whitely, Rev. Mr.	341
Wallace, Rev. R.	69	Whithead, Rev., S.	526
Wallis, Rev. J.	342	Wilkinson, Rev. H.	190
Walsh, Rev. T.	8	Wilkinson, Rev. T.	163
Wangaroa	323	Williams, Robert	61
Wangungu	342	Williamson, Rev. S.	287
War	63, 320, 388	Williamstown	283, 287
Warner, Charles	73	Wilson, Rev. F.	390
Warren, Rev. G.	166, 344	Windsor	276
Warrener, Rev. W.	113	Winnenden	38
Waterhouse, Rev. J.	345, 390, 427	Winscombe, Rev. Jasper	28
Watkins, Rev. Mr.	198, 372, 381	Witchcraft	249
Watsford, Rev. Mr.	280	Wittebergen	249
Watson, Rev. Mr.	197	Woon, Rev. Mr.	342
Wayte and Griffith, Messrs.	175	Work remaining to be done	539
Weatherstone, Rev. John	176	Worrell, Rev. T.	137
Webb, Captain	61	Wray and Hulbert	176
Wesley, John, Mission Ship	299	Wray, Rev. James	93
Wesleydale	328	Wrench, Rev. R.	175
Wesleyville	243	Wright, Rev. Richard	63
WEST INDIES	109	Wrigley, Rev. G. O.	196
West, Rev. D.	200	Wuchang District	528
West, Rev. T.	376	Wynberg Chapel	230
West, Rev. W.	200, 202		
Western Australia	296	Young, Rev. R.	308, 349, 393, 451
Whale-fishing	344	Young, Rev. S.	240, 241
Wharton, Rev. Henry	199, 201		
Whatcoat, Rev. Mr.	64	Zante	47
White and Sons	299	Zetland Islands	19
White, Rev. W.	87, 332	Zulus	251
Whippy, Mr. David	427		

NEW BOOKS

PUBLISHED BY

ELLIOT STOCK, 62, PATERNOSTER ROW, E.C.

"**Mr. Coley's Life of Collins will take its place among the classics of Methodist Biography.**"—WESLEYAN METHODIST MAGAZINE.

In crown 8vo, handsome cloth gilt, price 5s., also in Turkey morocco, gilt edges, price 10s. 6d. post free, Fourth Edition, with a Portrait.

The Life of the Rev. Thomas Collins,

By the REV. SAMUEL COLEY.

"Mr. Coley could scarcely have employed his pen on richer or more suggestive materials, and certainly Mr. Collins could not have a more painstaking, appreciative, and loving biographer. Mr. Coley has edited this choice volume with characteristic ability."—*The Watchman.*

"We are obliged to Mr. Coley for preserving a record of so devout and useful a man as Mr. Collins."—*Methodist Times.*

"It is now some years since there appeared a biography which more thoroughly represented Methodism in action than does Mr. Coley's life of his friend."—*Primitive Methodist Magazine.*

"The life of Thomas Collins is valuable, because it is a wonderful record of spiritual exercises, conflicts, and triumphs, and specially because it clearly shows the possibility of the spiritually feeble in our churches becoming even as this modern David."—*Bible Christian Magazine.*

"This is one of the best biographies of modern times, and the most adapted for usefulness."—*Methodist New Connexion Magazine.*

"In this biography we have the true portraiture of a veritable successor of the fathers and founders of the Wesleyan organisation."—*Literary World.*

THE BEST PRESENT FOR SUNDAY SCHOLARS.

In fcap. 8vo, cloth, with Portrait, price 1s. 6d., post free.

The Story of our Founder:

Being a Life of John Wesley, written for children. With an Introduction by the Rev. THOS. VASEY.

This little book gives an interesting narrative of the principal incidents in the life and labours of John Wesley. It is written in an entertaining style, such as will engage the interest of children, and at the same time inculcate those useful lessons of love to God and self-devotion, such as all good teachers are anxious to teach their scholars. In order that the little book may be very widely circulated, it is issued at a very low rate. Teachers are earnestly requested to send for a single copy before purchasing rewards.

ELLIOT STOCK, 62, PATERNOSTER ROW, LONDON, E.C.

Just published, price 3s. 6d., post free,

Won at Last.

Memoirs of Captain GEORGE and Mrs. HANNAH SMITH, of Bridlington Quay and York. By their eldest son, the Rev. THORNLEY SMITH.

"Mr. Thornley Smith has in this volume supplied portraits of Christian excellence which will find a place in many a home within and beyond the circle of the Methodist Churches. The tale of Captain Smith's incarceration at Dunkirk as a prisoner of war is particularly interesting. In this book there is enough of incident to keep alive the attention, and enough of true religion to render it extremely profitable."—*Methodist Recorder.*

THE WESLEYAN METHODIST ANNUAL, SECOND YEAR.
GREATLY IMPROVED.

In crown 8vo., containing over 200 pages, price 1s., post free,

The Wesleyan Methodist Year-Book,

Being a Manual of most important information relating to the Connexion for the year, condensed and arranged for ready reference.

This work has been carefully compiled, and contains much statistical matter which cannot be obtained elsewhere.

Some of the Principal Features of the Work are:—

A Wesleyan Almanac and Calendar—General Wesleyan Intelligence, including the Conference, its Presidents and Secretaries, places where it has been held, different Funds and Committees—Educational Returns—Home Mission and Chapel Fund Affairs, &c., &c.

The Conference of 1870, held at Burslem, an Epitome of its Proceedings—Inaugural of President Farrar—Official Conference Appointments—Death Roll of Ministers—Alphabetical List of Circuits, when formed, number of Members, of Chapels, &c., of Local Preachers, of S.S. Teachers and Scholars, with the Appointment of Ministers and Supernumeraries, showing the state of each Circuit at a single glance.

An Alphabetical List of Ministers and Supernumeraries; also, for the first time, and as far as can be ascertained, their precise Postal Addresses in all large towns.

The Irish Conference of 1870—a Digest of its Proceedings—Official Appointments—Circuit Lists and Statistics, with Lists of Ministers, &c.

Wesleyan Foreign Missions—Officers and Committees—Missionary Deputations—District Treasurers—Income and Expenditure—Statistical Returns and Lists of Circuits, Ministers, and Supernumeraries, alphabetically arranged.

Affiliated Conferences—viz., Canada—Australia—France—Eastern British North America—with an Account of each Conference held this year—and all Returns of Circuits, Ministers, and Supernumeraries, with statistics as above.

Local Preachers in Great Britain, not alphabetically arranged, but according to their several Districts and Circuits, with their Postal Addresses.

The Wesleyan Year-Book of Facts and Occurrences for the past year, *much enlarged.*

ELLIOT STOCK, 62, PATERNOSTER ROW, LONDON, E.C.